taste of home
family
favorites
made easy

taste of home
family favorites
made easy

Editor in Chief	Catherine Cassidy
Vice President & Executive Editor/Books	Heidi Reuter Lloyd
Creative Director	Ardyth Cope
Food Director	Diane Werner RD
Senior Editor/Books	Mark Hagen
Art Director	Rudy Krochalk
Content Production Supervisor	Julie Wagner
Design Layout Artist	Catherine Fletcher
Proofreader	Linne Bruskewitz
Recipe Asset Systems	Coleen Martin, Sue A. Jurack
Premedia Supervisor	Scott Berger
Recipe Testing & Editing	Taste of Home Test Kitchen
Food Photography	Taste of Home Photo Studio
Editorial Assistant	Barb Czysz

Chief Marketing Officer	Lisa Karpinski
Vice President/Book Marketing	Dan Fink
Creative Director/Creative Marketing	Jim Palmen

The Reader's Digest Association, Inc.

President and Chief Executive Officer	Mary G. Berner
President, RDA Food & Entertaining	Suzanne M. Grimes
President, Consumer Marketing	Dawn Zier

International Standard Book Number (10): 0-89821-716-4
International Standard Book Number (13): 978-0-89821-716-2
Library of Congress Control Number: 2008938982

Printed in U.S.A.

Cover Photography

Photographer	Dan Roberts
Food Stylist	Stephanie Marchese
Set Stylist	Diane Armstrong

Pictured on Front Cover: Poppy Seed Citrus Salad (p. 24);
Rosemary Infused Potatoes (p. 164); "Five Spice" Chicken (p. 83);
Sesame-Soy Broccoli Florets (p. 162); and Petite Mississippi Mud Pies (p. 204).

Pictured on Title Page: Fruit-Filled Cupcakes (p. 202).

Pictured on Back Cover: Chicken Au Gratin (p. 85).

Pictured Right: Sweet and Sour Meatball Skewers (p. 8);
Vegetarian Delight (p. 146); and San Diego Chicken Tacos (p. 448).

table of contents

serving up family favorites

it's true! You can set a hearty meal on the table...even when time is tight. You can also cut costs by avoiding the fast food drive-thru and skipping expensive, hard-to-find ingredients. You can even whip up fantastic desserts and impress weekend guests...with only a fraction of the effort you'd expect.

Take a look inside *Family Favorites Made Easy* and you'll find 356 sensational recipes, sure to set everyone's taste buds reeling. Whether you need a no-fuss entree for a busy weeknight, a quick contribution to a bake sale or a simple yet surprising menu for a Saturday night dinner party, this incredible collection has you covered. In addition to delivering mouth-watering flavor, each recipe includes a color photo as well as timelines that help beat the clock. You'll also find a cost-saving hint, ingredient substitution or clever kitchen tip with every recipe. And because we know you're interested in serving well-balanced meals, we've even included Nutrition Facts with each dish.

Best of all, with the variety of foods *Family Favorites Made Easy* offers, the perfect recipe is always at hand. Here's just a sampling of what's inside this new cookbook:

snacks & starters

Got the midday munchies? Need a few nibbles to round out an appetizer buffet? This chapter offers dozens of savory bites and no-stress snacks.

super salads & soups

Whether served alongside a meal or featured as the main course, a refreshing salad or velvety soup promises to satisfy. Consider any of these must-try options when planning your next menu.

best bets for beef

When it comes to true comfort, nothing satisfies like beef. Turn to this hearty chapter when you want to set a guaranteed winner on the table. With all of the meaty recipes in this section, finding a dish that fits your schedule is a breeze.

perfect poultry

Cider-Glazed Turkey, Rustic Stuffed Chicken, Arroz con Pollo...believe it or not, these sensational entrees are table-ready in less than half an hour. Surprise your family with any of these 48 unbeatable dishes tonight.

pork, ham & more

Switch up your dinner routine with flavorful pork chops, juicy sausages or savory ham. When you're looking for something new but don't have much time to spare, turn to this chapter. Most of the recipes are ready in 30 minutes.

has never been easier!

easy side dishes

With more than 50 recipes to choose from, this section makes it easier than ever to round a meal. Consider Florida Green Beans, Sweet & Savory Focaccia or Rosemary-Infused Potatoes the next time you need a quick dinner accompaniment.

delicious desserts

There's always room for dessert, and thanks to *Family Favorites Made Easy*, there's always time to prepare it, too. Featuring 48 scrumptious specialties, this chapter offers the ideal delight for any occasion.

you'll also find an entire chapter

featuring cookies, as well as a section on sandwiches, wraps, burgers and other handheld greats. Don't forget about the chapter devoted to seafood and meatless main courses. Those recipes truly shake up supper-time doldrums.

Still aren't sure what to serve tonight? Consider the 12 weeknight menus listed on pages 224 through 226. Not only will they give you plenty of meal ideas, but they're also sure to get you out of the kitchen and enjoying time with your family at the dinner table.

snacks & starters

red pepper hummus • p. 17

Turn to this chapter when you're looking for a tasty appetizer to start a meal or choosing a selection of delicious nibblers for an upcoming family gathering. Whether you're hosting a game-day get-together or you simply have the midday munchies, you'll find just what you need.

Your family and friends will rave about Hot Bacon Swiss Dip (p. 11), Jalapeno Corn Mini Muffins (p. 18) and Savory Cereal Snack Mix (p. 19). Need a sweet treat to add to your appetizer lineup? Consider Banana and Mango Fritters (p. 12) or tooth-tingling Nutty Butterscotch Fudge (p. 15).

sweet and sour meatball skewers

prep time: 25 minutes • total time: 25 minutes • serves: 8

Serve a sweet and savory taste of the Orient at your next party. Flavorful mini meatballs are skewered with colorful green peppers and fresh pineapple, then basted with a quick and simple sweet-and-sour dipping sauce.

1 small green pepper	2 tbsp. ketchup
6 green onions, *divided*	1 tbsp. soy sauce
1 inch piece of ginger	1/2 lb. ground pork
1/2 cup apricot preserves	1/4 tsp. salt
2 tbsp. red-wine vinegar	16 chunks fresh pineapple

1) If using bamboo skewers, soak 16 skewers in very hot water for 10 min. Preheat broiler to high and line shallow baking sheet with foil.

2) Cut pepper into 16 chunks. Finely chop enough green onions to equal 1/4 cup. Peel and finely chop enough ginger to equal 1 tbsp.

3) In small bowl, place preserves. Add vinegar, ketchup and soy sauce; blend well. Remove 1/3 cup to small serving bowl for use as dipping sauce.

4) In medium bowl, thoroughly combine pork, salt, chopped green onion and ginger. Shape mixture into 16 meatballs. Place each meatball on skewer, followed by 1 piece of pepper and 1 pineapple chunk. Place on prepared baking sheet.

5) Brush kabobs with half of preserves mixture. Place under broiler 4 inches from heat. Cook until first side is browned, about 4 min. Turn, baste with remaining preserves mixture and cook until done, 3-4 min. Garnish with remaining green onions and serve with dipping sauce.

nutritional facts: *Per serving: 150 calories • 19g carbohydrates • 6g protein • 6g fat • 250mg sodium • 20mg cholesterol • 1g fiber • 16g sugar*

hawaiian-style
Save the shell of the pineapple to use as a serving bowl. Fill the shell with cut-up mango and the remaining pineapple chunks and serve alongside the meatballs.

mini spinach frittatas

prep time: 9 minutes • total time: 29 minutes • serves: 6

Eggs aren't just for breakfast! Enjoy these mini frittatas as a heart-healthy snack or a starter for lunch, brunch or supper. For extra ease, they can be served warm or at room temperature.

1 (10 oz.) pkg. frozen chopped spinach	1-1/2 cups cottage cheese
6 large eggs	2/3 cup plain dry bread crumbs
	1/2 cup grated Parmesan cheese

1) Preheat oven to 400°F. Generously coat 12-cup muffin tin with cooking spray; set aside.

2) Place spinach in microwave-safe bowl with 2 tbsp. water. Cover and microwave on HIGH 4 min. Stir and microwave again, 3 min. Drain by pressing with wooden spoon in fine sieve, to remove excess liquid.

3) In large mixing bowl, whisk together eggs, cottage cheese, bread crumbs and Parmesan until well combined. Stir in spinach.

4) Drop by scant 1/3 cupfuls into prepared muffin cups. Bake until centers are set and tops are slightly puffed, about 18-20 min.

nutritional facts: *Per serving: 200 calories • 12g carbohydrates • 19g protein • 8g fat • 530mg sodium • 220mg cholesterol • 1g fiber • 3g sugar*

serve with waffles
Serve the frittatas as a brunch starter when you serve Belgian waffles. You can even sneak in the frozen kind and top them with fruit and cream for a filling meal.

parmesan chicken wings

prep time: 10 minutes • total time: 32 minutes • serves: 4

The savory cheese coating on these wings keeps the skin and meat incredibly moist while creating a crunchy coating that is baked, not fried.

2 lbs. chicken wings	1/2 tsp. salt
1 cup freshly grated Parmesan cheese	1/4 tsp. pepper
	1/3 cup butter
1/4 cup bread crumbs	1/2 tsp. Dijon-style mustard
1 tsp. dried oregano	

1) Preheat oven to 475°F. Line broiler pan with foil and set aside.

2) In medium bowl, mix Parmesan, bread crumbs, oregano, salt and pepper.

3) In medium saucepan over medium heat, melt butter. Remove from heat and stir in mustard. Toss chicken wings in butter mixture.

4) Roll wings, several at once, in Parmesan coating, pressing to adhere to chicken. Place in single layer on prepared broiler pan.

5) Bake until juices run clear when pricked with fork and coating starts to turn golden brown, about 22 min.

nutritional facts: *Per serving: 580 calories • 6g carbohydrates • 39g protein • 43g fat • 860mg sodium • 155mg cholesterol • 0g fiber • 1g sugar*

herbed yogurt dip

To make this dipping sauce, combine 1/2 cup each yogurt and sour cream, 2 tbsp. lemon juice, 2 tbsp. chopped chives, 1 tbsp. chopped parsley and salt and pepper to taste.

roasted veggie stacks

prep time: 5 minutes • total time: 29 minutes • serves: 9

A perfect nibble for any occasion, crunchy Parmesan cheese toasts are topped with tasty, balsamic vinegar-roasted vegetables dressed with pesto, then garnished with sliced tomato.

1 (9 inch) yellow summer squash	1/2 tsp. dried basil
	6 grape tomatoes
1 (9 inch) zucchini	8 large basil leaves
1 (9 inch) piece French bread	1/2 cup shredded Parmesan cheese
1/4 cup olive oil, *divided*	
1/2 tbsp. balsamic vinegar	1/4 cup prepared pesto

1) Preheat oven to 450°F. Cut squash, zucchini and bread into 1/4-inch slices. In large bowl, toss squash, zucchini, 1 tbsp. oil and vinegar. Place vegetables in single layer on baking sheet.

2) On second baking sheet, place bread in single layer. In small bowl, combine remaining oil and dried basil. Brush tops of bread with mixture. Place both pans in oven; bake bread 3 min. Meanwhile, cut tomatoes in quarters. Stack basil and roll into log. Cut through log to create thin strips. Set aside.

3) Remove bread from oven and sprinkle with Parmesan. Return to oven; bake 3 min.

4) Remove both pans from oven. Spoon 1/4 tsp. pesto on each piece of bread. Transfer to serving tray. Stack one of each vegetable on top. Spoon 1/4 tsp. pesto over vegetables. Top with shreds of basil and 1 piece of tomato. Serve immediately.

nutritional facts: *Per serving: 190 calories • 17g carbohydrates • 6g protein • 11g fat • 290mg sodium • 5mg cholesterol • 2g fiber • 3g sugar*

presto-pesto!

Blend or process garlic, fresh basil, pine nuts, extra-virgin olive oil, Parmesan cheese and a pinch of pepper. Freeze as ice cubes and use at will.

golden italian rice balls

prep time: 16 minutes • total time: 27 minutes • serves: 4

When you've got leftover rice (prepare extra next time!), this is the perfect dish to make. These little snacks are crunchy on the outside, soft and spicy on the inside and absolutely great any time!

2 large eggs	1 cup Italian bread crumbs
1/2 tsp. salt	1/4 cup refrigerated fresh basil
1/2 tsp. black pepper	pesto
1 slice thinly sliced prosciutto	olive oil for frying
2 cups cooked rice	1 cup prepared marinara sauce

1) In large bowl, whisk together eggs, salt and pepper. Mince prosciutto. Add prosciutto, rice, bread crumbs and pesto to egg mixture. Stir to combine completely and until pasty in texture.

2) Lay sheet of waxed paper on work surface. With 1/2-oz. ice cream scoop, make 28 (1-1/4-inch) balls and place on waxed paper.

3) In large skillet over medium, heat 1/2 inch oil. Add rice balls and fry, turning once, until golden brown on both sides, about 5 min. Drain on paper towels.

4) Meanwhile, place marinara sauce in small, microwave-safe serving dish. Microwave on HIGH until heated through, about 1 min. Place dish in center of serving platter, surround with rice balls and serve.

nutritional facts: *Per serving: 310 calories • 17g carbohydrates • 8g protein • 23g fat • 760mg sodium • 110mg cholesterol • 0g fiber • 0g sugar*

smart substitution

A slice of any ham you happen to have—Black Forest, Virginia or boiled—can be used in place of the more expensive prosciutto.

dutch indies quesadillas

prep time: 15 minutes • total time: 29 minutes • serves: 4

Fruity and smoky, fresh and flavorful, these are traditional-looking quesadillas with a twist! A combo of fresh papaya from the islands and a smoky Dutch Gouda is the tasty surprise.

1 large jalapeño	8 oz. smoked Gouda
1 small red pepper	1/2 large ripe papaya
1/2 large red onion	8 (8 inch) honey wheat flour
1 tbsp. vegetable oil	tortillas
1/4 cup fresh cilantro	1/4 cup sour cream

1) Preheat oven to 425°F. Seed and mince jalapeño. Mince red pepper and onion. In medium skillet over high, heat oil. Add all vegetables and cook, stirring, until soft, about 3 min. Meanwhile, chop cilantro. Add cilantro to skillet. Remove from heat and set aside.

2) Shred cheese. Seed, peel and thinly slice papaya.

3) Arrange 4 tortillas on 2 baking sheets. Top each tortilla with cheese, papaya, then vegetable mixture, reserving 1/4 cup of vegetable mixture for garnish. Top with remaining tortillas. Bake until cheese is melted, about 6 min.

4) Cut each into 6 wedges. To serve, spoon 1/2 tsp. sour cream onto each wedge and top with a garnish of vegetable mixture.

nutritional facts: *Per serving: 480 calories • 54g carbohydrates • 16g protein • 20g fat • 580mg sodium • 40mg cholesterol • 6g fiber • 8g sugar*

mexican ingredients

If you've got Mexican-style ingredients on hand, go more traditional with avocado and cheddar or Jack cheeses.

hot swiss bacon dip

prep time: 8 minutes • total time: 28 minutes • serves: 6

This dip is so rich, creamy and utterly irresistible that your guests will never believe how simple it is to make. Bacon and Swiss cheese are blended into flavored mayonnaise, then baked until bubbling hot.

2 slices bacon	2 tbsp. thinly sliced green
2 to 3 sprigs fresh dill (optional)	onions
1/2 cup mayonnaise	1 small head broccoli
1 tsp. Dijon-style mustard	1 red bell pepper
1/4 tsp. black pepper	3 ribs celery
1-1/2 cups shredded Swiss cheese	1/2 lb. button mushrooms
	1/2 (8 oz.) pkg. flatbread

1) Preheat oven to 350°F. Place bacon on several layers of paper towels; cover with 1 layer. Microwave on HIGH until crisp, about 2-3 min. Crumble and set aside. Finely chop dill to yield 1 tbsp.

2) In medium bowl, thoroughly blend mayonnaise, mustard and black pepper. Stir in cheese, bacon, green onions and dill.

3) Turn into small, shallow baking dish and bake, stirring once, until melted and bubbling, 20-25 min.

4) Cut crowns from broccoli. Arrange on serving platter. Cut red pepper into strips; arrange on platter. Trim both ends from celery and discard. Cut remainder into sticks. Arrange on platter with mushrooms and flatbread. Serve with dip.

nutritional facts: *Per serving: 480 calories • 46g carbohydrates • 16g protein • 27g fat • 620mg sodium • 35mg cholesterol • 11g fiber • 5g sugar*

chopped apple

Feel free to eliminate the bacon and use chopped apple for the crunch; punch up the flavor with a little chopped garlic, black olives, capers or diced jalapeños.

sweetie tomato bites

prep time: 20 minutes • total time: 20 minutes • serves: 24

If you often have guests dropping by, keep the seven ingredients for these tasty little morsels on hand so you can quickly and easily serve a crowd with flair. They're perfect any time of day.

1 lb. cherry tomatoes	2 tbsp. apricot preserves
1 tbsp. pecans	1 tbsp. prepared horseradish,
1 sprig curly parsley	drained
1/2 pkg. (4 oz.) Neufchatel cheese	2 tsp. Dijon-style mustard

1) Line plate with paper towels. Slice off top 1/4 of cherry tomatoes. With small spoon, scoop out and discard seeds. Place, cut-side down, on prepared plate to drain.

2) In food processor fitted with knife blade, place pecans. Process until finely chopped. Place in small skillet over medium heat, and cook until fragrant, 1-2 min. Remove to plate to cool. Remove parsley leaves from stem; finely chop. Stir into cooled pecans.

3) Meanwhile, wipe processor clean with damp paper towel. Add Neufchatel cheese, preserves, horseradish and mustard. Process until smooth.

4) Place cheese mixture into small, zippered plastic bag. Snip 1/2-inch opening from one corner. Pipe cheese mixture into each cherry tomato; sprinkle tops with pecan-parsley mixture.

nutritional facts: *Per serving: 25 calories • 2g carbohydrates • 1g protein • 1.5g fat • 30mg sodium • 5mg cholesterol • 0g fiber • 2g sugar*

no waste

Avoid needless waste by saving the cut-off tomato pieces and using them in a salad the next day.

banana and mango fritters

prep time: 8 minutes • total time: 20 minutes • serves: 6

So easy to make, these sweet, chunky banana and mango fritters can serve as a deliciously different snack or as an unexpected first course for a festive, Indian-inspired meal.

1 large banana	1/2 tsp. salt
1 medium mango	1 egg
1 cup all-purpose flour	1/4 cup milk
1 tsp. baking powder	canola oil, for frying
2 tbsp. granulated sugar	3 tbsp. confectioners' sugar, for dusting
1/2 tsp. pie spice	

1) Cut banana and mango into 3/8-inch pieces to yield 1-3/4 cups total; set aside. In large bowl, blend flour, baking powder, granulated sugar, pie spice and salt. Make a well in center of flour. Add egg and beat with fork. Pour in milk and stir until egg and milk are blended in well.

2) Stir banana and mango into egg mixture to coat. Mix with dry ingredients until combined. Meanwhile, in large saucepan over medium, heat 1-1/2 inches of oil to 375°F.

3) Drop batter by rounded tablespoonfuls into oil in batches, about 6 per batch. Fry until golden brown, turning frequently, about 1 to 1-1/2 min. Transfer to paper towels to drain, then to serving platter. Place confectioners' sugar in strainer and shake gently over fritters to dust. Serve immediately.

nutritional facts: *Per serving: 290 calories • 43g carbohydrates • 5g protein • 11g fat • 170mg sodium • 35mg cholesterol • 2g fiber • 18g sugar*

change to a dessert

You can change this recipe from a starter to an over-the-top dessert by serving these fritters warm with a generous scoop of vanilla ice cream or tropical fruit sorbet.

mexicali wontons

prep time: 15 minutes • total time: 25 minutes • serves: 6

Much lighter (and much easier to make) than jalapeño poppers, these mouth-watering appetizers are so tasty, they'll have your guests asking for more. Mexico and China have never been closer!

1/4 cup chopped canned green chiles (mild), drained	24 wonton wrappers
2 jalapeno peppers, canned	vegetable oil for frying
1 (8 oz.) pkg. shredded Monterey Jack cheese	1 cup prepared guacamole dip

1) Line baking sheet with paper towels. Cut peppers into thin wheels. In medium mixing bowl, stir together cheese, chiles and jalapeños with fork until just slightly lumpy but well mixed.

2) Working with several wonton skins at once, put 2 tsp. of cheese mixture in center of each wonton. Dampen 2 adjoining edges of wonton wrapper using finger dipped in cold water. Bring opposite dry edges to moist edges and press to form triangle.

3) In large skillet over medium, heat 1/2 inch vegetable oil. Add several wontons at once to skillet, but do not crowd. Cook until golden, about 20 seconds, turn and cook other side for about 20 seconds. Remove to prepared baking sheet using slotted spoon.

4) Place guacamole in small bowl on platter and surround with cooked wontons. Serve immediately.

nutritional facts: *Per serving: 100 calories • 6g carbohydrates • 3g protein • 7g fat • 190mg sodium • 10mg cholesterol • 0g fiber • 0g sugar*

easy guacamole

With one ripe avocado, it only takes a minute to make great guacamole: scoop out the avocado, mash it with a fork, add salt, garlic and either cilantro or diced tomato.

sausage cheese bites

prep time: 15 minutes • total time: 24 minutes • serves: 48

With only three ingredients and a clever trick that makes quick work of dividing the meat mixture, you can have a hot tidbit that's as perfect for family snacking as it is for cocktail parties.

---

1 lb. spicy bulk pork sausage	2 cups shredded cheddar cheese
3/4 cup baking mix	(about 8 oz.)

1) Preheat oven to 400°F. Line two baking sheets with foil; spray with cooking spray.

2) In food processor fitted with knife blade, combine sausage, baking mix and cheese. Process until thoroughly combined.

3) On cutting board, shape mixture into 8- x 6-inch rectangle. Cut into 48 (1-inch) squares. Roll each square into ball and place on baking sheet. Bake until cooked through, 9 to 11 min. Drain on paper towels; serve immediately.

nutritional facts: *Per serving: 120 calories • 3g carbohydrates • 6g protein • 9g fat • 330mg sodium • 20mg cholesterol • 0g fiber • 0g sugar*

make these in advance
Bake, cool and freeze them in small batches. They can be reheated in the oven or toaster oven when guests arrive.

---

ohio state fair fried pickles

prep time: 10 minutes • total time: 20 minutes • serves: 8

Hot and crunchy fried pickles, first seen at fairs and carnivals, are becoming more and more popular throughout the country—and in the cities, too. Surprise your family by making them at home!

---

1 (8 oz.) jar sweet pickle chips	1/2 tsp. paprika
1 (8 oz.) jar dill pickle spears	1 large egg
3/4 cup all-purpose flour	1 cup beer
1/4 cup cornmeal	vegetable oil for frying
1/2 tsp. salt	1/2 cup blue cheese dressing

1) Drain pickles on paper towels; set aside.

2) In medium bowl, stir together flour, cornmeal, salt and paprika.

3) Separate egg and place yolk and white in 2 small bowls. Add beer to yolk and beat with fork until blended. Whip egg white with wire whisk until soft peaks form.

4) Stir egg yolk mixture into flour mixture. Carefully fold in beaten egg white.

5) Heat oil in deep fryer to 350°F. Dip pickle chips into batter and fry, in batches, until golden, using tongs to turn once, about 2 min. Drain on paper towels. Repeat with pickle spears.

6) Place blue cheese dressing in small bowl on platter. Surround with fried pickles and serve immediately.

nutritional facts: *Per serving: 330 calories • 13g carbohydrates • 3g protein • 30g fat • 510mg sodium • 30mg cholesterol • 1g fiber • 5g sugar*

fresh pickles
Very crisp, jarred pickles can be hard to find in larger supermarkets; keep that purchase in mind when you get to a neighborhood delicatessen that may sell fresh pickles.

eggplant caviar

prep time: 10 minutes • total time: 27 minutes • serves: 4

This flavorful and colorful fresh eggplant dip is simply loaded with natural goodness, so it's perfect for any occasion. Onion, garlic, fresh herbs and tangy red-wine vinegar add a jolt to the subtle flavor.

1 large eggplant (about 1-1/2 lbs.)	4 fresh parsley sprigs
1 small onion	1 tbsp. red-wine vinegar
2 large cloves garlic	1/4 tsp. salt
1/2 cup olive oil	1/8 tsp. cayenne pepper
1/4 small red pepper	1/8 tsp. black pepper
8 medium, fresh basil leaves	wheat crackers

1) Peel and chop eggplant. Chop onion and garlic.

2) In large skillet over high, heat oil. Add eggplant, onion and garlic. Cover and cook, stirring every 3 min. until eggplant is very tender, about 10 min. total.

3) Meanwhile, mince red pepper. Chop basil and parsley.

4) In workbowl of food processor, add eggplant mixture and vinegar. Process until smooth. With rubber spatula, scrape down sides. Process again. Scrape into small bowl and, with spatula, stir in red pepper, basil, parsley, salt, cayenne and black peppers. Place bowl on large plate, surround with crackers and serve.

nutritional facts: *Per serving: 560 calories • 51g carbohydrates • 7g protein • 38g fat • 520mg sodium • 0mg cholesterol • 12g fiber • 5g sugar*

waste not

Don't waste the fresh red pepper. Cut the remainder into strips and serve it alongside the crackers with the "caviar."

groovy cheese fondue

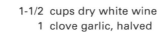

prep time: 20 minutes • total time: 20 minutes • serves: 8

Yes, that party staple from the '70s is back! And with good reason…it's easy to make and fun to eat. A simple mix of ingredients based on two tasty cheeses results in a dish full of flavor.

1-1/2 cups dry white wine	1/4 tsp. white *or* black pepper
1 clove garlic, halved	1/8 tsp. nutmeg
1/2 lb. imported Swiss cheese, shredded	2 tbsp. kirsch (optional)
1/2 lb. Gruyere cheese, shredded	1 lb. loaf crusty French, sourdough *or* pumpernickel bread
2 tbsp. cornstarch	

1) In large saucepan over high heat, bring wine and garlic to boiling point; reduce heat to low and simmer 2 min. Discard garlic.

2) In large bowl, toss cheeses with cornstarch. Add cheese mixture to saucepan in 1/4 cupfuls, stirring with fork after each addition.

3) Continue to cook at low simmer, stirring until mixture is smooth and creamy, about 10 min. Stir in pepper, nutmeg, and kirsch.

4) Meanwhile, cut bread into 1-inch cubes. Pour mixture into fondue pot set over flame and serve with bread.

nutritional facts: *Per serving: 380 calories • 27g carbohydrates • 20g protein • 18g fat • 360mg sodium • 55mg cholesterol • 1g fiber • 3g sugar*

fun fondue

The key to a great fondue is high quality cheese. Tossing the shredded cheese with cornstarch ensures that it melts smoothly and is rich and creamy.

nutty butterscotch fudge

prep time: 15 minutes • total time: 2-1/4 hours • serves: 32

This favorite sweet is easy enough to make for any event, whether you're having a party or need a hostess gift. Spend just 15 minutes working, chill for 2 hours and you've got a mouth-watering treat.

3/4 cup toasted pecans	1 (10.5 oz.) pkg. miniature
1 (11 oz.) pkg butterscotch chips, *divided*	marshmallows
1-1/2 cups sugar	1 tsp. vanilla extract
1 (5 oz.) can evaporated milk	1/2 tsp. ground cinnamon
2 tbsp. butter	1/2 cup white chocolate chips
1/2 tsp. salt	

1) Preheat oven to 400°F. Spread pecans on baking sheet. Bake until toasted, about 6 min.; set aside. Remove and reserve 1/2 cup butterscotch chips. Line 8- x 8-inch pan with foil.

2) In heavy saucepan over medium heat, combine sugar, evaporated milk, butter and salt. Bring to full boil, stirring constantly. Continue stirring for 5 min. Remove from heat.

3) Stir in marshmallows, remaining butterscotch chips, 1/2 cup nuts, vanilla and cinnamon. Stir until marshmallows and chips are melted. Pour into prepared pan. Sprinkle top with reserved butterscotch chips, nuts and white chocolate chips.

4) Chill until firm, about 2 hours. Lift from pan using foil; discard foil. Place fudge on cutting board; cut into 1-inch squares. Serve immediately, or store in airtight container in refrigerator.

nutritional facts: *Per serving: 170 calories • 26g carbohydrates • 2g protein • 6g fat • 65mg sodium • 5mg cholesterol • 0g fiber • 17g sugar*

almost anything goes

This is a recipe where almost any substitution works. Instead of butterscotch chips, use chocolate or peanut butter chips. Walnuts, almonds or even peanuts can replace the pecans.

pastrami canapes

prep time: 15 minutes • total time: 20 minutes • serves: 12

These attractive and tasty snacks will be a sure hit at your next party. The tang of roasted red pepper, the creamy, herbed cheese spread and the spicy pastrami are a wonderful flavor combination.

12 slices pastrami (about 1/2 lb.)	3 oz. cream cheese
1 (7.5 oz.) jar roasted red peppers	1 cup shredded Cheddar cheese
1 (4 oz.) container herb-flavored cream cheese spread	1 small bunch chives
	48 miniature toasts *or* crisp crackers

1) Cut each pastrami slice into fourths.

2) Drain liquid from roasted peppers. Place peppers, both cream cheeses and Cheddar in blender. Puree until smooth, about 1 min.

3) Cut chives into 1-inch pieces and set aside. Fold each piece of pastrami in half and place on cracker. Top with heaping tsp. of cheese mixture. Garnish each with 2 pieces of chives, crossed.

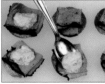

4) Arrange on platter and serve.

nutritional facts: *Per serving: 420 calories • 60g carbohydrates • 17g protein • 12g fat • 890mg sodium • 40mg cholesterol • 3g fiber • 6g sugar*

stress-free spread

The leftover cheese mixture makes a delicious sandwich spread—quite like a traditional pimiento-cheese spread.

festive presentation

When you're looking for a fun way to present these tasty finger foods, arrange them in a star pattern on a cake plate around a small saucer filled with the dip.

baked potato skins

prep time: 20 minutes • **total time:** 20 minutes • **serves:** 8

Both crisp and hearty, this snack's one that your gang will request often. They're perfect for casual get-togethers or even a no-fuss meal when you don't have much time to cook.

4 large baking potatoes, baked	1/8 tsp. pepper
3 tbsp. vegetable oil	8 bacon strips, cooked and
1 tbsp. grated Parmesan cheese	crumbled
1/2 tsp. salt	1-1/2 cups shredded cheddar cheese
1/4 tsp. garlic powder	1/2 cup sour cream
1/4 tsp. paprika	4 green onions, sliced

1) Cut potatoes in half lengthwise; scoop out pulp, leaving a 1/4-in. shell (save pulp for another use). Place potatoes skins on a greased baking sheet. Combine oil, Parmesan cheese, salt, garlic powder, paprika and pepper; brush over both sides of skins.

2) Bake at 475°F. for 7 minutes; turn. Bake until crisp, about 7 minutes more. Sprinkle bacon and cheddar cheese inside skins. Bake 2 minutes longer or until the cheese is melted. Top with sour cream and onions. Serve immediately.

nutritional facts: *Per serving: 338 calories • 35g carbohydrates • 11g protein • 17g fat • 408mg sodium • 38mg cholesterol • 3g fiber*

limeade slushie

Use the remaining limeade concentrate to make a refreshing beverage. Simply blend it with some crushed ice and a splash of lemon juice. Serve with fresh mint leaves.

ginger-glazed shrimp sticks

prep time: 16 minutes • **total time:** 20 minutes • **serves:** 4

Instead of marinating in sauce, these shrimp are brushed with an easy-to-make glaze that speeds preparation and creates a taste treat—inspired by the Caribbean—that's bursting with flavor.

1 small bunch chives	1/4 cup honey
1 inch piece fresh ginger	3 tbsp. soy sauce
1 lime	1 lb. large peeled and deveined
1/3 cup frozen limeade concentrate	shrimp (about 24)

1) Preheat grill or grill pan to medium-high. Chop chives to yield 2 tbsp.; set aside. Grate enough ginger to yield 2 tsp.; place in medium bowl. Grate rind of half of lime into bowl. Stir in limeade concentrate, honey, soy sauce and 1-1/2 tbsp. chives. Set aside 1/2 cup of glaze in small bowl.

2) Thread 2 shrimp on each skewer. Brush with glaze. Grill shrimp over medium-high heat until lightly golden on first side, about 2 min. Turn and brush with glaze. Grill until opaque in center, 1-2 min. per side. Place on serving platter and scatter with remaining chives. Serve with reserved sauce for dipping.

nutritional facts: *Per serving: 250 calories • 34g carbohydrates • 26g protein • 1.5g fat • 950mg sodium • 220mg cholesterol • 0g fiber • 32g sugar*

red pepper hummus

prep time: 15 minutes • total time: 150 minutes • serves: 8

Don't bother spending money on packaged hummus blends, when you can easily make your own and control the fat content. It's quick, tasty, healthy and inexpensive. What could be better?

3 cloves garlic, peeled	2 tbsp. lemon juice
1 (15.5 oz.) can chickpeas, drained	1 tbsp. mild cayenne pepper sauce
3/4 cup jarred roasted red pepper, drained well	4 ribs celery
2 tbsp. tahini	4 large carrots
	2 whole wheat pitas

1) In small glass dish, place garlic and add just enough water to cover. Cover dish with plastic wrap; microwave on HIGH for 45 seconds until garlic is slightly softened. Discard water.

2) Place in food processor and process until chopped. Add chickpeas, red pepper, tahini, lemon juice and pepper sauce. Process until smooth.

3) Thoroughly scrub celery ribs; cut sticks. Peel carrots, cut into sticks. Cut each pita into 8 wedges. Mound hummus in bowl in center of serving plate. Surround with vegetables and pita. Serve.

nutritional facts: *Per serving: 200 calories • 34g carbohydrates • 9g protein • 4g fat • 430mg sodium • 0mg cholesterol • 7g fiber • 5g sugar*

tahini trade

Tahini is made from ground sesame seeds and has a peanut-butter-like consistency. If you don't have any on hand, you can substitute 2 tsp. of sesame oil.

blue cheese bites

prep time: 15 minutes • total time: 25 minutes • serves: 4

Love to snack on those fancy, high-priced crackers found in gourmet shops, but don't want to overspend? Here's an easy way to get the fine taste but without the high price tag.

1 cup walnuts	1 (9 oz.) pkg. pie crust mix
1 cup crumbled blue cheese	4 tbsp. all-purpose flour, *divided*
1/2 cup grated Parmesan cheese	2 tsp. poppy seeds, *divided*

1) Preheat oven to 400°F. In workbowl of food processor, grind walnuts, blue cheese and Parmesan until chopped. Add pie crust mix and water indicated in package directions. Process just until mixture forms ball.

2) Divide dough in half. Coat dough ball in 2 tbsp. flour and place on plastic wrap. Pat to 8- x 6-inch rectangle. Top with plastic wrap and roll to 1/4-inch thickness. Set on small baking sheet; freeze 5 min. Repeat with remaining dough.

3) Remove top layer of plastic wrap from first sheet of dough and invert dough onto large baking sheet. Remove bottom layer of plastic wrap. Sprinkle dough with 1 tsp. poppy seeds. Repeat with remaining dough.

4) Using pastry wheel or pizza cutter, cut into 1-inch squares. Spread apart, leaving about 1/2-inch space between crackers. Bake, switching racks midway, until crisped and golden around edges, 12-14 min. Transfer to rack. Serve slightly warm or cooled. Store in airtight container for up to 2 weeks.

nutritional facts: *Per serving: 240 calories • 14g carbohydrates • 8g protein • 17g fat • 360mg sodium • 10mg cholesterol • 1g fiber • 0g sugar*

easy additions

These delicate bites are great to serve with drinks. On a serving tray, surround the crackers with a variety of nuts and clusters of fresh grapes.

jalapeno corn mini muffins

prep time: 10 minutes • total time: 22 minutes • serves: 24

A basketful of these tasty and slightly spicy little morsels are sure to please fans of Southwestern cooking. They're a great starter for dinner, but you can serve them with scrambled eggs, too.

1 large egg	1 (8.5 oz.) pkg. corn muffin mix
1/3 cup milk	1 jalapeno pepper
2 tbsp. vegetable oil	1/4 small red bell pepper
1/4 tsp. garlic powder	3/4 cup shredded pepper-Jack
1/8 tsp. hot pepper sauce	cheese

1) Preheat oven to 400°F. Coat two mini muffin pans (12 muffins each) with cooking spray. In medium bowl, combine egg, milk, oil, garlic powder and hot pepper sauce. Add corn muffin mix; blend ingredients together to form lumpy batter. Let rest 5 min.

2) Meanwhile, seed and mince jalapeno pepper. Finely chop bell pepper. Fold peppers and shredded cheese into muffin batter.

3) Spoon batter into prepared pans, about 1 tbsp. in each. Bake until toothpick inserted in center comes out clean, about 10–12 min. Let stand 5 min. Remove muffins from pan, using tip of paring knife, if needed, to loosen sides. Serve warm or cool completely before storing in airtight container.

nutritional facts: *Per serving (2 muffins): 140 calories • 15g carbohydrates • 4g protein • 8g fat • 200mg sodium • 30mg cholesterol • 0g fiber • 5g sugar*

want more heat?

No need to chop another jalapeño, just add some of the seeds—the source of the jalapeño's intense heat.

smoked salmon spirals

prep time: 5 minutes • total time: 25 minutes • serves: 18

This is an elegant appetizer for any meal. The pastel roll-ups are also great hors d'oeuvres for parties and can even serve as finger food at a more formal reception. Versatile and delicious!

1/2 lb. smoked salmon, sliced	1 tbsp. fresh lemon juice
1 tbsp. capers, rinsed and drained	1/2 tsp. dried dill weed
1 (8 oz.) pkg. cream cheese	2 medium cucumbers

1) Lay large piece of plastic wrap on work surface. Place salmon slices on plastic, overlapping edges to form 16- x 16-inch rectangle.

2) Place cream cheese on microwave-safe plate; microwave on HIGH until softened, 20 seconds. In mini food processor, mince capers. Add cream cheese, lemon juice and dill; process until smooth.

3) With plastic spatula, spread cream cheese mixture in thin layer over salmon slices. Carefully lift 1 short edge of plastic wrap; roll salmon down length into tight log, pressing gently against plastic while rolling and keeping wrap on outside edge of salmon. Place in freezer until firm, 20 min.

4) Meanwhile, slice each cucumber into 9 (1/2-inch) rounds. Arrange on serving tray. Remove salmon from freezer; discard plastic wrap. Slice into 18 (3/4-inch) rounds. Top each cucumber slice with salmon roll; serve.

nutritional facts: *Per serving: 60 calories • 0g carbohydrates • 3g protein • 5g fat • 90mg sodium • 15mg cholesterol • 0g fiber • 0g sugar*

super secret

If you are buying the smoked salmon at the deli counter, ask to have each slice placed on the paper separate from one another so they don't stick together.

savory cereal snack mix

prep time: 10 minutes • total time: 30 minutes • serves: 6

Even more addictive than salted nuts, the subtle barbecue flavor of this snack mix makes it perfect for snacking at home or on the run. Make a double batch and have plenty on hand!

2 cups corn & rice (square-shaped) cereal	3/4 cup baked thin wheat crackers
1 cup mini pretzel twists	2 tbsp. barbecue sauce
1 cup bite-size fish-shaped cheese crackers	1/2 tsp. garlic powder
	1/2 tsp. onion powder

1) Preheat oven to 325°F. Lightly coat rimmed baking sheet with cooking spray.

2) In large bowl, combine cereal, pretzels, cheese crackers and wheat crackers. Stir gently to combine.

3) In small bowl, combine barbecue sauce, garlic powder and onion powder. Spoon over cereal/cracker mixture and toss lightly to coat. Spread seasoned mix onto prepared baking sheet.

4) Bake until coating is completely dry, about 20 min., turning with spatula after the first 10 min. Pour into bowl and serve.

nutritional facts: *Per serving: 370 calories • 65g carbohydrates • 8g protein • 9g fat • 400mg sodium • 0mg cholesterol • 2g fiber • 2g sugar*

sweet surprise
Combine some yogurt-covered raisins, candy-coated chocolate pieces, cashews and flaked coconut to create a sweet mix of flavor to serve alongside the cereal mix.

zucchini bites

prep time: 10 minutes • total time: 22 minutes • serves: 6

Need a great appetizer to pass at your next party? Enjoy these crunchy disks of coated zucchini served with a dollop of a feta and fresh mint dip. It's an exotic and ever-so-easy veggie snack.

2 cups instant stuffing mix	1/4 cup olive oil
1 lb. zucchini (3-4 medium)	1/4 cup loosely packed fresh mint leaves
1/2 cup mayonnaise	1 lemon
1/2 tsp. garlic powder	
1/4 lb. feta cheese	

1) Preheat oven to 425°F. Line baking sheet with foil. Place stuffing mix in workbowl of food processor and pulse until finely chopped, 30 seconds. Remove crumbs to shallow bowl or pie plate. Trim and slice zucchini into 1/2-inch-thick rounds. Set aside.

2) In small bowl, stir together mayonnaise and garlic powder.

3) Working with several at once, dip zucchini rounds into mayonnaise mixture to lightly coat. Dredge slices in crumbs and place on prepared baking sheet. Repeat with remaining slices. Bake until crumbs are light golden brown and slices are firm, but tender, about 12-14 min. Transfer to rack to cool slightly.

4) Meanwhile, place feta, olive oil and mint leaves into workbowl of food processor. Cut lemon in half and squeeze in juice of both halves. Process until smooth, about 30 seconds.

5) Transfer zucchini rounds to large platter. Place 1 dollop of feta spread on top of each zucchini round. Serve slightly warm or at room temperature.

nutritional facts: *Per serving: 470 calories • 38g carbohydrates • 12g protein • 30g fat • 1180mg sodium • 25mg cholesterol • 4g fiber • 3g sugar*

low-cost crumbs
Dry, seasoned bread crumbs are an easy, less costly substitute for the stuffing mix. Or make your own with a loaf of day-old bread and a bit of Italian seasoning.

tips for
snacks & starters

selecting snacks for a party

When planning what appetizers to serve, don't overdo it. It's better to prepare a few good choices than be stressed by trying to prepare a wide variety of items.

- Make one spectacular appetizer and fill in with other easy but delicious foods.

- Prevent last-minute fuss with recipes that have make-ahead aspects.

- Provide hot, cold and room temperature choices and items with a good variety of color textures and flavors.

- Choose one or two lighter options to cater to guests concerned about their diet.

- Scatter bowls of nuts and snack mixes throughout other rooms.

how much to serve

The number of appetizers per person varies on the length of the party, the number of guests and the purpose of the appetizers.

- For a social hour before dinner, plan on serving 3 or 4 different appetizers and allow 4 to 5 pieces per person.

- For an open-house affair, plan on serving 4 to 5 different appetizers and allow 4 to 6 pieces per person per hour.

- For an appetizer buffet that is served in place of a meal, plan on serving 6 to 8 different appetizers and allow 10 to 14 pieces per person.

- In general, for larger groups you should offer more types of appetizers. For 8 guests three types may be sufficient, 16 guests about four to five types and for 25 guests serve six to eight types. The more variety of appetizers you serve, the fewer servings of each type each person will take.

food quantities for appetizers

When serving appetizers, no one wants to run out of food…but you also don't want to have lots of leftovers either. Here are some guidelines to estimate how much you'll need per person. The more appetizers you serve, the less of each type you will need.

3 tablespoons dips

2 ounces cheese

3 to 4 cocktail wieners

1 to 2 ounces deli meat

3 tablespoons dips

2 to 4 small egg rolls

3 to 4 meatballs

1 to 2 slices pizza

2 to 4 miniature quiches

elegant serving dishes

Use stemware to dish out single-serving portions for a shrimp cocktail or other appetizers. If you're concerned about breakage, serve them up in inexpensive plastic stemware.

have snacks, will travel

The 1/2-cup size of reusable plastic containers is ideal for individual snacks. Fill them with healthy foods for a quick, portable treat. Good choices are fat-free cottage cheese, sliced fruit, no-sugar-added applesauce, sugar-free gelatin or instant pudding. Tape a plastic spoon on the container to make it super easy to grab and go.

perfect cheese fondue

To serve a smooth and delicious cheese fondue, keep these tips in mind:

- Cheese can curdle easily when overheated. So reduce the heat to low before stirring the cheese into hot liquids. Keep the heat at low while the cheese melts.

- Cheese will melt faster and easier if it is shredded or cut into small cubes.

- Cheese fondues are traditionally made with white wine, which not only adds flavor but helps prevent the cheese from becoming stringy. Don't substitute red wine, which will adversely affect the color of the fondue.

crunchy bagel snacks

Bagel chips are a crispy snack all by themselves but are also great with dips. Making chips is also a fun way to recycle leftover bagels! To make chips, slice bagels very thin, and arrange in a single layer in a baking pan. Then spritz with cooking spray and sprinkle with different seasonings, such as garlic powder or dried basil on savory bagels, or cinnamon and sugar on sweet bagels. Toast in a 350°F. oven for about 15-20 minutes or until the bagel slices are crispy.

great cheese flavor

Select sharp cheddar when using packaged shredded cheese for recipes that you'd like to have a bolder flavor. If you will be shredding cheese at home from bulk cheddar, you can choose from mild, medium, sharp and extra sharp.

keeping foods warm

Warm dips can be prepared ahead and then heated in a slow cooker instead of the oven. A slow cooker will also keep your dip warm during the party. When foods need to be cooked in batches, such as Banana and Mango Fritters, you'll want to keep each batch warm until the entire recipe is cooked. Drain fried foods on paper towels, then place on an ovenproof platter. Cover loosely with foil and place in a 200°F. oven until the entire recipe is completed.

pretty dippers

Don't stick with the same old carrot or celery sticks for dippers. Many vegetables and fruits make excellent and colorful choices. Try radishes, sweet red pepper strips, sugar snap peas, broccoli, cauliflower and cherry tomatoes. Depending on the dip, fruit choices to consider are apples, pears, bananas, strawberries and dried apricots.

Green beans can also be used as dippers, but should be tenderized first. They can be blanched in boiling water for 3 minutes, then immediately plunged into ice water to stop the cooking. Drain and pat dry and they're ready to serve.

preparing a cherry tomato for stuffing

With a small sharp knife, cut the top off of each tomato. Scoop out the pulp with a small spoon, and place each tomato cut side down on paper towels to drain liquid.

super salads & soups

vegetable chowder • p. 28

Whether cool and crunchy or warm and wonderful, a salad can be served as a meal starter, a side dish or the main course. You'll find all three in this handy chapter, plus salad dressings that range from creamy to surprisingly tangy. See Field Greens with Basil Vinaigrette (p. 37) to see exactly what we mean.

In addition, a steaming bowl of soup can chase away the winter chills, warming you up inside and out. For savory broth- or cream-based soups that comfort the soul, check out Santa Fe Corn Tortilla Soup (p. 25) and family-pleasing Macaroni and Cheese Soup (p. 30).

poppy seed citrus salad

prep time: 15 minutes • total time: 15 minutes • serves: 4

Everyone knows we should all be eating our leafy greens every day. A delicious and easy poppy seed dressing will inspire you to make this salad a regular part of your meal plan. What a great and easy way to eat healthy!

1/3 cup canola oil	2 tsp. poppy seeds
1/4 cup sugar	2 medium oranges
2 tbsp. apple cider vinegar	1/2 small red onion
1 tbsp. minced yellow onion	1 large head Boston lettuce
1 tsp. dry mustard	(10 oz.)

1) In blender, process oil, sugar, vinegar, onion and mustard until combined and sugar is dissolved. Stir in poppy seeds. Set aside.

2) Peel and section oranges. Thinly slice onion. Clean lettuce and evenly divide leaves among 4 salad plates. Arrange orange segments and onion on top of greens.

3) Drizzle dressing over top of salad and serve.

nutritional facts: *Per serving: 270 calories • 26g carbohydrates • 2g protein • 19g fat • 5mg sodium • 0mg cholesterol • 5g fiber • 21g sugar*

citrus secret

Nothing beats fresh oranges, but in a pinch, you can use canned mandarin oranges.

thai shrimp soup

prep time: 10 minutes • total time: 29 minutes • serves: 4

Thai soups such as this popular one of shrimp and coconut milk are usually a mix of spicy and mellow flavors. The resulting taste is always light and refreshing—never heavy or oily.

2 large carrots	1 tbsp. cornstarch
3 to 4 oz. shiitake mushrooms	3 green onions
1 tbsp. vegetable oil	3 oz. angel hair pasta
2 tsp. grated fresh ginger	1/2 lb. medium shrimp, cleaned
1 tsp. minced garlic	2 tbsp. lime juice
1/8 tsp. red pepper flakes	1/4 tsp. salt
1 (13.5 oz.) can coconut milk, unsweetened	

1) Thinly slice carrots. Remove and discard stems from mushrooms and thinly slice caps.

2) In large saucepan over medium, heat oil. Add carrots, mushrooms, ginger, garlic and pepper flakes. Cook, stirring constantly, until fragrant, about 2 min. Add coconut milk and 2-1/2 cups hot tap water. Cover and bring to boil; reduce heat and simmer, covered, 5 min.

3) Meanwhile, diagonally slice green onions; set aside. Break pasta in half and add to saucepan. Bring to boil; reduce heat and simmer until pasta and carrots are almost tender, 4 min.

4) In small bowl, stir together cornstarch and 1/2 cup water; add to saucepan and, over high heat, bring to boil. Stir in shrimp and about 2/3 of green onions; boil until shrimp are cooked through, about 2 min. Remove soup from heat. Stir in lime juice and salt. Spoon into 4 serving bowls and garnish with remaining green onions before serving.

nutritional facts: *Per serving: 260 calories • 18g carbohydrates • 12g protein • 17g fat • 180mg sodium • 55mg cholesterol • 2g fiber • 2g sugar*

easy adjustment

You can use 1/2 cup diced boneless chicken in place of the shrimp, and to have a more generous-looking amount of shrimp, slice the shrimp in half along the vein line.

santa fe corn tortilla soup

prep time: 23 minutes • total time: 23 minutes • serves: 4

This soup is the best of Southwestern cuisine—fresh, light and full of flavor and texture. Corn, pan roasted, stars in a spicy broth. Lime and crispy tortilla strips add the final flavors and a surprising crunch.

6 (6 inch) corn tortillas	3/4 tsp. salt
2 tbsp. oil, *divided*	1 (48 oz.) can chicken broth
1 (11 oz.) can corn, well drained	4 green onions
4 Roma tomatoes	1 cup shredded cooked chicken
1 clove garlic	1/4 cup cilantro leaves
2 tsp. chili powder	1 lime
3/4 tsp. ground cumin	

1) Preheat oven to 375° F. Lightly brush both sides of tortillas with 1 tbsp. olive oil. Cut tortillas in half, then stack and cut into 1/2-inch strips. Place on baking sheet and separate into single layer. Bake until light golden brown, about 15 min.

2) In Dutch oven over medium-high heat, cook corn in remaining oil, stirring occasionally until golden brown, about 5 min.

3) Meanwhile, finely chop tomatoes and garlic; add to corn with chili powder, cumin and salt and cook about 2 min. Raise heat to high and add broth; bring to boil, then simmer 5 min.

4) Slice green onions thinly; add to soup along with chicken. Simmer 2 min., then stir in cilantro. Ladle into 4 soup bowls and top with tortilla strips. Cut lime into wedges and garnish soup bowls.

nutritional facts: *Per serving: 370 calories • 36g carbohydrates • 25g protein • 15g fat • 2740mg sodium • 45mg cholesterol • 5g fiber • 7g sugar*

great garnish

While the tortillas are baking in the oven, prepare the soup. Sprinkle the soup with tortilla strips just before serving.

dilled garden vegetable salad

prep time: 13 minutes • total time: 13 minutes • serves: 4

With crunchy garden vegetables and an ample dash of dill, this lovely salad and its cool, sour cream and vinegar dressing will keep them coming back for more. It's an easy way to get in those veggies!

1/2 large English cucumber	3 sprigs fresh dill, *divided*
1/2 medium yellow pepper	2/3 cup sour cream
1/2 medium red pepper	1 tbsp. apple cider vinegar
1/4 head of fresh broccoli	1/2 tsp. salt
1 small carrot	1/4 tsp. black pepper
1/4 of a small red onion	

1) Trim end off cucumber. Chop cucumber and peppers into 1/2-inch pieces. Place in large bowl. Chop broccoli into small florets; peel and grate carrot. Mince onion to yield about 1/4 cup. Add broccoli, carrot and onion to bowl.

2) Mince 2 sprigs fresh dill to yield 2 tbsp. In small bowl, combine sour cream, vinegar, dill, salt and pepper. Pour sour cream mixture over cucumber mixture. Stir to coat. Garnish with remaining dill and serve.

nutritional facts: *Per serving: 130 calories • 12g carbohydrates • 5g protein • 9g fat • 280mg sodium • 15mg cholesterol • 5g fiber • 3g sugar*

mighty mint

As an alternative to dill, try fresh mint—a perennial plant that grows like a weed (so keep it in a large pot); it gives this dish that fresh, Middle Eastern flair.

tomato bowls

Dress up this salad with this tasty presentation idea. Hollow out firm tomatoes and fill with the salad. Serve them on a plate lined with curly leaf lettuce.

tuscan tuna salad

prep time: 20 minutes • total time: 20 minutes • serves: 4

Hold the mayo! This meal in a bowl combines many of the flavors as well as the heart-healthy ingredients of southern Italy in one dish that elevates simple tuna salad to new heights of taste.

2 (6 oz.) cans chunk white albacore tuna in water, drained	1 medium red pepper
	1/4 cup nonpareil capers, drained
	1 lemon
2 (15 oz.) cans cannellini beans, drained and rinsed	1/3 cup olive oil
	2 tsp. fresh thyme leaves
1 small red onion	1 tsp. salt
1/2 cup pitted black olives	1/4 tsp. ground black pepper
1 small bunch parsley	

1) Drain tuna; separate into chunks with fork. Place in large bowl. Drain beans and add to bowl.

2) Chop red onion; add to bowl. Chop olives, parsley and red pepper; add to bowl. Stir in capers. In large salad bowl, combine tuna, beans, red onion and capers.

3) Into small bowl, squeeze juice of lemon; add olive oil, thyme, salt, and pepper. Stir to combine. Pour over ingredients in large bowl. Mix gently; serve immediately or cover tightly and store in refrigerator.

nutritional facts: *Per serving: 490 calories • 45g carbohydrates • 31g protein • 22g fat • 1370mg sodium • 20mg cholesterol • 17g fiber • 3g sugar*

lighten up

Sugar can be easily eliminated in this recipe. For sweetness you can use a sugar substitute.

robust romaine salad

prep time: 15 minutes • total time: 15 minutes • serves: 4

This simple recipe yields a hearty and healthy salad. It's a perfect combo…crispy romaine lettuce, warm "charred" onions, juicy tomatoes and shreds of Cheddar tossed in a sweet and tangy dressing.

2 large sweet onions	1 tbsp. Dijon-style mustard
2 tsp. plus 1/4 cup oil	1 tbsp. sugar
1 cup grape *or* cherry tomatoes	1/2 tsp. salt
4 oz. cheddar cheese	1/4 tsp. pepper
2 tbsp. balsamic vinegar	2 heads romaine lettuce

1) Preheat broiler to high and adjust rack as close as possible to element. Line large, shallow baking sheet with foil.

2) Slice onion into 1/2-inch rings; separate and place on prepared baking sheet; toss with 2 tsp. oil. Broil 8 min., turning once, until starting to char, but still crisp-tender.

3) Meanwhile, halve tomatoes and shred cheese. In small bowl, whisk together remaining oil, vinegar, mustard, sugar, salt and pepper.

4) Cut romaine in half lengthwise, then cut crosswise into bite-size pieces. Place in large bowl. Drizzle on dressing and toss to coat. Divide among 4 plates. Evenly top with tomatoes, warm onions and cheese

nutritional facts: *Per serving: 360 calories • 25g carbohydrates • 10g protein • 26g fat • 580mg sodium • 30mg cholesterol • 4g fiber • 16g sugar*

healthy cabbage soup

prep time: 12 minutes • total time: 32 minutes • serves: 4

Savor the flavors of summer in this lean and luscious soup. Although the ingredient list is long, everything is roughly chopped and it goes into one big pot for a simple, delicious (and healthy!) dish.

1 large sweet onion	1 (14.5 oz.) can chicken broth
2 stalks celery	4 cups coleslaw mix
1 tsp. olive oil	1 tsp. Italian seasoning
1 green pepper	1 tsp. salt
1 zucchini	2 cups fresh leaf spinach
4 cloves garlic	1 tbsp. packed brown sugar
1 (15 oz.) can diced tomatoes	1/2 tsp. hot pepper sauce

1) Chop onion and celery. In large saucepan over medium, heat oil. Add onion and celery; cook, covered, until softened, about 6 min., stirring occasionally.

2) Meanwhile, chop green pepper. Quarter zucchini lengthwise, then slice crosswise. Thinly slice garlic.

3) In same saucepan, add 2 cups water, tomatoes, broth, coleslaw mix, Italian seasoning, salt, green pepper, zucchini and garlic. Bring to boil, reduce to simmer and cook 12 min. Stir in spinach and sugar. Cook until vegetables are tender, about 2 min. Stir in hot sauce. Ladle into bowls and serve.

nutritional facts: *Per serving: 160 calories • 30g carbohydrates • 7g protein • 2.5g fat • 990mg sodium • 10mg cholesterol • 7g fiber • 16g sugar*

use what you have

When that crisper drawer is full, use this recipe as a guide to profit from the vegetables on hand.

colorful chickpea salad

prep time: 14 minutes • total time: 14 minutes • serves: 4

Don't be fooled by this brightly colored lemony mix atop greens—this is no lightweight, hungry-again-in-minutes salad! It's packed with satisfying chickpeas and full of great flavor from the infused oil.

2 cloves garlic	3-4 sprigs fresh parsley
1/4 cup olive oil	1/8 tsp. salt
1 lemon	1/8 tsp. pepper
2 plum tomatoes	1 large heart of romaine lettuce
1/8 medium red onion	1/4 cup crumbled feta cheese
1/2 cup canned chickpeas, drained	

1) Mince garlic. In medium, microwave-safe bowl, combine garlic and oil. Microwave on HIGH until garlic flavor infuses oil, about 30 seconds.

2) Juice lemon to yield 2-1/2 tbsp.; add to bowl. Coarsely chop tomato and onion; add to bowl with chickpeas. Finely chop parsley to yield 1/4 cup; add to bowl with salt and pepper. Toss to combine.

3) Chop lettuce to yield about 4 cups. Place one cup lettuce on each of 4 salad plates. Evenly spoon chickpea-tomato mixture over top. Sprinkle evenly with feta cheese and serve.

nutritional facts: *Per serving: 220 calories • 13g carbohydrates • 5g protein • 17g fat • 190mg sodium • 10mg cholesterol • 5g fiber • 4g sugar*

fast fix

Salad for dinner is a real option when served with hearty bread like focaccia. Look for fresh focaccia in the bakery section of your supermarket.

oriental salad

prep time: 10 minutes • total time: 10 minutes • serves: 4

This colorful, healthy salad has a snappy Asian flavor thanks to a dressing made of soy sauce, sesame oil and rice vinegar. Start off an Asian-themed meal with it or serve it for lunch.

1/2 cup snow peas	2 tsp. sesame seeds, toasted
1 small red pepper	2 tsp. soy sauce
1 small yellow pepper	1/4 tsp. sugar
2 tbsp. vegetable oil	1 (8 oz.) bag mixed salad greens
1 tbsp. toasted sesame oil	with grated carrots
1-1/2 tbsp. rice vinegar	

1) In medium saucepan fitted with steamer basket, bring a 1/2 inch of water to boil. Lightly steam snow peas until bright green, 2-3 min. Remove and set aside.

2) Cut red and yellow peppers in half. Remove seeds and discard. Cut peppers into thin strips.

3) In small jar with tight-fitting lid, combine oils, vinegar, sesame seeds, soy sauce and sugar.

4) In large bowl, place greens and all vegetables. Shake dressing well and drizzle over greens. Toss and serve.

nutritional facts: *Per serving: 130 calories • 7g carbohydrates • 3g protein • 12g fat • 170mg sodium • 0mg cholesterol • 3g fiber • 3g sugar*

no-stress dressing

If you don't use rice vinegar and sesame oil in other recipes, just purchase bottled Oriental salad dressing so the ingredients won't go to waste.

vegetable chowder

prep time: 14 minutes • total time: 24 minutes • serves: 6

This hearty chowder will warm your family on a chilly evening. It's chock-full of chunky and wholesome veggies, so you'll feel good about serving it. Best of all, your family won't know it's good for them.

1 medium onion	1/2 tsp. salt
2 tbsp. butter	1/4 tsp. pepper
1 (8 oz.) pkg. sliced mushrooms	1 (10 oz.) pkg. frozen broccoli
2 tbsp. all-purpose flour	florets, thawed
1-1/4 cups vegetable broth	1 (10 oz.) pkg. frozen mixed
2 tbsp. sherry	vegetables (peas, corn,
1-1/4 cups half-and-half	carrots, green beans)
1/2 tsp. poultry seasoning	

1) Chop onion to yield 1/2 cup. In large saucepan over medium heat, melt butter. Add onion and cook, stirring, until softened, about 2 min.

2) Add mushrooms to pan and cook, stirring, until beginning to release moisture, 4 min. Add flour and cook, stirring, until lightly browned, about 3 min.

3) Add vegetable broth and sherry to mixture in pan; whisk until smooth. Slowly stir in half-and-half, poultry seasoning, salt and pepper.

4) Add broccoli and mixed vegetables to pan and simmer until heated through, about 10 min. Evenly divide among 6 bowls and serve immediately.

nutritional facts: *Per serving: 180 calories • 18g carbohydrates • 5g protein • 10g fat • 490mg sodium • 30mg cholesterol • 3g fiber • 5g sugar*

fresh herbs

Parsley, basil, thyme or oregano will bring out all the flavors of the vegetables while a small can of chopped tomatoes adds depth and texture.

great gazpacho

prep time: 15 minutes • **total time: 15 minutes** • **serves: 4**

The refreshing taste of fresh-from-the garden vegetables (even if yours come from the market!) makes this flavorful chilled soup so enjoyable. With just a bit of spice, it's surprisingly rich and satisfying.

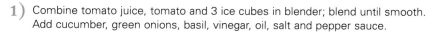

2 cups tomato juice	1 tbsp. red-wine vinegar
1 large tomato, cut into eighths	1 tbsp. extra-virgin olive oil
1 (4 inch) piece of cucumber, peeled seeded and cubed	1/4 tsp. salt
2 green onions, cut in 1-inch pieces	1/2 tsp. red pepper sauce *or* to taste
3 tbsp. basil *or* parsley leaves (about 12 basil leaves), plus leaves for garnish	1 cup canned Mexican-style corn, drained

1) Combine tomato juice, tomato and 3 ice cubes in blender; blend until smooth. Add cucumber, green onions, basil, vinegar, oil, salt and pepper sauce.

2) Blend just until vegetables are chopped, about 30-60 seconds. Remove pitcher from blender base. Reserve 3 tbsp. of corn for garnish. Add remaining corn to blender pitcher and stir in by hand.

3) Pour into 4 bowls; garnish with reserved corn and basil leaves.

nutritional facts: *Per serving: 110 calories • 19g carbohydrates • 3g protein • 3.5g fat • 820mg sodium • 0mg cholesterol • 3g fiber • 9g sugar*

get creative

This refreshing, chilled soup can be garnished with an array of items, including crunchy croutons, chopped fresh chives, chopped avocado or a dollop of yogurt.

shrimp cocktail salad

prep time: 15 minutes • **total time: 20 minutes** • **serves: 6**

Classic, and always popular, the flavors of shrimp cocktail make a welcome appearance as a salad. This tangy, tasty presentation is great for your budget, too, since you can use the tiniest, least expensive shrimp.

1 small rib celery	6 drops red pepper sauce
1 large shallot	2 lbs. cooked shrimp, cleaned and deveined
1/3 cup chili sauce	1 lemon
1/4 cup ketchup	1 large head Boston lettuce
1 tsp. prepared horseradish	
1/4 tsp. salt	
1/4 tsp. Cheasapeake-style seasoning	

1) Finely chop celery. Finely mince shallot to yield 2 tbsp. In large bowl, combine chopped celery, shallots, chili sauce, ketchup, horseradish, salt, Cheasapeake-style seasoning and red pepper sauce.

2) Chop shrimp into 1/2-inch pieces and add to chili sauce mixture. Toss gently to combine.

3) Cut lemon into 6 slices. Line 6 salad bowls or plates with lettuce leaves. Evenly divide shrimp mixture among salad bowls. Garnish each serving with lemon slice and serve.

nutritional facts: *Per serving: 190 calories • 10g carbohydrates • 33g protein • 2g fat • 1020mg sodium • 295mg cholesterol • 1g fiber • 7g sugar*

money saver

Frozen, cooked shrimp are usually a better bargain—and have a fresher taste—than the ones in the seafood case. And, since you'll be chopping the shrimp, purchase whatever size cooked shrimp is least expensive.

easy add-on

Pair this family-pleasing soup with your favorite crusty grilled sandwich for a comforting meal.

macaroni and cheese soup

prep time: 12 minutes • total time: 22 minutes • serves: 6

If you've got mac and cheese fans at your house, this is a perfect soup for a casual supper. Because it's so quick and easy to fix, there's no need to reach for the preservative-laden packaged variety.

3-1/2 cups chicken broth	3 cups shredded, sharp
1-1/2 cups small shell-shaped pasta	cheddar cheese
3 tbsp. butter	1 tsp. salt
3 tbsp. all-purpose flour	1/2 tsp. Dijon-style mustard
2 cups milk	

1) In large saucepan over high heat, bring chicken broth to boil. Add pasta and cook until tender, about 10 min.

2) Meanwhile, in another large saucepan over medium heat, melt butter. Sprinkle flour over butter; stir with whisk until smooth. Cook, stirring constantly, until mixture is light golden brown and slightly thickened, about 2 min.

3) Slowly whisk in milk. Cook until mixture thickens to consistency of yogurt, about 5 min. Stir in Cheddar cheese, salt and mustard. Cook until cheese is melted and sauce is smooth, 1 min. Remove from heat.

4) Into colander over large bowl, drain pasta, reserving broth in bowl. Stir broth into cheese sauce, whisking until smooth. Add cooked pasta and stir to combine. Transfer to bowls and serve.

nutritional facts: *Per serving: 420 calories • 26g carbohydrates • 19g protein • 26g fat • 1380mg sodium • 70mg cholesterol • 1g fiber • 4g sugar*

dressed up

You can use bottled ranch dressing if you like, but add the lime juice for a fresh, zesty flavor.

mexican cornbread salad

prep time: 15 minutes • total time: 15 minutes • serves: 10

This sweet and savory bread salad has lots of delicious flavors and textures. It pairs well with grilled meats or fish but can also stand alone as a main dish, since it has plenty of protein.

1/3 cup sour cream	2-3 sprigs fresh cilantro
1/3 cup mayonnaise	1 (15 oz.) can pinto beans
1 tbsp. ranch dressing mix	1 (8.75 oz.) can corn
1 tbsp. lime juice	1 cup shredded Monterey Jack
1/2 lb. loaf crusty Italian bread	& cheddar-blend cheese
1 large corn muffin	1 (4.5 oz.) can chopped green
4 green onions	chiles
1 orange bell pepper	1/2 cup sliced black olives
2 medium tomatoes	

1) In small bowl, combine sour cream, mayonnaise, ranch dressing mix and lime juice. Set aside.

2) Cut Italian bread and corn muffin into 3/4-inch cubes; place in large serving bowl.

3) Slice green onions and dice orange pepper; add to bowl. Seed and chop tomatoes; chop cilantro to yield 3 tbsp. Add to bowl. Drain beans and corn and add to bowl. Add cheese, chiles and olives to bowl; toss to combine.

4) Add dressing mixture to bowl and toss gently until thoroughly combined. Serve immediately.

nutritional facts: *Per serving: 290 calories • 34g carbohydrates • 10g protein • 14g fat • 460mg sodium • 25mg cholesterol • 5g fiber • 6g sugar*

gingered chicken salad

prep time: 10 minutes • total time: 26 minutes • serves: 4

Exotic and aromatic, ginger—which lends a punch of flavor to most dishes and is used three different ways here—is the real heart of this simple and satisfying chicken recipe.

1 qt. chicken broth	2 tbsp. dried crystallized ginger
1 small piece fresh ginger	1/4 cup mayonnaise
1 lb. boneless, skinless chicken breasts	1 tbsp. plain yogurt
	1/2 tsp. low-sodium soy sauce
1 tsp. coarse salt	3/4 tsp. ground ginger
1 large rib celery	1/4 tsp. pepper
2 green onions	1 small head radicchio
1/3 cup macadamia nuts	

1) In large, covered pot over high, heat chicken broth. Slice 3 quarter-sized rounds from fresh ginger and add to broth; set remainder aside. Bring to boil. Sprinkle chicken breasts with salt and add to pot; reduce heat to low and poach until cooked through, about 8 min.

2) Meanwhile, dice celery and cut green onions thinly; place in medium bowl. Chop nuts and add to bowl.

3) Rinse crystallized ginger to remove sugar; pat dry and coarsely chop; place in small bowl. Finely grate remaining fresh ginger to yield 1 tsp.; add to bowl. Add mayonnaise, yogurt, soy sauce and ground ginger. Stir to combine.

4) Remove poached chicken to colander; rinse under cool water. Pat dry; cut into bite-sized pieces. Add chicken to bowl with celery mixture. Stir in mayonnaise mixture. Sprinkle with pepper and stir to combine.

5) Line 4 salad plates with radicchio leaves. Evenly mound with chicken mixture and serve.

nutritional facts: *Per serving: 380 calories • 13g carbohydrates • 29g protein • 24g fat • 820mg sodium • 70mg cholesterol • 1g fiber • 4g sugar*

saving ginger

Ginger can be stored in the freezer for up to six months. Freeze and save any unused portion to have on hand for your next recipe.

carrot-raisin salad

prep time: 15 minutes • total time: 15 minutes • serves: 6

The beautiful orange of carrots never looked so good as it does in this light, fresh salad. Crunch from the carrots and apple and chewiness from the raisins combine for a wonderful taste sensation.

2 (8 oz.) pkgs. shredded carrots	3/4 cup reduced-fat mayonnaise
1-1/4 cups raisins	1 tsp. sugar
1 Granny Smith apple	1/2 tsp. salt
1 lemon	1/4 tsp. pepper

1) In medium salad bowl, combine shredded carrots and raisins.

2) With skin on, cut apple into eighths and remove core. Dice apple and add to carrot mixture.

3) Into small bowl, juice lemon. Stir in mayonnaise, sugar, salt and pepper.

4) Pour dressing over salad and toss to coat.

nutritional facts: *Per serving: 240 calories • 39g carbohydrates • 2g protein • 10g fat • 490mg sodium • 10mg cholesterol • 4g fiber • 26g sugar*

cut calories

Cut calories by using one part mayonnaise to one part plain yogurt, and add even more sweetness with some drained, crushed pineapple.

sun-dried tomatoes

Make your own oil-packed sun-dried tomatoes. Simmer dry-packed "sun-dried" tomatoes in water till plump; remove and pat dry. Place in a container with olive oil and refrigerate.

sunny day salad

prep time: 10 minutes • total time: 20 minutes • serves: 4

Chewy, crunchy, salty, sweet—this dish has it all! The flavors and colors combine beautifully to create a salad that's great served icy cold on a hot day or at room temperature any time of the year.

1/3 cup oil-packed sun-dried tomatoes, drained & patted dry	1-1/4 tsp. salt, *divided*
	1/2 lb. elbow-shaped pasta
1/2 cup pitted kalamata olives	1/3 cup raisins
3/4 cup crumbled feta cheese	1/4 cup olive oil
1/3 cup pine nuts	2 tbsp. balsamic vinegar
	1/4 tsp. pepper

1) Bring large pot of hot water to boil over high heat.

2) Meanwhile, roughly chop sun-dried tomatoes and olives; place in medium salad bowl. Add feta cheese and pine nuts.

3) Add 1 tsp. salt and pasta to boiling water. Boil, uncovered, until cooked al dente, 10-12 min. Add raisins to pasta during last 2 min. of cooking time.

4) Drain pasta and raisins in colander. Rinse under cold running water and drain thoroughly. Add cooled, drained pasta mixture to salad bowl.

5) In small plastic container with tight-fitting lid, combine olive oil, vinegar, remaining salt and pepper. Shake well. Pour dressing over salad and toss gently to coat.

nutritional facts: *Per serving: 660 calories • 69g carbohydrates • 15g protein • 37g fat • 950mg sodium • 25mg cholesterol • 4g fiber • 19g sugar*

scandinavian crisp bread

Pick up a box of rye or sourdough crisp bread to go along with this lovely, Scandinavian-inspired soup.

chilled beet soup

prep time: 6 minutes • total time: 29 minutes • serves: 4

This thick, chilled beet soup, with its hint of caramelized onions and orange, is not only hearty but also refreshing. Whether you make it as a first course or a light main dish, you can't go wrong.

6 small beets (about 1-1/4 lbs.)	1 orange
1 medium onion	3/4 cup orange juice
1 tbsp. oil	1 cup milk
1/2 tsp. sugar	

1) Trim and discard end of beets. Cut beets into quarters. Fit large pot with steam basket and fill with 1-inch hot tap water. Place beets in steamer. Cover and bring to boil over high heat. Cook until tender, 15 min.

2) Meanwhile, chop onion. In small skillet, heat oil. Add onion and sugar. Cook, stirring, until very tender and browned, 6 min. Grate 1 tsp. zest from orange and set aside.

3) Fill large bowl with ice and water. With tongs, remove beets from steamer and place in ice water. One by one, peel and discard skin from beets.

4) Place onion, orange juice, orange zest and 1/2 cup cold water in blender. Add peeled beets. Puree until smooth, 1 min. Add milk and puree until smooth and combined. Pour into 4 bowls. If desired, peel several strips of orange rind and slice thinly. Garnish soup with orange rind strips and serve.

nutritional facts: *Per serving: 220 calories • 38g carbohydrates • 5g protein • 6g fat • 140mg sodium • 5mg cholesterol • 4g fiber • 30g sugar*

green and white soup

prep time: 10 minutes • total time: 26 minutes • serves: 5

This satisfying soup tastes so good, you'll forget it's good for you, too, with its loads of fresh-from-the-garden vegetables and chunky, protein-rich beans. Enjoy a bowl in good health!

2 (14 oz.) cans reduced-sodium chicken broth	1/2 tsp. oregano
1 large onion	1/2 tsp. pepper
1 rib celery	2 (15 oz.) cans cannellini beans
1 carrot	1/2 head escarole (8 oz.)
8 large cloves garlic	1 cup grape tomatoes
2 tbsp. olive oil	1/3 cup shredded Parmesan cheese
1 tsp. basil	

1) In medium saucepan over high heat, bring broth to boil. Meanwhile, chop onion to yield 1 cup. Chop celery and carrot to yield 1/2 cup each. Thinly slice garlic.

2) In 5-qt. pot over high, heat oil. Add onion, celery, carrot, garlic, basil, oregano and pepper. Cook, stirring, until onions are translucent, 2 min.

3) Drain and rinse beans. Add broth and beans to onion mixture. Cover and bring to boil. Meanwhile, chop escarole into 1/2-inch pieces. Add to pot; cover and return to boil. Reduce to medium-high heat and cook until vegetables and beans are tender, about 4 min. Add tomatoes and cook until heated through, 1 min.

4) Transfer to 4 serving bowls; sprinkle evenly with cheese and serve.

nutritional facts: *Per serving: 220 calories • 28g carbohydrates • 11g protein • 7g fat • 430mg sodium • 5mg cholesterol • 8g fiber • 2g sugar*

money-saving tip

Dried beans soaked overnight are always less expensive than canned beans. You can easily stretch this for extra savings by adding cooked chunked chicken with another can of broth.

roasted corn and bean salad

prep time: 15 minutes • total time: 15 minutes • serves: 4

Roasting corn brings out a sweet, caramelized flavor from its natural sugars. Toss the corn in this colorful mix of chickpeas, black beans, grape tomatoes and green onions for a delicious twist.

1 bunch green onions	6 sprigs basil
2 cups frozen corn kernels	2 limes
1 cup canned chickpeas, rinsed and drained	1 tbsp. olive oil
1 cup canned black beans, rinsed and drained	2 tbsp. brown sugar
	2 tsp. jalapeno sauce
1 cup grape tomatoes	1/2 tsp. salt

1) Slice green onions. Coat large, nonstick skillet with cooking spray. Add corn; spread in single layer and set over medium-high heat. Cook, without stirring, until corn begins to brown, 7 min. Stir in green onions and cook 1 min. Scrape into medium bowl. Add chickpeas and black beans.

2) Cut tomatoes lengthwise in half, then chop basil to make 1/2 cup; add to bowl. Juice limes; add 3 tbsp. juice to bowl, along with oil, sugar, jalapeno sauce and salt. Toss well to combine. Serve immediately at room temperature or chill before serving.

nutritional facts: *Per serving: 280 calories • 53g carbohydrates • 11g protein • 6g fat • 370mg sodium • 0mg cholesterol • 11g fiber • 13g sugar*

farmers market veggies

Corn, green onions, tomatoes and basil are in great supply when they're garden-fresh or at the farmers market. Make this dish when the produce is at its peak.

one-stop pantry salad

prep time: 15 minutes • total time: 15 minutes • serves: 6

Keep your pantry stocked with a variety of high-quality jarred and canned vegetables, and you'll always have the makings for a tasty salad. This one's a can't-miss dish on a busy night.

1 (14.5 oz.) can diced tomatoes with basil, garlic & oregano	1 (6 oz.) jar marinated mushrooms, partially drained
1 (14 oz.) can artichoke hearts, drained	1 (6 oz.) can pitted black olives, drained
1 (15 oz.) can hearts of palm, drained	1 small red onion
1 (7 oz.) jar roasted peppers, drained	1/3 cup olive oil
	2 tsp. dried parsley
	1 tsp. sugar

1) Place strainer over small bowl. Place tomatoes in strainer to separate from liquid; let stand while preparing other vegetables.

2) Cut artichokes into halves and arrange in large serving bowl. Cut hearts of palm crosswise in half, then lengthwise into quarters; place in bowl. Cut roasted peppers into strips and add to bowl.

3) Add mushrooms (with about half of marinade), then olives and drained tomatoes to bowl.

4) Slice red onion crosswise very thinly and separate into rings; arrange over vegetables.

5) In small bowl, combine oil, parsley, sugar and 1/4 cup of tomato liquid; blend well and pour over vegetables.

nutritional facts: *Per serving: 300 calories • 35g carbohydrates • 7 protein • 16g fat • 1080mg sodium • 0mg cholesterol • 5g fiber • 14g sugar*

quick tip

Serve this dish as a main course with crusty bread and an olive oil dip. For the dip, place 1/4 cup of olive oil in a shallow bowl and sprinkle with salt, black pepper and lemon juice.

marinated cucumber salad

prep time: 15 minutes • total time: 15 minutes • serves: 6

This salad is a wonderful and unexpected accompaniment to grilled sausages, marinated steaks and even dresses up burgers and hot dogs. Moist and cool, it's a welcome side dish on a hot day.

3 large cucumbers	2 tbsp. chopped fresh dill
1/4 small red onion	1/2 tsp. salt
1 cup cider vinegar	1/8 tsp. pepper
2/3 cup sugar	

1) Peel and thinly slice cucumbers. Thinly slice red onion.

2) In two-quart covered container, place vinegar and sugar, stirring until dissolved. Stir in dill, salt and pepper. Add cucumber and onion.

3) Fill two-cup glass measure with ice. Add enough cold water to fill in air pockets between ice chunks to yield full volume. Pour over cucumber mixture.

4) Cover and chill at least 15 min. or until ready to serve. Discard any unmelted ice. Serve by spooning from container with slotted spoon.

nutritional facts: *Per serving: 160 calories • 42g carbohydrates • 1g protein • 0g fat • 300mg sodium • 0mg cholesterol • 2g fiber • 40g sugar*

using dill

A teaspoon of dried dill weed can take the place of fresh dill when fresh herbs are hard to come by.

nutty napa ribbons

prep time: 10 minutes • total time: 10 minutes • serves: 6

If you've never tried Napa cabbage, you are in for a pleasant surprise. Crunchy but tender, it is perfect for this Asian-flavored dish—simple, colorful and oh-so-tasty.

3 tbsp. rice-wine vinegar	1/2 small head Napa cabbage
1 tbsp. sesame oil	(about 3/4 lb.)
1 tbsp. sugar	1 small red pepper
1/2 tsp. salt	4 green onions
	1/4 cup sliced almonds

1) In large serving bowl, whisk together vinegar, oil, sugar and salt until sugar is dissolved.

2) Thinly slice enough cabbage to yield 4 cups. Cut red pepper in half horizontally, then cut into thin julienne strips. Thinly slice green onions on sharp diagonal.

3) Add cabbage, red pepper and onions to bowl with dressing; toss to combine. Top with almonds and serve.

nutritional facts: *Per serving: 70 calories • 7g carbohydrates • 2g protein • 4.5g fat • 200mg sodium • 0mg cholesterol • 2g fiber • 4g sugar*

simple stir-fry

Shred the remaining 1/2 head Napa cabbage and use it in a quick stir-fry with canned Asian-style veggies and chunks of uncooked chicken.

roasted pear salad

prep time: 15 minutes • total time: 29 minutes • serves: 4

Looking for something new? Consider this gourmet salad combo of oven-roasted pears, Parmesan curls and a homemade pecan dressing. It delights the eye as well as the palate.

2 firm, ripe pears	2 tbsp. honey
1/8 tsp. dry mustard	1/4 tsp. salt
1/8 tsp. ground ginger	1/8 tsp. pepper
1/2 cup pecan pieces	1/2 cup vegetable oil
2 oz. wedge Parmesan cheese	3 tbsp. white-wine vinegar
1/4 medium red onion	1 (10 oz.) bag salad greens,
1 clove garlic	about 7 cups
2 tbsp. Dijon-style mustard	1/3 cup dried cranberries

1) Preheat oven to 400°F. Core each pear and cut into 8 wedges. In medium bowl, toss pears with mustard and ginger. Cover 1/4 of baking pan with foil; place pecans on foil. Cover remainder of baking pan with foil coated with cooking spray; place pears on coated foil. Bake until pecans are toasted and fragrant, 5 min. Remove pecans; place in refrigerator. Turn pears; bake until just tender, 10 to 12 min.

2) Shave 16 Parmesan curls; set aside. In food processor, chop garlic. Add vinegar, mustard, honey, salt and pepper. Add 2 tbsp. pecans; blend until combined. With unit running, gradually add oil, processing until combined.

3) Transfer pears to medium bowl. Remove 2 tbsp. dressing; toss with pears. Slice onion; place in large bowl with salad greens, cranberries and remaining pecans. Add dressing; toss well. Divide among 4 salad plates; top each with 4 pear pieces and 4 Parmesan curls.

nutritional facts: *Per serving: 540 calories • 35g carbohydrates • 9g protein • 44g fat • 580mg sodium • 10mg cholesterol • 6g fiber • 25g sugar*

flavor boost

If you are wondering what to do with the dried mangoes or crystallized ginger you have on the shelf, add them to this salad for an added boost of flavor and texture.

spinach success

Make this salad even healthier by preparing it with spinach—the bags of tender baby leaves are on the shelf next to the lettuce—which is richer in vitamins A and K.

blt salad with avocado

prep time: 13 minutes • total time: 18 minutes • serves: 4

The smoky flavor, crispness of bacon and the creaminess of avocado make this a hearty salad, packed with contrasting textures. Fresh salad greens and cherry tomatoes lend bright color.

1/2 lb. reduced-sodium bacon	1 (8 oz.) bag lettuce greens with shredded carrots
1/4 cup reduced-fat mayonnaise	
1-1/2 tbsp. 2% milk	1/2 cup cherry *or* grape tomatoes
1/4 tsp. garlic powder	1 avocado, pitted and diced
1/8 tsp. black pepper	1/2 cup unseasoned croutons

1) In large skillet over medium heat, fry bacon until both sides are cooked crisp. Drain on paper towel. Crumble and set aside.

2) Meanwhile, in small bowl, combine mayonnaise, milk, garlic powder and pepper.

3) In large bowl, toss lettuce with the mayonnaise mixture. Add bacon, tomatoes, avocado and croutons. Toss again and serve.

nutritional facts: *Per serving: 340 calories • 11g carbohydrates • 12g protein • 29g fat • 530mg sodium • 40mg cholesterol • 5g fiber • 2g sugar*

take-along favorite

This salad is wonderfully flavorful at room temperature, making it an ideal tasty take-along to a summer barbecue, a fall picnic or even a winter holiday buffet.

fruity lentil & rice salad

prep time: 29 minutes • total time: 29 minutes • serves: 6

The citrusy zing of orange and lemon and zip of parsley and chives lend a flavorful balance to the sweet dried cherries in this protein-rich salad made with healthful lentils and rice.

1 cup long-grain white rice	1 orange
1/2 cup lentils	1 small bunch fresh parsley
3 shallots	1 small bunch fresh chives
1 lemon	1/2 cup dried cherries
1/3 cup balsamic vinegar	1/3 cup olive oil
3/4 tsp. salt	

1) In medium saucepan over high heat, bring 1-1/2 cups water to boil. Add rice; reduce heat to medium-low. Cover and cook until tender, 20 min.

2) In large saucepan over high heat, bring 8 cups water and lentils to boil. Reduce heat to medium and gently boil until tender, 20 min. Drain.

3) Finely chop shallots to yield 1/3 cup. Squeeze lemon to yield 2 tbsp. juice. In small glass measure, stir together oil, vinegar, shallots, lemon juice and salt. Set aside.

4) Finely grate zest from orange; add to shallot mixture. Cut away remaining peel and pith from orange, cut sections from membranes. Cut orange sections into thirds.

5) Chop parsley to yield 1/4 cup and chives to yield 2 tbsp. In large, serving bowl, place cherries, parsley and chives.

6) Add rice, lentils, shallot mixture and orange pieces to bowl. Toss thoroughly to combine and serve.

nutritional facts: *Per serving: 320 calories • 44g carbohydrates • 6g protein • 13g fat • 300mg sodium • 0mg cholesterol • 5g fiber • 14g sugar*

ranch chicken salad

prep time: 15 minutes • total time: 23 minutes • serves: 4

You'll never go back to bland, bottled ranch dressing after you see how easy and flavorful this homemade dressing is, especially atop a fresh green salad with delicious grilled chicken.

1 lb. skinless, boneless chicken breasts
2 tbsp. olive oil
2 tsp. lemon pepper seasoning
1 clove garlic
1/4 tsp. salt
1-1/2 cups buttermilk
3 tbsp. sour cream
2 tbsp. mayonnaise
1 tsp. dried parsley
1/2 tsp. dried tarragon
12 cherry tomatoes
1/2 small red onion
4 cups mixed salad greens, washed
1 cup croutons

1) Preheat grill or grill pan to medium-high. Coat chicken breasts with olive oil and sprinkle with lemon pepper seasoning. Grill chicken on first side until golden, 4-5 min. Turn and cook until done, about 4 min. Transfer to plate and cover with foil to keep warm.

2) Meanwhile, mince garlic. In small bowl, mash garlic with salt. In medium bowl, whisk together buttermilk, sour cream, mayonnaise, parsley, tarragon and garlic mixture. Set aside.

3) Transfer chicken to cutting board. Slice crosswise into strips and set aside. Cut tomatoes into quarters and chop red onion to yield about 2 tbsp.

4) Arrange 1 cup of salad greens on each of 4 plates. Evenly divide tomatoes, croutons, onions and chicken strips and place on top of salad greens.

5) Drizzle about 3 tbsp. dressing over each salad. Keep remaining dressing, covered, in refrigerator up to 5 days.

nutritional facts: *Per serving: 430 calories • 16g carbohydrates • 41g protein • 22g fat • 510mg sodium • 110mg cholesterol • 2g fiber • 7g sugar*

in-a-dash dip

Add 1/4 cup sour cream to 1/2 cup leftover dressing to make a delicious dip for cut vegetables.

field greens with basil vinaigrette

prep time: 12 minutes • total time: 12 minutes • serves: 4

A generous side dish, this Italian-inspired salad uses basil in the dressing for a refreshing taste of the sunny Tuscan countryside. Mix a few large pieces of basil with packaged salad greens for a coordinated taste.

1 bunch basil
1/2 cup cherry *or* grape tomatoes
1/4 lb. mesclun salad greens
3 tbsp. olive oil
1-1/2 tbsp. red-wine vinegar
1 clove garlic
1/8 tsp. salt
1/8 tsp. pepper

1) Remove enough small basil leaves from bunch to equal 1/4 cup; gently tear in half down length of leaf. Slice tomatoes in half. Divide salad greens among 4 serving plates. Top each with basil leaves then tomatoes.

2) Remove 10 large basil leaves from bunch; place in blender with oil, vinegar, garlic, salt and pepper. Pulse until smooth, scraping sides of blender. Drizzle vinaigrette over salads.

nutritional facts: *Per serving: 110 calories • 4g carbohydrates • 1g protein • 11g fat • 85mg sodium • 0mg cholesterol • 2g fiber • 1g sugar*

basil turnabout

When fresh basil is not available, use 1 tsp. dry basil in the vinaigrette and omit the basil leaves in the salad.

beef it up

Thinly sliced beef fajitas will be just as good as the chicken. This salad is a perfect way to use up some of your leftover roast beef or steak in a new and delicious way.

sizzling hot fajita salad

prep time: 20 minutes • total time: 20 minutes • serves: 6

This will be the hottest salad you've ever tasted! Top the cool, crunchy greens with a delicious, spicy, sizzling chicken fajita and pepper mixture, then drizzle on a creamy ranch-style dressing.

1 lime	1 (8.75 oz.) can corn kernels
3/4 cup sour cream	1 (2.25 oz.) can sliced black
1 (1.25 oz.) pkg. fajita seasoning mix	olives
1/4 cup salsa	1 (10 oz.) pkg. precut romaine hearts
1-1/4 lb. boneless, skinless chicken breast	1 (16 oz.) pkg. frozen pepper stir-fry
1 tbsp. vegetable oil	6 tbsp. shredded cheddar cheese *divided*
1 (15 oz.) can black beans	

1) Squeeze lime juice into small bowl. Stir in sour cream, 1-1/2 tsp. fajita seasoning and salsa. Set aside.

2) Slice chicken breasts into 1/2-inch strips. In large, nonstick skillet over medium-high, heat oil. Add chicken and cook, stirring, until golden on all sides, about 5-7 min.

3) Meanwhile, drain black beans, corn and olives. Toss with romaine in large bowl.

4) Add pepper stir-fry, 1/2 cup water and remaining fajita seasoning to chicken. Cook until sauce begins to thicken and vegetables are heated through, about 5 min.

5) To serve, divide romaine mixture evenly among 6 plates. Top each salad with hot fajita chicken. Drizzle dressing over salad and sprinkle 1 tbsp. cheese over each. Serve immediately.

nutritional facts: *Per serving: 360 calories • 29g carbohydrates • 29g protein • 14g fat • 1350mg sodium • 80mg cholesterol • 8g fiber • 6g sugar*

dollar stretcher

Walnut oil can be pricey. If it's not in your cupboard, increase the olive oil to 1/2 cup and omit the walnut oil.

fennel salad with walnuts

prep time: 15 minutes • total time: 15 minutes • serves: 6

Elegant and easy describes this salad. Fennel, also known as anise, has a slight licorice flavor that goes well with the tart, crisp apple. A sprinkling of toasted walnuts adds extra crunch and flavor.

1/4 cup walnuts	1/4 cup red-wine vinegar
2 fennel bulbs	1/4 cup extra-virgin olive oil
1 Granny Smith apple	1/4 cup walnut oil
1 shallot	1 tsp. salt

1) In small nonstick skillet over medium-low, toast walnut halves until fragrant, about 5 min. Remove from heat and set aside to cool.

2) Meanwhile, trim tops of fennel bulbs. Remove core and slice thinly. Core and thinly slice apple. Thinly slice shallot and set aside.

3) In large salad bowl, toss together fennel and apple. Add cooled walnuts and toss.

4) Place shallot and red-wine vinegar in jar with tight-fitting lid. Shake to combine. Add olive and walnut oils and salt. Cover and shake vigorously for 30 seconds to combine. Pour over salad and toss gently. Serve immediately.

nutritional facts: *Per serving: 230 calories • 10g carbohydrates • 2g protein • 22g fat • 430mg sodium • 0mg cholesterol • 3g fiber • 3g sugar*

summer harvest chopped salad

prep time: 16 minutes • total time: 16 minutes • serves: 4

The essence of summer is captured with every forkful of this simple salad. Enjoy the bounty of the season—fresh corn, juicy tomatoes, abundant, aromatic basil—in a delicious chopped salad you can put together in minutes.

1/3 cup olive oil	2 ears corn, husked
1 tbsp. red-wine vinegar	1 medium zucchini
2 tsp. sugar	3 medium tomatoes
1 tsp. Dijon-style mustard	1/2 cup fresh basil leaves
1/2 tsp. salt	1/2 small red onion

1) In medium bowl, whisk together oil, vinegar, sugar, mustard and salt.

2) On cutting board, hold corn cob upright, stem end down. Carefully slice kernels from cob and place in bowl with dressing. Repeat with remaining cob.

3) Finely chop zucchini, tomatoes and basil and add to bowl. Finely chop onion to yield 2 tbsp. and add to bowl. Toss well to combine with dressing and serve.

nutritional facts: *Per serving: 130 calories • 25g carbohydrates • 4g protein • 3.5g fat • 340mg sodium • 0mg cholesterol • 3g fiber • 9g sugar*

extra nutrition

For protein, add a can of drained black beans, chickpeas or some cheddar, and serve this salad in scooped-out red peppers or atop lettuce leaves.

pronto dinner salad

prep time: 7 minutes • total time: 15 minutes • serves: 4

Tortellini, salty-sweet ham and fresh asparagus get tossed with a lemon-tarragon mustard dressing in this main-dish salad. The easy part? The asparagus and tortellini cook together in one pot!

2 (9 oz.) pkg. refrigerated cheese tortellini	2 tbsp. vegetable oil
1-1/2 tsp. salt, *divided*	1 tbsp. Dijon-style mustard
1 lb. asparagus	1 tsp. sugar
1/2 lb. deli ham (unsliced)	1/4 tsp. pepper
1 lemon	2-3 sprigs tarragon

1) In large pot, bring 3 quarts hot water to boil over high heat. Add 1 tsp. salt and tortellini and cook according to package directions, about 8 min. Slice asparagus into 3/4-inch pieces; add to tortellini during last 3 min. of cooking.

2) Meanwhile, cut ham into small dice. Grate lemon to yield 2 tsp. zest; set aside Squeeze lemon to yield 2 tbsp. juice. In large bowl, whisk together lemon, oil, mustard, sugar, remaining salt and pepper.

3) Reserve 1/4 cup of cooking liquid, then drain tortellini and asparagus. Run under cold water for several seconds; drain well.

4) Whisk cooking liquid into dressing. Add tortellini and asparagus, ham and lemon zest. Finely chop tarragon; add to bowl and toss to coat. Serve immediately at room temperature or chill.

nutritional facts: *Per serving: 570 calories • 70g carbohydrates • 30g protein • 20g fat • 1180mg sodium • 85mg cholesterol • 6g fiber • 10g sugar*

tool time

If you have the time to use a potato peeler to take off the tough skin from the lower third of the asparagus, you won't have to snap off the bottoms and throw them away.

jazzy gelatin

prep time: 10 minutes • total time: 12 hours • serves: 12

Finish things off with a bang with this colorful gelatin garnished with a chorus of fresh grapes. Chock-full of mandarin oranges and crushed pineapple, it's so refreshing that guests won't be able to refrain from seconds.

1 package (6 ounces) orange gelatin	1 (8 ounces) can unsweetened crushed pineapple, undrained
2 cups boiling water	1 (6 ounces) can frozen orange juice concentrate, thawed
1 cup ice cubes	Green grapes and fresh mint, optional
1 (15 ounces) can mandarin oranges, drained	

1) In a large bowl, dissolve gelatin in boiling water. Add ice cubes, oranges, pineapple and orange juice concentrate. Pour into a 6-cup ring mold coated with cooking spray. Refrigerate overnight or until firm.

2) Just before serving, unmold onto a serving plate. Fill center with grapes and garnish with mint if desired.

nutritional facts: *Per serving: 107 calories • 26g carbohydrates • 2g protein • trace fat • 35mg sodium • 0 cholesterol • 1g fiber*

it's in the can

For extra appeal, replace some of the boiling water with the juices from the can of mandarin oranges.

italian squash salad

prep time: 12 minutes • total time: 12 minutes • serves: 4

It's so simple, so tasty and so Italian to take so few ingredients to create a really memorable dish! A light "slaw" of shredded squash is tossed with oil, lemon and Parmesan and served on a bed of arugula.

1/4 cup olive oil	3/4 lb. zucchini
4 tsp. fresh lemon juice	3/4 lb. yellow summer squash
1 tsp. sugar	1/4 cup shredded Parmesan cheese
1/4 tsp. salt	1/2 bunch arugula
1/4 tsp. pepper	

1) In medium bowl, whisk together oil, lemon juice, sugar, salt and pepper.

2) Using large holes of box grater or shredding disc of food processor, shred zucchini and yellow squash. Add to dressing and toss to coat. Add Parmesan and toss thoroughly.

3) Arrange arugula onto 4 plates and evenly top with squash mixture. Serve immediately.

nutritional facts: *Per serving: 180 calories • 8g carbohydrates • 4g protein • 16g fat • 240mg sodium • 5mg cholesterol • 2g fiber • 5g sugar*

summer squash

If using larger summer squash, discard the inner "pulpy" portion that can be too wet and stringy and simply use the outer, more firm section for better results.

summer strawberry soup

prep time: 6 minutes • total time: 10 minutes • serves: 4

Very pretty and delightfully refreshing, this cold dessert soup is a great option when you just need "a little something" to end a meal. It's an easy, splendid finale to serve both guests and family.

1 (16 oz.) pkg. frozen whole strawberries (about 3 cups)
1-1/2 cups vanilla yogurt, *divided*
1/2 cup plus 1 tbsp. orange juice
1/2 cup sugar
1/8 tsp. ground cardamom *or* ginger
1 (12 oz.) can lemon *or* lemon-lime soda, chilled

1) In glass bowl, place strawberries. Microwave on LOW 4 min., stirring once, to partially thaw berries.

2) In blender, combine strawberries, 1-1/4 cups yogurt, 1/2 cup orange juice, sugar and cardamom. Process until smooth. Transfer mixture to bowl; stir in soda.

3) Ladle into 4 serving bowls. Stir remaining orange juice into remaining yogurt. Spoon dollop of yogurt onto each serving. Using tip of a knife, swirl into soup to create spiral design.

nutritional facts: *Per serving: 270 calories • 61g carbohydrates • 5g protein • 1.5g fat • 70mg sodium • 5mg cholesterol • 2g fiber • 54g sugar*

strawberry smoothies

Reduce the sugar and omit the soda: You'll have a Strawberry Smoothie the kids will love.

honeydew fruit salad

prep time: 15 minutes • total time: 15 minutes • serves: 8

Here's a refreshing medley that's a colorful addition to most any meal. It's particularly lovely for brunch or even special occasions such as Easter dinner. Best of all, it comes together in no time!

1 can (20 ounces) unsweetened pineapple chunks
4-1/2 teaspoons cornstarch
1 large honeydew, cut into balls *or* cubes
1 can (15 ounces) mandarin oranges, drained
1 tablespoon minced fresh mint

1) Drain pineapple, reserving juice; set pineapple aside. In a small saucepan, combine cornstarch and pineapple juice until smooth. Bring to a boil; cook and stir for 2 minutes or until thickened. Cover and refrigerate until cool.

2) In a large serving bowl, combine the honeydew, oranges, mint and reserved pineapple. Stir in pineapple juice mixture. Cover and refrigerate until serving.

nutritional facts: *Per serving 117 calories • 30g carbohydrates • 1g protein • trace fat • 22mg sodium • 0mg cholesterol • 2g fiber • 0g sugar*

instant flair

Jazz up the fruit salad with a can of lemon-lime soda. Simply pour a small amount of the soda over the fruit medley immediately before serving. It's a fast, citrus addition to this light recipe.

removing an avocado pit

1) Wash avocado. Cut in half lengthwise, cutting around the seed. Twist halves in opposite directions to separate.

2) Use a tablespoon and slip under the seed to loosen it from the fruit.

3) To remove half an avocado from skin, loosen from skin with a large spoon and scoop out avocado.

4) Slice peeled avocado as desired. Or, cut into unpeeled wedges and slice between the skin and the avocado.

snappy fruit salad

Add a sweet tang to ordinary fruit salad (cut-up apples, oranges, bananas, grapes) by sprinkling powdered lemonade mix over the fruit. Gently stir to distribute the lemonade mix. Start with just a light sprinkle, then taste and add a little more if you like. Your guest will never guess what your secret ingredient is.

cutting down on fat

If you are using canned broth that is not fat-free, just chill it in the refrigerator. After it's cold, remove the top of the can and lift off the solidified fat.

garnishes for soups

Dress up a soup with a sprinkle of nuts, chopped fresh herbs, sliced green onions, slivers of fresh vegetables, croutons, shredded cheese or crumbled bacon.

nutritious way to cool soup

Do you ever serve soup that is too hot to drink? To quickly cool the soup without diluting the flavor, add some frozen vegetables such as peas, corn and carrots. The veggies will cool the soup quickly, and they add some extra nutrition to the dish as well.

lightening up soups

It's easy to add soup to a food-smart meal plan. Keep the following pointers in mind when you're lightening up your favorites.

- **Skip the salt**—Set down the salt shaker and stir in additional herbs or a salt-free seasoning blend into your soup instead. When recipes call for canned chicken broth, substitute the reduced-sodium variety.

- **Thin thickeners**—Watching your weight doesn't mean writing off creamy soups. Puree a cooked peeled potato and reduced-fat milk or fat-free half-and-half to a creamy consistency. Slowly stir the mixture into the heated soup to thicken it. Then heat through, but do not boil. To thicken up southwestern soups and chili, add cooked and pureed beans.

- **Cut back on beef**—Try preparing a recipe with additional vegetables or pasta in place of beef. Or, consider replacing beef with cooked poultry now and again.

about freezing soup

Soups are great to make when you have time, then freeze for fast future meals. Here are some hints for freezing:

- Most soups freeze nicely. The exceptions are soups made with cream and potatoes. Those are better when eaten fresh.

- To cool soup quickly before freezing, place the kettle in a sink filled with ice water. When cool, transfer to airtight freezer-safe containers, leaving 1/4-in. headspace for expansion.

- Pasta in soup can get mushy in the freezer. It's best to add the pasta when ready to eat, not before freezing.

- To help retain their fantastic flavor, don't freeze soups for longer than 3 months.

- Thaw soup completely in the refrigerator and reheat in a saucepan.

handling beets

Once beets are cut, the color will bleed onto the cutting surface, knife and your hands. To protect your hands, wear plastic gloves when peeling and cutting beets.

bringing salads to potlucks

Resealable plastic bags make a great container for transporting marinated or creamy salads to a potluck. The bags don't take up much space in the cooler, and they won't spill! Once you arrive, just pour the salad into a serving bowl.

plan-ahead for potato salad

If you're baking potatoes for dinner add some extra for potato salad on the following day. Cool the extras and store them in the refrigerator until you're ready to make the potato salad. The cold baked potatoes are easy to peel with a knife.

the perfect container for transporting soup

A 5-quart slow cooker is ideal to transport soups or chili. Once you're at the potluck, just plug in the slow cooker to keep the food hot. Serve your contribution directly from the slow cooker.

shortcut to vegetable soup

If you don't like to chop up fresh vegetables for homemade soup, here's some ideas to eliminate the task. Use frozen vegetables instead of fresh. There are some great vegetable mixes you can use. Also, visit your grocer's salad bar and pick the mix you like best.

from leftover macaroni salad to hearty tuna salad

To create a tasty main dish salad from leftover macaroni salad, stir in a can of drained and flaked tuna and some frozen peas. Serve on a lettuce leave and add a little fruit on the side or a corn muffin and you'll have a delicious lunch.

handheld greats

monte cristo sandwich • p. 50

Here's a whole new take on fast food. Quick to make, yes. But these handheld delights are wholesome, delicious and made in the comfort of your own home.

It's a snap to whip up a refreshing, no-fuss bite with California Stuffed Croissants (p. 47) or Turkey Waldorf Sandwiches (p. 48). Or, get cozy with a warm sandwich such as Favorite Pepperoni Pizza Bagels (p. 47) or Spicy Meatball Sandwiches (p. 54).

And don't forget that "Handheld Greats" include items such as San Diego Chicken Tacos (p. 48) and Old-Fashioned Beer Brats (p. 52), too!

italian country pork sandwiches

prep time: 20 minutes • total time: 20 minutes • serves: 4

Face the triple threat: Hot, crunchy, and gooey! These hearty and savory pork sandwiches offer a great combination of flavors and are guaranteed to satisfy your hungriest crowd.

1 (12 oz.) jar roasted red peppers	1/4 tsp. garlic powder
1/3 cup mayonnaise	4 oblong sandwich rolls (about 2 oz. *each*)
3/4 lb. pork tenderloin	1/4 lb. hard salami
2 tsp. oil, *divided*	1/2 lb. fresh mozzarella cheese
1/4 tsp. salt	12 fresh basil leaves
1/8 tsp. pepper	

1) Preheat broiler to high. Drain peppers; pat dry. Process in blender or food processor with mayonnaise until smooth, 1 min.; set aside.

2) Cut pork diagonally into 1/2-inch slices. Place between sheets of waxed paper and pound thin. In large, nonstick skillet over medium-high, heat 1 tsp. oil. Add half of pork and cook until pork begins to turn color, about 2 min. Turn and cook until tender and done, 2-3 min. Remove to plate and season with salt, pepper and garlic powder. Repeat with remaining oil and pork.

3) Cut rolls open and place on baking pan. Broil until toasted. Spread all cut sides with red pepper mayonnaise. Remove half of pieces to plates and top with pork and salami. Thinly slice cheese and place on remaining bread. Return to broiler until cheese is just melted, 1 min. Top each piece with 3 basil leaves. Close sandwiches, cut in half and serve.

nutritional facts: *Per serving: 840 calories • 43g carbohydrates • 53g protein • 45g fat • 2340mg sodium • 145mg cholesterol • 2g fiber • 0g sugar*

grilling peppers

Grill a pepper until it's blackened; seal it in a zippered plastic bag so the skin loosens. When completely cool, remove the peel and seeds, then puree the pepper.

pilgrim's turkey sandwich

prep time: 20 minutes • total time: 20 minutes • serves: 4

Don't wait for the day after Thanksgiving to enjoy a turkey sandwich. The twist on this delicious version includes stuffing and cranberry sauce. Yum!

8 slices whole grain *or* white bread	1 lb. cooked, sliced turkey breast
3/4 cup cranberry sauce	1/4 cup chipotle *or* regular mayonnaise
4 lettuce leaves	
2 cups prepared stuffing, at room temperature	

1) Toast 4 slices of bread; lay out on cutting board. Spread 3 tbsp. cranberry sauce on each slice. Top with lettuce leaves.

2) Spoon on stuffing and top with sliced turkey, dividing evenly. Toast remaining bread. Spread on mayonnaise and place, mayonnaise-side down, on sandwiches.

3) Cut each sandwich in half (or fourths) and secure with picks. Serve immediately.

nutritional facts: *Per serving: 640 calories • 66g carbohydrates • 43g protein • 22g fat • 940mg sodium • 100mg cholesterol • 7g fiber • 20g sugar*

"soup-er" addition

These satisfying sandwiches become a meal when served with a piping hot bowl of minestrone soup.

california stuffed croissants

prep time: 19 minutes • total time: 19 minutes • serves: 4

Overstuffed with fresh turkey, garlic-parsley mayonnaise, tomato, avocado and sprouts, this delicious, West-coast inspired croissant sandwich can satisfy even those with the heartiest of appetites.

1 clove garlic	1 tbsp. butter
4 sprigs fresh parsley	4 slices Swiss cheese (about
3 tbsp. mayonnaise	1/4 lb.)
1/4 tsp. pepper, *divided*	1 large tomato
4 turkey cutlets (about	1-1/2 medium avocados
1 lb. total)	4 large croissants
1/4 tsp. salt	1/3 cup broccoli sprouts

1) Mince garlic and finely chop parsley to yield 1/4 cup. In small bowl, combine mayonnaise, garlic, parsley and 1/8 tsp. pepper. Set aside.

2) Sprinkle turkey cutlets with salt and remaining pepper. In large skillet over high heat, melt butter. Add turkey and cook until browned on first side, about 3 min. Turn and cook until done, 3-4 min. During last minute of cooking, top each cutlet with 1 slice cheese.

3) Meanwhile, cut tomato into 8 slices and avocados into 12 slices. Cut croissants horizontally. Spread mayonnaise mixture onto inside tops of croissants.

4) With fork, push cutlets around in pan to coat with pan juices. Place each piece on 1 croissant bottom. Top cutlets with 2 slices tomato, 3 pieces avocado and 1/4 of sprouts. Cover with top of croissant and serve.

nutritional facts: *Per serving: 740 calories • 38g carbohydrates • 50g protein • 45g fat • 840mg sodium • 175mg cholesterol • 4g fiber • 9g sugar*

pennywise

Broccoli sprouts are loaded with antioxidents so they're definitely worth the price tag. But if they're just out of reach, try less-expensive alfalfa sprouts or even red-leaf lettuce to keep that West-coast feel.

favorite pepperoni pizza bagels

prep time: 9 minutes • total time: 21 minutes • serves: 4

Pepperoni is the top-selling pizza in America, so why not make it at home atop thick mini bagels for a fun and satisfying lunch for the kids? It's a perfect treat on a half-day of school!

4 mini bagels	1/8 tsp. pepper
1/2 cup tomato and basil pasta	16 slices pepperoni
sauce	1/2 cup part-skim shredded
1/2 tsp. dried oregano	mozzarella cheese (2 oz.)

1) Preheat oven to 375°F. Split bagels in half and place on baking sheet. Top each with equal amount of pasta sauce. Sprinkle with oregano and pepper.

2) Stack pepperoni and cut in half. Place 4 pepperoni halves onto each bagel half, then evenly sprinkle each with cheese.

3) Bake until cheese is melted and bagel is browned on bottom, 12 min. Cool 1-2 min., then transfer to plates and serve.

nutritional facts: *Per serving: 220 calories • 18g carbohydrates • 11g protein • 12g fat • 700mg sodium • 35mg cholesterol • 1g fiber • 3g sugar*

deep-dish-style

For an old-world touch, make these pizzas deep-dish-style by scooping out the insides of the bagels so the mozzarella cheese can melt into the boat-shaped pizza crust.

san diego chicken tacos

prep time: 15 minutes • total time: 29 minutes • serves: 4

Bring home the flavors of sunny Southern California with these jalapeño chicken tacos that have a slightly sweet mango and black bean salsa—wrapped in a soft flour tortilla for perfect summer fare.

1 large mango	1 lb. thin-sliced boneless, skinless chicken breast
2 large radishes	
1/4 cup fresh cilantro	1 tbsp. vegetable oil
1/2 cup canned black beans	1/8 tsp. salt
1-1/2 tbsp. lime juice, *divided*	1/2 tsp. ground cumin
1 large jalapeno	1/8 tsp. pepper
1 medium onion	8 (6-inch) flour tortillas
2 large cloves garlic	1 cup prepared guacamole

1) Cut mango in half around pit. With spoon, remove pit from flesh. Working from cut side, cut flesh into 1/4-inch dice, being careful not to cut through skin. Turn skin inside-out; scrape mango from skin.

2) Mince radishes. Chop cilantro. In medium bowl, combine mango, radishes, cilantro, beans and 1/2 tbsp. lime juice. Set aside.

3) Seed jalapeño. Mince jalapeño, onion and garlic. Cut chicken into 1/2-inch strips.

4) In large skillet over high, heat oil. Add jalapeño, onion and garlic. Cook, stirring, 3 min. Add chicken; cook until no longer pink, 3-4 min. Add remaining lime juice, salt, cumin and pepper. Stir to coat.

5) Place tortillas on work surface. Evenly mound chicken on half of each tortilla. Spoon on guacamole and salsa. Fold over tortilla. Place 2 on each plate; serve.

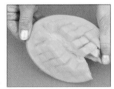

nutritional facts: *Per serving: 520 calories • 52g carbohydrates • 31g protein • 21g fat • 830mg sodium • 65mg cholesterol • 8g fiber • 12g sugar*

taco twists

There are many good variations to these. Busy cooks might prefer to shred a few previously made chicken breasts—or even some leftover cooked fish—for the family taco night.

turkey waldorf sandwiches

prep time: 12 minutes • total time: 12 minutes • serves: 4

Originated at New York's Waldorf-Astoria hotel as a salad made with fruits, nuts and celery, this clever version adds turkey and dried cranberries to transform this well-known classic into a hearty and delicious sandwich filling.

1/2 cup reduced-fat mayonnaise	1 large rib celery, diced (3/4 cup)
2 tbsp. lemon juice	
1 tsp. honey	1/3 cup chopped walnuts
1/4 tsp. salt	1/3 cup dried cranberries
10 oz. cooked turkey	8 slices whole grain bread
1 apple, cored and diced (1-1/4 cups)	8 lettuce leaves

1) Preheat broiler. In medium bowl, blend together mayonnaise, lemon juice, honey and salt. Cut turkey into 1/4-inch cubes; add to bowl. Add apple and celery to bowl, then walnuts and cranberries; stir until combined.

2) Meanwhile, toast bread slices under broiler. Arrange lettuce leaves on 4 slices of bread. Top with salad mixture, dividing evenly. Place remaining bread on top and cut each sandwich in half diagonally. Serve immediately.

nutritional facts: *Per serving: 590 calories • 45g carbohydrates • 30g protein • 33g fat • 650mg sodium • 70mg cholesterol • 6g fiber • 19g sugar*

skip the bread

With such a healthy, fruit-and-protein packed filling, you can skip the bread and serve the mixture within endive or arugula leaves for a satisfying lunch.

fennel, prosciutto and pear panini

prep time: 4 minutes • total time: 25 minutes • serves: 4

This springtime-in-Italy-inspired grilled sandwich is light and so delicious—loaded with fennel, pear, prosciutto and cheese. It makes for a simple, satisfying lunch or light supper.

1 baby fennel bulb (about 8 oz.)	8 oz. sliced mozzarella cheese
1 red pear	6 oz. thinly sliced prosciutto
1 tbsp. butter	12 large leaves basil
1/4 cup mayonnaise	
8 slices Italian bread (large round loaf)	

1) Trim and discard fennel top. Core fennel and thinly slice. Core and thinly slice pear.

2) In medium skillet over medium-high heat, melt butter. Add fennel and cook, stirring, until tender, about 5 min.

3) Meanwhile, spread mayonnaise on 1 side of each bread slice. Place 4 slices of bread, mayonnaise-side down, on work surface. Evenly layer each with cheese, prosciutto, fennel, pear and basil. Top each with bread slice mayonnaise-side up.

4) Heat large skillet over medium-high heat. When hot, place 2 sandwiches into skillet. Cover with second skillet topped with filled kettle of water to press down and flatten sandwiches. Cook until browned and crisp on first side, 4 min. Turn over and replace skillet and kettle. Cook until browned and crisp on second side, about 3-4 min. Transfer to cutting board. Repeat with remaining sandwiches. Cut each sandwich in half, transfer to plates and serve.

nutritional facts: *Per serving: 600 calories • 44g carbohydrates • 32g protein • 33g fat • 1990mg sodium • 75mg cholesterol • 5g fiber • 5g sugar*

sweet potato chips

Make your own homemade sweet potato chips. Slice sweet potatoes very thin and fry in hot oil until lightly browned; drain and sprinkle with coarse salt.

french quarter muffuletta

prep time: 20 minutes • total time: 20 minutes • serves: 6

This unusual, stuffed sandwich of savory meats and cheese was invented in New Orleans. The tangy olive salad, which flavors the cold cuts mounded on round bread, is what makes this a "Muffuletta."

1 (1 lb.) round loaf French bread	1/4 tsp. dried oregano
1/2 cup bottled red-wine vinaigrette dressing	1/8 tsp. pepper
1/2 cup pimento-stuffed olives, drained and chopped	1/4 lb. thinly sliced Genoa salami
1/4 cup chopped kalamata olives	1/4 lb. thinly sliced baked ham
1/4 tsp. dried basil	1/4 lb. thinly sliced Provolone cheese

1) Slice off top third of bread, reserving top portion as a "lid." Scoop out soft bread from center of larger portion of loaf, creating 1-inch-deep bowl.

2) In medium mxing bowl, stir together dressing, olives, basil, oregano and pepper. Brush dressing mixture onto inside of bread "lid" and "bowl," then spoon olives in.

3) Arrange layers of salami, Provolone and ham inside bread. Add lid; cut into wedges to serve.

nutritional facts: *Per serving: 460 calories • 42g carbohydrates • 19g protein • 23g fat • 1630mg sodium • 40mg cholesterol • 2g fiber • 3g sugar*

stacked shortcut

Buy whole country French or sourdough bread rounds. Cut through crosswise, the large round slices are big enough to contain all the ingredients.

monte cristo sandwiches

prep time: 25 minutes • total time: 25 minutes • serves: 4

A throwback to the Los Angeles of the 1940s, this perennially popular sandwich is a delicious cross between luscious, sweet French toast and a classic, savory grilled ham and cheese.

3 large eggs	4 thin slices Black Forest ham
1 cup milk	8 slices Swiss cheese
4 tsp. mayonnaise	4 thin slices roast turkey
8 slices soft white bread	2 tbsp. butter, *divided*
4 tsp. spicy brown mustard	4 tbsp. raspberry jam

1) In shallow bowl, whisk together eggs and milk. Set aside.

2) Spread 1 tsp. mayonnaise over 1 side of each of 4 slices of bread. Spread 1 tsp. mustard over 1 side of each of remaining 4 slices bread.

3) Layer 1 slice ham, 2 slices Swiss cheese and 1 slice turkey over mayonnaise-covered bread. Top with remaining bread, mustard-side down.

4) In large, nonstick skillet over medium-low heat, melt 1 tbsp. butter. Working with 2 sandwiches at a time, dip each side of bread into egg mixture, allowing excess to drip back into bowl.

5) Place in heated skillet and cook until brown on first side, about 4 min. Gently flip and press down cooked side with spatula. Cook until browned on second side and cheese is melted, 4 min. Repeat with remaining sandwiches.

6) Place each sandwich on serving plate and serve immediately with 1 tbsp. raspberry jam alongside.

nutritional facts: *Per serving: 570 calories • 44g carbohydrates • 31g protein • 30g fat • 990mg sodium • 170mg cholesterol • 1g fiber • 17g sugar*

special touch

Thick-sliced Brioche bread slices and a Russian-dressing (ketchup, mayo and a bit of horseradish) dip make these Monte Cristo sandwiches extra special.

pizza burgers

prep time: 5 minutes • total time: 23 minutes • serves: 4

Want something new instead of the same old cheeseburger? Try this Italian-style burger made from a fresh-tasting meat loaf mix. It's topped with a zesty tomato sauce, fresh mozzarella and oregano.

1-1/4 lbs. ground meat loaf mixture (beef, pork, veal)	1 tsp. dried basil
2 tbsp. finely grated Parmesan cheese	1 tsp. coarse salt
	1 cup tomato sauce
1-1/4 tsp. dried oregano, *divided*	1/3 lb. fresh mozzarella
	4 Italian sandwich rolls

1) Adjust rack to 4-5 inches below heat; preheat broiler. In medium bowl, using wooden spoon, thoroughly combine ground meat with Parmesan cheese, 1 tsp. oregano, basil and salt. Divide into 4 patties. Place on broiler pan and broil 5 min. Turn and broil 2-4 min., until almost to desired doneness.

2) Meanwhile, in small saucepan over medium, heat tomato sauce. Thinly slice mozzarella cheese into 8 pieces.

3) Remove pan from broiler and spoon several tbsp. warmed sauce over each burger. Place two slices cheese overlapping each burger. Sprinkle with remaining oregano. Return to broiler and cook until cheese melts, 1-2 min.

4) Trim ends off rolls and slice each roll in half horizontally. Place burgers on rolls and serve immediately.

nutritional facts: *Per serving: 620 calories • 53g carbohydrates • 49g protein • 25g fat • 1700mg sodium • 125mg cholesterol • 8g fiber • 11g sugar*

money stretcher

You'll probably have more tomato sauce than you need. Freeze the remainder in individual-size portions so you'll have a pasta topper almost instantly for those on-the-go family members.

grilled brie & fig sandwiches

prep time: 18 minutes • total time: 24 minutes • serves: 4

This simple pairing of ingredients results in a very special sandwich. With layers of creamy Brie cheese and fruity fig spread in between two slices of toasty brown bread, it's totally unique and delicious.

1 large orange	1/4 lb. wedge Brie cheese
1/2 cup dried figs (about 10)	1 tsp. butter, *divided*
1 (1 lb.) can brown bread	

1) Peel 1 inch of zest from orange. Squeeze orange to yield 1/4 cup juice. In small saucepan over high, combine figs, 1/4 cup water, zest and orange juice. Bring to boil; cover and reduce heat to medium. Cook until figs are softened, about 10 min. Remove and discard orange zest.

2) Place mixture in blender; puree 1 min. Set aside.

3) Remove both ends of can containing brown bread. Gently push bread from can. Slice into 8 rounds.

4) Slice Brie into wedges and cover 4 bread slices. Spread 1 tbsp. fig mixture on remaining bread slices. Top cheese with fig-covered bread, bread side out.

5) In large, nonstick skillet over medium heat, heat 1/2 tsp. butter. Place all sandwiches in skillet; top with second skillet weighted down with cans. Cook until slightly crispy on first side, 4 min. Add remaining butter to skillet. Turn sandwiches and replace skillet and weight. Cook second side until crispy and cheese is soft, 4 min. Transfer to plates and serve.

nutritional facts: *Per serving: 620 calories • 99g carbohydrates • 20g protein •18g fat • 1160mg sodium • 60mg cholesterol • 10g fiber • 61g sugar*

switch it up

Other dried fruit can be used instead of the figs. Some options are dried plums or dried apricots. Or use apple butter or marmalade if you have those on hand.

cheesy chicken & broccoli quesadillas

prep time: 7 minutes • total time: 27 minutes • serves: 4

This satisfying sandwich can be eaten with a knife and fork or cut into small wedges for anytime munching. It's a great change of pace from boring, old grilled cheese.

3/4 cup frozen broccoli pieces	2 small green onions, thinly sliced
2 cups refrigerated cooked chicken strips (about 10 oz.)	8 (8 inch) whole wheat tortillas
1-1/2 cups shredded sharp cheddar cheese	1 cup salsa

1) In a small, covered microwave-safe bowl, heat broccoli and 2 tbsp. water on HIGH for 1 min. Let stand for 1 min. Drain excess water. Mince broccoli.

2) Chop chicken into 1/4-inch pieces. In medium bowl, combine broccoli, chicken, cheese and green onions.

3) Place one tortilla in large nonstick skillet. Spoon generous cup of cheese mixture over entire surface. Top with another tortilla. Turn heat to medium. Cook until cheese begins to melt and tortilla is toasted, about 2 min. Turn and cook another until cheese is completely melted and both sides are toasted. Remove to plate; keep warm. Repeat with remaining ingredients. Serve with salsa.

nutritional facts: *Per serving: 570 calories • 55g carbohydrates • 29g protein • 31g fat • 1500mg sodium • 40mg cholesterol • 5g fiber • 2g sugar*

authentic flair

For authenticity, use half Monterrey Jack cheese or substitute it for the cheddar altogether. To add spice to the dish, look for jalapeno-seasoned cheese.

fast flavor

For a fast sauce, whip up a quick blend of 1/4 cup horseradish, 2 tablespoons each sour cream and chopped dill, and a teaspoon of mustard.

old-fashioned beer brats

prep time: 5 minutes • total time: 25 minutes • serves: 4

Savory brats simmered in beer, then grilled until crisp—it's a long-held tradition that everyone enjoys. These are served with a flavorful onion-kraut mixture.

2 medium red onions	1 tbsp. brown sugar
1 (12 oz.) bottle dark *or* amber beer	1 tbsp. caraway seeds
4 fresh (uncooked) bratwurst links	1 tsp. mustard
	2 tbsp. chopped fresh dill
1 (16 oz.) bag sauerkraut	4 hoagie *or* Kaiser rolls

1) Preheat grill or broiler. Peel and cut onions in half lengthwise, then thinly slice into half rings. In large saucepan over high heat, place onions and beer and bring to boil.

2) Pierce bratwurst 1 or 2 times with fork; add to saucepan. Reduce heat and simmer 10 min. Remove bratwurst.

3) In strainer, rinse sauerkraut with cold running water; let drain. Reserving 3 tbsp. beer, pour remaining beer and onions over sauerkraut in strainer to drain. Return mixture to saucepan, adding reserved beer, sugar, caraway and mustard. Cook over medium-low heat for 10 min.; stir in dill.

4) Meanwhile, grill or broil bratwurst, turning frequently, until crisp and golden, about 5 min. During last min of cooking, split rolls and grill or broil. Place each bratwurst on roll and mound with sauerkraut mixture.

nutritional facts: *Per serving: 550 calories • 69g carbohydrates • 31g protein • 17g fat • 1230mg sodium • 80mg cholesterol • 8g fiber • 14g sugar*

"cents-ible" substitution

If Napa cabbage is too costly or difficult to find, use strips of iceberg lettuce instead.

chinese chicken tacos

prep time: 10 minutes • total time: 24 minutes • serves: 4

Mexico and Asia unite for a great taste sensation! A crunchy taco shell is the perfect vessel for a delicious and easy Asian-inspired chicken sauté topped with tasty shredded cabbage.

8 taco shells	2 green onions
1 red pepper	1/4 cup jarred sweet-and-sour sauce
1 piece fresh gingerroot	
1 tsp. sesame oil	2 tsp. chili-garlic sauce
3/4 lb. ground chicken	4 Napa cabbage leaves

1) Preheat oven to 250°F. Place taco shells on baking sheet and place in oven. Chop red pepper into 1/2-inch dice and set aside 1/4 cup. Thinly slice cabbage; set aside. Grate 2 tsp. ginger.

2) In large, nonstick skillet over medium-high, heat sesame oil. Add red pepper and cook, stirring, 3 min. Add chicken and ginger and cook, breaking up meat with spoon, until no longer pink, about 4 min.

3) Meanwhile, slice green onions for topping. Stir sweet-and-sour sauce and chili-garlic sauce into skillet. Cook until heated through, about 1 min. Remove taco shells from oven. Spoon chicken mixture into taco shells and top with sliced cabbage, remaining red pepper and green onion. Place 2 on each serving plate and serve.

nutritional facts: *Per serving: 290 calories • 26g carbohydrates • 16g protein • 14g fat • 240mg sodium • 55mg cholesterol • 3g fiber • 7g sugar*

prosciutto pesto baguettes

prep time: 5 minutes • total time: 15 minutes • serves: 4

You can't go wrong with this: Pesto, red peppers, provolone and prosciutto combine all the best Italian flavors into one spectacular deli-style sandwich. Enjoy it any time of day or night!

1 loaf French bread	2 tbsp. prepared pesto
3 tbsp. olive oil	1 (7 oz.) jar roasted red peppers
1 clove garlic	1/4 lb. pound thinly sliced
1/4 lb. sliced provolone cheese	prosciutto

1) Preheat broiler. Line broiler pan with aluminum foil; set aside.

2) Slice bread in half crosswise, then slice again lengthwise. Brush olive oil over cut side of each piece. Broil bread 6 inches from heat until bread starts to turn golden, about 3-4 min. Meanwhile, peel garlic clove and cut in half.

3) Remove toasted bread from broiler and rub with cut side of garlic clove. Fold cheese slices in half. Place on top halves of bread. Return top halves to broiler until cheese is melted, about 3-4 min.

4) Spread both bottom halves of bread with 1 tbsp. pesto each. Drain red peppers, pat dry and tear into small chunks; place on top of pesto.

5) Remove top halves of bread from broiler and top melted cheese with sliced prosciutto. Press top and bottom halves of bread together. Cut each half into quarters before serving.

nutritional facts: *Per serving: 840 calories • 96g carbohydrates • 29g protein • 37g fat • 2240mg sodium • 45mg cholesterol • 7g fiber • 0g sugar*

pile on the taste

Scoop some of the dough out of the baguette—with fingers or a sharp grapefruit spoon—so the roasted peppers and prosciutto will stuff the sandwich nicely.

three-bacon pizza

prep time: 11 minutes • total time: 23 minutes • serves: 4

With a taste like the best meat-lover's pie at the pizzeria, what could be better? How about that this delicious pizza comes straight from your own oven in no time, with just seven ingredients!

1 cup tomato sauce	1/2 lb. fresh mozzarella cheese
4 strips bacon	1 (14 oz.) prepared pizza crust
2 oz. sliced Canadian bacon	1 tsp. dried oregano
1 oz. sliced prosciutto	

1) Preheat oven to 450°F. Adjust rack to lower third of oven. In small saucepan over medium, heat sauce until warmed through, 1-2 min.

2) Cut bacon strips in half crosswise. In medium skillet over medium heat, cook bacon until crisp, about 4 min. Remove and drain on paper towels, about 4 min. Drain excess drippings from pan and return to heat. Add Canadian bacon and sear on both sides, about 30 seconds per side. Cut into small strips.

3) Cut prosciutto into small strips. Slice mozzarella.

4) Place pizza crust on back of baking sheet. With large spoon, spread tomato sauce evenly over top of crust, leaving 1/4-inch border all around. Arrange cheese over sauce and spread strips of prosciutto and Canadian bacon over cheese. Place bacon strips in crisscross pattern over top and sprinkle with oregano. Bake until cheese is melted, 10 min. Cool slightly; cut into 4 wedges and serve.

nutritional facts: *Per serving: 510 calories • 53g carbohydrates • 32g protein • 0g fat • 1740mg sodium • 55mg cholesterol • 3g fiber • 5g sugar*

say "cheese"

Don't be tempted to skimp on the cheese in this recipe—there is a big difference in the taste of this important ingredient. Buy and slice fresh mozzarella cheese for the best flavor.

spicy meatball sandwich

prep time: 29 minutes • total time: 29 minutes • serves: 6

A new way to think about a meatball hero! Ground beef is blended with spices, soft bread crumbs and fresh spinach to create these meatballs with a spicy kick. Serve on rolls spread with zesty mayo.

3	slices white bread	1	large egg
4	cups fresh spinach, *divided*	6	ciabatta *or* French rolls
1-1/2	tsp. chili powder, *divided*	1-1/2	cups grated Jack cheese
1	tsp. dried oregano	3 to 4	sprigs cilantro
1	tsp. ground cumin	3/4	cup mayonnaise
1/2	tsp. salt	1	small red pepper
1	lb. lean ground beef		

1) Preheat oven to 400°F. Line 1 shallow baking sheet with foil. Coat another with cooking spray.

2) In food processor, process bread to fine crumbs; turn into large bowl. Into processor, add 2 cups spinach and process until finely chopped; add to bowl. Into spinach and bread crumbs, stir 1/2 tsp. chili powder, oregano, cumin and salt. Add ground beef and egg; blend well. With small scoop, make 24 meatballs. Place on coated baking pan. Bake until cooked through, 15 min.

3) Meanwhile, split rolls and place bottom halves onto lined baking sheet. Top with cheese and place in oven during last 2 min. meatballs are baking.

4) Chop cilantro to yield 1/4 cup. In small bowl, blend mayonnaise, remaining chili powder and cilantro. Spread mixture onto inside of tops of rolls. Thinly slice red pepper. To make sandwiches, evenly divide remaining spinach among bottoms of rolls. Top each with 6 meatballs and red pepper strips. Cap with mayonnaise-coated tops and serve.

nutritional facts: *Per serving: 550 calories • 28g carbohydrates • 28g protein • 37g fat • 890mg sodium • 110mg cholesterol • 3g fiber • 1g sugar*

fast fix

If you wish, one (10 oz.) package of frozen spinach can be substituted for the fresh leaves, but be sure to completely squeeze out all the water and drain it very well.

light chili-cheese dogs

prep time: 15 minutes • total time: 17 minutes • serves: 6

Using ground turkey breast and reduced-sodium tomato sauce in the chili helps to keep down the fat and sodium in these ballpark favorites. The bold flavors of these franks really come through!

1	lb. ground turkey breast *or* lean ground beef	3/4	tsp. ground cumin
1-1/2	cups frozen chopped onions	6	turkey hot dogs
2	(8 oz.) cans reduced-sodium tomato sauce	6	hot dog rolls
1	(1.25 oz.) pkg. chili seasoning mix	3/4	cup shredded cheddar cheese

1) In nonstick skillet over medium-high heat, cook turkey and onions, breaking up meat with spoon, until no longer pink, about 6 min. Drain, if necessary.

2) Stir in tomato sauce, chili seasoning and cumin. Simmer until thickened, about 6 min.

3) Meanwhile, in grill pan or large skillet over medium heat, cook hot dogs until heated through and browned on all sides, about 5 min. Place hot dogs in rolls and top each with about 1/2 cup chili and 2 tbsp. shredded cheese.

nutritional facts: *Per serving: 500 calories • 35g carbohydrates • 30g protein • 27g fat • 1430mg sodium • 125mg cholesterol • 4g fiber • 6g sugar*

crunchy touch

This fun and fast meal will be a hit with your family. Let the kids crush a few corn chips to place on top of their chili dogs—the colorful corn chips add the perfect crunch.

knockwurst reuben

prep time: 20 minutes • total time: 20 minutes • serves: 4

Here's a tasty—and economical—take on the classic Reuben. This one has all the familiar components, but with a twist: a split knockwurst instead of corned beef, and dressing made with just three ingredients.

1 medium onion	4 slices rye bread
1 tbsp. vegetable oil	2 stalks chives
1 (16 oz.) pkg. sauerkraut, drained	1 cup mayonnaise
	1/3 cup chili sauce
4 knockwurst	4 slices Swiss cheese

1) Preheat broiler; line baking sheet with foil. Chop onion. In large saucepan over medium, heat oil. Add onion and cook until almost tender, about 4 min. Add sauerkraut and stir; place knockwurst on top; reduce heat to medium-low. Cover and simmer, stirring occasionally, 10 min.

2) Meanwhile, place bread on baking sheet. Place under broiler until toasted on first side, about 2 min. Turn and toast second side, 1 min.

3) Chop chives to yield 2 tbsp. In small bowl, blend mayonnaise, chili sauce and chives. Spread 1 side of each piece of toast with 1 tbsp. dressing mixture.

4) Remove each knockwurst from pan and split in half lengthwise; place on bread. Evenly mound sauerkraut on top of knockwurst; add 1 slice of cheese. Broil until cheese is melted, 1-2 min. Remove from broiler, cut in half and serve.

nutritional facts: *Per serving: 940 calories • 31g carbohydrates • 21g protein • 80g fat • 430mg sodium • 100mg cholesterol • 6g fiber • 8g sugar*

easy option

If you don't have chili sauce for the Russian dressing, substitute ketchup and add a bit of horseradish or a dash of red pepper sauce for heat.

chorizo & pepper quesadillas

prep time: 3 minutes • total time: 19 minutes • serves: 4

Quesadillas are a delicious alternative to a sandwich for an easy lunch or simple supper. Even with the time it takes cooking the peppers and heating the chorizo, just about nothing is faster!

1 red pepper	1 (7 oz.) pkg. chorizo
1 green pepper	4 (10 inch) flour tortillas
3 tbsp. canola oil, *divided*	1/2 lb. sliced cheddar cheese
1/8 tsp. salt	4 tsp. minced pepperoncini

1) Thinly slice red and green pepper. In large skillet over medium, heat 1 tbsp. oil. Add red and green peppers. Cook until softened, 4-5 min.; sprinkle with salt. Meanwhile, slice chorizo in 1/4-inch rounds and add to pan. Cook, stirring occasionally, until heated through, 1 min. Transfer to plate; wipe out skillet.

2) Lay tortillas on work surface. Place three slices Cheddar cheese on bottom half of each tortilla, overlapping as necessary. Evenly spread pepper-chorizo mixture over cheese. Sprinkle 1 tsp. pepperoncini over peppers. Fold top half of tortilla over cheese and peppers.

3) In same skillet over medium, heat 1 tsp. oil. Place 2 tortillas in pan and cook until golden on first side, 1-2 min. Carefully turn and cook until golden on second side, 1-2 min. Transfer to plate; keep warm. Repeat with remaining oil and tortillas. Cut each quesadilla into 3 wedges and serve.

nutritional facts: *Per serving: 800 calories • 42g carbohydrates • 35g protein • 55g fat • 1650mg sodium • 110mg cholesterol • 3g fiber • 4g sugar*

true colors

Orange or yellow peppers are sweeter and add a bit more of a special touch than green peppers and can be used for green peppers in most dishes.

tips for handheld greats

about muffuletta

A muffuletta is a classic New Orleans sandwich. It consists of a hallowed out round loaf of Italian bread. The bread is spread with an olive-based mixture, then the bread is filled with cheese, like provolone and deli meats, such as salami and ham. There are many variations of this hearty sandwich.

mayo substitute

Out of mayo? Try spreading your bread or roll with ranch or creamy Caesar salad dressing.

sun-dried tomato sandwich spread

Add a little interest to a sandwich of deli meat by jazzing up some mayonnaise. To 2 tbsp. mayonnaise add, 2 tbsp. chopped oil-packed sun-dried tomatoes and 2 tsp. minced red onion.

tasty sandwiches

- If you enjoy grilled sandwiches, you may want to invest in an electric or stovetop griddle, which will allow you to grill four to six sandwiches at a time. Or purchase a panini maker or indoor grill to toast both sides at one time.

- When assembling sandwiches ahead, spread them with butter or margarine to seal the bread and keep the meat's moisture from being absorbed into the bread.

- Enhance a sandwich with toppings, such as guacamole, salsa, cheese spreads, mayonnaise, Swiss cheese, blue cheese, sautéed mushrooms or strips of crisp bacon.

battering a sandwich

Combine filling ingredients and spread over half the bread slices. Top with remaining bread; set aside. In a shallow bowl, whisk batter ingredients together. Dip both sides of the sandwich into the batter.

soggy sandwich solution

When you brown bag your lunch, sometimes the sandwich is soggy from the ketchup and mayonnaise by lunchtime. To prevent a soggy sandwich, spread mustard, mayonnaise, ketchup, etc. between slices of meat or cheese instead of directly on the bread. Or, plastic the condiment in a small plastic container and spread it on just before eating.

sandwiches with character

Add character to your kid's brown-bag sandwiches by cutting out their sandwiches with large cookie cutters. Try various shapes, such as hearts, cloves, animals, Christmas trees or Easter bunnies. As a bonus, the bread crust is trimmed away for those fussy eaters who don't like the crust.

garlic lovers' sandwiches

What to have a fabulous sandwich? Use heated garlic bread instead of French or sourdough bread for toasted cheese sandwiches. Experiment with other fillings to create your own favorite.

mini muffuletta

Make an individual muffuletta with a hard roll. Just cut off the top of a hard roll and hollow it out. Brush your favorite vinaigrette inside the roll and top. Sprinkle inside with some chopped green olives. Fill with cheese and deli meat, tuna salad or egg salad. Add a little onion, lettuce and tomato if you like, then put the top back on.

lunch-box sandwiches

Add a little flavor twist to sandwiches that go into a lunch box. Sprinkle the filling with dried minced onion. By the time lunch has arrived, the onion will have soaked up some moisture from the sandwich, making it a tender and tasty addition.

a la parmesan

When making veal, chicken or eggplant Parmesan for dinner, plan to make a few extra pieces. The leftovers will make a great sandwich the next day. Reheat in the microwave and place on a toasted roll. Top with a little warm spaghetti sauce and enjoy.

meatball sandwiches

Extra meatballs can be turned into a tasty sandwich and simple, but quick meal. Fry bell pepper strips until crisp-tender, then add sliced meatballs to the pan. Serve on French or Italian bread.

meat loaf sandwiches

After serving meat loaf for dinner, cut the leftovers into thick slices. Place two pieces of waxed paper between each slice and place in a freezer bag. When you're in the mood for a meat loaf sandwich, you can easily remove a slice. Defrost and warm the meatloaf and then build you sandwich.

boring bread

Change out the bread in sandwiches by rolling the filling in a tortilla, or using a pita or bagel.

smart start

Leftover dinner biscuits make great grab-and-go breakfast items. Simply warm them in the microwave or toaster. Top them with a little butter or your favorite jam, and you have a no-fuss, economical meal on-the-run. And if you don't have time to sit down and enjoy a bacon-and-egg breakfast with the rest of the family, simply toast two frozen waffles and layer the bacon and eggs between them. It's a fast handheld great that won't interfere with your schedule.

tortilla tip

If your flour tortillas are too stiff to roll into wraps, place them between two damp microwave-safe paper towels and warm them in the microwave oven. Check them every few seconds, and remove them when they are pliable.

best bets for beef

aegean skillet dinner • p. 66

Nothing beats the versatility of beef. If you're short on time or money, ground beef always cooks up quickly and inexpensively. If you're hosting a gathering, a savory roast with gravy will be the talk of the party, and if you are in the mood for something ethnic, a Southwestern entree will do the trick.

You'll find something for every palate right here. Whip up Texas Grilled Steaks (p. 60) when you're craving some flame-broiled fare. Or, serve Mini Beef Wellingtons (p. 63) when entertaining weekend guests. For hurried nights, consider Sweet-Sour Beef & Broccoli (p. 69). It's ready in just 10 minutes.

cowboy beef and beans

prep time: 6 minutes • total time: 24 minutes • serves: 4

Turn to this simple recipe when you need an all-in-one dish that's hearty. It's great for nights when your family is on different schedules because it keeps on the stovetop and reheats so well.

2 chorizo sausages (about 3.5 oz.)	1 (16 oz.) can kidney beans
1 onion	1 (16 oz.) can maple-flavored baked beans
1 yellow pepper	3/4 cup barbecue sauce
2 cloves garlic	1 tbsp. Worcestershire sauce
3/4 lb. lean ground beef	1 cup frozen baby lima beans

1) Quarter chorizo lengthwise and cut into slices. Chop onion and yellow pepper. Finely chop garlic. In large, nonstick skillet over medium-high heat, add beef, chorizo, onion, pepper and garlic. Cook, breaking up meat with a spoon, until browned and no longer pink, 8 min. Pour off excess fat.

2) Drain kidney beans and stir into skillet. Add baked beans, barbecue sauce, Worcestershire, baby limas and 1/4 cup water. Bring to simmer and cook until flavors are combined and baby limas are tender, about 6 min. Transfer to bowls and serve.

nutritional facts: *Per serving: 640 calories • 81g carbohydrates • 45g protein • 16g fat • 1100mg sodium • 70mg cholesterol • 15g fiber • 30g sugar*

buttermilk cheddar biscuits

Arrange refrigerated buttermilk biscuits on baking sheet; sprinkle with shredded cheddar cheese. Bake as directed.

spice rubs

Don't be tempted to buy those expensive, ready-made spice rub mixtures. For less money, you can double or triple the rub in this recipe and store it in a glass jar in your cupboard. The next time you grill, it's ready to go!

texas grilled steak

prep time: 5 minutes • total time: 24 minutes • serves: 4

Designed to bring the barbecue indoors, this recipe calls for grilling both the steak and the toast. This perfectly spiced steak has flavor as big as Texas itself.

1 tsp. peanut oil	1/4 tsp. allspice
1-1/2 tbsp. ground ancho chili pepper	1/4 tsp. cayenne pepper
1 tbsp. garlic powder	1-1/2 lbs. boneless beef sirloin steak
1 tbsp. plus 1 tsp. coarse salt	4 cloves garlic
1 tsp. cumin	7 tbsp. unsalted butter
1/4 tsp. ground cinnamon	1 loaf country-style white bread, unsliced

1) Brush grill pan lightly with peanut oil and place over high heat.

2) Place ancho chili pepper, garlic powder, 1 tbsp. salt, cumin, cinnamon, allspice and cayenne into small bowl; stir to combine. Rub half of spice mixture into each side of steak. Place onto hot grill pan and cook until browned on first side, about 5 min. Turn and cook until desired doneness, about 5-8 min. Remove to cutting board to rest.

3) Meanwhile, peel and mince garlic. In small pan, combine garlic with butter and heat over medium until butter is melted. Slice bread into eight 1/2-inch-thick slices. Brush both sides of each slice with garlic butter and sprinkle with remaining salt.

4) Place four slices of bread on grill pan, and cook until lightly browned on first side, about 1 min.; turn and cook until browned on second side, about 1 min. Grill marks will appear on bread when toasted. Place two pieces of toast on each plate. Slice steak and serve over grilled bread.

nutritional facts: *Per serving: 790 calories • 48g carbohydrates • 59g protein • 38g fat • 2060mg sodium • 205mg cholesterol • 3g fiber • 9g sugar*

family feast bracciole

prep time: 50 minutes • total time: 1-3/4 hours • serves: 6

Bracciole is a classic Italian-American Sunday dinner. Thin slices of beef are rolled with a savory filling, then simmered to tenderness in a simple homemade sauce. They taste even better when made a day or two ahead.

1 bunch parsley	1/4 tsp. pepper
1/2 bunch basil	18 thin slices salami
4 cloves garlic	2 tbsp. olive oil, *divided*
1 cup shredded Parmesan cheese	1 cup finely chopped onions
18 very thin slices beef top round (4 x 5 inches *each*)	2 (28 oz.) cans crushed tomatoes
1/2 tsp. salt	1 cup red wine
	1 tsp. sugar

1) Finely chop parsley to yield 1-1/2 cups and basil to yield 1/2 cup. Chop garlic cloves. In medium bowl, combine parsley, cheese, basil and half of the garlic. Lay beef slices on work surface; season both sides with salt and pepper. Top each piece with cheese mixture, spreading to within 1/4-inch of edges. Top with salami. Roll beef up jelly-roll fashion, tucking in sides. Secure with toothpicks.

2) In Dutch oven over medium-high, heat 1 tbsp. oil. Add half of beef rolls, and brown on all sides, about 6 min. total. Set aside and repeat with remaining oil and rolls. Remove and set aside.

3) Lower heat to medium. Add onion and remaining garlic, cook until soft, about 5 min. Add tomatoes, wine and sugar; bring to boil. Reduce heat to low; add rolls and simmer, partially covered, until tender, 1-1/2 hours. Remove toothpicks from rolls and serve with sauce.

nutritional facts: *Per serving: 410 calories • 24g carbohydrates • 41g protein • 15g fat • 1430mg sodium • 85mg cholesterol • 5g fiber • 11g sugar*

pasta with cheese

A bowl of pasta sprinkled with freshly grated Parmesan is the classic side dish for traditional Bracciole.

quarter hour steak

prep time: 4 minutes • total time: 15 minutes • serves: 6

Make this steak when your family is really on the go. The herb topping adds so much zest, you'll hardly believe it's ready in just 15 minutes.

3 tbsp. olive oil	1/2 tsp. paprika
3 tbsp. cilantro, minced	1/4 tsp. cayenne pepper
3 cloves garlic, minced	1-1/2 lbs. New York strip *or* top round steak
1 tbsp. cumin	
2 tsp. salt	

1) Heat large skillet or stovetop grill pan over medium-high heat. Meanwhile, in small bowl, stir together olive oil, cilantro, garlic, cumin, salt, paprika and cayenne.

2) If steak is too large to fit in skillet, cut into two pieces. Rub herb mixture over both sides of steak.

3) Place steak in hot skillet. Cook until browned on first side, about 5 min. Turn over; cook until done, about 5 min. Remove to a cutting board; let rest 1 min. Cut steak into thin slices and serve.

nutritional facts: *Per serving: 310 calories • 1g carbohydrates • 41g protein • 14g fat • 830mg sodium • 100mg cholesterol • 0g fiber • 0g sugar*

easy slicing

For safety and easy slicing of the steak, sharpen your knife by holding the sharpening steel rod steady and stroking the knife blade downward five times on each side.

lemon beef and rice skillet

prep time: 10 minutes • total time: 25 minutes • serves: 4

With a hint of lemon and oregano, this dish of tender beef strips and brown rice is rich in Greek flavor. The addition of carrots, tomatoes and a bit of feta makes it a one-dish meal.

1/2 lemon	1 (14.5 oz.) can petite-diced tomatoes, drained
1 lb. boneless, beef sirloin steak	
1 tbsp. extra-virgin olive oil	1-2/3 cup quick-cooking brown rice
1 tbsp. fresh oregano leaves	1 cup shredded carrots
1 large green onion	1/3 cup crumbled feta cheese
1 (14.5 oz.) can beef broth	1/4 tsp. black pepper

1) Zest lemon to yield 1 tsp. Juice lemon to yield 2 tsp. Thinly slice steak into strips. In large, nonstick skillet over high, heat oil. Add steak and cook, stirring, until browned and almost cooked through, about 2 min. Meanwhile, mince oregano. Thinly slice green onion.

2) Add beef broth, tomatoes, oregano, lemon juice and zest to skillet. Bring to boil.

3) Stir in rice, carrots, and green onion. Return to boil, then reduce heat to low. Simmer, covered, until rice is tender, about 10 min. Transfer to serving dish, sprinkle with cheese and black pepper and serve immediately.

nutritional facts: *Per serving: 390 calories • 37g carbohydrates • 32g protein • 13g fat • 570mg sodium • 80mg cholesterol • 4g fiber • 5g sugar*

spread for bread

Combine some shredded mozzarella, softened butter, chopped green onions, sliced olives, minced garlic and a touch of mayonnaise. Spread on halved bread and bake until cheese melts.

tuscan veal chop

prep time: 14 minutes • total time: 28 minutes • serves: 2

Simple, elegant and flavored to perfection, these grilled veal chops are served on a healthy mix of rosemary-scented vegetables. They're just perfect for a delightful supper for the two of you!

1 large carrot	1/4 tsp. pepper
1 medium tomato	1 sprig fresh rosemary
1 small red onion	1/4 cup nonfat Italian dressing
1/4 lb. green beans	2 tbsp. dry white wine
2 bone-in rib *or* loin veal chops (about 3/4-inch thick, 5 oz. *each*)	

1) Cut carrots into matchsticks; place in 11- x 7-inch baking dish. Cut tomato into wedges and slice onion thinly; place in dish with carrots. Add green beans. Season chops on both sides with pepper; add to dish. Chop rosemary to yield 1 tsp.; set aside.

2) In small container with tight-fitting lid, add Italian dressing and wine. Close lid; shake well to combine. Pour over chops and vegetables; toss to coat. Let stand for about 5 min.

3) Coat nonstick grill pan with cooking spray and set over medium. Add chops. Cook until golden on first side, about 7 min. Turn and cook until golden but slightly pink in center, about 7 min.

4) Meanwhile, coat large, nonstick skillet with cooking spray. Add vegetables and marinade. Sprinkle with rosemary. Cook, stirring constantly, until vegetables are tender, about 6 min. Divide between serving plates. Top each with 1 chop and serve.

nutritional facts: *Per serving: 300 calories • 17g carbohydrates • 29g protein • 12g fat • 330mg sodium • 100mg cholesterol • 5g fiber • 7g sugar*

chops on the grill

If you prefer to cook your chops on the barbecue, marinate the chops separately from the vegetables. Grill the chops and cook the veggies in an aluminum-foil package.

mini beef wellingtons

prep time: 10 minutes • total time: 29 minutes • serves: 4

This restaurant classic may seem too intimidating to try on a weeknight, but you really can make this gourmet-style dish at home in under 30 minutes. It's a truly wonderful treat.

1 tsp. olive oil	1 sheet frozen puff pastry,
4 (6 oz.) slices filet mignon	thawed (half of one
1/2 tsp. salt	17.25 oz. pkg.)
1/4 tsp. pepper	4 oz. mushroom pate
1 egg	

1) Heat oven to 425°F. Line baking sheet with foil; set aside. In heavy, nonstick skillet over medium-high, heat oil. Season filets with salt and pepper. Place in hot oil and sear, 2 min. per side. Set aside to cool.

2) Meanwhile, on lightly floured surface, roll out pastry to 14-inch square. With pastry wheel, cut four 1/4-inch wide strips; set aside. Cut remaining pastry into four 7-inch squares. Beat egg in small bowl and brush on pastry squares.

3) Cut pate into four portions. Top each filet with pate. Place each filet, pate side down, in center of pastry square. Fold pastry over to enclose; press edges to seal. Place, seam side down, on foil-lined baking sheet. Cut reserved pastry strips in half lengthwise. Place two crossed strips on each pastry packet. Brush pastry with egg.

4) Bake until pastry is golden brown and the beef is medium-rare (internal temperature 145°F.) 15 to 18 min.

nutritional facts: *Per serving: 650 calories • 20g carbohydrates • 55g protein • 37g fat • 320mg sodium • 195mg cholesterol • 1g fiber • 2g sugar*

money savers

Four pieces of pork tenderloin can be used in place of the beef. Cook it to an internal temperature of 150°F. You could also substitute a thick slice of good-quality liverwurst for the pate.

korean steak

prep time: 9 minutes • total time: 29 minutes • serves: 4

Once you taste this delicious steak, you'll understand why it is such a popular dish in most Korean restaurants. It's soaked in a tasty marinade, then quickly cooked for intense flavor.

1 lb. flank steak	1 tbsp. sesame oil
1 medium onion	2 tbsp. sugar
1 shallot	2 tbsp. sesame seeds
2 cloves garlic	3 green onions
1/4 cup low-sodium soy sauce	1 tsp. vegetable oil
2-1/2 tbsp. mirin (sweet Japanese wine)	

1) Slice steak across grain into very thin strips. Thinly slice onion. Chop shallot and mince garlic.

2) In large bowl, combine soy sauce, mirin, sesame oil, sugar, sesame seeds, onion, shallot and garlic. Add beef; let stand 20 min.

3) Cut green onions into 1-inch pieces and set aside. Heat wok or large skillet over high heat. When hot, add vegetable oil and steak mixture. Stir-fry until steak is no longer pink, about 4 min.

4) Add green onions and stir-fry 30 seconds. Transfer to plates and serve.

nutritional facts: *Per serving: 300 calories • 16g carbohydrates • 26g protein • 14g fat • 440mg sodium • 40mg cholesterol • 1g fiber • 11g sugar*

rice wine vinegar

If you don't want to purchase mirin just for this recipe, you can substitute the same amount of rice wine vinegar instead.

lettuce-wrapped picadillo

prep time: 5 minutes • total time: 20 minutes • serves: 4

Picadillo (pronounced pee-kah-DEE-yoh) is a Spanish dish of mildly spiced meat. In this version, the filling is folded into healthy lettuce "wraps." Your entire family will love it!

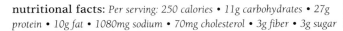

2 tsp. canola oil	1/8 tsp. cayenne pepper
1/3 cup chopped red onion	1 (4.5 oz.) can chopped green chiles, drained
2 tsp. minced garlic	
1 lb. ground beef	1/3 cup frozen corn
2-1/2 tsp. chili powder	8 large Boston lettuce leaves
1-1/2 tsp. coarse salt	1/4 cup prepared salsa
1/2 tsp. cumin	1 (2.25 oz.) can sliced ripe olives, drained
1/2 tsp. ground cinnamon	

1) In large saute pan over medium, heat oil; swirl to cover pan. Add onion and garlic, cook until softened, 1-2 min.

2) Add ground beef to pan; use a spoon to break up meat. Sprinkle chili powder, salt, cumin, cinnamon and cayenne over meat; stir. Cook until meat is browned, about 4 min. Mix in chopped chiles. Pour 1/4 cup water into pan; stir in corn. Reduce heat and cook until liquid is absorbed, 6-8 min. Remove from heat.

3) Place 2 lettuce leaves on each plate. Place spoonful of meat filling in center of lettuce leaves, dividing evenly among 8 leaves. Garnish with salsa and olives. Fold up lettuce; serve immediately.

nutritional facts: *Per serving: 250 calories • 11g carbohydrates • 27g protein • 10g fat • 1080mg sodium • 70mg cholesterol • 3g fiber • 3g sugar*

ground beef

Freshly ground chuck is juicier than ground round and has more flavor. Just pour off the excess fat from the pan.

roadhouse beef

prep time: 20 minutes • total time: 20 minutes • serves: 4

When you're in a hurry but need a great dinner, ready-cooked meats are a terrific starting point. Dress up some roast beef and make a western-style supper fit for hearty appetites.

1 red onion	4 (10-inch) flour tortillas
1 green bell pepper	1 small bunch chives
2 tsp. olive oil	1/2 cup reduced-fat sour cream
1 (17 oz.) pkg. ready-cooked beef roast in gravy	1 tbsp. adobo sauce
	1/4 tsp. cumin
1/2 cup smoky barbecue sauce	

1) Cut onion into slices; cut peppers into short strips. In nonstick skillet over medium, heat oil. Add onion and pepper; cook, stirring occasionally, until softened, 6 min. Meanwhile, cut beef crosswise into 1-inch-thick slices; shred each slice into 1/2-inch pieces with 2 forks. Discard gravy or save for another use.

2) Add beef to pan. Cook, stirring occasionally, until heated through, 4 min. Stir in barbecue sauce and cook 1 min. Remove from heat.

3) Meanwhile, wrap tortillas in paper towels and microwave on HIGH until heated through, 1 min. Place 1 tortilla on each serving plate.

4) Chop enough chives to make 1 tbsp. In small bowl, stir together sour cream, adobo, cumin and chives until combined. Evenly mound beef mixture on each tortilla. Serve with dollop of spiced sour cream.

nutritional facts: *Per serving: 470 calories • 52g carbohydrates • 30g protein • 16g fat • 2300mg sodium • 65mg cholesterol • 4g fiber • 8g sugar*

onion flavor

Use 1 tbsp. finely chopped red onion for the chives. To remove the strong onion flavor, rinse it under cold running water and pat dry with paper towels.

beef "birds"

prep time: 15 minutes • total time: 29 minutes • serves: 6

Tender strips of sirloin are rolled around savory stuffing, then placed on "nests" of angel hair pasta. The rich, creamy sauce is the crowning touch.

1 (9 oz.) pkg. refrigerated fresh angel hair pasta	1/4 tsp. pepper
1/2 tsp. salt, *divided*	2 tbsp. oil
1 carrot	2 tbsp. butter
1-1/4 cups herb-seasoned stuffing mix	2 tbsp. all-purpose flour
1-1/2 lbs. boneless beef sirloin	1 (14.5 oz.) can beef broth
	2 tbsp. fresh parsley leaves
	1/4 cup sour cream

1) Over high heat, bring pot of water to boil. Add 1/4 tsp. salt and pasta; cook according to package directions, about 5 min. Drain and divide among 6 plates.

2) Meanwhile, mince carrot; place in small bowl with stuffing mix and 2-1/2 tbsp. hot water. Stir until water is absorbed.

3) Cut steak into 3 pieces. Season both sides with pepper and remaining salt. Evenly spread stuffing mixture on each steak, leaving 1/4-inch border all around. Roll up; secure with kitchen twine.

4) In large skillet over high, heat oil. Add steaks and cook, turning every 2 min. until browned and almost cooked through. Transfer steaks to plate.

5) Reduce heat to medium; melt butter in skillet. Whisk in flour until lightly browned, 2 min. Add broth and cook, stirring constantly, until thickened, 2 min.

6) Chop parsley; add to skillet along with sour cream. Stir until blended. Return beef to skillet; cook, covered, until heated through, 4 min. Remove steak; cut each in half. Place 1 steak in each dish of pasta. Spoon sauce over and serve.

nutritional facts: *Per serving: 420 calories • 36g carbohydrates • 30g protein • 17g fat • 580mg sodium • 80mg cholesterol • 2g fiber • 2g sugar*

lower-sodium stuffing

If you're watching your salt intake, avoid the high sodium content of stuffing mix by cubing and toasting some bread and adding oregano, thyme or any Italian seasoning.

chili-rubbed gorgonzola steaks

prep time: 10 minutes • total time: 22 minutes • serves: 4

You can't go wrong with this quick and simple crowd-pleasing steak that gets its distinctive flavor from a spice rub. It's complemented by the nutty flavor of gorgonzola cheese.

1 tsp. fennel seeds	1 sirloin steak (1-inch thick, about 1-1/2 pounds)
1/2 tsp. dried thyme	3/4 cup crumbled gorgonzola cheese
1 tbsp. sweet paprika	
1/2 tbsp. chipotle chili pepper	
1/4 tbsp. salt	

1) Preheat grill, grill pan or broiler. In small bowl, crush fennel seeds and thyme; add paprika, chili powder and salt. Stir to combine. Place steaks on waxed paper or foil. Sprinkle spice mixture evenly over both sides of steaks, rubbing into meat.

2) Grill steak for 10 to 12 min., turning halfway during cooking for medium-rare (internal temperature 145˚F). Sprinkle gorgonzola on top of steaks during final 2 min. of cooking.

3) Place cooked steak on serving platter and let stand 5 minutes for juices to set. Carve into 1/2-inch thick slices. Serve immediately.

nutritional facts: *Per serving: 390 calories • 2g carbohydrates • 36g protein • 25g fat • 540mg sodium • 120mg cholesterol • 1g fiber • 0g sugar*

mexican rice

For a quick and festive side dish, stir 1 can of diced tomatoes flavored with green chilies into a bowl of hot cooked instant white rice. What could be easier?

aegean skillet dinner

prep time: 22 minutes • total time: 22 minutes • serves: 4

This Greek-inspired skillet dinner is truly unique. Ground beef and white beans are simmered with wine, stewed tomatoes and aromatic spices, then finished with fresh parsley, feta cheese and olives.

1 large onion	1 (19 oz.) can white kidney beans
1 clove garlic	small bunch fresh parsley
1 lb. lean ground beef	1 cup crumbled feta cheese
1/2 tsp. ground cinnamon	1/2 cup pitted kalamata olives
1/2 tsp. dried mint leaves	
1/2 cup red wine	
2 (14.5 oz.) cans stewed tomatoes	

1) Coarsely chop onion and finely chop garlic. In large, nonstick skillet over high heat, brown ground beef, breaking up meat with a spoon. Add onion and garlic and cook until tender, about 5 min. Stir in cinnamon and mint, then add wine and cook until reduced, about 1 min.

2) Add tomatoes, breaking up slightly if pieces are very large. Drain and rinse beans and add to skillet. Cover and simmer for 10 min. Meanwhile, finely chop parsley to yield 1-1/2 cups.

3) Remove skillet from heat; top meat mixture with parsley, feta and olives. Cover and let stand until cheese has softened, 1-2 min. Transfer to rimmed plates and serve immediately.

nutritional facts: *Per serving: 610 calories • 49g carbohydrates • 39g protein • 27g fat • 1310mg sodium • 75mg cholesterol • 3g fiber • 10g sugar*

easy add-on

Lightly brush pita bread with oil and sprinkle with a dash of oregano or thyme. Wrap in foil and heat in the oven.

oven-braised beef brisket

prep time: 20 minutes • total time: 5 hours • serves: 8

Here's a great "set it and forget it" meal that feeds a crowd. It's perfect for entertaining.

1/2 cup dried mushrooms	1/2 tsp. pepper
4 cloves garlic	1/2 cup ketchup
4 large onions	1/2 cup steak sauce
1 thin-cut beef brisket (6 to 7 lbs.)	1 tsp. dried crushed rosemary
1/2 tsp. salt	1 (12 oz.) bottle pale ale *or* beer
	1 (1 lb) pkg. baby carrots

1) Preheat oven to 350°F. Break large mushroom pieces in half and scatter in large roasting pan (15- x 11-inch). Thinly slice garlic. Peel, halve and slice onions. Scatter half of onions and garlic in pan.

2) Trim and discard any visible fat from brisket; place in pan. Sprinkle with salt and pepper. Scatter remaining onions on top. In small bowl, stir together ketchup, steak sauce and rosemary. Drizzle evenly over meat. Pour beer over meat. Cover pan tightly with foil.

3) Bake for 3 hours. Meanwhile, cut carrots in half lengthwise. Scatter over beef and bake, covered, until meat and carrots are fork-tender, 1 hour. Remove carrots and onions to serving bowl. Transfer meat to board; cover with foil and let rest at least 30 min. (Or refrigerate for up to 2 days.) Slice meat against grain. Skim fat from pan juices and serve with beef and vegetables.

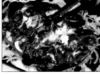

nutritional facts: *Per serving: 810 calories • 22g carbohydrates • 116g protein • 24g fat • 730mg sodium • 235mg cholesterol • 4g fiber • 10g sugar*

cuts of brisket

There are two cuts of brisket. The point half (also called second cut) is thicker and marbled with fat. The thin cut or first cut, is the thinner and leaner end of the brisket.

margarita steaks

prep time: 15 minutes • total time: 21 minutes • serves: 4

A lively mixture is used to marinate the steak and add some extra zest to the peach-mango salsa topping. The large, sweet grilled onion slices make a great side.

1/3 cup tequila	2 cups peach-mango *or* regular salsa
3 tbsp. lime juice	
2 tbsp. triple sec	1 large Vidalia *or* Maui sweet onion
2 tbsp. oil, *divided*	
2 tsp. cumin	salt and pepper
1-1/4 lbs. skirt steak	1 avocado

1) In medium bowl, combine tequila, lime juice, triple sec, 1 tbsp. oil and cumin. Remove 1/3 cup mixture and place in shallow dish; add steak. Turn to coat and let stand 10 min. Stir salsa into remaining mixture.

2) Preheat grill pan or cast-iron skillet over medium-high heat. Peel and slice onion crosswise into 1/4-inch slices; brush with remaining oil and sprinkle with salt and pepper. Cook, turning once, just until crisp-tender, about 2 min. per side. Remove and keep warm.

3) Remove steak from marinade, letting excess drip off. Add steaks to grill pan and cook until browned on first side, about 4 min. Turn and cook until desired doneness, another 4 min. for medium-rare.

4) Meanwhile peel and dice avocado; stir into salsa mixture. Thinly slice steak and serve with onions and salsa.

nutritional facts: *Per serving: 660 calories • 38g carbohydrates • 39g protein • 32g fat • 460mg sodium • 85mg cholesterol • 5g fiber • 23g sugar*

wooden skewers

Before adding the meat to the marinade, use it to soak wooden skewers. Then spear them through the onion slices. They'll stay together and turn easily while grilling.

bacon-smothered chopped steaks

prep time: 10 minutes • total time: 17 minutes • serves: 4

Here's an updated family favorite—a variation on Salisbury steak—with a gravy made rich from mushrooms and chopped bacon. It's sure to please the meat lovers in your home.

3 strips precooked bacon	1 egg white
1/2 small sweet onion	1-1/2 tsp. Worcestershire sauce
10 sprigs fresh parsley	3/4 tsp. seasoned salt
1 lb. lean ground beef	1 (8 oz.) pkg. sliced baby Bella mushrooms
2 tbsp. dry seasoned bread crumbs	1 (12 oz.) jar fat-free beef gravy

1) Chop bacon and set aside. Grate onion into medium bowl to yield about 1/4 cup. Chop parsley to yield 1/3 cup. Add 3 tbsp. parsley to bowl. Add beef, bread crumbs, egg white, Worcestershire sauce and salt. Mix together just until combined. Shape into four oval patties, about 4 inches long x 1/2-inch thick.

2) Coat large, nonstick skillet with cooking spray. Into skillet over medium heat, add patties and cook until no longer pink in center, 5-6 min. per side. Transfer to plate. Pour off any excess fat if needed.

3) Increase heat to medium-high and add mushrooms and bacon. Cook until browned and softened, 4 min. Add gravy and patties (plus any accumulated juices). Bring to simmer and cook until heated through, 1 min. Transfer to platter. Sprinkle with reserved parsley and serve.

nutritional facts: *Per serving: 230 calories • 14g carbohydrates • 28g protein • 7g fat • 880mg sodium • 65mg cholesterol • 2g fiber • 4g sugar*

richer flavor

For even richer flavor, substitute 1 lb. meat loaf mix for the ground beef and consider adding 1/4 cup crumbled blue or shredded cheddar or Jack cheese to the patties.

mexican-style cheese

Making Mexican-style cheese is easy. Shred whatever cheese is in your refrigerator and sprinkle with cumin or red pepper flakes for a do-it-yourself blend.

beef & tortilla bake

prep time: 12 minutes • total time: 28 minutes • serves: 6

This recipe delivers everyone's favorite Mexican flavors in one easy-to-prepare dish. By using lean ground beef, baked tortilla chips and tomato, it's also good for you.

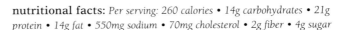

1 cup baked tortilla chips	1 (10 oz.) can mild enchilada sauce
1 lb. lean ground beef	
1 clove garlic	1 cup shredded Mexican 4-cheese blend
1 medium onion	
1 (4 oz.) can diced mild green chiles	1 medium tomato
	1/2 cup sour cream
	6 sprigs fresh cilantro

1) Preheat oven to 375°F. Place tortilla chips in zippered plastic bag. With rolling pin, crush chips to fine crumbs. Set aside.

2) In large skillet over high heat, cook beef, breaking up lumps with a spoon, until browned, about 4 min. Meanwhile, mince garlic; chop onion to yield about 1/2 cup.

3) Drain beef and return skillet to stovetop. Reduce heat to medium-high; add onion and garlic. Cook, stirring, until onion is softened, about 3 min. Add chiles and enchilada sauce.

4) Transfer mixture to medium, shallow casserole. Sprinkle with cheese and reserved tortilla crumbs. Bake until cheese is bubbly, about 15 min.

5) Seed and chop the tomato. Divide the baked mixture among six serving plates. Top each serving with chopped tomato and a dollop of sour cream. Garnish with a cilantro sprig and serve.

nutritional facts: *Per serving: 260 calories • 14g carbohydrates • 21g protein • 14g fat • 550mg sodium • 70mg cholesterol • 2g fiber • 4g sugar*

chop your own

Precut veggies are a real time-saver but definitely add to the grocery bill. Chop your own peppers and onions when time permits and opt for precut veggies only rarely.

beef sausage & red beans

prep time: 7 minutes • total time: 27 minutes • serves: 4

Thick and hearty with a kick from hot sauce, this saucy casserole is just right on a wintry day. The beans take on a creamy texture so they're rich and delicious.

1/3 lb. smoked beef kielbasa sausage	1 stalk celery
	1 small green pepper
2 (14.5 oz.) can kidney beans, undrained	1/2 small onion
	1 tbsp. sugar
1/4 cup lightly packed fresh parsley leaves	1 tsp. hot sauce
	1 tsp. garlic powder

1) Preheat oven to 425°F. Cut kielbasa into 1/2-inch pieces. Set aside.

2) In large mixing bowl, place beans and half of liquid. With handheld masher, mash beans lightly, leaving about half intact.

3) Chop parsley and celery; dice green pepper and onion. Add sausage, green pepper, onion, parsley, celery, sugar, hot sauce and garlic powder to beans; stir to combine.

4) Pour into 13- x 9-inch baking dish. Bake, covered, for 15 min. Remove cover and bake until juices are bubbling and vegetables are tender, about 5 min. Transfer to shallow bowls or rimmed plates and serve.

nutritional facts: *Per serving: 450 calories • 63g carbohydrates • 29g protein • 10g fat • 450mg sodium • 25mg cholesterol • 24g fiber • 4g sugar*

sweet-sour beef & broccoli

prep time: 10 minutes • **total time:** 10 minutes • **serves:** 4

Stir-fry is one of the fastest techniques for getting dinner on the table. When you use precut beef strips and broccoli florets, it's even faster. The sweet, tangy sauce is a snap, too!

1 small onion	1 tsp. cornstarch
1 piece (1 inch) fresh gingerroot	1/2 cup chicken broth
1/2 cup ketchup	1 tbsp. vegetable oil
1/2 cup grape jelly	1 lb. stir-fry beef strips
1/2 tsp. crushed red pepper flakes	4 cups broccoli florets
1/4 cup soy sauce	(about 1 lb.)

1) Cut onion and thinly slice; set aside. Peel and mince gingerroot and place in medium mixing bowl. Stir in the ketchup, grape jelly, red pepper flakes and soy sauce.

2) In small bowl, stir cornstarch into broth until dissolved.

3) In large, nonstick skillet or wok over high, heat oil. Add onion and beef to skillet and cook, stirring frequently, until beef is brown, 2-3 min. Add broccoli florets and cook about 1 min.

4) Stir in jelly mixture and chicken broth. Cook until sauce bubbles and starts to thicken, 1 min. Transfer to platter and serve immediately.

nutritional facts: *Per serving: 470 calories • 43g carbohydrates • 30g protein • 21g fat • 1410mg sodium • 60mg cholesterol • 4g fiber • 32g sugar*

sauce secrets

Ketchup and grape jelly are a pantry-shelf solution for sweet-and-sour chicken, stuffed cabbage or beef dishes. But marmalade or a berry jelly work, too.

salisbury steak

prep time: 5 minutes • **total time:** 27 minutes • **serves:** 4

Smothered in rich mushroom gravy, these diner-inspired patties are a blast from family dinners of years past. But they're simple enough that you can make them any night—they're always a hit.

1 egg	2 tbsp. butter
1/4 cup dry bread crumbs	1 (8 oz.) pkg. sliced white
2 tbsp. finely chopped onion	mushrooms
2 tbsp. Worcestershire sauce, *divided*	3 tbsp. flour
	1 cup beef broth
1/2 tsp. salt	1/2 cup milk
1/2 tsp. pepper	1/4 tsp. nutmeg
1 lb. ground beef	2 tsp. fresh parsley

1) In medium bowl, combine egg, bread crumbs, onion, 1 tbsp. Worcestershire sauce, salt and pepper. Add ground beef and mix well. Shape into 4 oval patties, each about 3/4-inch thick.

2) Heat large nonstick skillet over medium-high. Add patties and cook until first side is lightly browned, about 3 min. Flip and cook second side, about 3 min. Remove patties from skillet.

3) In same skillet, melt butter and cook mushrooms until they begin to release liquid, about 3 min.

4) In small bowl, combine flour and broth. Stir into skillet; add milk, nutmeg and remaining Worcestershire sauce. Cook until mixture starts to thicken. Return patties to skillet and simmer, covered, over medium-low heat, about 10 min. Sprinkle with parsley and serve.

nutritional facts: *Per serving: 320 calories • 15g carbohydrates • 32g protein • 14g fat • 1020mg sodium • 140mg cholesterol • 1g fiber • 4g sugar*

reduce the fat

To make this dish a little more healthy, discard the fat in the skillet after cooking the patties and before adding the butter.

steak sandwiches

For great, open-faced sandwiches, brush slices of toasted bread with some Chimichurri sauce. Then pile on slices of cooked steak and peppers.

chimichurri steak and bell peppers

prep time: 7 minutes • total time: 25 minutes • serves: 4

A fresh herb sauce with bold flavors of garlic and parsley, chimichurri is popular in Argentina—a country that loves beef! Once you've tried the tasty sauce, you'll use it on everything from burgers to tenderloin.

2 boneless rib-eye *or* loin steaks (about 1-1/2 lbs.)	4 large cloves garlic
1/2 tsp. salt, *divided*	2 tbsp. red-wine vinegar
1/2 tsp. pepper, *divided*	2 tsp. dried oregano
3 bell peppers	1/8 tsp. crushed red pepper flakes
1 bunch flat-leaf parsley	1/4 cup olive oil

1) Preheat broiler. Season steak with 1/4 tsp. each salt and pepper and arrange on broiler pan. Cut peppers in half. Gently press down to flatten slightly. Place cut side down around steak.

2) Holding bunch of parsley near leaves, twist to remove tough stems. Discard stems. In food processor, with knife blade spinning, drop in garlic cloves to chop. Add parsley sprigs to food processor; add vinegar, oregano, crushed red pepper flakes and remaining salt and pepper. Process until parsley is chopped. With machine running, gradually add oil; set aside.

3) Meanwhile, broil steak and peppers until done as desired, about 5 min. per side for medium-rare. Cut peppers into strips and toss with half the parsley sauce. Cut steak into thin strips. Serve with remaining sauce.

nutritional facts: *Per serving: 610 calories • 7g carbohydrates • 47g protein • 43g fat • 390mg sodium • 215mg cholesterol • 2g fiber • 2g sugar*

sauce variations

If you have family members who don't care for steak sauce, substitute your favorite barbecue sauce. Or try going a bit more upscale with a red wine reduction.

saucy beef in bread baskets

prep time: 10 minutes • total time: 24 minutes • serves: 4

This easy dish brings a dash of fun to any weeknight dinner. Bread bowls catch all the savory sauce surrounding the beef and mushrooms. The fun continues after dinner with fewer dishes to wash.

4 (4-inch) unsliced whole wheat rolls	2 tsp. all-purpose flour
3 shallots	1/2 cup red wine
2 tsp. olive oil	1/3 cup steak sauce
1 (8 oz.) pkg. sliced baby bella *or* cremini mushrooms	1/2 tsp. dried tarragon *or* basil
3/4 lb. chunk deli roast beef (1-inch thick slice)	1 cup no-salt-added canned peas, drained

1) Preheat oven to 350°F. Trim off tops of rolls. Hollow out soft centers and discard. Arrange rolls and tops on baking sheet. Bake until outsides are crisp, about 6 min.

2) Meanwhile, chop shallots. In nonstick skillet over medium-high, heat oil. Add mushrooms and shallots. Cook until mushrooms are softened, 6 min. Cut beef into bite-sized pieces.

3) Stir flour into skillet until blended. Add wine, steak sauce and tarragon. Simmer until thickened and reduced to saucy consistency, 4 min. Stir in peas and beef; cook until heated through, 2 min. Spoon into baskets and serve.

nutritional facts: *Per serving: 450 calories • 63g carbohydrates • 29g protein • 9g fat • 1300mg sodium • 30mg cholesterol • 10g fiber • 12g sugar*

greek porcupine meatballs

prep time: 5 minutes • total time: 23 minutes • serves: 4

If you fondly remember "porcupine" meatballs, you'll love this Greek version. Herbs star in these tender, rice-studded meatballs that are served in a zesty, classic lemon sauce.

1 cup fresh parsley leaves	1/3 cup instant rice
1/4 cup fresh dill *or* mint leaves, *or* a combination	1/3 cup dry bread crumbs
	1/2 tsp. salt
1 lb. meat-loaf mix *or* ground beef	1 (14.5 oz.) can chicken broth
	2 tbsp. cornstarch
2 large eggs, *separated*	1 lemon

1) Finely chop parsley to equal 1/2 cup. Finely chop dill and mint together to equal 2 tbsp. Place in large bowl with meat loaf mix, egg whites, rice, crumbs, salt and 2 tbsp. water. Blend well. Shape mixture into 1-1/2-inch-thick square. Cut into 16 pieces and roll each into a ball.

2) In small bowl, blend cornstarch with 3/4 cup water. Place in large skillet over medium heat with broth and bring to simmer. Add meatballs and cook, covered, 15 min., turning meatballs occasionally. Remove meatballs to serving dish and keep warm. Reduce heat to low.

3) Squeeze lemon to yield 2 to 3 tbsp. juice. In small bowl, whisk egg yolks with lemon juice. Stirring constantly, add 3 tbsp. hot broth to yolk mixture. Gradually add back to skillet, stirring constantly. Simmer 2 min. or until sauce thickens; do not boil. Pour over meatballs. Serve immediately.

nutritional facts: *Per serving: 380 calories • 31g carbohydrates • 31g protein • 14g fat • 500mg sodium • 180mg cholesterol • 2g fiber • 1g sugar*

lighter meatballs

When time permits, whip the egg whites by hand with a whisk and fold them into the meat mixture. This will make the meatballs fluffier and lighter in texture.

sirloin tips with braised onions

prep time: 5 minutes • total time: 25 minutes • serves: 4

Meat eaters will appreciate these savory steaks served on a bed of braised onions. The cook's bonus? It's prepared in just minutes, all in one pan!

2 large sweet onions	2 tbsp. butter
4 beef round sirloin tip steaks (3/4-inch thick, about 1-1/4 lbs.)	1/4 tsp. salt
	1/8 tsp. pepper
1 tsp. lemon pepper seasoning	1 cup beef broth, *divided*
2 to 3 sprigs fresh parsley	1/3 cup heavy cream

1) Preheat oven to 275°F. Slice onions into 1/4-inch rings. Rub steaks with seasoning. Finely chop parsley to yield 2 tbsp.; set aside.

2) In large, nonstick skillet over high heat, melt butter. Add onions; sprinkle with salt and pepper. Cook, stirring occasionally, until onions begin to soften, 5 min., Add 2/3 cup broth and cook, covered, until onions are completely soft, 5 min. Turn onto ovenproof serving platter; place in oven.

3) Into same skillet over medium-high heat, add steaks. Cook until browned on first side, 5 min. Turn and cook until rare to medium-rare, 2-3 min. Arrange steaks on onions and place in oven.

4) Reduce heat to medium. Into skillet, add remaining broth and cream. Cook, stirring constantly, until thickened, about 2 min. Stir in parsley. Remove platter from oven; drizzle sauce over steaks and serve.

nutritional facts: *Per serving: 410 calories • 22g carbohydrates • 34g protein • 21g fat • 500mg sodium • 105mg cholesterol • 4g fiber • 10g sugar*

skip the sauce

The cream sauce is a nice touch, but the steak and braised onions are also delicious alone. Just be careful not to overcook the meat; it is best cooked rare to medium-rare and served thinly sliced.

chili pot pie

With a couple of simple substitutions, you can make a chili pot pie: use a jar of chili sauce rather than BBQ sauce and red kidney beans instead of baked ones.

bbq beef cups

prep time: 6 minutes • total time: 25 minutes • serves: 6

Most meat pies are fully enclosed in pastry dough. But for a delicious change of pace, try this open-faced version, which features savory baked beans in addition to ground beef.

2 refrigerated ready-made pie crusts	1/4 tsp. pepper
	1 cup beans
1 small white onion	1/2 cup BBQ sauce
2 tsp. canola oil	1 oz. white cheese
1 lb. ground round	2 green onions
3/4 tsp. salt	

1) Preheat oven to 450°F. Flatten each piece of dough with rolling pin. Cut 12 rounds from dough. Gently press each round into muffin tin. Prick bottoms with fork. Place in freezer, uncovered, for 5 min. Bake until golden, 9 min.

2) Meanwhile, peel and dice onion. In large skillet over medium, heat oil. Add onion and cook, stirring until softened, about 2 min. Add beef. Sprinkle with salt and pepper; cook until no longer pink, 6 min. Drain. Pour in beans and mash with fork. Stir in BBQ sauce; reduce heat to low and cover.

3) Meanwhile, grate cheese and thinly slice green onions. Remove muffin tin from oven; turn oven to broil. Divide meat mixture between cups. Top with cheese and green onions. Broil until cheese is melted, about 1 min. Remove muffin tin from oven; place on wire rack until cool enough to handle, about 5 min. Lift pastry cups onto serving plate with small spatula.

nutritional facts: *Per serving: 570 calories • 48g carbohydrates • 29g protein • 29g fat • 900mg sodium • 90mg cholesterol • 3g fiber • 4g sugar*

steak tenderizer

Although tasty, skirt steaks benefit from tenderizing; use a meat mallet, a tenderizing powder or marinate in the rub for an hour or more before grilling.

mexican cheese steaks

prep time: 10 minutes • total time: 22 minutes • serves: 4

Whip up these delicious steaks, rubbed with flavorful spices and topped with cheese and avocado, any time you need to satisfy a craving for Mexican food and a hearty appetite.

1 pound skirt steak, trimmed	1 cup shredded pepper-Jack cheese
2 tsp. ancho *or* regular chili powder	
	1 (4 oz.) can whole green chiles
1 tsp. cumin	1 ripe avocado
1/4 tsp. salt	lime wedges and cilantro sprigs
3 tbsp. chopped cilantro	

1) Cut steak into 4 equal pieces. Combine chili powder, cumin and salt. Sprinkle on both sides of steaks and rub into meat. Toss cilantro with cheese in second bowl. Split chiles in half lengthwise.

2) Preheat grill to medium-high heat or heat heavy-bottomed skillet over medium heat. Add steaks and cook until browned on first side, about 4 min. Turn steaks over and place chiles on top. Cook until medium-rare (145°F. on an instant-read thermometer), about 4 min.

3) Turn off heat or move steaks away from heat source. Sprinkle cheese over steaks. Cover with pan lid until cheese is melted, about 2-3 min.

4) Meanwhile, pit, peel and slice avocado. Transfer steaks to serving plates and top with avocado. Garnish with lime wedges and cilantro sprigs, if desired.

nutritional facts: *Per serving: 550 calories • 8g carbohydrates • 44g protein • 40g fat • 580mg sodium • 130mg cholesterol • 2g fiber • 1g sugar*

pepper-vinegar sirloin steak

prep time: 12 minutes • total time: 22 minutes • serves: 6

This is a spicy food-lover's dream come true! These delicious steaks are served with two kinds of peppers for a real kick.

1-1/2 tsp. Italian seasoning	2 tbsp. brown sugar
1/2 tsp. coarse-ground pepper	1/2 cup jarred sliced hot cherry
1/4 tsp. salt	peppers, drained
2 cloves garlic	1/2 cup jarred roasted red
1 sirloin steak (1-inch thick,	peppers, drained
1-1/2 lbs.)	2 green onions
1/2 cup balsamic vinegar	2 large sprigs fresh basil

1) Preheat grill or broiler. In small dish, combine Italian seasoning, pepper and salt. Crush garlic and rub on both sides of steak. Sprinkle seasoning mixture on both sides of steak.

2) Place steak on grill or under broiler and cook until browned on first side, about 8-10 min. Turn and cook until desired doneness, about 10 min. for medium-rare. Let stand 5 min. and thinly slice. Place on serving platter.

3) Meanwhile, in small saucepan over medium heat, simmer vinegar and sugar until syrupy and reduced to 1/4 cup, about 5 min. Place in medium bowl. Slice peppers and onions; coarsely chop basil. Stir into vinegar mixture. Pour mixture over steak and serve.

nutritional facts: *Per serving: 240 calories • 17g carbohydrates • 21g protein • 8g fat • 620mg sodium • 55mg cholesterol • 1g fiber • 11g sugar*

mild peppers

Not everyone likes spicy food. For a more mild flavor, substitute roasted red peppers for the cherry peppers and serve with a mild, bottled chili sauce.

beef & coriander skillet

prep time: 17 minutes • total time: 24 minutes • serves: 6

Ready in a flash, this one-dish meal is perfect for any weeknight. The coriander and cumin lend exotic flavor to the simple beef and potatoes.

1-1/4 lbs. lean ground beef	1/2 tsp. cumin
1 small onion	1/4 tsp. crushed red pepper flakes
1 clove garlic	1 cup frozen hash brown
1 (1.2 oz.) pkg. brown gravy mix	potatoes
1 cup water	1-1/2 cups frozen mixed vegetables
1/2 cup red wine	1 large tomato
1 tsp. ground coriander	2 to 3 sprigs fresh parsley

1) In large skillet over high heat, cook ground beef until completely browned, breaking up with a spoon, about 5 min. Drain and return to skillet.

2) Meanwhile, chop onion to yield 1/2 cup. Mince garlic. Add onion and garlic to beef; reduce heat to medium-high. Cook, stirring constantly, until onions are softened, about 3 min.

3) Reduce heat to medium; add gravy mix, 1 cup water, wine, coriander, cumin and red pepper flakes. Stir until mixture begins to thicken.

4) Add potatoes and mixed vegetables to skillet. Cook and stir for 7 min. Meanwhile, chop tomato and parsley. Gently stir in tomatoes; cook until heated through, 1 min.

5) Transfer to serving dish. Sprinkle with parsley and serve.

nutritional facts: *Per serving: 210 calories • 18g carbohydrates • 20g protein • 4g fat • 420mg sodium • 50mg cholesterol • 2g fiber • 1g sugar*

bread bowl

Serve this chili-style dish in a bread bowl. Cut the top off a small loaf of round bread. Hollow out bread, leaving a 1/2-inch shell; fill with the chili and serve.

stuffed summer squash

prep time: 18 minutes • total time: 24 minutes • serves: 4

This recipe packs a tasty filling into rounds of yellow squash for an all-in-one dish.

3 large summer squash (1-3/4 lbs.)	1 tsp. dried oregano
3/4 tsp. salt, *divided*	1 tsp. cumin
3/4 lb. lean ground beef	1/4 tsp. allspice (optional)
4 green onions	1/2 tsp. sugar
1 clove garlic	2 tbsp. tomato paste
	3 tbsp. pine nuts, *divided*

1) Trim off flower ends of squash. Cut each squash into 4 cylinders, 1-1/4-inches thick. With melon ball cutter, hollow out center of slices, about 2/3 of the way through cylinder. Arrange hollowed-side up in microwave-safe, 9-inch pie plate or 1-1/2 qt. casserole. Sprinkle with 1/4 tsp. salt and cover with plastic. Microwave on HIGH just until tender, about 4 min.

2) Meanwhile, in nonstick skillet over medium heat, brown ground beef, about 4 min., breaking up lumps with spatula. Slice green onions and chop garlic. Add to beef with oregano, cumin, allspice, sugar and remaining salt. Cook and stir until meat is cooked and liquid is evaporated, about 3 min. Drain fat if needed.

3) Stir in tomato paste, 2 tbsp. pine nuts and 2 tbsp. water. Spoon mixture into squash hollows, spooning any extra filling around them. Top with remaining 1 tbsp. pine nuts. Garnish with chopped green onions and serve.

nutritional facts: *Per serving: 240 calories • 12g carbohydrates • 22g protein • 13g fat • 380mg sodium • 30mg cholesterol • 4g fiber • 7g sugar*

use zucchini instead

If you (or a friendly neighbor) has an abundance of zucchini from a productive garden, feel free to use that instead of summer squash.

ancho chili beef fajitas

prep time: 10 minutes • total time: 23 minutes • serves: 4

Fajitas are a Mexican version of a stir-fry—a quick skillet meal with nearly endless variations.

1 tbsp. ancho chili powder	1 tbsp. green (jalapeno) pepper sauce
2 tsp. cumin	1 lb. stir-fry beef strips
1 tsp. dried oregano	2 ears corn on the cob
1 red bell pepper	2 tsp. olive oil, *divided*
1 green pepper	4 (10-inch) whole wheat tortillas
1 small red onion	
1 lime	

1) In medium bowl, stir together chili powder, cumin and oregano. Remove 1 tbsp. and set aside. Thinly slice peppers and onion; set aside. Cut lime in half. Cut 1 half into 4 wedges; set aside. Squeeze remaining half to yield 1 tbsp. juice; place in medium bowl. Add pepper sauce and beef strips; toss to combine. Holding corn cob upright on a cutting board, carefully slice down side of cob to remove kernels. Repeat with remaining cob.

2) In large, nonstick skillet over medium-high, heat oil. Add onion and peppers. Cook, stirring occasionally, until crisp-tender, about 7 min. Stir in corn and reserved chili powder mixture. Cook and stir until corn is just tender, 2 min. Spoon mixture onto serving platter. Wipe out skillet with paper towels.

3) Heat remaining 1 tsp. oil in skillet. Add beef and stir-fry until beef is browned, but still pink inside, 1-2 min. Add to platter. Garnish with lime wedges. Wrap tortillas in paper towels; microwave on HIGH until heated, 1 min. Transfer tortillas to plate; serve with beef and peppers.

nutritional facts: *Per serving: 510 calories • 41g carbohydrates • 31g protein • 24g fat • 280mg sodium • 60mg cholesterol • 7g fiber • 11g sugar*

avoid a mess

To avoid a mess and be safe when cutting corn kernels off cobs, place the cobs upright on a small cutting board that's set within a flat-bottomed, high-sided pan or bowl.

easy empanadas

prep time: 40 minutes • total time: 50 minutes • serves: 24

These exotic South-American meat pies are easier to make than they appear. They'll add a unique flair to any party fare and will have your guests clamoring for more! They can be served as a main dish or appetizer.

2 tbsp. rum	1 tbsp. capers
1/3 cup currants	1/2 tsp. salt
1 medium onion	1/4 tsp. pepper
1/4 cup pimiento-stuffed olives	1/4 tsp. oregano
1 medium tomato	1/4 tsp. ground cinnamon
2 to 3 sprigs parsley	1 tbsp. all-purpose flour
3/4 lb. lean ground beef	3 refrigerated pie crusts
2 tbsp. pine nuts	1 large egg

1) Preheat oven to 400°F. Line 2 baking sheets with parchment paper. In small bowl, combine rum and currants; set aside. Chop onion and dice olives. Seed and dice tomato; chop parsley to yield 1 tbsp.

2) In large skillet over high, brown ground beef, about 4 min. Reduce heat to medium; add onion. Cook and stir until onion is softened, 3 min.

3) Add currants, olives, tomato, pine nuts, capers, parsley, salt, pepper, oregano and cinnamon to skillet. Cook and stir 2 min. Remove from heat.

4) Sprinkle flour on work surface. Unroll pie crusts. With rolling pin, smooth wrinkles. Using 5-inch-diameter glass, cut 8 circles from each crust, re-rolling scraps as needed.

5) Place 1 tbsp. beef mixture in center of each circle. Moisten edges of dough with water; fold dough over to form half-circle. Press edge with fork to seal. Transfer to baking sheets.

6) In small bowl, beat egg. Brush each empanada with egg. Bake until golden brown, 10 min. Serve.

nutritional facts: *Per serving: 160 calories • 16g carbohydrates • 4g protein • 9g fat • 220mg sodium • 20mg cholesterol • 0g fiber • 3g sugar*

spanish-style salad

Toss crisp green lettuce with a few kalamata olives and chopped tomato and red onion. Sprinkle with a light vinaigrette and a few croutons.

---

hobo dinner

prep time: 5 minutes • total time: 50 minutes • yield: 1 serving

The meat and vegetables in this dinner are all wrapped in a piece of foil and cooked together, resulting in a juicy burger and tender vegetables.

1/4 pound ground beef	1 carrot, sliced
1 sheet heavy-duty aluminum foil (18 inches x 13 inches)	2 tablespoons chopped onion
1 potato, sliced	salt and pepper to taste (optional)

1) Shape beef into a patty; place in the center of foil with potato, carrot and onion. Sprinkle with salt and pepper if desired.

2) Fold foil over and seal well; place on a baking sheet.

3) Bake at 350° for 45 minutes. Open foil carefully.

nutritional facts: *Per serving: 374 calories • 46 g carbohydrates • 27 g protein • 9 g fat • 84 mg sodium • 69 mg cholesterol • 6 g fiber*

grilled great

Hobo Dinner can also be made on the grill. Just set the packet over medium heat. Cover and grill for 45-60 minutes or until the potatoes are tender.

quick steak dinner

Turn leftover steak into a quick dinner. Just slice the steak into thin strips. Then saute some chopped garlic and slice onions and mushrooms in olive oil. Add the meat and cook until heated through. You can season this with soy sauce or Worcestershire sauce. Add some garlic sauce or herbs such as basil, thyme or oregano. Serve over rice or on a sandwich roll. If you like your meat a little saucy, add some beef broth and thicken with cornstarch.

super steak stew

For a simple, tender stew try using steak. Cut the meat into small cubes then brown it in olive oil in a skillet. Add about 2 cups of beef broth, two cubed potatoes, sliced carrots and diced onion. Season as desired. Bring to a boil and simmer about 20 minutes or until the vegetables are done. Thicken liquid with flour or cornstarch. This is a delicious meal served with hot biscuits.

cut the fat from ground beef

To reduce the fat from ground beef in your recipes, cook it in a microwave-safe strainer over a microwave-safe bowl. Break up the ground beef with a fork and stir it frequently. You should cook it until it is just no longer pink. The fat will collect at the bottom of the bowl and be discarded. Finish cooking according to the recipe; just omit the browning step.

tips for grilling steaks

Trim steaks to avoid flare-ups, leaving a thin layer of fat, if desired, to help maintain juiceness. Pat dry with paper towels before grilling—a dry steak will brown better than a moist one.

stretching your grocery dollar

Here's a way to stretch ground beef for recipes, such as tacos, sloppy joes and soups. For every pound of ground beef that the recipe calls for, replace a half pound with 1-1/2 cups cooked brown rice. It's a tasty and healthy way to beat the bank.

ground beef labels

Ground beef is often labeled using the cut of meat that it is ground from, such as ground chuck or ground round. (Ground beef comes from a combination of beef cuts.) Ground beef can also be labeled according to the fat content of the ground mixture or the percentage of lean meat to fat, such as 85% or 90% lean. The higher the percentage, the leaner the meat.

doneness test for steak

To test for doneness, insert an instant-read thermometer horizontally from the side, making sure to get the reading in the center of the steak.

keep the meat in your tacos

To keep ground beef from falling out of burritos or enchiladas, add a can of refried beans to the meat mixture and heat thoroughly. The filling not only stays in place, but the beans stretch the mixture so you can serve more.

complementing veal's flavor

Veal has a delicate taste, which allows the more flavorful ingredients in a recipe to shine. Herbs and spices that complement veal include marjoram, rosemary, sage, oregano, black pepper, cinnamon, garlic, mustard, nutmeg, bay leaf and thyme.

making meatballs of equal size

1) Lightly pat meat mixture into a 1-inch-thick rectangle. Cut the rectangle into the same number of squares as meatballs in the recipe.

2) Using your hands, gently roll each square into a ball.

purchasing beef

When purchasing beef and ground beef, select beef with a bright, cherry-red color and without any gray or brown patches. Make sure the package is cold and free of holes or tears. Also make sure the package does not have excessive liquid, as this might indicate that the meat was subjected to improper temperatures. Always purchase items before the sell-by date for best quality. If the sell-by date is the actual date you purchase the meat and you're not using it that day, wrap the meat and store it in the freezer.

cutting uncooked beef into strips

To easily slice raw beef, first place the meat in the freezer for about 30 minutes or until it is firm but not solidly frozen. Slice to desired thinness.

rub it in

Apply a rub or blend of seasonings, such as fresh or dried herbs and spices to the surface of uncooked steaks or roasts. A rub adds a burst of flavor to the beef, but does not tenderize the meat.

make a salad

Turn leftover cooked beef into a tasty salad. Simply cut the beef into thin strips. Add some onions and sweet pepper and toss with Italian salad dressing. Let it chill while the flavors blend. Then serve it over some salad greens.

freeze browned ground beef

If you're pressed for time when making weeknight dinners, try this easy trick. Crumble and brown several pounds of ground beef at one time. Spread in a shallow baking pan and freeze until solid. Transfer to freezer bags in 1/2- or 1-pound amounts...whatever your favorite recipes call for. On busy days, pull out a bag and add to chili, tacos or any recipe that uses browned ground beef.

perfect poultry

chicken au gratin • p. 85

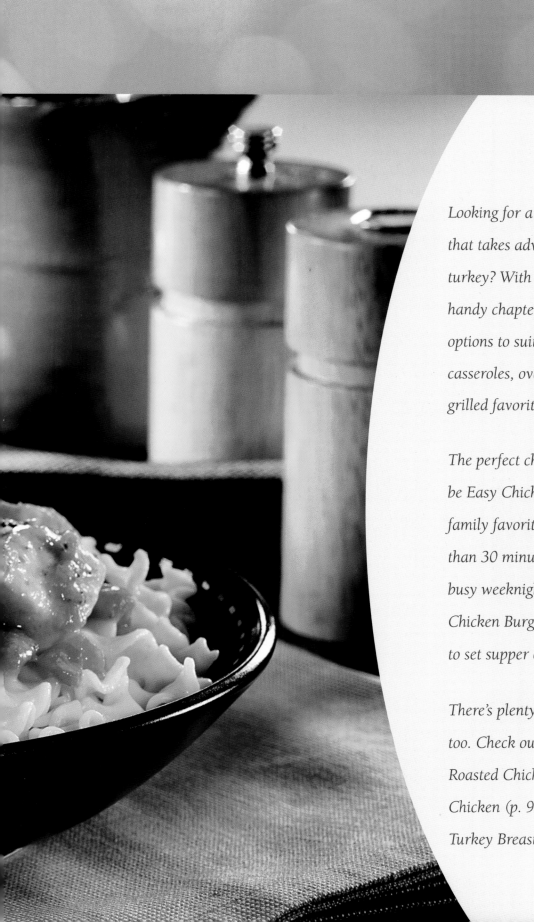

Looking for a palate-pleasing recipe
that takes advantage of chicken or
turkey? With 48 succulent recipes, this
handy chapter offers plenty of delicious
options to suit any occasion. You'll find
casseroles, oven entrees, skillet suppers,
grilled favorites and more.

The perfect choice for dinner just may
be Easy Chicken Piccata (p. 82). This
family favorite is table-ready in less
than 30 minutes, making it ideal for
busy weeknights. Or consider Buffalo
Chicken Burgers (p. 88) when you need
to set supper on the table in a flash.

There's plenty of options for company,
too. Check out the recipes for Herb
Roasted Chicken (p. 87), Salsa Verde
Chicken (p. 92) or Sausage-Stuffed
Turkey Breasts (p. 99).

ginger peachy glazed chicken

prep time: 15 minutes • **total time:** 25 minutes • **serves:** 4

Don't just consider this recipe—give it a try tonight! The grilled peaches are truly delicious and the sauce lends great flavor to the quickly cooked chicken. Your family will love it, too.

4 boneless, skinless chicken breast halves	1 bunch green onions, *divided*
1-1/2 tbsp. ginger, *divided*	3 peaches
1-1/2 tsp. salt, *divided*	2 cups white grape & peach juice blend, *divided*
1/2 tsp. garlic powder	1/4 cup lemon juice
1/4 tsp. pepper	2 tsp. cornstarch
2 tsp. oil	

1) Preheat grill to medium. Pound chicken to even thickness between sheets of waxed paper. In small bowl, combine 2 tsp. ginger, 1-1/4 tsp. salt, garlic powder and pepper. Coat chicken with oil, then rub with spice mixture.

2) Thinly slice one green onion; set aside. Quarter peaches; remove pits. Place peaches skin-side down on grill; cook 3 min. Turn peaches; add chicken to grill and cook, turning peaches and chicken occasionally until almost done, 6 min. Add whole onions and cook until done, 2 min. Remove to platter.

3) Reserve 2 tbsp. juice blend; place in small bowl. In large skillet over medium-high heat, combine remaining juice blend, lemon juice, remaining ginger and salt. Bring to boil and cook over medium-high heat until mixture is reduced by half, 5-7 min. Stir in cornstarch and reserved juice. Add to skillet; return to boil. Stir in sliced green onion. Place chicken, peaches and whole green onions in skillet; turn to coat with sauce. Transfer to platter; serve.

nutritional facts: *Per serving: 280 calories • 30g carbohydrates • 28g protein • 6g fat • 950mg sodium • 75mg cholesterol • 3g fiber • 24g sugar*

make it simple

If you can't easily find a white grape and peach juice blend, you can use white grape juice instead.

quicker barbecued chicken 'n' rice

prep time: 10 minutes • **total time:** 35 minutes • **serves:** 4 to 6

This chicken is sure to appear regularly on your weekly meal plan. Because it bakes in the oven, it's a terrific way to bring a bit of summer to the table even on the chilliest night.

1-1/2 cups uncooked instant rice	1-1/4 cups barbecue sauce
1 cup chicken broth	1 tablespoon dried minced onion
6 boneless, skinless chicken breast halves	1/4 teaspoon celery seed

1) Combine the rice and broth in a greased 11 x 7-in. baking dish. Top with the chicken.

2) Combine barbecue sauce, onion and celery seed; pour over chicken.

3) Bake, uncovered, at 375°F. for 25-30 minutes or until a meat thermometer reads 170°F.

nutritional facts: *Per serving: 256 calories • 27g carbohydrates • 26g protein • 4g fat • 636mg sodium • 63mg cholesterol • 1g fiber*

kids in the kitchen

Little chefs can help prepare this dish by measuring the instant rice, stirring up the barbecue sauce mixture and assembling the items in the baking dish.

cider-glazed turkey

prep time: 8 minutes • total time: 20 minutes • serves: 4

Tender turkey cutlets are glazed in a sweet but tangy apple cider and sage sauce. They're then crowned with a garnish of tart dried cranberries and crunchy pecans. It's a mini Thanksgiving feast that can be made in a snap!

1 lb. turkey cutlets	1 large shallot
1/4 tsp. salt	1/4 tsp. sage
1/8 tsp. pepper	1 tbsp. fresh parsley
2 tbsp. butter	2 tbsp. dried cranberries
1 cup apple cider, *divided*	2 tbsp. chopped pecans
2 tsp. cornstarch	

1) Sprinkle turkey cutlets with salt and pepper. In large skillet over high heat, melt butter. Add cutlets and cook until browned on first side, about 3 min. Turn and cook until done, about 3-4 min. Remove and keep warm.

2) Meanwhile, in small bowl, combine 2 tbsp. cider with cornstarch. Set aside.

3) Finely chop shallot to yield 1/4 cup; add to skillet. Cook and stir 1 min. Add remaining cider and sage. Bring to boil; cook until reduced to 1/2 cup. Stir in cider and cornstarch mixture. Return to boil; cook and stir until thickened. Return turkey and any juices to skillet. Stir to coat cutlets. Remove skillet from heat.

4) Chop parsley. In small bowl, combine parsley, cranberries and pecans. Transfer turkey to serving dish; spoon sauce over top; sprinkle with cranberry mixture. Serve immediately.

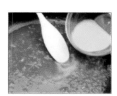

nutritional facts: *Per serving: 250 calories • 13g carbohydrates • 29g protein • 9g fat • 650mg sodium • 60mg cholesterol • 1g fiber • 10g sugar*

sweet tastes

For a little sweeter glaze, try adding a teaspoon of honey when you stir in the cider and cornstarch mixture. You could also add a spoonful of maple syrup.

rustic stuffed chicken

prep time: 11 minutes • total time: 28 minutes • serves: 4

Here goat cheese and prepared tapenade (a savory mix of olive paste, garlic and herbs), lend country flair to chicken breasts.

3 sprigs fresh tarragon	4 boneless, skinless chicken
2 tbsp. prepared tapenade	breasts (about 1-3/4 lbs.)
(drained if necessary)	1/4 tsp. salt
1 (4 oz.) log goat cheese,	2 tsp. olive oil
divided	1/4 cup white wine
1/4 tsp. pepper, *divided*	1/4 cup sour cream

1) Chop tarragon to yield 3 tsp.; place 2 tsp. in small bowl. Stir in tapenade, half of goat cheese and 1/8 tsp. pepper until combined.

2) With sharp, paring knife, cut pocket in thick side of each breast, being careful not to cut through back. Stuff each breast with 1 tbsp. tapenade mixture. Secure opening with toothpicks; sprinkle with salt and remaining pepper.

3) In large, nonstick skillet over medium, heat oil. Add chicken; cook until browned on first side, 6 min. Turn chicken over; add wine. Cook, covered, until cooked through, 6 min. Transfer chicken to serving platter and cut into slices. Sprinkle with remaining tarragon.

4) Reduce heat to low. Add remaining goat cheese to pan. Cook and stir until melted. Remove from heat; stir in sour cream until blended. Serve with chicken.

nutritional facts: *Per serving: 410 calories • 2g carbohydrates • 53g protein • 18g fat • 510mg sodium • 150mg cholesterol • 0g fiber • 2g sugar*

bone-in chicken

Chicken breasts on the bone are a terrific variation of this recipe. You can easily push the stuffing under the skin, then simply secure it with a skewer.

easy chicken piccata

prep time: 5 minutes • **total time:** 28 minutes • **serves:** 6

Chicken cutlets lightly covered with flour are quickly sauteed and smothered in a tasty chicken broth and lemon juice sauce enlivened by capers and mushrooms. Every bite has a fresh burst of flavor.

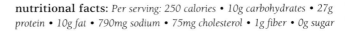

1 egg, beaten	1 cup chicken broth
1 lemon, cut in half	1 cup sliced white mushrooms
1/2 cup all-purpose flour	1/4 cup capers, rinsed and
1 tsp. salt	drained
1/2 tsp. pepper	1 tbsp. butter
2 tbsp. extra-virgin olive oil	
6 thin-sliced chicken cutlets (about 1 pound)	

1) In shallow bowl, stir together egg and juice of half of lemon. In another shallow dish, combine flour, salt and pepper.

2) In large skillet over medium-high, heat oil. Dip each cutlet into the egg mixture, then dredge in the seasoned flour to coat. Place in skillet and brown for about 3 min. on each side.

3) Add chicken broth, mushrooms and juice of remaining lemon to skillet. Cook, covered, over medium-low heat, until flavors combine, about 15 min.

4) Remove cutlets to serving plate. Stir capers and butter into the sauce in the skillet to thicken. Season with additional salt and pepper. Spoon sauce over chicken and serve.

nutritional facts: *Per serving: 250 calories • 10g carbohydrates • 27g protein • 10g fat • 790mg sodium • 75mg cholesterol • 1g fiber • 0g sugar*

the best capers

Capers are packed in salt and sold in specialty food markets. Before adding them to a recipe, rinse the desired amount in water twice to remove some of the salt.

bacon vinaigrette grilled chicken

prep time: 2 minutes • **total time:** 22 minutes • **serves:** 4

This tempting grilled chicken topped with a zesty bacon vinaigrette is made from just six common ingredients, so it's very quick and easy. It's destined to be a new favorite!

1/2 lb. sliced bacon	2 medium tomatoes, seeded
4 thin-sliced chicken cutlets (about 1 lb.)	1/4 cup extra-virgin olive oil
1 small onion	3 tbsp. red wine vinegar

1) Preheat outdoor grill or indoor grill pan.

2) In large skillet over medium heat, lay bacon strips in single layer. Cook, turning frequently, until crispy, about 5 min. Remove to paper towel-lined plate. Pour off excess fat; set skillet aside.

3) Cook chicken cutlets on grill or grill pan until juices run clear, about 4-5 min. per side. Cut into slices and place on serving platter.

4) Meanwhile dice the onion and tomato. Place the diced tomato on top of the chicken.

5) Add the olive oil and diced onion to skillet. Cook until the onion is translucent, about 5 min.

6) Pour vinegar into the skillet and stir for 1 min. Remove from heat. Crumble bacon and add to vinaigrette. Spoon over chicken and serve.

nutritional facts: *Per serving: 460 calories • 10g carbohydrates • 29g protein • 33g fat • 370mg sodium • 90mg cholesterol • 3g fiber • 3g sugar*

bacon bonus

Bacon enhances many recipes. Cook the entire package and remove a half pound before it is fully crisp; wrap slices in paper towels and freeze in a zippered bag. Remove as many slices as needed and reheat.

"five spice" chicken

prep time: 5 minutes • total time: 29 minutes • serves: 6

This dish uses Chinese Five-Spice powder, a blend of spices including star anise. Brown sugar, soy sauce, sherry, ginger and garlic round out the marinade and give it body.

2 tbsp. brown sugar	4 tsp. Chinese Five-Spice Powder
2 tbsp. soy sauce	
1/4 cup dry sherry	6 chicken thighs (about 3 lbs.), excess skin trimmed
1 tsp. minced fresh ginger	
1 clove garlic, minced	

1) Preheat oven to 425°F. Line baking sheet with foil. In small bowl, stir together brown sugar, soy sauce, sherry, ginger, garlic and Five-Spice Powder.

2) Dip each chicken thigh into the sauce. Place, skin side up, on prepared baking sheet. Bake for 15 min., brushing periodically with remaining sauce.

3) Switch oven to broil and broil chicken 10 inches from heat until juices run clear, about 6-8 min. Remove to platter and serve.

nutritional facts: *Per serving: 590 calories • 6g carbohydrates • 58g protein • 35g fat • 500mg sodium • 210mg cholesterol • 0g fiber • 4g sugar*

jazz it up

Make this a company meal by stuffing each thigh with some chopped apples, pears or mangos that have been sauteed in a bit of olive oil and ginger-studded soy sauce.

turkey roll-ups with gravy

prep time: 24 minutes • total time: 29 minutes • serves: 4

A flavorful sausage and bread stuffing fills turkey rolls that simmer with pearl onions in a rich savory gravy. This is one meal that will have both the cook and diners feeling thankful.

2 tbsp. butter, *divided*	1/4 tsp. pepper
2 links sweet Italian sausage (about 4 oz.)	2 sprigs fresh parsley
3/4 cup finely chopped celery	1/2 (16 oz.) pkg. frozen pearl onions
2 slices firm white sandwich bread	2 tbsp. all-purpose flour
8 turkey cutlets (about 1-1/2 lbs.), pounded 1/8-inch thick	1 cup chicken broth
1/4 tsp. salt	1/2 cup dry white wine *or* chicken broth

1) In large, nonstick skillet over medium-high heat, melt 1 tbsp. butter. Remove sausage from casing; add to skillet, breaking into small pieces with spatula. Add celery and cook, stirring occasionally, until sausage is no longer pink, about 5 min.

2) Meanwhile, cut bread into 1/4-inch cubes. Lay turkey cutlets on cutting board; season with salt and pepper. Roughly chop parsley to yield 2 tbsp.

3) Remove skillet from heat; stir in bread cubes and 1 tbsp. parsley. Evenly mound stuffing onto cutlets and roll up, tucking in sides slightly. Secure with toothpicks.

4) In same skillet over high heat, melt remaining butter. Add turkey rolls, seam side down. Top with onions. Cook rolls 2 min.; turn and cook 2 min., stirring onions occasionally. Continue cooking and turning chicken until cooked through.

5) In medium bowl, place flour. Gradually whisk in broth and wine. Stir in remaining parsley. Add to skillet, stirring to combine. Reduce heat to medium-low and simmer, covered, 5 min., turning rolls once. Transfer to plates; remove toothpicks and serve.

nutritional facts: *Per serving: 370 calories • 15g carbohydrates • 50g protein • 10g fat • 460mg sodium • 90mg cholesterol • 1g fiber • 5g sugar*

fresh idea

Instead of cutting the day-old bread into cubes, put the slices into a small food processor and make fluffy bread crumbs. It's fast and the bread crumbs will work nicely in this stuffing.

thai-style chicken & cashews

prep time: 25 minutes • total time: 25 minutes • serves: 4

Stir-fry dishes are so popular not only because they're quick and tasty but also because the veggies retain their beautiful colors. Enjoy the taste and presentation of this chicken!

3/4 lb. green beans, trimmed and halved crosswise (4 cups)	1-1/2 tsp. olive oil
1 small red onion, cut into slivers	1 lb. boneless, skinless chicken breasts
1/2 cup jarred teriyaki sauce	1 tbsp. chopped fresh ginger
1 tsp. anchovy paste, optional	1/3 cup roasted cashews, *divided*
1 to 2 tsp. jalapeno hot sauce	1/3 cup torn basil leaves
1 lime, halved	

1) Bring medium saucepan of water to boil over high heat. Add beans; cook until crisp-tender, 5 min. Add onions and cook 1 min. more. Rinse under cold water and drain well.

2) In small dish, stir together teriyaki sauce, anchovy paste and hot sauce. Cut chicken into 3/4-inch pieces.

3) In wok or skillet over medium-hight, heat oil. Add chicken and stir-fry until almost cooked through, about 5 minutes. Add green bean mixture, ginger and half of cashews; stir-fry 3 min.

4) Stir teriyaki mixture and cook, stirring continuously, until thickened and bubbly. Remove from heat and stir in basil. Squeeze on juice from half of lime; toss to combine. Transfer to serving platter; sprinkle with remaining cashews. Cut remaining lime into wedges to garnish chicken.

nutritional facts: *Per serving: 280 calories • 22g carbohydrates • 30g protein • 9g fat • 1410mg sodium • 65mg cholesterol • 4g fiber • 7g sugar*

play it safe

To avoid cross-contamination, use a plastic, dishwasher-safe cutting board exclusively for cutting chicken. Ideally, it should have a ridge to catch juices.

blackened chicken

prep time: 8 minutes • total time: 24 minutes • serves: 4

This delightful Cajun-inspired dish can be cooked in a skillet indoors in bad weather or on a grill outdoors when the weather is fine. The secret to its great flavor? It's all in the blend of special spices.

2 tsp. paprika	3/4 tsp. dried oregano
2 tsp. onion powder	1/2 tsp. salt
1 tsp. garlic powder	1/2 tsp. cayenne pepper
1 tsp. black pepper	6 to 8 boneless, skinless chicken thighs (about 1-1/2 lbs.)
3/4 tsp. dried thyme	2 tbsp. melted butter

1) In small dish, combine paprika, onion powder, garlic powder, black pepper, thyme, oregano, salt and cayenne pepper.

2) Place chicken between sheets of plastic and pound to even thickness, about 3/8 inch. Brush with half of butter and sprinkle with half of seasoning. Turn over chicken; repeat with butter and seasoning.

3) Heat cast-iron or very heavy skillet over medium-high. Add chicken, in batches if necessary, and cook until first side is blackened and cooked through, about 4 min. Turn and cook until second side is blackened, 4 min. Serve immediately. Note: If cooking in batches, wipe out skillet between batches, using wadded paper towels held with tongs.

nutritional facts: *Per serving: 360 calories • 6g carbohydrates • 31g protein • 23g fat • 430mg sodium • 125mg cholesterol • 1g fiber • 1g sugar*

creole mustard sauce

Combine 1/2 cup mayonnaise with 1/4 cup Creole-style mustard in a small bowl. Stir gently. Add a drop of hot sauce and serve as a sauce for the chicken.

chicken au gratin

prep time: 10 minutes • total time: 24 minutes • serves: 6

This is the recipe you've been waiting for! Tender chicken pieces and chopped broccoli are cooked in a wonderful, au gratin cheese sauce with a hint of wine.

2 cups frozen chopped broccoli	1/2 cup dry white wine
1-1/4 lbs. boneless, skinless chicken breasts	1/2 cup chicken broth
1 small onion	1/2 cup canned petite diced tomatoes
1 tbsp. oil	1/4 tsp. salt
3 tbsp. butter, *divided*	1/4 tsp. pepper
1/2 tbsp. chopped garlic in oil	1-1/4 cups shredded cheddar-Jack cheese, *divided*
2 tbsp. all-purpose flour	

1) In medium, microwave-safe bowl, place broccoli and 2 tbsp. water. Cover; microwave on HIGH until thawed, 3 min.

2) Cut chicken into 1-inch pieces. Mince onion. In large, nonstick skillet over medium, heat oil and 1 tbsp. butter. Add chicken, onion and garlic. Cook and stir, until chicken is almost cooked through, 4 min. Remove chicken, leaving onion, garlic and juices in pan.

3) Add remaining butter; stir until melted. Sprinkle in flour and cook, whisking constantly, 1 min. Add white wine and chicken broth; bring to boil, stirring constantly. Cook, scraping up bits from bottom of pan, until thickened, 1 min.

4) Add chicken, broccoli, tomatoes, salt and pepper; return to boil for 1 min. Remove from heat; stir in 1 cup cheese. Transfer to serving dish; sprinkle with remaining the cheese and serve.

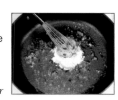

nutritional facts: *Per serving: 340 calories • 8g carbohydrates • 32g protein • 19g fat • 410mg sodium • 105mg cholesterol • 2g fiber • 2g sugar*

broccoli spears

If you prefer spears of broccoli, use fresh broccoli and peel the stems so they'll be tender when cooked in the microwave.

moroccan grilled chicken

prep time: 10 minutes • total time: 24 minutes • serves: 4

Create the exotic flavors of Morocco by combining fragrant spices with oil, lemon and parsley to make a rub that clings to the chicken. Making slashes in the chicken allows the flavors to penetrate.

2 boneless skinless chicken breasts (about 1-1/2 lbs.)	3 tbsp. oil
1 tbsp. coriander	1-1/2 tbsp. lemon juice
2 tsp. cumin	1/2 cup finely chopped parsley, *divided*
2 tsp. paprika	lemon wedges for serving
1/2 tsp. allspice	

1) If using grill, brush grate with oil. If using broiler, line shallow baking sheet with foil and set rack about 3 inches from heat. Preheat grill or broiler to high.

2) Cut each chicken breast in half to form cutlets. Make 3 or 4 diagonal slashes about 1/4-inch deep in thickest part of each cutlet.

3) In small bowl, thoroughly blend spices with oil and lemon. Stir in 1/4 cup parsley. Rub mixture thoroughly on chicken, being sure to rub into slashed areas. Let stand about 5 min.

4) Grill or broil chicken, turning once, until cooked through, about 9-12 min. Sprinkle with remaining parsley and lemon wedges; serve immediately.

nutritional facts: *Per serving: 410 calories • 2g carbohydrates • 51g protein • 21g fat • 130mg sodium • 145mg cholesterol • 1g fiber • 0g sugar*

a dash of heat

Add 1/4 teaspoon cayenne pepper to the mix. You can also try adding 1/2 teaspoon ground ginger or 1/4 teaspoon ground cloves.

flavored butter

Serve a loaf of fresh bread with
this flavorful butter: Combine
1 stick softened butter with
1/4 cup freshly grated Parmesan;
season with salt and pepper.

basil balsamic chicken

prep time: 17 minutes • total time: 24 minutes • serves: 4

With just a few simple ingredients, you can make a dish with a whole world of flavor. Balsamic vinegar and wine blend to create a rich sauce with tons of taste without a lot of calories.

8	boneless, skinless chicken thighs (about 1-1/2 lbs.)	2	tsp. all-purpose flour
1/4	tsp. salt	1/2	cup white wine
1/8	tsp. pepper	1/3	cup balsamic vinegar
1	tbsp. butter	1/3	cup water
3	shallots	1/4	cup basil leaves

1) Sprinkle chicken with salt and pepper. In large skillet over medium-high heat, melt butter. Add chicken and cook until just golden on first side, about 4 min. Turn and cook until golden on second side, 4 min. Remove and keep warm.

2) Meanwhile, finely slice shallots to yield 1/2 cup. Add to skillet; cook and stir 1 min. Add flour; cook and stir, 1 min. Gradually whisk in wine, then vinegar and water. Bring to boil; reduce heat to medium-low.

3) Add chicken and simmer until chicken is cooked through, about 7 min. Meanwhile, finely chop basil; stir into skillet just before removing from heat.

nutritional facts: *Per serving: 420 calories • 11g carbohydrates • 45g protein • 19g fat • 590mg sodium • 160mg cholesterol • 1g fiber • 6g sugar*

chicken chili

Serve a chicken chili delight:
Add a can of drained and rinsed
white beans and a drained can of
corn kernels to the mixture—
a teaspoon of chili powder
completes the dish.

italian chicken casserole

prep time: 5 minutes • total time: 29 minutes • serves: 4 to 6

You can come home after a long day of work or an outing with the kids and have this hot, hearty casserole on the table in just about 30 minutes!

1	small onion	1	lb. ground chicken
2	large cloves garlic	1/2	cup sliced black olives
1	medium red bell pepper	1	(14.5 oz.) can petite-cut diced tomatoes, drained
1	small zucchini		
2	tbsp. olive oil, *divided*	1	large egg
1/2	tsp. salt	1	cup shredded Parmesan cheese, *divided*
1/4	tsp. pepper		
1	tsp. dried oregano	1 to 2	sprigs fresh basil

1) Preheat oven to 400°F. Chop onion into large pieces. Peel and mince garlic. Cut red pepper into small strips and zucchini into half-rounds. In large skillet over medium, heat 1 tbsp. olive oil. Add onion and garlic, cook and stir until fragrant, about 2 min. Add pepper and zucchini; season with salt, pepper and oregano. Cook, stirring occasionally, until vegetables are tender, about 5 min. Transfer to plate and set aside.

2) Heat the remaining olive oil. Add the chicken and cook, breaking up lumps with wooden spoon, until no longer pink, 5 min. Add the olives and tomatoes; cook until heated through.

3) Meanwhile, in small bowl, lightly beat egg. Mix in 1/2 cup Parmesan. Finely chop basil leaves and add to egg mixture.

4) Remove chicken mixture from heat and fold in egg mixture. Transfer chicken to baking dish. Spread reserved vegetables evenly over top of chicken. Sprinkle with remaining Parmesan cheese. Bake until vegetables are soft and mixture is heated through, 12 min.

nutritional facts: *Per serving: 220 calories • 8g carbohydrates • 19g protein • 13g fat • 660mg sodium • 95mg cholesterol • 2g fiber • 4g sugar*

herb roasted chicken

prep time: 15 minutes • total time: 2 hours • serves: 6

Once this chicken is in the oven, you can move on to making side dishes or relaxing with family.

4 cloves garlic, minced	2 medium onions, cut into
1 1/2 tsp. dried thyme, *divided*	1/2-inch slices
1/2 tsp. crushed dried rosemary	1/4 cup all-purpose flour
1 tsp. coarse salt	1 (14 oz.) can reduced-sodium
1/4 tsp. coarse ground-pepper	chicken broth
1 lemon	1/4 cup dry white wine
1 roasting chicken (about 4 lbs.)	

1) Preheat oven to 425°F. In small bowl, combine garlic, 1 tsp. thyme, rosemary, salt and pepper. Zest lemon; reserve 1/2 tsp. for sauce. Place remaining zest with herbs. Cut lemon into wedges; squeeze juice into bowl. Season chicken with mixture inside and out. Place squeezed lemon wedges inside chicken. Tie legs together; tuck under wings.

2) In center of roasting pan, arrange onions; place chicken on onions. Roast until an instant-read thermometer reads 180°F. in breast, about 1-1/2 hours, basting occasionally. Tent with foil if skin becomes too dark. Remove chicken to cutting board. Loosely cover with foil and let stand 10 min.

3) Meanwhile, place roasting pan over medium heat. Stir in flour; cook until flour is slightly browned. Gradually add chicken broth; bring to boil, scraping up any browned bits. Stir in wine, remaining thyme and reserved lemon zest. Cook until mixture is thickened. Strain gravy and serve with carved chicken.

nutritional facts: *Per 6-oz. serving: 250 calories • 3g carbohydrates • 19g protein • 17g fat • 240mg sodium • 80mg cholesterol • 0g fiber • 1g sugar*

smart shopping

Buy an extra chicken when they are on sale. Don't bother rewrapping it; it actually freezes better in the original wrapping.

chicken 'n' dumplings

prep time: 19 minutes • total time: 29 minutes • serves: 4

With a couple of shortcuts, this old country favorite is done in just under half an hour.

1 cup instant baking mix	1 (6 oz.) pkg. shredded carrots
1/3 cup milk	1 (14.5 oz.) can reduced-sodium
3 sprigs fresh flat-leaf parsley,	chicken broth
chopped	1/8 tsp. pepper
2 sprigs fresh tarragon, chopped	2 cups shredded, cooked
1 large onion, diced	chicken
3 ribs celery	2 (14.5 oz.) cans chicken gravy
1/4 lb. green beans, chopped	

1) Fill 6-qt. saucepot with 4 inches very hot water. Cover and bring to boil. Combine baking mix, milk and half of parsley and tarragon. Drop by 4 large spoonfuls into boiling water. Reduce heat and simmer 10 min.; cover and gently simmer, reducing heat again if necessary, 10 min.

2) In large saucepan, combine celery, onion, green beans, carrots and broth. Cover and boil gently, until vegetables are tender, about 10 min. Stir in remaining herbs, chicken and gravy; heat through. Ladle chicken mixture into serving bowls. Top each with a dumpling.

nutritional facts: *Per serving: 320 calories • 28g carbohydrates • 22g protein • 13g fat • 1140mg sodium • 45mg cholesterol • 3g fiber • 4g sugar*

sweet stew

For those who like a sweet stew, you can add 1/2 cup diced yams to the vegetables. Or, for a different flavor, try adding a bay leaf, but remember to remove it before serving.

today's duck a l'orange

prep time: 15 minutes • total time: 45 minutes • serves: 6

Boneless duck breasts are now available in supermarkets, making this one-time "restaurant only" dish possible at home. It's a treat for guests, especially when served with the luscious sauce.

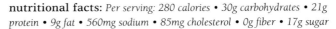

3/4 cup apricot preserves
1/2 cup fresh orange juice
3 tbsp. sherry wine vinegar
2 tbsp. sweet sherry
1 tsp. salt, *divided*
1/2 tsp. pepper, *divided*

1 tbsp. chopped fresh tarragon
2 tbsp. grated orange rind
3 (1 lb.) boneless Muscovy duck breasts with skin *or* 6 (8 oz.) Peking duck breasts with skin

1) In medium saucepan over low heat, combine preserves, juice, vinegar, sherry, 1/2 tsp. salt and 1/4 tsp. pepper. Simmer, stirring occasionally, 5 min. Remove from heat and stir in tarragon and orange rind.

2) Meanwhile, preheat broiler to high. Line broiler pan with heavy-duty aluminum foil and add 1 cup water. Place rack on top. Score skin of duck in crosshatch pattern, being careful not to cut through to meat. Season with remaining salt and pepper.

3) Place skin-side down on rack and broil (with door slightly open) for 15 min (7 min. for Peking breasts); turn and broil 10 min. for medium-rare (150°F on instant-read thermometer). To cook further, switch setting to bake at 450°F. Roast duck for 15-20 min. (165°F on instant-read thermometer). Remove to cutting board and cover loosely with foil; let rest 5 min.

4) To serve, slice thinly on diagonal and arrange on 6 plates; drizzle with some of warm sauce and pass remaining sauce at table.

nutritional facts: *Per serving: 280 calories • 30g carbohydrates • 21g protein • 9g fat • 560mg sodium • 85mg cholesterol • 0g fiber • 17g sugar*

peking duck

If you're using a Peking duck breast, you can also try this dish on the stovetop. Simply heat a cast-iron skillet to high, then cook the scored breast skin-side down until done.

healthy addition

Crisp, well-chilled celery and carrot sticks are the best partners for these spicy burgers.

buffalo chicken burgers

prep time: 12 minutes • total time: 22 minutes • serves: 4

Bring the fun and fabulous taste of Buffalo wings to another weekend favorite—the burger! These zippy, hearty chicken patties will have you skipping the beef any time and never even missing it.

1 large celery stalk
2 green onions
1 lb. lean ground chicken
2 tbsp. dry bread crumbs
4 tbsp. cayenne pepper sauce, *divided*

1/2 cup crumbled blue cheese, *divided*
4 romaine leaves
4 rolls
1/4 cup blue cheese dressing

1) Chop celery and green onions in mini processor; scrape mixture into large bowl. Add chicken, bread crumbs, 2 tbsp. pepper sauce and 1/4 cup blue cheese. Stir together just until combined. Shape into 4 patties, about 4 inches in diameter.

2) Coat grill or grill pan with cooking spray; heat over medium heat. Place burgers on grill and cook until browned on first side, 5 min. Turn and grill until browned on second side and no longer pink in center, about 5 min.

3) Meanwhile, shred romaine and slice rolls in half horizontally. Mound romaine on roll bottoms; sprinkle on remaining blue cheese. Top with burgers, dressing, remaining pepper sauce and roll top. Serve immediately.

nutritional facts: *Per serving: 420 calories • 25g carbohydrates • 27g protein • 25g fat • 1130mg sodium • 90mg cholesterol • 2g fiber • 4g sugar*

cheddar-crowned turkey tenderloins

prep time: 11 minutes • total time: 205 minutes • serves: 4

Turkey tenderloins get the royal treatment of buttery, honey-mustard glaze and a crunchy, savory "crown" of cheddar and buttered soft bread crumbs.

4	turkey tenderloins (about 2 lbs.)	3	tbsp. honey
1/2	tsp. salt	3	tbsp. Dijon-style mustard
1/4	tsp. pepper	3/4	cup parsley leaves
4	tbsp. butter	2	slices white bread
		1	cup shredded cheddar cheese

1) Adjust oven rack to 6 inches below heat and preheat broiler to high. Line large, shallow baking sheet with foil and coat with cooking spray. Place tenderloins on sheet and season with salt and pepper.

2) Place butter in small, microwave-safe dish and microwave on HIGH until melted, 1 min. In small bowl, mix together 3 tbsp. melted butter, honey and mustard. Spread about 1-1/2 tbsp. onto each tenderloin; broil until almost cooked through, 8-10 min.

3) Meanwhile, in food processor, chop parsley; place in medium bowl. Place bread in the food processor; pulse until medium crumbs form. Add to the parsley with the remaining melted butter and toss well. Add cheddar cheese and toss again.

4) Turn tenderloins over and spread remaining honey-mustard mixture on each. Evenly top with crumb mixture. Broil until turkey is cooked through and crumbs are golden, about 3 min. Transfer to individual plates and serve.

nutritional facts: *Per serving: 550 calories • 23g carbohydrates • 65g protein • 22g fat • 1110mg sodium • 150mg cholesterol • 1g fiber • 14g sugar*

rosy apple rings

Core 2 unpeeled, red-skinned apples and slice into 1/2-inch thick rings. Place on baking sheet with turkey and broil for the full time. There's no need to turn.

caribbean chicken amandine

prep time: 1 minute • total time: 11 minutes • serves: 4

A spicy rub gives zesty flavor to these updated chicken cutlets. Then sauteed bananas and almonds whisk you away to a tropical island!

1	tbsp. paprika	2	tbsp. butter, *divided*
1	tsp. allspice	2	small bananas
1	tsp. ginger	1	tsp. sugar
1	tsp. curry powder	1/4	cup sliced almonds
1/2	tsp. salt	1	lime, cut into wedges, optional
4	thin sliced chicken cutlets (about 3/4 lb.)		

1) In small bowl, combine seasonings. Sprinkle over chicken. In large nonstick skillet over medium-high heat, melt 1 tbsp. butter. Add chicken and saute 2-3 min. per side, until cooked through. Remove to serving platter and keep warm. Remove pan from heat and let cool 2 min.; wipe with paper towels to remove spices and any drippings.

2) Meanwhile, peel bananas and slice in half crosswise, then lengthwise. In skillet over medium heat, meet remaining butter. Add bananas and saute just until golden, about 30 seconds. Turn and sprinkle with sugar and almonds. Saute just until sugar begins to melt, 45 seconds. Do not overcook. Serve with chicken and lime wedges if desired.

nutritional facts: *Per serving: 230 calories • 19g carbohydrates • 20g protein • 10g fat • 360mg sodium • 55mg cholesterol • 3g fiber • 10g sugar*

coconut rice

Prepare 1 cup of your favorite rice as usual, but just before serving, stir in 2 tablespoons each of toasted coconut and chopped fresh parsley.

royal chicken

prep time: 20 minutes • **total time:** 29 minutes • **serves:** 4

Inspiration for this recipe was found in the classic Kung Pao Chicken, a spicy dish invented long ago for a Chinese monarch. This mild version will suit everyone.

1 lb. boneless, skinless chicken breasts	1/8 tsp. hot pepper sauce
1 tbsp. sherry	1 small red pepper
1 tbsp. plus 1 tsp. cornstarch, *divided*	3 large green onions
	2 cloves garlic
1/4 cup reduced-sodium soy sauce	1/3 cup fresh cilantro leaves
	1 tbsp. oil
1 tbsp. brown sugar	2 tsp. chopped fresh ginger
1 tsp. apple cider vinegar	1/4 cup lightly salted peanuts

1) Cut chicken into 1/2 inch chunks. In medium bowl, combine chicken, sherry and 1 tsp. cornstarch. Set aside.

2) In small bowl, combine 1/4 cup water, soy sauce, brown sugar, vinegar, hot pepper sauce and remaining cornstarch. Set aside.

3) Slice red pepper into small thin strips. Diagonally slice green onions into 1/2-inch pieces to yield 1 cup. Mince garlic. Chop cilantro.

4) In large skillet or wok over high, heat oil. Add chicken, garlic and ginger. Cook, and stir for 2 min. Add peppers; cook until chicken is almost cooked through, 2 min.

5) Add soy sauce mixture, green onions and cilantro. Bring to boil and cook 1 min. Meanwhile, chop peanuts. Transfer chicken to serving platter; sprinkle with peanuts and serve.

nutritional facts: *Per serving: 210 calories • 11g carbohydrates • 25g protein • 7g fat • 700mg sodium • 65mg cholesterol • 1g fiber • 5g sugar*

marinate ahead

Plan ahead by putting the chicken in a resealable plastic storage bag and add the soy sauce mixture. Seal the bag and marinate for an hour, or even the day before, for more intense flavor.

island spiced chicken legs

prep time: 5 minutes • **total time:** 29 minutes • **serves:** 4

The aroma and flavor of these chicken legs will spice up a weeknight meal. They are so easy and quick to make, you'll have time to prepare a special side dish or dessert to serve with them.

2 limes	1-1/2 tsp. pumpkin pie spice
1 tbsp. olive oil	1-1/2 tsp. dried thyme
1 tbsp. rum	1/2 tsp. Cajun seasoning
1/4 cup sesame seeds	1/2 tsp. coarse salt
1 tbsp. brown sugar	4 chicken legs

1) Preheat oven to 400°F. Squeeze 1 lime to yield 1 tbsp. juice. Cut second lime into wedges and set aside.

2) In pie plate, combine the olive oil, rum and lime juice. In second pie plate, combine sesame seeds, brown sugar, pumpkin pie spice, thyme, Cajun seasoning and salt.

3) Dip each chicken leg in olive oil mixture, then roll in spice mixture. Place in 9- x 9-inch baking dish. Pour remaining olive oil mixture around chicken. Bake until chicken is cooked through, about 24 min.

4) Transfer chicken to serving platter. Garnish with lime wedges and serve.

nutritional facts: *Per serving: 440 calories • 8g carbohydrates • 32g protein • 30g fat • 500mg sodium • 140mg cholesterol • 2g fiber • 4g sugar*

sesame seeds

Fresh sesame seeds are actually quite perishable. Store them, tightly sealed in the freezer to keep them from becoming rancid. Bring them to room temperature before using.

chicken saltimbocca

prep time: 10 minutes • total time: 25 minutes • serves: 4

"Saltimbocca" recipes were originally created in Rome. In Italian, the name refers to getting a punch of flavor in your mouth from the onion, prosciutto and lemon. And that's certainly the case with this delicious chicken!

2 large boneless, skinless chicken breasts (about 1-1/4 lbs.)	1 tbsp. olive oil
1/4 tsp. salt	1 tsp. fresh lemon juice
1/8 tsp. pepper	1/3 cup minced red onion
4 thin slices prosciutto	1/2 cup chicken broth
4 fresh sage leaves	1 tbsp. nonpareil capers
	1 tbsp. butter

1) Cut each chicken breast in half to form cutlets. Cut each cutlet in half lengthwise; place between sheets of waxed paper. Pound until 1/4-inch thick. Season both sides of cutlets with salt and pepper.

2) Lay each cutlet on top of a prosciutto slice. Fold prosciutto over cutlet. Lay one piece of sage on top of prosciutto; Secure with toothpick.

3) In large skillet over medium, heat oil. Place chicken in pan, sage side down. Cook until browned on first side, 2-3 min. Turn and cook until done. Place on platter; remove toothpicks and keep warm.

4) Add the onion to pan and cook until translucent, about 3 min. Add broth and capers; simmer, scraping up browned bits with wooden spoon. Stir in the butter and lemon juice; cook until the sauce is smooth, about 2-3 min. Pour sauce over chicken and serve.

nutritional facts: *Per serving: 170 calories • 3g carbohydrates • 18g protein • 10g fat • 610mg sodium • 55mg cholesterol • 1g fiber • 1g sugar*

purchasing prosciutto

Look for "all natural," presliced prosciutto in the refrigerator section of your supermarket rather than at the deli counter. The paper-thin slices are perfect for this recipe.

mustard-crumbed turkey

prep time: 7 minutes • total time: 20 minutes • serves: 4

Hungry for Thanksgiving? Try these tasty turkey cutlets. Brushing the turkey with a mustard sauce and coating with crumbs ensures the meat stays moist.

1-1/2 cups whole wheat baked pita chips	1/3 cup plus 1 tbsp. apricot jam
1 small bunch chives	1/2 tsp. dried thyme
5 tbsp. grainy mustard, *divided*	4 turkey cutlets (about 1 lb.)
	1/2 tsp. jalapeno pepper sauce

1) Preheat oven to 425°F. Line jelly-roll pan with foil. Place pita chips in heavy bag. With rolling pin, crush until medium-coarse crumbs form to yield about 1 cup. Chop chives to yield 3 tbsp. In small dish, stir together 3 tbsp. mustard, 1 tbsp. jam, 2 tbsp. chives and thyme.

2) Arrange cutlets on prepared pan. Evenly spread mustard mixture over each cutlet. Sprinkle crumbs evenly over mustard mixture. Bake until turkey is cooked through and crumbs are golden brown, 12-14 min.

3) Meanwhile, in small dish, stir together the pepper sauce and the remaining jam mustard. Transfer turkey to serving platter. Sprinkle with the remaining chives and serve with sauce.

nutritional facts: *Per serving: 290 calories • 39g carbohydrates • 31g protein • 2g fat • 380mg sodium • 45mg cholesterol • 2g fiber • 17g sugar*

use leftover bread

Here's a way to use any extra bread you have on hand. Bake at 325°F. for 20 minutes; let cool, then crush in a zippered plastic bag. Sprinkle over these cutlets.

tropical fruit rice

Jazz up instant rice with fruit salad to make a tropical side dish. Stir 1 (15 oz.) can, drained, fruit cocktail into the rice while cooking.

tender coconut chicken

prep time: 3 minutes • total time: 29 minutes • serves: 4

These crispy chicken tenders get their sweet crunch from a combination of Panko and flaked coconut. Then added flavor is poured on with the creamy coconut milk and pineapple sauce.

1 cup reduced-fat coconut milk	1 cup Panko bread crumbs
4 tbsp. crushed pineapple, undrained	1 cup shredded coconut flakes
1 tsp. chopped fresh ginger	2 tsp. Chinese Five-Spice Powder
2 tsp. sugar	1/8 tsp. cayenne pepper
3 egg whites	1/2 tsp. coarse salt
1/2 cup all-flour	6 tbsp. canola oil
1-1/2 lbs. chicken tenders	

1) In small saucepan over medium heat, combine coconut milk and crushed pineapple. Stir ginger into saucepan with sugar. Bring to simmer and cook until slightly thickened and flavors are combined, 5 min. Pour into blender; set aside uncovered.

2) In wide, shallow bowl, lightly stir egg whites. Place flour on plate. On second plate, combine Panko, shredded coconut, Five-Spice Powder and cayenne.

3) Cut each tender in half crosswise and sprinkle with salt. Coat each piece of chicken in flour, dip in egg whites and roll in Panko mixture.

4) In large skillet over medium, heat oil. Add chicken in batches. Cook, turning once, until golden and crispy, about 4-6 min. Remove to paper towels. Repeat with remaining chicken. Transfer chicken to serving plates.

5) Pulse coconut sauce in blender until smooth, about 20 seconds. Evenly place in 4 small dishes and serve on plates with chicken.

nutritional facts: *Per serving: 640 calories • 29g carbohydrates • 41g protein • 41g fat • 990mg sodium • 90mg cholesterol • 2g fiber • 9g sugar*

delicious leftovers

Buy some tortillas and grill quesadillas with shredded cheese and leftover pieces of this chicken. You'll probably have some salsa and sour cream on hand to serve on the side.

salsa verde chicken

prep time: 3 minutes • total time: 28 minutes • serves: 6

This Mexican-inspired recipe will be welcomed at your house on busy nights when a one-dish meal is absolutely critical. It's great tasting, easy to prepare and very quick to clean up.

1 whole chicken, cut-up (about 4 lbs.)	1 (16 oz.) jar mild green salsa
1 (1.25 oz.) pkg. taco seasoning mix	1 cup shredded cheddar cheese
1 tbsp. vegetable oil	6 tbsp. sour cream
	1 green onion, thinly sliced

1) In large skillet over medium-high, heat oil. Sprinkle taco seasoning over each piece of chicken.

2) Place chicken pieces in skillet, skin side down, and cook until browned, about 5 min. Drain excess oil from pan.

3) Pour salsa over chicken. Cover and reduce heat to medium. Cook, turning chicken once, until chicken is cooked through, about 19-20 min.

4) Sprinkle cheese evenly over chicken; cover for 1 min. to allow cheese to melt.

5) Transfer chicken to serving plate; spoon salsa from pan on top of chicken. Top with dollops of sour cream and sprinkle with green onion.

nutritional facts: *Per serving: 810 calories • 7g carbohydrates • 63g protein • 58g fat • 1230mg sodium • 255mg cholesterol • 1g fiber • 1g sugar*

secret cauliflower casserole

prep time: 5 minutes • total time: 29 minutes • serves: 4

This hearty casserole uses ground chicken instead of beef and pureed cauliflower instead of potatoes. So it's lower in fat, calories and carbs than the traditional shepherd's pie that inspired it.

1 head fresh cauliflower	1/2 tsp. pepper, *divided*
2 tsp. coarse salt, *divided*	1/2 cup chicken broth
1-1/2 tbsp. olive oil	1/2 cup frozen corn
1 large clove garlic	2 tbsp. light cream
1 small carrot	3 tbsp. Greek-style fat-free
1 lb. ground chicken	yogurt
1 tsp. dried basil	2 tsp. Dijon-style mustard
1/4 tsp. sweet paprika, *divided*	1/2 cup shredded Asiago cheese

1) Preheat oven 450°F. Bring large pot of hot water to boil over high. Remove leaves and inner core of cauliflower. Chop cauliflower into small pieces. Add to pot with 1 tsp. salt. Cover and cook until tender, about 4 min.

2) Meanwhile, peel and mince garlic. Peel carrot and slice lengthwise; thinly slice into half-circles. In large skillet over medium-low, heat olive oil. Add garlic and carrots; cook until soft, 1-2 min.

3) Add chicken to skillet; break into small chunks with wooden spoon. Season with 1/2 tsp. salt and 1/4 tsp. pepper, basil and 1/8 tsp. paprika. Cook, stirring occasionally, until chicken is no longer pink. Add chicken broth, corn and light cream. Stir to combine.

4) Drain cauliflower; puree in food processor. Add yogurt, mustard and remaining salt and pepper; blend until combined.

5) Spread chicken mixture evenly over bottom of medium casserole dish. Spread pureed cauliflower evenly over top. Sprinkle with cheese and remaining paprika. Bake until top just begins to brown, 10 min.

nutritional facts: *Per serving: 340 calories • 18g carbohydrates • 26g protein • 21g fat • 1150mg sodium • 95mg cholesterol • 5g fiber • 7g sugar*

supper standbys

Some rustic Italian bread and a tossed salad will round out the meal. Replace the butter on the table with a seasoned olive oil for a continental touch.

chicken with fig sauce

prep time: 8 minutes • total time: 27 minutes • serves: 4

This clever dish capitalizes on sweet, fruity figs and the kick of chili powder and cayenne pepper to dress up ordinary chicken thighs, resulting in an unforgettable meal.

1 sweet onion	1/2 tsp. dried thyme
1 tsp. olive oil	1/4 tsp. salt
1-1/4 lbs. bone-in, skinless chicken thighs	1/8 tsp. cayenne pepper
	1/3 cup fig jam
3/4 tsp. chili powder	1/3 cup port *or* red wine

1) Cut onion into 1-inch strips. In large, nonstick skillet over medium-high, heat oil. Add chicken and cook until golden, 6 min. Turn chicken over and scatter onion into skillet. Cook, covered, until onion is soft, 6 min.

2) Stir in the chili powder, thyme, salt and cayenne pepper; cook until fragrant, about 30 seconds. Stir in the jam and port. Increase heat to high; turn the chicken and boil until liquid is thickened reduced to a glaze, about 5 min. Transfer to platter; spoon on remaining sauce from pan and serve.

nutritional facts: *Per serving: 280 calories • 19g carbohydrates • 29g protein • 7g fat • 280mg sodium • 120mg cholesterol • 1g fiber • 15g sugar*

brown rice pilaf

Round out the meal with brown rice pilaf blended with chopped pecans and sweetened cranberries or currants.

awesome orzo

This recipe is delicious with pasta, too. Instead of serving the tomato and feta mixture as a relish, use it as a sauce for three cups of cooked orzo; serve the chicken cutlets on top.

mint-infused chicken

prep time: 10 minutes • total time: 22 minutes • serves: 6

Savory feta and salty kalamata olives make a robust, relish for mild and minty chicken cutlets. These are quickly grilled to lock in their juices and are a spectacular summertime dinner.

1 bunch fresh mint	15 pitted kalamata olives
1/3 cup plus 1/4 cup olive oil, *divided*	4 oz. crumbled feta cheese
1-1/4 lbs. thin-sliced chicken cutlets	1 to 2 sprigs fresh dill
1 tsp. coarse salt	2 to 3 sprigs fresh flat-leaf parsley
1/2 pint grape tomatoes	1/4 tsp. pepper

1) Remove enough mint leaves from stem to yield 1 cup plus 2 tbsp. Place 1 cup mint leaves and 1/3 cup olive oil in blender; pulse to chop, about 30 seconds. Season both sides of cutlets with 1/2 tsp. salt; brush mint oil over both sides of cutlets. Set aside.

2) Cut tomatoes and olives into quarters; place in medium bowl. Sprinkle with feta. Chop dill, parsley and remaining mint; add to bowl. Sprinkle with remaining salt and pepper. Drizzle on remaining olive oil and toss to coat.

3) Coat grill pan with cooking spray and heat over high until hot, but not smoking. Add half of cutlets and cook until golden on first side, about 3 min. Turn and cook through, about 2 min. Remove to platter and keep warm. Repeat with remaining cutlets.

4) Spoon tomato-feta relish over top of cutlets and serve.

nutritional facts: *Per serving: 300 calories • 4g carbohydrates • 22g protein • 21g fat • 570mg sodium • 70mg cholesterol • 1g fiber • 1g sugar*

mango slices

Whether served alongside or sprinkled on top, slivers or diced fresh, juicy mango taste great with this dish.

paradise chicken

prep time: 5 minutes • total time: 22 minutes • serves: 4

After just a single bite, you'll know how this dish got its name. The exotic flavors of rum and fragrant herbs in the spicy, creamy sauce are a little taste of paradise.

2 cloves garlic	1/4 tsp. salt
1 cup cilantro leaves	1/4 tsp. crushed red pepper flakes
1/2 cup mint leaves	1 tbsp. brown sugar
2 tsp. cornstarch	1 tbsp. oil
1/2 cup chicken broth	1/4 cup rum
8 bone-in chicken thighs (about 1-1/4 lbs.)	1/3 cup heavy cream

1) Finely chop garlic, cilantro and mint seperately; set aside. In small bowl, blend cornstarch with broth; set aside. Sprinkle chicken with salt, red pepper flakes and sugar.

2) In large, nonstick skillet over high, heat oil. Add chicken and garlic; cook until chicken is just golden on first side, 2 min. Turn chicken and cook until just golden on second side, 2 min. Remove chicken to plate and keep warm. Add rum to skillet and cook until slightly reduced, about 1 min.

3) Reduce heat to medium-low. Stir in broth mixture, then cream and half of cilantro and mint. Cook and stir until mixture is smooth and begins to thicken, 2 min. Return chicken to skillet and cook, partially covered, 8 min., turning chicken once. Add remaining cilantro and mint. Simmer, uncovered, until sauce is thickened and chicken is cooked through, 2 min.

nutritional facts: *Per serving: 400 calories • 6g carbohydrates • 21g protein • 28g fat • 250mg sodium • 120mg cholesterol • 0g fiber • 2g sugar*

arroz con pollo

prep time: 8 minutes • total time: 29 minutes • serves: 4

Chicken with saffron rice is a classic dish in Spain and very simple to make. Once all the ingredients are in the pan, all you need to do is enjoy the aroma until the cooking is complete.

1 tbsp. garlic oil	3/4 cup dry white wine
1 lb. chicken tenders	1 tsp. saffron threads
3/4 tsp. coarse salt, *divided*	1/2 cup black beans, drained and rinsed
1/2 tsp. sweet paprika	3/4 cup sliced green olives with pimientos
1/2 tsp. garlic powder	
1/2 cup diced fresh green pepper	
1 cup basmati rice	1/2 cup frozen baby peas
1-1/4 cups chicken broth	2 to 3 sprigs flat-leaf parsley

1) In large skillet with tight-fitting lid over medium-high, heat 1 tbsp. garlic oil. Sprinkle the chicken evenly with 1/2 tsp. salt, paprika and garlic powder; add in a single layer to pan. Sear on both sides, 1-2 min. per side. Remove to a plate and keep warm.

2) Reduce heat to medium; add green pepper to pan. Cook until softened, about 2 min. Add rice to pan and stir to coat with oil. Pour in broth and wine. Sprinkle saffron, beans and olives with remaining salt. Stir to combine. Return chicken to pan, placing on top of rice mixture. Increase heat to high; bring to boil. Reduce heat to low. Cover and simmer until liquid is mostly absorbed, 15 min.

3) Sprinkle peas over mixture. Turn off heat; let stand 5 min. Finely chop parsley. Evenly divide chicken and rice among 4 plates; sprinkle each with parsley. Serve.

nutritional facts: *Per serving: 310 calories • 28g carbohydrates • 28g protein • 5g fat • 1080mg sodium • 60mg cholesterol • 3g fiber • 1g sugar*

skip the saffron

Saffron will give a true yellow color and traditional Spanish flavor to the dish. But it can be very pricey. So this dish is still wonderful without it.

peachy chicken and vegetables

prep time: 12 minutes • total time: 2 hours • serves: 6

This one-dish, sweet and spicy chicken entree is welcome for a family dinner or a special occasion. The unique technique of tilting the chicken to one side, then the other, keeps the breast moist.

3 large carrots	1/2 cup peach preserves
3 large parsnips	1/4 cup thick barbecue sauce
3 large red potatoes	1/4 tsp. onion powder
2 tbsp. oil	1/4 tsp. salt
1 roasting chicken (6 lb.)	

1) Place oven racks at lowest level. Preheat oven to 375°F. Remove and discard giblets from chicken cavity. Rinse chicken under cold water; pat dry. Peel carrots and parsnips. Chop carrot, parsnips and potatoes into 1-1/2-inch chunks. In large bowl, combine vegetables with oil, set aside.

2) Place small rack in roasting pan. Place chicken on side on rack, using vegetables on either side to keep chicken balanced. Roast chicken, about 40 min.

3) Turn chicken to rest on opposite side, adjusting vegetables as needed. Roast another 40 min. Meanwhile, combine preserves, barbecue sauce, onion powder and salt.

4) Turn chicken breast-side up. Baste chicken and vegetables with sauce. Cook until internal temperature is 180°F., about 30 min. Let stand 5 min before carving. Serve with vegetables.

nutritional facts: *Per serving: 760 calories • 51g carbohydrates • 57g protein • 35g fat • 430mg sodium • 170mg cholesterol • 6g fiber • 25g sugar*

home-style bbq sauce

Blend your own barbecue sauce by combining ketchup, Worcestershire, brown sugar, salt and pepper.

mediterranean turkey cutlets

prep time: 18 minutes • total time: 18 minutes • serves: 4

This is one of those great simple recipes that you'll come back to time and again. Tender turkey tenderloins are cooked in a zesty sauce and served over a bed of pasta.

1-1/2 tsp. salt, *divided*	2 cloves garlic
8 oz. fettuccine	3/4 cup parsley leaves
3 tbsp. olive oil, *divided*	1/2 cup pitted kalamata olives
4 turkey tenderloins	1 (15 oz.) can diced tomatoes
(6 to 8 oz. *each*)	2 tbsp. capers
1/4 tsp. pepper	1/4 tsp. crushed red pepper flakes

1) In large pot over high heat, bring 3 quarts water to boil. Add 1 tsp. salt and fettuccine. Cook according to package directions, 8-9 min.

2) Meanwhile, in a large, nonstick skillet over medium-high, heat 1 tbsp. oil. Season turkey with remaining salt and pepper add to skillet. Cook until no longer pink on first side, about 3 min. Turn and cook until almost cooked through, 3 min.; remove and keep warm.

3) Chop garlic, parsley and olives. Reserve 1/4 cup chopped parsley.

4) Into skillet over medium heat, add 1 tbsp. oil and garlic; cook 30 seconds. Add 1/2 cup parsley, olives, tomatoes and capers; cook 3 min. Add turkey and cook until cooked through, 2 min.

5) Drain fettuccine and toss with remaining oil and pepper flakes. Evenly divide among 4 plates. Top each with 1 turkey tenderloin and 1/4 of sauce. Sprinkle with reserved parsley and serve.

nutritional facts: *Per serving: 590 calories • 50g carbohydrates • 52g protein • 20g fat • 1580mg sodium • 70mg cholesterol • 3g fiber • 5g sugar*

uncanny resemblance

When fresh tomatoes aren't in season, use canned tomatoes from Italy (San Marzano) or from California. Try to find a product without additional ingredients.

dreamy coconut chicken

prep time: 25 minutes • total time: 25 minutes • serves: 4

Tender chicken and crispy sugar snap peas are simmered in a sauce flavored with ginger, garlic, lime, basil and coconut. One bite and you'll be dreaming of exotic places.

1 lb. thin-sliced chicken cutlets	1 tbsp. lime juice
2 tbsp. oil, *divided*	1 tbsp. brown sugar
1 small red bell pepper	3/4 tsp. salt
2 cloves garlic	1/4 tsp. crushed red pepper flakes
1 piece fresh ginger (1 inch)	(optional)
1 (13.5 oz.) can unsweetened	8 oz. fresh sugar snap peas
coconut milk	1 cup fresh basil leaves

1) Cut chicken into 1-inch strips. In large, nonstick skillet over medium-high, heat 1 tbsp. oil. Add chicken and cook until lightly browned, 3-4 min. Remove and keep warm.

2) Meanwhile, finely dice red pepper into small dice; finely chop garlic and ginger. Into skillet over medium-high heat, add remaining oil, red bell pepper, garlic and ginger. Cook until pepper begins to soften, 2 min. Stir in coconut milk, lime juice, brown sugar, salt and red pepper flakes. Bring to simmer; cook 5 min.

3) Add snap peas; cook 2 min. Add chicken and saute until cooked through, 3 min. Roughly shred basil and stir into skillet; simmer 30 seconds. Transfer to plate and serve immediately.

nutritional facts: *Per serving: 360 calories • 13g carbohydrates • 15g protein • 29g fat • 490mg sodium • 30mg cholesterol • 3g fiber • 6g sugar*

sauce thickener

The recipe creates a typically thin, Thai-style sauce. If you prefer a thicker sauce, stir in 2 teaspoons cornstarch mixed with 2 tablespoons cold water, then add the snap peas.

orange-avocado salsa chicken

prep time: 15 minutes • total time: 25 minutes • serves: 4

Plain chicken breasts sparkle when quickly cooked with oranges and garlic. Add more oranges to a tasty, chunky salsa and serve it with the chicken for added fresh flavor and texture.

3 oranges	1/4 tsp. pepper
4 boneless, skinless chicken breast halves (about 1-1/2 lbs.)	2 tbsp. oil
	1 clove garlic
	1/8 tsp. crushed red pepper flakes
1/3 cup all-purpose flour	1 ripe avocado
1/2 tsp. plus 1/8 tsp. salt	2 green onions
1/2 tsp. garlic powder	1/2 red bell pepper

1) Zest 1 orange; reserve 1 tsp. Juice the orange to yield 1/3 cup; set aside. Place chicken between sheets of waxed paper; pound to even thickness. In plastic, zippered bag, place remaining zest, flour, 1/2 tsp. salt, garlic powder and black pepper. Add chicken; shake to coat.

2) In large skillet over medium, heat oil. Add chicken. Cook, turning occasionally, until tender, about 10 min. Remove chicken to platter; keep warm. Thinly slice garlic, add to skillet. Stir in orange juice. Cook until thickened, stirring up any browned bits from pan. Spoon over chicken.

3) Meanwhile, peel remaining oranges over medium bowl to catch any juices. Cut into bite-size pieces and place in bowl. Add red pepper flakes. Peel and cut avocado into bite-size pieces; add to bowl. Thinly slice green onions; chop red pepper. Add to bowl and stir to combine. Place on serving platter alongside chicken.

nutritional facts: *Per serving: 430 calories • 23g carbohydrates • 39g protein • 20g fat • 310mg sodium • 100mg cholesterol • 5g fiber • 8g sugar*

ripe avocados

If you buy avocados that are ripe, keep them from getting too soft by storing them in the refrigerator for up to two days.

strawberry-balsamic chicken

prep time: 20 minutes • total time: 29 minutes • serves: 4

Every bit as tasty as it is pretty, this sumptuous dish is perfect when you're entertaining guests on a summer evening. Serve it with a green salad, French bread and a no-fuss dessert.

2 tbsp. butter, *divided*	2 to 3 sprigs parsley
1 tbsp. olive oil	1/4 cup chicken broth
8 chicken thighs	3 tbsp. balsamic vinegar
3 to 4 shallots	1/3 cup strawberry preserves
1 pint strawberries	1/4 cup heavy cream

1) In large, nonstick skillet over medium-high heat, melt 1 tbsp. butter in olive oil. Add chicken. Saute until golden, turning once, until cooked through, about 25 min.

2) Meanwhile, finely chop shallots to yield 1/4 cup. Hull and slice strawberries; set aside. Chop parsley to yield 2 tbsp.; set aside.

3) In small saucepan over medium heat, melt remaining butter. Add shallots; cook, and stir until softened, about 3 min.

4) Add chicken broth, balsamic vinegar, strawberry preserves and cream to shallots. Stir to combine. Remove from heat. When chicken is cooked through, pour sauce over chicken and stir to coat. Add strawberries; cook until heated through, 1 min.

5) Transfer chicken to platter. Sprinkle with parsley and serve.

nutritional facts: *Per serving: 640 calories • 35g carbohydrates • 35g protein • 40g fat • 200mg sodium • 180mg cholesterol • 2g fiber • 25g sugar*

in-a-dash dessert

End the meal with a simple fruity dessert. Stuff canned pear halves with gorgonzola cheese and walnuts. Drizzle with raspberry vinaigrette.

gourmet cheese

Try substituting an interesting semi-soft cheese, such as a Mercadel, for the mozzarella. Or if you prefer to go dairy-free, you can skip the cheese entirely.

chicken with white beans

prep time: 18 minutes • total time: 27 minutes • serves: 4

Both tasty and colorful, this nutritious one-dish meal is packed with tons of protein.

1 lb. boneless, skinless chicken breasts	1 medium shallot
1/4 lb. turkey bacon	1/2 cup shiitake mushrooms
1 (9 oz.) bag spinach	1 (16 oz.) can cannellini beans
2 tbsp. olive oil, *divided*	1 cup chicken broth
1/2 tsp. salt	1 tsp. dried thyme
1/4 tsp. pepper	1/2 cup finely shredded mozzarella cheese

1) Cut chicken into 1-1/2-inch pieces. Cut turkey bacon into 1-inch pieces. Reserve 1 cup spinach leaves and set aside.

2) In large, nonstick skillet over medium-high, heat 1 tbsp. oil; add chicken. Cook, stirring occasionally, until golden on all sides, about 7 min. Season chicken with salt and pepper. Remove from skillet.

3) Meanwhile, chop shallot and mushrooms. Drain and rinse beans. Add remaining oil to skillet. Add shallot and turkey bacon. Cook and stir until bacon starts to become crispy, about 4 min. Stir in mushrooms; cook and stir 3 min.

4) Stir in broth and thyme. Return chicken pieces to pan; simmer 5 min. Add beans and spinach. Stir gently until spinach just begins to wilt, about 2 min. Sprinkle with cheese. Remove from heat.

5) Evenly divide reserved spinach leaves among 4 serving plates. Spoon the chicken mixture over the spinach leaves and serve.

nutritional facts: *Per serving: 460 calories • 26g carbohydrates • 42g protein • 21g fat • 1520mg sodium • 105mg cholesterol • 7g fiber • 1g sugar*

making crepes

To ensure that each crepe will be the same size, use a standard ice cream scoop or a long, coffee measuring spoon when measuring out the crepe batter.

chicken pesto crepes

prep time: 20 minutes • total time: 28 minutes • serves: 4

Crepes are so simple to make, you'll soon understand why they're always popular.

crepes:	filling:
2/3 cup milk	1 (10 oz.) pkg. cooked chicken strips
2 large eggs	
1 cup all-purpose flour	8 tbsp. prepared pesto
1/4 tsp. salt	1 cup ricotta cheese
2 tbsp. butter, *divided*	

1) Preheat oven to 450°F. Coat 11- x 7-inch baking dish with cooking spray. In blender, combine milk, 2/3 cup water, eggs, flour, salt and1 tbsp. butter. Blend just until smooth.

2) In medium, nonstick skillet over medium heat, melt remaining butter; set plate nearby. Half-fill 1/4-cup measure with batter (about 2 tbsp.) Pour in pan; quickly tilt and swirl to coat bottom. Cook until edge is light brown, 20-30 seconds. Remove with thin spatula, place on plate and repeat with remaining batter to make 8 crepes.

3) Working in batches, spoon 1/8 chicken strips, 1 tbsp. pesto and 2 tbsp. ricotta down center of each crepe. Fold over sides and place in baking dish. Bake until heated through, 8 min. Place 2 crepes on each plate and serve.

nutritional facts: *Per serving: 700 calories • 39g carbohydrates • 33g protein • 45g fat • 1040mg sodium • 155mg cholesterol • 2g fiber • 2g sugar*

gardener's roasted chicken

prep time: 11 minutes • total time: 29 minutes • serves: 4

This light but satisfying dish is completely cooked in the oven, making it easy to prepare and serve often. The fennel and fresh summer vegetables add color and a distinctive taste.

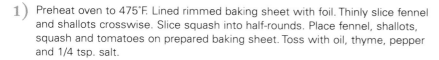

1/2 fennel bulb	1/8 tsp. pepper
2 shallots	1/2 tsp. salt, *divided*
2 summer squash	1 lemon
1 pint cherry *or* grape tomatoes	1-1/4 lbs. boneless, skinless chicken breasts
2 tsp. olive oil	
1/2 tsp. dried thyme	4 sprigs fresh basil

1) Preheat oven to 475°F. Lined rimmed baking sheet with foil. Thinly slice fennel and shallots crosswise. Slice squash into half-rounds. Place fennel, shallots, squash and tomatoes on prepared baking sheet. Toss with oil, thyme, pepper and 1/4 tsp. salt.

2) Bake 10 min. Meanwhile, zest lemon over medium bowl. Squeeze lemon to yield 2 tbsp. juice. Add 1 tbsp. to bowl; reserve remainder. Slice chicken crosswise into thin strips; add to bowl. Sprinkle with remaining salt and toss to coat.

3) Remove vegetables from oven. Add chicken and toss to combine. Return to oven and bake until chicken is cooked through, 12 min.

4) Meanwhile, tear basil leaves into small pieces to equal 1/3 cup. Remove baking sheet from oven. Sprinkle with basil; drizzle with remaining lemon juice. Toss to coat. Transfer to platter. Garnish with remaining basil and serve.

nutritional facts: *Per serving: 230 calories • 13g carbohydrates • 31g protein • 6g fat • 380mg sodium • 80mg cholesterol • 3g fiber • 5g sugar*

roasted asparagus

If you don't think your family will favor licorice-flavored fennel, make roasted asparagus instead. Cut spears into thirds on a diagonal and they'll be done in 10 minutes.

sausage-stuffed turkey breast

prep time: 28 minutes • total time: 2-1/2 hours • serves: 8

When you're craving a traditional roast turkey dinner but only have a few guests to feed, try this delicious dish. It's tender and juicy—and perfect for those who only like white meat.

1 small onion	6 lb. bone-in turkey breast
1 large stalk celery	1-1/2 tbsp. oil
1/2 lb. bulk Italian sausage	1 tsp. dried poultry seasoning
4 cups herb-seasoned stuffing	1 tsp. dried thyme
1 cup chicken *or* vegetable broth	

1) Preheat oven to 425°F. Grease 13- x 9-inch roasting pan. Chop onion and celery. In large skillet over high heat, cook sausage, onion and celery, breaking sausage into tiny pieces, until sausage is cooked through, about 8 min. Add stuffing and broth. Stir until combined and stuffing cubes are moistened.

2) Rinse turkey breast and pat dry. Stuff turkey cavity. Mound remaining stuffing in center of pan. Place turkey on top so that it stands breast side up. Rub turkey with oil. Sprinkle with poultry seasoning and thyme. Cover exposed stuffing with strips of aluminum foil, pressing foil to touch stuffing.

3) Roast turkey for 1 hour. Baste, then loosely cover top of breast with foil. Bake 1 hour longer, uncovering during the last 15 minutes, until internal temperature reaches 160°F. in thickest part of breast. Allow to rest 15 min. before carving.

nutritional facts: *Per serving: 860 calories • 43g carbohydrates • 112g protein • 24g fat • 1600mg sodium • 320mg cholesterol • 3g fiber • 1g sugar*

in a rush?

Ask the supermarket butcher to bone and divide a turkey breast for you. You can pound it flat, stuff it, then roll and bake the two breasts in an hour.

chicken cordon bleu

prep time: 20 minutes • **total time:** 27 minutes • **serves:** 4

This is a classic…and for good reason. Chicken that is crisp and crunchy on the outside reveals savory ham and melting cheese on the inside.

4 boneless, skinless chicken breasts (about 1-1/2 lbs.)	1 cup dry seasoned bread crumbs
4 thin slices deli ham	3 tbsp. butter, *divided*
4 thin slices Swiss cheese	1 tbsp. oil
1/4 cup plus 2 tbsp. all-purpose flour	1-1/4 cups milk, heated
1 large egg, lightly beaten	salt and pepper

1) Preheat oven to 475°F. Place chicken breasts in heavy freezer bag. Pound with flat side of meat mallet to 1/4-inch thickness.

2) Layer ham, then cheese on each breast, leaving 1/4-inch margin on all sides. Tuck in long sides slightly. Roll up; secure with toothpicks.

3) Place 1/4 cup flour, egg and bread crumbs in individual shallow bowls. Roll chicken in flour. Dip into egg, then roll in bread crumbs.

4) In large, ovenproof skillet over medium-high, heat 1 tbsp. butter and oil. Add chicken rolls. Cook, turning so that all sides are well browned, about 4 min.

5) Place skillet in oven and bake until chicken is cooked through, about 7 min. Remove toothpicks.

6) Meanwhile, in saucepan over medium heat, melt remaining butter; add remaining flour. Cook, stirring constantly, until bubbly, about 2 min. Add warm milk; bring to boil, stirring constantly. Add salt and pepper to taste. Cook and stir, 2-3 min. more, until sauce is thickened. Serve with chicken.

nutritional facts: *Per serving: 590 calories • 15g carbohydrates • 64g protein • 29g fat • 650mg sodium • 205mg cholesterol •1g fiber • 1g sugar*

easy cleanup

For easy-as-pie cleanup, place flour, beaten egg and bread crumbs in individual aluminum pie plates that originally held frozen crusts. Toss tins away when you're done.

holiday chicken casserole

prep time: 9 minutes • **total time:** 29 minutes • **serves:** 4

This time-saving dish is truly a one-dish wonder! A savory stuffing topping over a light, creamy chicken and vegetable base is a crowd pleaser. It's perfect for festive potlucks or at-home family dinners.

2 cups stuffing mix, *divided*	1/2 cup sour cream
3/4 cup chicken broth	1 (16 oz.) bag frozen mixed vegetables, thawed and drained (liquid reserved)
1 lb. boneless, skinless chicken breasts	
1 (10.75 oz.) can condensed cream of celery soup	

1) Preheat oven to 500°F. Sprinkle 1/2 cup dry stuffing mix evenly on bottom of 13- x 9-inch baking dish.

2) In medium bowl, stir chicken broth into remaining stuffing mix and set aside.

3) Cut chicken into 1-inch cubes. Place chicken over stuffing mix in baking dish.

4) In medium bowl, stir together soup, sour cream and vegetables. Spread over chicken. Top chicken mixture with reserved stuffing.

5) Bake until chicken is cooked through, 20 min.

nutritional facts: *Per serving: 270 calories • 23g carbohydrates • 21g protein • 10g fat • 760mg sodium • 55mg cholesterol • 3g fiber • 5g sugar*

sodium-free broth

There's plenty of salt in both the stuffing mix and the cream of celery soup, so this dish will be fine using sodium-free chicken broth—and no additional salt.

sweet-spiced marrakesh chicken

prep time: 10 minutes • total time: 26 minutes • serves: 4

The surprising combination of spices—ginger, cinnamon and cumin—gives this simple, boneless chicken an exotic taste. Assorted dried fruits lend to its sweetness and texture.

2 tbsp. oil	1/2 tsp. cumin
1 lb. boneless, skinless chicken breast	1 (14.5 oz.) can chicken broth
1/4 tsp. salt	3 tbsp. all-purpose flour
1/8 tsp. pepper	1/2 cup chopped prunes
1 large onion	1/2 cup chopped apricots
2 large cloves garlic	3 tbsp. lemon juice
1 tsp. ground cinnamon	2 tbsp. honey
1/2 tsp. ginger	sliced almonds and chopped cilantro, for garnish

1) In large skillet over medium-high, heat oil. Cut chicken into 1-inch cubes and season with salt and pepper. Add chicken to skillet and cook, stirring occasionally, until cooked through, about 5 min. With slotted spoon, remove chicken to plate. Set aside. Reduce heat to medium.

2) Quarter and thinly slice onion; add to skillet. Cook until onion begins to soften, about 2 min. Thinly slice garlic and stir into pan. Stir in cinnamon, ginger and cumin. Return chicken to skillet; cook and stir, about 1 min.

3) In small bowl, whisk together broth and flour. Gradually stir broth into skillet. Add prunes, apricots, lemon juice and honey. Bring to boil, stirring frequently.

4) Simmer, covered, until chicken is tender, about 5 min. Sprinkle with almonds and cilantro.

nutritional facts: *Per serving: 400 calories • 43g carbohydrates • 27g protein • 14g fat • 670mg sodium • 70mg cholesterol • 4g fiber • 27g sugar*

drumstick substitution

You can also make this recipe with whole, skinless drumsticks. Just extend the cooking time until the chicken reads 170°F. when tested with an instant-read thermometer.

italian crusted chicken

prep time: 5 minutes • total time: 29 minutes • serves: 4

This simple baked chicken gets a delicious coating of garlic and Parmesan. It can be served with steamed veggies, over wilted greens or on a bed of pasta with either a red or white sauce.

4 boneless, skinless chicken cutlets (about 1-1/2 lbs.)	2 to 3 sprigs fresh thyme leaves
1 tbsp. olive oil, *divided*	1/2 cup shredded Parmesan cheese
3 cloves garlic	1/4 cup mayonnaise

1) Preheat oven to 400°F. Line rimmed baking sheet with foil. Brush foil with 1/2 tsp. olive oil.

2) Mince garlic; finely chop thyme to yield 1 tsp. Combine 1/2 tsp. olive oil, garlic and thyme in small, microwave-safe bowl. Cover with plastic wrap, venting 1 corner. Microwave on HIGH until garlic is soft, about 90 seconds.

3) Remove from microwave; stir in Parmesan and mayonnaise.

4) Place chicken on prepared baking sheet and brush with remaining olive oil. Bake 10 min. Turn cutlets. Evenly divide Parmesan-garlic mixture and spread on top of cutlets.

5) Bake until crust is lightly golden and juices run clear when pierced with fork, about 12-14 min. Transfer to plates and serve.

nutritional facts: *Per serving: 290 calories • 1g carbohydrates • 31g protein • 17g fat • 230mg sodium • 85mg cholesterol • 0g fiber • 0g sugar*

homemade buttermilk

Buttermilk is a healthy alternative to mayonnaise and a wonderful marinade for any battered or crusted chicken. If you don't have any on hand, add 1 tbsp. vinegar to 1 cup milk.

puff pastry baskets

You can dress up this dish a bit by replacing the refrigerated biscuits with frozen puff pastry shells. Bake them separately and use them as "nests" for the turkey mixture.

biscuit-topped turkey a la king

prep time: 12 minutes • total time: 22 minutes • serves: 6

"A la king" describes cooked poultry in cream sauce with vegetables, traditionally peas and pimiento. This updated version uses onions and broccoli and is covered with Parmesan biscuits.

6 refrigerated biscuits	1 (16 oz.) pkg. frozen broccoli cuts
1 tsp. olive oil	1 (14.75 oz.) can chicken broth
1/4 cup plus 2 tsp. grated Parmesan cheese, *divided*	1/4 cup all-purpose flour
1/4 tsp. plus 1/8 tsp. cracked pepper, *divided*	3 cups cubed cooked turkey
1 (9 oz.) pkg. frozen pearl onions in cream sauce	

1) Preheat oven to 350°F. Arrange biscuits on greased baking sheet. Brush with oil; sprinkle with 2 tsp. Parmesan and 1/8 tsp. pepper. Bake until partially cooked, 10 min.

2) Meanwhile, microwave onions according to package directions. In large skillet over high heat, place broccoli and 1/2 of chicken broth. Bring to boil. Stir flour into remaining broth and add to skillet. Stir in turkey; cook over medium heat until thickened. Stir in onions and remaining Parmesan and pepper. Bring to boil again.

3) Remove from heat. Spoon turkey mixture into deep-dish pie plate or casserole. Arrange partially baked biscuits on top. Bake until casserole is bubbly and biscuits are done, about 10 min.

nutritional facts: *Per serving: 320 calories • 26g carbohydrates • 35g protein • 8g fat • 610mg sodium • 80mg cholesterol • 3g fiber • 5g sugar*

lo mein noodles

Serve the stir-fry over a bed of tender lo mein noodles. The noodles can then be tossed with the sauce, chicken and vegetables.

basil chicken stir-fry

prep time: 18 minutes • total time: 26 minutes • serves: 4

This dish is a budget-saver, especially in summer, when basil and tomatoes are at their peak.

1 small bunch fresh basil leaves	1 tbsp. Asian fish sauce
3 medium tomatoes	1 tbsp. honey
1 onion	1 tbsp. cornstarch
1 piece (1 inch) fresh gingerroot	1 lb. boneless, skinless chicken breasts
2/3 cup chicken broth	1-1/2 tsp. canola oil
2 tbsp. reduced-sodium soy sauce	

1) Remove enough basil leaves to equal 2 cups; rinse and place in sieve to drain. Following contour of tomato, cut off sides and discard centers. Cut tomato portions into thick strips. Halve onion and slice into strips. Cut ginger into matchsticks. Cut chicken crosswise into thin strips.

2) In small bowl, stir together chicken broth, soy sauce, fish sauce, honey and cornstarch until smooth.

3) In large, nonstick skillet over medium-high, heat oil. Add onion and cook, stirring, 1 min. Add chicken; cook and stir until no longer pink, about 4 min.

4) Stir broth mixture; add to skillet. Bring to boil; stir. Reduce heat to simmer for 1 min. Stir in tomatoes; remove from heat. Add basil; cook and stir, just until it begins to wilt, 30 seconds. Transfer to platter; serve.

nutritional facts: *Per serving: 210 calories • 15g carbohydrates • 26g protein • 5g fat • 720mg sodium • 65mg cholesterol • 2g fiber • 9g sugar*

white chicken chili

prep time: 10 minutes • total time: 27 minutes • serves: 6

This chicken chili is topped with a wonderfully cool, lime-infused sour cream. The balance of hot and chunky versus cold and creamy is delicious.

1 tbsp. vegetable oil	2 (15.5 oz.) cans white beans, drained and rinsed
1 lb. ground chicken	1 (15.25 oz.) canned corn, drained
1 medium yellow onion	
2 cloves garlic, peeled	1 (7 oz.) jar chopped jalapenos, undrained
2 tsp. cumin	
2 tsp. chili powder	1 lime
1 tsp. dried oregano	1/2 cup sour cream
3 tbsp. all-purpose flour	2 tbsp. chopped cilantro
3 cups chicken broth	

1) In large stockpot over medium-high, heat oil. Add chicken and cook until browned, about 5 min. Meanwhile, finely chop onion and garlic. Add to browned chicken and cook until onion is translucent, about 5 min.

2) Add cumin, chili powder and oregano; cook and stir 1 min. Sprinkle flour over top; cook and stir for 1 min. Add broth; stir until smooth. Add beans, corn, and jalapenos. Cook until thickened, about 15 min.

3) Meanwhile, zest and juice lime into small bowl. Add sour cream and cilantro; stir until combined. Spoon chili into 4 individual serving bowls; garnish with generous dollop of sour cream mixture.

nutritional facts: *Per serving: 350 calories • 37g carbohydrates • 22g protein • 14g fat • 1080mg sodium • 60mg cholesterol • 10g fiber • 4g sugar*

taco shells

This chili makes great tacos. Fill crispy taco shells with a scoop of chili and garnish with traditional taco toppings such as shredded lettuce and cheese, salsa, guacamole or olives.

chicken enchiladas picante

prep time: 12 minutes • total time: 22 minutes • serves: 4

Make this Southwestern favorite tonight. Frozen veggies, precooked chicken from the supermarket's meat case and your microwave make it possible to put this guaranteed hit on the table in minutes.

1 (8 oz.) jar picante sauce	1-1/2 tsp. chili powder
1 (8 oz.) can tomato sauce	2/3 cup sour cream, *divided*
1 cup frozen chopped onion	8 (6-inch) flour tortillas
1 cup frozen chopped green pepper	3/4 cup shredded reduced-fat Mexican blend cheese
3 cups precooked, sliced chicken (about 3/4 lb.)	chopped cilantro

1) In medium bowl, stir together picante and tomato sauce; set aside. In medium, microwave-safe bowl, combine onion and pepper. Microwave on HIGH for 2-1/2 min.; drain well. Stir in chicken, chili powder and 1/3 cup sour cream.

2) Wrap tortillas in paper towels; microwave on HIGH for 30 seconds. Spoon half of picante sauce mixture into 11- x 7-inch microwave-safe dish. Spoon 1/2 cup chicken mixture down center of each tortilla. Roll up and place, seam side down, in dish. Spoon remaining sauce mixture over tortillas.

3) Cover with vented plastic; microwave on HIGH until bubbly around the edges, 7-9 min. Sprinkle on cheese; microwave on HIGH until cheese is heated through, 1 min. Serve with sour cream and cilantro.

nutritional facts: *Per serving: 570 calories • 51g carbohydrates • 38g protein • 23g fat • 1440mg sodium • 75mg cholesterol • 5g fiber • 10g sugar*

quick fix

If you've got salsa on hand, you can quickly puree it in a blender and use it instead of purchasing the picante sauce.

tips for
perfect poultry

defrosting poultry

- Defrosting times for poultry depend on the weight and thickness of the package. For refrigerator defrosting, place a tray under the package to catch any liquid or juices and to keep the refrigerator clean. Allow 1 to 2 days for bone-in parts and 1 day for every 4 pounds of a whole chicken or turkey.

- For cold water defrosting, place the poultry in a leakproof bag or heavy-duty resealable plastic bag. Submerge the wrapped poultry in cold tap water. Change the water every 30 minutes until the bird is thawed. For this method, allow 30 minutes for every pound.

storing leftovers

- Any perishable food should not stand at room temperature for longer than 2 hours. So within 2 hours of roasting, the poultry meat should be removed from the carcass and put away in the refrigerator or freezer. If desired, slice, cube or cut the meat into strips. Leftover poultry pieces can be packaged without being cut up.

- Meat and leftover poultry casseroles can be refrigerated for 3 to 4 days, stuffing for up to 3 days and gravy for 2 days. Stuffing can be frozen for 1 to 2 months and meat and casseroles for 6 months. Homemade gravy does not freeze well.

flavorful chicken drumsticks

For a very tasty baked drumsticks without any fuss, combine an envelope of ranch salad dressing mix and an 8-1/2-ounce box of corn bread/muffin mix. Dip the drumsticks in milk, then coat with the ranch mix. Place in a greased baking dish and bake.

chicken skin color

The skin color of chicken ranges from white to deep yellow. The skin color is due to the chicken's diet and is not an indication of freshness or quality.

cooking without stuffing

If you don't plan to stuff a whole chicken or turkey, place 1 to 2 cups total of chopped celery, carrots, onions and, if desired, apples into the cavity. The veggies and fruit will add some flavor to the pan juices, which will make a delicious gravy. Discard the vegetables before carving the bird.

flattening chicken breasts

Place boneless chicken breasts between two pieces of waxed paper or plastic wrap, or place in a resealable plastic bag. Starting in the center and working out to the edges, pound the chicken breast lightly with the flat side of a meat mallet until the chicken is even in thickness.

poultry stuffing tips

Stuff the poultry just before you are ready to bake. Loosely spoon stuffing into the neck and body cavities to allow for expansion as the poultry roasts. Stuffed poultry requires a longer roasting time—add 15 to 45 min. to the time required of unstuffed poultry. The internal temperature of the stuffing must reach 165°F. in order to be fully cooked. If the bird is completely cooked and the stuffing has not reached 165°F., remove from the bird and transfer to a baking dish. Continue baking the stuffing until it reaches 165°F.

a neat trick to remove stuffing

Before roasting a whole chicken or turkey, place the stuffing in a large piece of cheesecloth. Bring the ends together and tie in a loose knot, then insert into the cavity. After roasting, simply pull the cheesecloth bag out of the cavity. There's no scooping to get out the stuffing.

no-mess breaded chicken

When breading chicken, replace the egg wash with mayonnaise. Just brush mayonnaise onto the chicken pieces and coat with the crumb mixture. The mayonnaise won't drip like the eggs and it also adds a bit of flavor.

cooked chicken math

Generally, 3/4 pound of boneless skinless chicken breasts will yield 2 cups of cubed cooked chicken. A 3-1/2-pound whole chicken will yield about 3 cups of diced, cooked chicken.

removing chicken skin before cooking

To save calories, many recipes call for skinless breasts or thighs. The uncooked skin is very greasy and hard to grip. If you use a paper towel to grip it, the skin will come off easily.

testing for doneness

When checking chicken for doneness, use an instant-read thermometer. Breasts should register 170°F. and dark meat 180°F. If a recipe calls for bone-in chicken breast and you've substituted boneless, start testing about 20 minutes before the time stated in a recipe.

a hen or a tom

The designation hen or tom turkey indicates whether the turkey was female (hen) or male (tom). Tom turkeys are usually larger than hen turkeys. A hen or tom turkey should be equally tender.

about ground turkey

If you're looking to cut calories and fat, make sure you buy ground turkey breast and not just ground turkey. Ground turkey breast is just white meat and has a fat content of 1 to 3 percent. Ground turkey is either mixture of white and dark meat or all dark meat. The fat content can be as high as 17 percent.

jazzed up gravy

Make your gravy unique and add some flavor with these suggestions...replace half of the water needed with wine, substitute chicken broth for all of the water or, after the gravy is done, turn the heat to low and stir in some sour cream (do not boil).

pork, ham & more

cajun sausage & succotash • p. 113

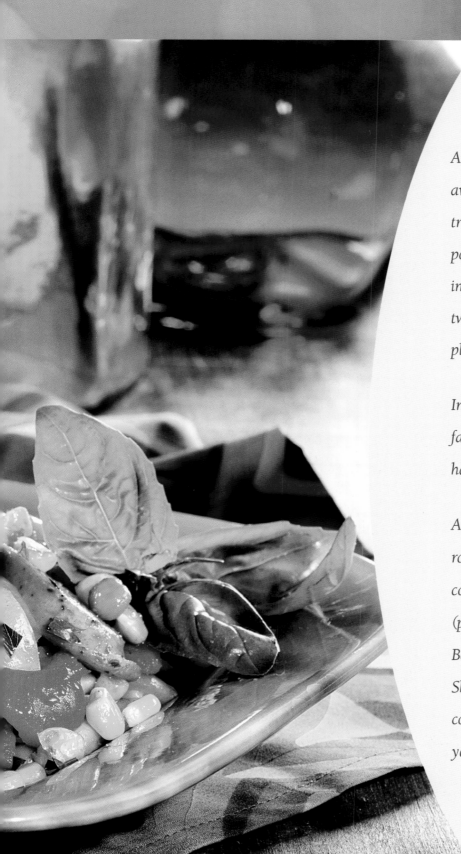

An enticing entree is only minutes away with this chapter of tried-and-true recipes featuring various cuts of pork. Whether you want to cook indoors or out, you'll find more than two dozen options here that are sure to please your family and friends.

In addition to pork chop and pork roast favorites, you'll find many ideas for ham, sausage and even lamb.

Add versatility to your menus year-round with mouth-watering main courses such as Cheesy Chili Casserole (p. 108), Havana Pork with Black Beans (p. 111) and Sausage Potato Skillet (p. 120). You won't believe the comforting flavors that are in store for you and your family!

pork chops mole

prep time: 10 minutes • **total time:** 22 minutes • **serves:** 4

Traditional mole takes hours to cook, and uses many ingredients. But this recipe captures the essence of the flavorful Mexican sauce in just minutes and pairs it with pork chops.

2 green onions	1 (8 oz.) can tomato sauce
1 clove garlic	1 tbsp. honey
1 tsp. olive oil	2 tbsp. peanut butter
1-1/2 tsp. cocoa powder	4 boneless, center-cut pork
3/4 tsp. cumin	chops (about 2 lbs.)
1/8 tsp. allspice	2 tbsp. chopped cilantro
1 tbsp. chili powder, *divided*	

1) Finely chop green onions and garlic in mini-processor or by hand. In nonstick saucepan or small skillet over medium-low, heat oil. Add green onion and garlic; cook until softened, 2 min.

2) Stir in cocoa, cumin, allspice and 1/2 tbsp. chili powder; cook and stir 30 seconds. Stir in tomato sauce, 1/3 cup water, honey and peanut butter until blended. Bring to simmer and cook 6 min.

3) Meanwhile, heat grill pan or nonstick skillet over medium-high. Sprinkle both sides of pork chops with remaining chili powder. Coat pan with cooking spray. Add chops. Cook until internal temperature reads 160°F on an instant-read thermometer, about 12 min. total, turning once halfway during cooking. Remove to serving platter; spoon sauce over. Garnish with cilantro and serve.

nutritional facts: *Per serving: 250 calories • 13g carbohydrates • 28g protein • 10g fat • 440mg sodium • 70mg cholesterol • 2g fiber • 7g sugar*

mole sauce

Mole may be made with chocolate but not the sweet variety; it is traditionally made with unsweetened cocoa powder. Look for one that's 70 percent cocoa.

cheesy chili casserole

prep time: 15 minutes • **total time:** 29 minutes • **serves:** 6

Folks who favor spicy-food will want to eat this dish again and again. Sausage, store-bought chili mix and tomatoes with jalapenos come together to lend great flavor in short order.

3/4 lb. ground pork	1 (10 oz.) can diced tomatoes
1/4 lb. spicy Italian sausage	with jalapenos
1 (1 lb.) bag frozen stir-fry	1 (16 oz.) can light kidney beans,
peppers with onions	drained
1 (1.25 oz.) pkg. chili mix	1 (8 oz.) pkg. shredded
2 (8 oz.) cans tomato sauce	Monterey Jack cheese (about
flavored with basil, garlic and	2 cups)
oregano	2 green onions
	1 small tomato

1) Preheat oven to 425°F. In large skillet over medium heat, brown pork and sausage until fully cooked, breaking up meat with spoon, about 8-10 min. Add peppers, onions, chili mix, tomato sauce and diced tomatoes. Cover and cook until bubbly, about 4-5 min. Stir in beans; remove from heat.

2) Spoon half of mixture into 2-1/2-qt. casserole. Sprinkle with half of cheese. Repeat layers. Bake until mixture is heated through and cheese is melted, 10 min.

3) Meanwhile, thinly slice green onions. Cut tomato in half crosswise and gently squeeze to remove seeds. Chop the tomato. Top casserole with the green onions and tomato.

nutritional facts: *Per serving: 520 calories • 40g carbohydrates • 30g protein • 29g fat • 1570mg sodium • 80mg cholesterol • 8g fiber • 13g sugar*

chili mix

You can add chili powder and crushed red pepper flakes to the meat mixture instead of chili mix. But simmer a bit longer to blend the flavors.

pasta with smoked mozzarella

prep time: 15 minutes • total time: 25 minutes • serves: 4

Simple and satisfying but never dull, this hearty pasta dish is bursting with flavor and texture from the earthy mushrooms and the piquant arugula that complements the smoked mozzarella.

1/2 tsp. salt	1 (14.5 oz.) can petite diced tomatoes, undrained
1/2 lb. cellantani (long elbow) shaped pasta	1 bunch arugula, washed, stems trimmed
1/2 lb. hot *or* sweet Italian sausage	1 tsp. dried oregano
1 small red onion	7 oz. smoked mozzarella
1 tbsp. olive oil	
3/4 cup sliced baby bella mushrooms	

1) Preheat oven to 475°F. Lightly coat 8- x 8-inch baking pan with cooking spray. Bring large pot of hot water to boil over high heat. Add salt, then pasta, and cook just until tender, about 10-11 min.

2) Meanwhile, remove sausage from casing. Peel and chop onion. In large skillet over high, heat oil. Add sausage and onion; cook until sausage just starts to brown, breaking up any lumps of sausage with spatula, 5 min. Add mushrooms. Cook until mushrooms start to release moisture and sausage is fully browned, about 2 min.

3) Stir tomatoes, arugula and oregano into sausage mixture until arugula wilts, about 2 min. Dice mozzarella into 1/2-inch cubes and set aside.

4) Drain pasta and return to cooking pot. Combine with sauce and cheese. Spoon into prepared baking dish. Bake, uncovered, until cheese melts, 10 min.

nutritional facts: *Per serving: 430 calories • 53g carbohydrates • 33g protein • 9g fat • 370mg sodium • 20mg cholesterol • 4g fiber • 9g sugar*

pressed for time?
When time is short you can combine the sauce, cooked pasta and cheese on the stovetop and skip the baking. Cook over low heat just until cheese melts.

pork and apple kebabs

prep time: 29 minutes • total time: 29 minutes • serves: 4

Kabobs turn ordinary meals into something special. Here cubes of pork are skewered with apples and shallots and then brushed with a tangy glaze.

1-1/2 lbs. pork tenderloin	2 tbsp. bourbon *or* apple juice
8 small shallots	1/4 tsp. allspice
2 apples	1/4 tsp. pepper
1/3 cup packed brown sugar	1 tbsp. oil
1/4 cup prepared mustard	

1) Preheat broiler to high. Line shallow baking sheet with foil.

2) Cut pork into 1-1/4-inch cubes. Peel and halve shallots lengthwise through root end. Quarter apples; core, then cut in half crosswise. Thread pork, shallots and apples onto 8 skewers and place on baking sheet.

3) In small bowl, blend sugar, mustard, bourbon, allspice and pepper; transfer half to small serving dish to use as a drizzling sauce. To remaining mixture, add oil. Brush lightly onto apples and shallots, and more heavily onto pork.

4) Broil 5 min.; turn and brush with remaining mixture as before. Broil until pork is cooked through, 5 min. Serve with reserved sauce.

nutritional facts: *Per serving: 410 calories • 40g carbohydrates • 37g protein • 9g fat • 460mg sodium • 110mg cholesterol • 3g fiber • 32g sugar*

packaged tenderloins
Vacuum-sealed pork tenderloins have a long refrigerator life and are handy for quick meals. Buy an extra one when they go on sale.

sweet-and-sour pork chops

prep time: 5 minutes • total time: 20 minutes • serves: 4

This colorful entree is quick to prepare in one skillet. Plus, it's nutritious and kid-pleasing. What more can you ask from a recipe? No wonder it's a classic!

maraschino cherries

To tempt your little ones, add a few maraschino or fresh, pitted cherries during the last few minutes of cooking and make sure they end up on the kids' plates.

4 boneless pork chops (about 1/2-inch thick and 1-1/4 lbs. *each*)	1 tbsp. cornstarch
	3 tbsp. sugar
	1/2 cup cold water
salt and pepper	3 tbsp. rice wine *or* white wine
1 tbsp. oil	vinegar
1 green pepper, cut into chunks	3 tbsp. ketchup
1 orange pepper, cut into chunks	2 tbsp. soy sauce
1 large onion, cut into chunks	1-1/2 cups fresh pineapple chunks

1) Sprinkle chops with salt and pepper. In large, nonstick skillet over medium heat, heat oil, add chops and cook, turning once, until browned on both sides and almost cooked through, about 4 min. Remove to platter and keep warm.

2) Add peppers to skillet and cook, stirring constantly, for 1 min. Add onion and cook, stirring constantly, until vegetables are just crisp-tender, about 5 min.

3) In small bowl, mix cornstarch and sugar; gradually add water, stirring until smooth. Add vinegar, ketchup and soy sauce.

4) Lower heat to medium; add pineapple to skillet. Add cornstarch mixture; cook and stir until the sauce begins to thicken. Add the chops and simmer until cooked through, about 3 min.

nutritional facts: *Per serving: 320 calories • 24g carbohydrates • 27g protein • 13g fat • 500mg sodium • 65mg cholesterol • 2g fiber • 18g sugar*

balsamic maple-glazed pork

prep time: 8 minutes • total time: 12 minutes • serves: 4

You'll win the prize for best "instant chef" every time you make this flavorful and elegant pork dinner, which is prepared and cooked in minutes.

paprika pointer

Regular paprika is a bit more readily available than the smoky variety, which is more rare and sometimes expensive.

1-1/4 lbs. pork tenderloin	1/2 tsp. mild smoky paprika,
5 tbsp. maple syrup, *divided*	*divided* (optional)
4 tbsp. balsamic vinegar, *divided*	1/2 tsp. salt, *divided*
	1/4 tsp. pepper
3/4 tsp. dried sage, *divided*	1 small bunch chives

1) Trim off silver skin from pork. Starting at narrower end, slice pork diagonally into 1/2-inch thick slices; place in food storage bag. Add 1 tbsp. maple syrup, 2 tbsp. balsamic vinegar, 1/2 tsp. sage, 1/4 tsp. paprika, 1/4 tsp. salt and pepper. Seal the bag and knead to combine; set aside. Chop enough chives to yield 2 tbsp.; set aside.

2) In small saucepan over medium heat, combine remaining syrup, balsamic vinegar, sage, paprika and salt. Cook until reduced to about 3 tbsp. of syrupy glaze, 3 min. (If glaze is too thick, thin with 1 or 2 tsp. vinegar.)

3) Coat grates of grill or grill pan with cooking spray. Preheat to medium-high. Add pork and grill just until cooked on first side, 2 min. Turn and cook until done, 1-2 min. Place on serving platter. Drizzle with maple glaze; top with chives. Serve.

nutritional facts: *Per serving: 260 calories • 23g carbohydrates • 30g protein • 5g fat • 370mg sodium • 90mg cholesterol • 0g fiber • 20g sugar*

havana pork with black beans

prep time: 12 minutes • total time: 22 minutes • serves: 4

Cuban-style cooking brings together a variety of flavors and textures. A marinade of garlic and lime coats this pork, which is quickly sauteed and covered in a mix of onion, radishes and black beans.

2 cloves garlic	4 large radishes
2 tbsp. lime juice	1/4 cup cilantro, *divided*
1 tsp. dried oregano	2 tsp. olive oil, *divided*
1 tsp. cumin, *divided*	1 cup canned black beans, rinsed and drained
1/4 tsp. salt	
1 lb. pork tenderloin,	1 tbsp. packed brown sugar
1 red onion	2 tsp. balsamic vinegar

1) Finely chop garlic. In medium bowl, place garlic, lime juice, oregano, 3/4 tsp. cumin and salt. Holding knife at angle, diagonally slice pork 1 inch thick. Add to bowl and toss to coat; let stand 10 min.

2) Meanwhile, chop onion, radishes and 1 tbsp. cilantro. Remove pork and pat dry on paper towels. In large nonstick skillet, heat 1 tsp. oil over medium heat. Add pork and cook first side until lightly golden, 2 min. Turn and cook until done, about 2 min. Place on serving dish and cover to keep warm.

3) Add remaining oil to pan. Add onion, cook and stir until translucent, 2 min. Add radishes and cook until heated through, 2 min. Remove from heat. Stir in the beans, sugar, vinegar, remaining cilantro 1/4 tsp. cumin and 2 tbsp. water, combining thoroughly. Spoon over pork on serving dish; garnish with cilantro and serve.

nutritional facts: *Per serving: 260 calories • 18g carbohydrates • 28g protein • 9g fat • 210mg sodium • 75mg cholesterol • 4g fiber • 5g sugar*

use fresh juice

Fresh lime juice gives a more intense flavor than bottled. To juice a lime, cut the fruit in half and squeeze it through your fingers to catch any seeds. This technique works well with lemons, too.

smoky kielbasa casserole

prep time: 14 minutes • total time: 28 minutes • serves: 6

You and your family will love this hearty shepherds' pie, featuring the smoky sweetness of kielbasa. The addition of mashed potatoes makes it a complete meal.

1 lb. kielbasa sausage, diced	1 (14.5 oz.) can diced tomatoes, drained
1 medium onion	
2 cloves garlic	1 tbsp. tomato paste
1 red bell pepper	salt and pepper to taste
1 green pepper	1 (2 lb.) pkg. prepared refrigerated mashed potatoes

1) Preheat oven to 400°F. In large, nonstick skillet over medium-high heat, cook kielbasa for 5 min. Drain fat from pan.

2) Meanwhile, chop onion and mince garlic; add onion and garlic to sausage. Saute 2-3 min. Seed and dice peppers. Add to pan and cook until softened, 2-3 min.

3) Stir diced tomatoes and tomato paste into sausage mixture. Season with salt and pepper to taste. Cook until slightly thickened, 2-3 min.

4) Spoon mixture into 13- x 9-inch baking dish. Spread mashed potatoes over top. Bake until top just starts to brown and liquid bubbles around edges, 12-14 min.

nutritional facts: *Per serving: 350 calories • 27g carbohydrates • 13g protein • 22g fat • 1250mg sodium • 50mg cholesterol • 4g fiber • 5g sugar*

mashed potatoes

Next time you're making mashed potatoes from scratch, simply double the recipe and freeze the extra.

ham and artichoke frittata

prep time: 10 minutes • total time: 25 minutes • serves: 4

Here's a great dinner that includes veggies, protein and starch in one delicious and versatile dish. Once you've mastered this frittata, you'll find you can make it in dozens of varieties.

1 tbsp. olive oil, *divided*	1/4 tsp. crushed dried rosemary
2 cups frozen hash brown potatoes	1/2 tsp. salt
3/4 cup frozen chopped onion	1/2 tsp. jalapeno pepper sauce
1-1/2 cups thick-sliced ham, cut into 1/2-inch cubes (6 oz.)	3/4 cup shredded Italian cheese blend (3 oz.)
8 large eggs	1 cup canned, drained artichoke hearts, halved
4 green onions, sliced	

cooked potatoes

Frozen hash browns are a great time-saver, but if you have leftover cooked potatoes, you can dice them up instead.

1) Preheat oven to 450°F. In 10-inch nonstick, ovenproof skillet over medium-high, heat 1/2 tbsp. oil. Add potatoes, onion and ham; cook until potatoes are tender, about 8 min. Remove onion and ham from skillet; wipe pan clean.

2) In medium bowl, whisk together eggs, green onions, rosemary, salt and pepper sauce. Stir in potato mixture and half of cheese.

3) Heat remaining oil in pan over medium. Pour in egg mixture; sprinkle with artichokes. Cook until bottom is lightly browned, about 3 min. Tilt skillet, and using nonstick spatula, lift edges of frittata to allow liquid to run underneath. Cook about 3 min. more.

4) Sprinkle remaining cheese around edge of frittata. Bake until egg is set in the center, about 7 min. Cut into wedges to serve.

nutritional facts: *Per serving: 440 calories • 22g carbohydrates • 29g protein • 28g fat • 1140mg sodium • 460mg cholesterol • 5g fiber • 3g sugar*

pineapple glazed bone-in ham

prep time: 10 minutes • total time: 1 hour • serves: 10-12

Dotted with the usual pineapple and cherries, this elegant ham gets a modern-day twist from a cranberry and apple chutney glaze that's sweet with just a little bit of a tang.

1 fully cooked, spiral-cut, bone-in ham (about 9 to 10 lbs.)	1/4 cup maraschino cherry juice
1 (10.5 oz.) jar cranberry apple chutney	1 (20 oz.) can sliced pineapple, drained (about 8 slices)
1/3 cup spicy brown mustard	1/4 cup maraschino cherries (about 8)
1/2 cup packed light brown sugar	

cranberry apple chutney

If cranberry apple chutney is unavailable, you can substitute another type, such as mango or apricot. Or thin down some orange marmalade with a bit of warm water.

1) Preheat oven to 350°F. Place ham in large, heavy roasting pan. In food processor or blender, combine chutney, mustard, brown sugar and cherry juice. Process for 30 seconds until smooth.

2) With pastry brush, completely coat surface of ham with glaze. Cover ham with pineapple slices, securing slices with toothpicks. Place 1 cherry in center of each pineapple ring and secure with toothpick.

3) With pastry brush, lightly coat fruit with glaze. Place remaining glaze in small serving dish. Bake ham, uncovered, until heated through, 1 hour. Transfer to platter and serve with remaining glaze.

nutritional facts: *Per serving: 290 calories • 20g carbohydrates • 37g protein • 6g fat • 1760mg sodium • 110mg cholesterol • 1g fiber • 18g sugar*

fiery lamb with three onions

prep time: 23 minutes • total time: 23 minutes • serves: 4

A traditional favorite in northern China, tender lamb is sauteed with a variety of onions and flavored with a tangy, sweet-and-spicy sauce. It's served in lettuce cups for a cool crunch that helps tame the heat.

3 tbsp. reduced-sodium soy sauce, *divided*	1 large leek
1 tbsp. cornstarch	1 bunch green onions
3 tsp. Chinese chili sauce with garlic, *divided*	1/3 cup hoisin sauce
	2 tbsp. white vinegar
1 lb. boneless lamb	3 tbsp. oil, *divided*
1 large sweet white onion	8 Boston *or* Bibb lettuce leaves

1) In large bowl, blend 2 tbsp. soy sauce, cornstarch and 1 tsp. chili sauce. Slice lamb into 1/4-inch slices; cut slices into julienne strips. Add to bowl and toss thoroughly to coat. Marinate 10 min.

2) Meanwhile, thinly slice onion. Cut leek into 1-1/2 inch julienne pieces; wash thoroughly to remove any grit. Cut green onions into 1-1/2 inch lengths; set aside green portion.

3) In small bowl, mix hoisin sauce, vinegar and remaining soy and chili sauces.

4) In large, nonstick skillet, heat 2 tbsp. oil over high. Add lamb; cook and stir 2 min. Remove to plate. Add remaining oil, onion, leek and white portion of green onions. Cook and stir 2 min. Return lamb and add sauce to skillet; cook and stir about 1 min. Stir in green portion of green onions.

5) Place two lettuce leaves on each plate. Evenly divide meat mixture among leaves. Serve immediately.

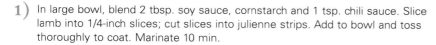

nutritional facts: *Per serving: 420 calories • 30g carbohydrates • 26g protein • 21g fat • 1110mg sodium • 75mg cholesterol • 4g fiber • 13g sugar*

flavored oils

Flavored oils lend considerable flavor to any dish. For an authentic Asian touch, use sesame oil in the skillet. You could also try walnut oil or even garlic oil for variety.

cajun sausage & succotash

prep time: 8 minutes • total time: 20 minutes • serves: 4

Here's a wholesome and fresh meal-in-a-skillet that's ready for the table in just 20 minutes. Baby lima beans can be used in place of edamame if you wish.

1 sweet onion	1 (1 lb.) pkg. precooked spicy chicken sausages (4 links)
1 red bell pepper	
3 sprigs fresh basil	2 cups frozen corn
2 tsp. olive oil	1 cup frozen shelled edamame
1 (15 oz.) can diced tomatoes	2 to 3 tsp. Cajun seasoning

1) Chop onion and pepper. Chop basil to yield 3 tbsp. In nonstick skillet over medium, heat oil. Add onion and pepper. Cook and stir until softened, 6 min. Meanwhile, drain tomatoes and discard liquid. Cut sausages into 1/2-inch slices on the diagonal.

2) Add corn, edamame, Cajun seasoning and tomatoes to skillet. Bring to simmer; cook until vegetables are tender, 4 min. Stir in sausages and cook until heated through, 1 min. more. Transfer to dish and serve.

nutritional facts: *Per serving: 380 calories • 34g carbohydrates • 26g protein • 17g fat • 1370mg sodium • 70mg cholesterol • 6g fiber • 12g sugar*

niblets of corn

Niblets of corn—whether fresh, frozen or the best canned products—are crunchy and easy to use in this dish. Or go a bit fancier and try it with canned baby corn.

oriental slaw

Combine the remainder of
coleslaw mix with 2 tbsp. each
of honey and rice vinegar and
1 tbsp. of soy sauce and toasted
sesame oil. Chill and serve
alongside the pork.

mu shu pork

prep time: 10 minutes • total time: 15 minutes • serves: 4

This simplified version of a popular restaurant dish makes good use of supermarket staples like flour tortillas and coleslaw mix. Add julienned pork, green onions, eggs and a quick sauce and dinner is on the table!

3/4 lb. pork tenderloin	3 tbsp. vegetable oil
1 bunch green onions	4 large eggs, lightly beaten
2 tbsp. soy sauce	1/2 (16 oz.) pkg. coleslaw mix
2 tbsp. sherry	(about 2 cups)
4 tsp. toasted sesame oil	hoisin sauce
8 (8-inch) flour tortillas	

1) Preheat oven to 350°F. Slice the pork into very thin slices, then cut into julienne strips.

2) Cut green onion tops and bottoms into 1-1/2-inch pieces, then into julienne strips, keeping white and green portions separate.

3) In small bowl, mix soy sauce, sherry and sesame oil. Wrap tortillas in foil and place in oven to warm.

4) In large, nonstick skillet over high heat, add 1 tbsp. vegetable oil. When very hot, add eggs, and cook, stirring constantly, until eggs are just scrambled; remove.

5) In another skillet over high heat, add remaining vegetable oil. When very hot, add pork and white portion of green onions. Cook, stirring constantly, until pork begins to lose pink color, about 1 min. Add coleslaw mix and soy sauce mixture; cook, stirring constantly, until crisp-tender, about 1 min. Add eggs and green portion of onions; stir just until heated through.

6) To serve, spoon hoisin sauce onto tortillas. Add pork mixture and roll or fold up.

nutritional facts: *Per serving: 650 calories • 56g carbohydrates • 35g protein • 32g fat • 1210mg sodium • 270mg cholesterol • 5g fiber • 5g sugar*

use fresh rosemary

Dried rosemary does not work
well in this recipe. If fresh
rosemary is too expensive, simply
omit it. The prosciutto still lends
plenty of flavor.

pork cutlets with prosciutto

prep time: 15 minutes • total time: 15 minutes • serves: 6

Enjoy the sunny flavors of the Sorrento coast in these juicy pork cutlets filled with fresh rosemary and prosciutto. Fancy enough to serve unexpected company, it's a perfect party dish.

12 thin-sliced pork cutlets	1 tbsp. olive oil
1/4 lb. very thinly sliced prosciutto	1/2 tsp. salt, *divided*
1 to 2 sprigs fresh rosemary	1 lemon

1) Place pork cutlets between sheets of plastic wrap. With meat mallet, gently pound to 1/2-inch thickness.

2) Fold prosciutto slices in half and lay over 6 cutlets, being careful not to extend over edges. Mince fresh rosemary to yield 1 tsp. Sprinkle rosemary evenly over proscuitto and top with remaining cutlets.

3) In large skillet over medium-high, heat olive oil. Sprinkle 1/4 tsp. salt over top of cutlets. Place salted side down in skillet. Sprinkle remaining salt over top. Cook until golden on first side, 4-5 min. Turn and cook until outside is golden on second side and pork is cooked through, 4 min. Squeeze lemon juice over top, transfer to plates and serve.

nutritional facts: *Per serving: 520 calories • 40g carbohydrates • 22g protein • 31g fat • 1260mg sodium • 65mg cholesterol • 4g fiber • 21g sugar*

mexicali meatballs

prep time: 12 minutes • total time: 27 minutes • serves: 4

These tender little bites are not your ho-hum, typical old meatballs! They get their flavor from sun-dried tomatoes, a bit of garlic and jalapeño combined with pork and a quick simmer in a spicy sauce.

1 small jalapeno	1/4 tsp. salt
1/4 cup oil-packed sun-dried tomatoes	1/8 tsp. pepper
	2 tbsp. oil
1 large clove garlic	1 (14.5 oz.) can petite-cut diced tomatoes with jalapenos
1 lb. ground pork	
1/4 cup dried bread crumbs	1/4 tsp. dried oregano
1 large egg	2 sprigs fresh parsley

1) Halve, seed and roughly chop jalapeno. In food processor, process jalapeno, sun-dried tomatoes and garlic until finely chopped. Transfer the mixture to large bowl. Add the pork, bread crumbs, egg, salt and pepper. Combine until thoroughly blended together.

2) With 1/2-oz. ice cream scoop, divide mixture into 28 portions. With slightly moistened hands, roll each portion into a ball.

3) In large skillet over medium-high, heat oil. Add meatballs. Cook, turning frequently with tongs, until browned on all sides, about 6 min. Remove to plate. Discard oil from skillet.

4) Add tomatoes and oregano to skillet. Bring to boil, scraping bottom of pan. Return meatballs to skillet. Spoon sauce over top of meatballs and simmer, about 2 min. Meanwhile, chop parsley. Transfer meatballs to serving dish. Sprinkle with parsley and serve.

nutritional facts: *Per serving: 440 calories • 11g carbohydrates • 23g protein • 33g fat • 590mg sodium • 135mg cholesterol • 2g fiber • 4g sugar*

jalapeno peppers

If you purchase a large jalapeno, finely chop it first, then use half for the meatballs and half in the sauce with a can of plain diced tomatoes.

island salsa ham steaks

prep time: 12 minutes • total time: 22 minutes • serves: 4

Try this fun combination: chunks of delightfully cool fruits and spicy pepper sauce atop quick-cooking ham steaks. It makes for a speedy summer supper that's as pretty as it is tasty.

2 kiwifruit	3 tsp. jalapeno pepper sauce, *divided*
1/2 large mango	
8 oz. pre-cut seedless watermelon	1 tbsp. fresh lime juice
	4 boneless ham steaks (97 percent fat-free), about 1-1/2 lbs.
1/2 cucumber	
8 sprigs cilantro	
4 tbsp. apricot jam, *divided*	

1) Peel kiwifruit and mango; pit mango. Cut watermelon, cucumber, kiwi and mango into 1/2-inch pieces. Place in medium bowl. Chop cilantro to yield 3 tbsp.; add to bowl. Add 2 tbsp. jam and 1-1/2 tsp. jalapeno sauce; toss to combine.

2) Coat grill with cooking spray. Preheat grill or grill pan over medium heat. Combine remaining 2 tbsp. jam and remaining jalapeño sauce in small dish.

3) Brush ham with jam mixture and grill until marked on first side, about 3 min. Baste top and turn. Baste with remaining sauce and cook until heated through, 2-3 min. Transfer steaks to plates, evenly mound with salsa and serve.

nutritional facts: *Per serving: 260 calories • 28g carbohydrates • 31g protein • 4.5g fat • 2150mg sodium • 70mg cholesterol • 2g fiber • 19g sugar*

outdoor grilling

If you are using a high flame or an outdoor grill, carefully baste the jam sauce on the ham steaks during the last minute of cooking each side so it doesn't smoke and burn.

apricot preserves

No plum sauce on your shelf?
Don't fret. Substitute apricot
preserves instead or stir in a few
teaspoons of raspberry preserves
to 1/2 cup grape jelly.

eternal sun crispy pork

prep time: 22 minutes • total time: 22 minutes • serves: 4

Adding a simple topping of juicy orange slices and a quick, sweet-and-tangy sauce really enhances the goodness of an already delicious, crispy pork cutlet. Make it for guests on a weekend.

2 oranges	1/8 tsp. pepper
1/2 cup plum sauce	2 tbsp. all-purpose flour
4 tsp. rice wine vinegar	2 large eggs, beaten
1 tbsp. sherry	1 cup dry, seasoned bread
8 pork cutlets, 1/2-in. thick	crumbs
1/4 tsp. salt	oil for frying

1) Peel and thinly slice 1 orange; set aside. Grate 1 tbsp. zest from remaining orange into small, microwave-safe bowl. Juice zested orange to yield 1/2 cup adding water if needed. Add to bowl. Stir in plum sauce, vinegar and sherry. Microwave on HIGH, 5 min., stirring once.

2) Meanwhile, season pork with salt and pepper. Dust chops with flour. Dip into egg, then roll in bread crumbs.

3) In medium skillet over high, heat 1/8-inch oil. Reduce heat to medium and add 4 cutlets. Cook until golden on first side, 2 min.; turn and cook until cooked through, about 1 min. Remove and keep warm. Repeat with remaining cutlets, adding additional oil if needed.

4) To serve, arrange orange slices on cutlets and drizzle with some sauce. Serve remaining sauce alongside.

nutritional facts: *Per serving: 840 calories • 47g carbohydrates • 35g protein • 56g fat • 900mg sodium • 165mg cholesterol • 4g fiber • 18g sugar*

cast-iron skillet

It pays to have a black, cast-iron
skillet on hand. With it, you can
sear any meat or fish on top of the
stove, then transfer it to the oven
or broiler without dirtying
another dish.

low-fat pesto pork chops

prep time: 15 minutes • total time: 23 minutes • serves: 4

The typical cheese and pine nuts are omitted from this homemade pesto, resulting in a reduced-fat version that piles on the flavor of basil and garlic. It really locks in the pork's succulent juices.

2 cups fresh basil leaves	2 tbsp. dry bread crumbs
3 large garlic cloves	2 tbsp. olive oil
1/2 tsp. salt, *divided*	4 center-cut pork loin chops, (about
1/4 tsp. pepper, *divided*	1/2 inch thick and 4 oz. *each*)

1) Preheat broiler. Place basil, garlic and half of salt and pepper in food processor; pulse until roughly chopped, 20-30 seconds. Add bread crumbs and process until incorporated, about 30 seconds. With motor running, slowly add oil through feed tube until pureed, 1 min. Set aside.

2) Coat broiler pan with cooking spray; set aside. Heat large, heavy skillet over high until very hot but not smoking. Sprinkle both sides of chops with remaining salt and pepper. Place chops in skillet and sear on first side until browned, 1 min. Turn and sear second side, about 1 min. Remove from heat.

3) Place chops on work surface and spread 1 side of each chop with pesto. Place chops pesto-side down on prepared broiler pan. Evenly spread remaining pesto over uncoated side of chops.

4) Broil chops until pesto is slightly darker on first side, about 2 min. Turn and broil until pork juices run clear, about 2 min. Transfer to plates and serve.

nutritional facts: *Per serving: 310 calories • 4g carbohydrates • 35g protein • 16g fat • 380mg sodium • 95mg cholesterol • 1g fiber • 0g sugar*

nana's moussaka

prep time: 60 minutes • total time: 2 hours • serves: 8

Moussaka, sometimes called "Greek lasagna," is a delicious casserole of mildly spiced ground lamb and slices of eggplant topped by a creamy, golden sauce. It's sure to please guests and family alike.

2 medium eggplants	3 tbsp. chopped parsley
1/2 cup olive oil, *divided*	2 tsp. dried oregano
1 medium onion, minced	2-1/2 cups milk
2 cloves garlic, minced	1 tsp. salt
1/4 tsp. ground cinnamon	4 tbsp. butter
1/4 tsp. allspice	1/2 cup all-purpose flour
1 lb. ground lamb	2 egg yolks
1 (28 oz.) can crushed tomatoes	1/2 cup grated Parmesan cheese
2 tbsp. tomato paste	1/4 tsp. black pepper
1/2 cup white wine	

1) Cut eggplants into 1/4-inch-thick slices. Layer slices in colander, sprinkling each with salt. Let stand for 30 min., then rinse; pat dry.

2) Meanwhile, in large saucepan over medium, heat 2 tbsp. olive oil. Add onion and garlic, saute until soft, 5 min. Stir in cinnamon and allspice. Add lamb; increase heat to medium-high. When meat is browned, stir in tomatoes, tomato paste, white wine, parsley and oregano. Lower heat; simmer until thickened.

3) In large, nonstick skillet over medium, heat 1 tbsp. oil. Add eggplant slices in batches; cook until golden on one side. Add oil as needed. Turn slices; cook until golden. Remove to platter. Preheat oven to 350°F.

4) In medium saucepan over low, heat milk. In medium saucepan over medium-low, melt butter. Stir flour into butter; cook for 3 min. Add milk to butter mixture, whisking until smooth. Add salt and pepper. Remove from heat; stir in egg yolks and Parmesan until smooth.

5) Spoon one-third of sauce into 13- x 9-inch baking dish. Cover with one-third of eggplant slices, then meat mixture. Repeat eggplant and meat layers twice, ending with eggplant. Spread on white sauce. Bake until top is golden brown, about 45 min. Let stand 5 min.; serve.

nutritional facts: *Per serving: 520 calories • 26g carbohydrates • 19g protein • 37g fat • 670mg sodium • 120mg cholesterol • 6g fiber • 11g sugar*

making this ahead?

If you're preparing this casserole in advance, let the uncooked moussaka cool, then cover and refrigerate. Bake it covered for 45 minutes, then uncover and bake for 20 minutes more.

ham in currant sauce

prep time: 10 minutes • total time: 20 minutes • serves: 6

This recipe combines grilled ham steaks with a sweet currant sauce and a dash of port wine.

1/2 cup raisins	3 thin-cut ham steaks
1/4 cup port wine	(about 1-1/4 lbs.)
	1 (12 oz.) red currant jelly

1) Place raisins in small bowl; pour in port wine. Set aside. Cut each ham steak in half. In large skillet over medium-high heat, cook ham steaks until browned on first side, about 5 min. Turn and cook until browned on second side, 4-5 min. Remove to platter and keep warm.

2) Add currant jelly, raisins and port wine to skillet, stirring until jelly dissolves and sauce is smooth. Spoon sauce and raisins over ham. Serve.

nutritional facts: *Per serving: 330 calories • 53g carbohydrates • 19g protein • 4g fat • 1200mg sodium • 45mg cholesterol • 1g fiber • 46g sugar*

apple cider

Try apple cider as a cost-effective substitute for the port wine.

curry paste

For an added punch, try rubbing the pork with a store-bought, jarred curry paste (instead of the fennel-seed rub) before you prep the fruit.

pork medallions with apple chutney

prep time: 12 minutes • total time: 24 minutes • serves: 4

This traditional autumn recipe is wonderful at any time of year, since it cooks up so quickly but is impressive enough for guests, too. Pork and sweetly spiced apples are a natural pairing.

2 Granny Smith apples (about 1 lb.)	3 tbsp. cider vinegar
2 stalks chives	1/4 tsp. ginger
1/2 cup frozen chopped onion	1-1/2 tsp. seasoned salt, *divided*
1/4 cup dried cranberries	1 tsp. fennel seeds
1/4 cup packed brown sugar	1-1/4 lbs. pork tenderloin
3 tbsp. brandy	2 tsp. olive oil

1) Peel, halve and core apples. Chop into 1/2-inch pieces. Chop chives and set aside. In medium saucepan over medium-high heat, bring apples, onions, cranberries, brown sugar, brandy, vinegar, ginger and 1/4 tsp. seasoned salt to brisk simmer. Cook until the apples are tender and liquid has mostly evaporated, about 12 min.

2) Meanwhile, crush fennel seeds with mortar and pestle or flatten with knife on cutting board and finely chop. Combine with remaining seasoned salt in small dish. Diagonally slice pork into 8 slices; place on board. Cover with plastic wrap and press lightly with palm of hand to flatten slightly. Remove plastic wrap and sprinkle both sides of meat with fennel mixture.

3) In large, nonstick skillet over medium, heat oil. Add pork and cook until golden on first side, about 2 min. Turn and cook until done, 1 to 2 min. Transfer to plates; top with apple mixture. Garnish with chives and serve.

nutritional facts: *Per serving: 450 calories • 41g carbohydrates • 42g protein • 10g fat • 440mg sodium • 110mg cholesterol • 3g fiber • 25g sugar*

zesty garnishes

Slice up some green onions or chop a few chives and use them as a zesty garnish. Sliced lime and orange wedges on the side are also always pretty.

pork with citrus vermouth sauce

prep time: 10 minutes • total time: 22 minutes • serves: 4

Orange and lemon rind, orange juice and vermouth bring bright, fresh flavor to a simple plate of pork chops, elevating them from a simple, humble dish to an exciting meal.

4 thin-cut boneless pork chops (about 1-1/4 lbs.)	2 tsp. olive oil
1 navel orange	1 large shallot
1 lemon	3/4 cup orange juice
1/4 tsp. pepper	2 tbsp. dry vermouth
1/2 tsp. salt, *divided*	1/2 tsp. dried tarragon

1) Trim off silver skin on side of pork. Place chops between 2 sheets of plastic wrap and pound to 1/4-inch thickness. Grate rind from orange and lemon; place in medium bowl. Squeeze lemon to yield 2 tbsp. juice; add 1 tbsp. to bowl with pepper and 1/4 tsp. salt. Add pork and toss to coat.

2) In large, nonstick skillet over medium, heat oil. Add pork and cook until golden on first side, about 4 min. Turn and cook until done, 4 min. Transfer to serving plate and keep warm.

3) Meanwhile, trim pith from orange and coarsely chop flesh; set aside. Finely chop shallot; add to skillet. Cook and stir 30 seconds. Add orange juice, vermouth, tarragon, remaining lemon juice and salt; simmer until reduced to about 1/2 cup, about 2-3 min. Stir in chopped orange and any pork juices from platter; spoon over pork and serve immediately.

nutritional facts: *Per serving: 320 calories • 14g carbohydrates • 28g protein • 16g fat • 830mg sodium • 75mg cholesterol • 1g fiber • 8g sugar*

greek stuffed pork pockets

prep time: 10 minutes • total time: 25 minutes • serves: 4

Delightful Mediterranean flavors abound in these succulent pork chops that are stuffed to overflowing with a combo of dill, parsley, feta cheese and olives. Your family will love them!

1 tbsp. olive oil	1/2 cup pitted kalamata olives
1 small bunch fresh dill	1/4 cup crumbled feta cheese
1 small bunch fresh flat-leaf parsley	4 center-cut pork chops (about 3/4-inches thick)
1/3 cup oil-packed sun-dried tomatoes	1/2 tsp. coarse salt
	1/4 tsp. pepper

1) Coat grill or grill pan with olive oil and preheat to medium.

2) Roughly chop dill and parsley to yield 1 cup each; set aside. Place sun-dried tomatoes and olives in food processor. Pulse to form rough paste. Add parsley and dill; pulse once or twice to combine. Scrape mixture into small bowl and fold in feta cheese. Set aside.

3) Place 1 chop on cutting board. With sharp knife held parallel to cutting board, cut deep slit into center of chop, being careful not to cut through to opposite side. Repeat with remaining chops.

4) Evenly divide olive mixture and stuff into pocket of each chop. Press chops lightly with palm of hand to flatten slightly. Season each side of chops with salt and pepper.

5) Place chops on grill or in grill pan. Cook on first side until lightly browned, about 6 min. Turn and cook until desired doneness, about 6-7 min.

nutritional facts: *Per serving: 570 calories • 6g carbohydrates • 52g protein • 37g fat • 930mg sodium • 150mg cholesterol • 1g fiber • 0g sugar*

rice pilaf

A boxed rice pilaf mix is the perfect side dish for this flavorful pork. Rice pilaf mixes are convenient and offer authentic—and sometimes even exotic—flavor.

pizza patties

prep time: 10 minutes • total time: 25 minutes • serves: 4

If you like lots of sauce, you may want to serve extra spaghetti sauce on the side of these patties for dipping.

1/3 cup finely chopped green pepper	1 cup spaghetti sauce
1 small onion, finely chopped	4 sandwich buns, split
1/4 cup grated Parmesan cheese	1/2 cup shredded part-skim mozzarella cheese
1 lb. bulk Italian sausage	

1) In a large bowl, combine the green pepper, onion and Parmesan cheese. Crumble sausage over mixture and mix just until combined. Shape into four patties.

2) In a large skillet, cook patties over medium heat for 7-8 minutes on each side or until meat is no longer pink; drain. Add the spaghetti sauce; bring to a boil. Reduce heat; cover and simmer for 7-8 minutes or until heated through.

3) Place a patty on the bottom of each bun; drizzle with spaghetti sauce. Sprinkle with mozzarella cheese; replace tops.

nutritional facts: *Per serving: 720 calories • 45g carbohydrates • 31g protein • 46g fat • 1645mg sodium • 100mg cholesterol • 3 g fiber*

simple shortcut

To cut preparation at mealtime, mix and shape these patties the night before. Cover and refrigerate.

cost crusher

Make your own bread crumbs by lightly toasting Italian bread and then crushing with a rolling pin.

crispy pork and apple fry

prep time: 15 minutes • **total time:** 29 minutes • **serves:** 4

Super-crisp on the outside and moist on the inside, the pork chops and apple rings, accented with cinnamon and lemon, are perfect together.

1 lb. boneless, center-cut pork loin chops (1/2-inch thick)	3 eggs
1/4 tsp. salt	3/4 cup oil
1/4 tsp. pepper	1 large McIntosh apple
1/3 cup all-purpose flour	1 tbsp. brown sugar
2-1/4 cups Panko bread crumbs	1/8 tsp. ground cinnamon
	1 lemon

1) Place pork between sheets of waxed paper; pound to 1/4-inch thickness. Season both sides with salt and pepper.

2) Into large, zippered plastic bag, place flour. Add pork; shake to coat. Place bread crumbs on plate. In shallow bowl, lightly beat egg. Dip pork into egg, then into bread crumbs, coating both sides.

3) In large skillet over medium, heat oil. Add pork and fry until golden brown on first side, 3 min. Turn and cook until golden brown on second side, 3 min. Remove to paper-towel-lined platter to drain.

4) Core apple and cut into 8 rings. Whisk brown sugar and cinnamon into remaining beaten egg. Place apple rings in bag with remaining flour; shake to coat. Dip rings into egg mixture; roll in bread crumbs, coating evenly.

5) Add apples to oil and fry until golden and crisp on first side, about 1-2 min. Turn and cook until golden on second side, about 1-2 min. Remove to paper-towel-lined platter. Slice lemon into 4 wedges. Transfer pork and apples to serving plates. Garnish with lemon and serve.

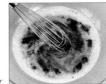

nutritional facts: *Per serving: 500 calories • 29g carbohydrates • 26g protein • 32g fat • 760mg sodium • 140mg cholesterol • 3g fiber • 13g sugar*

swift side

Use this recipe for a no-fuss side dish. Simply leave out the sausage links for unbeatable hash browns.

sausage potato skillet

prep time: 10 minutes • **total time:** 30 minutes • **serves:** 4

If you love meaty sausages and potatoes at breakfast, now you can enjoy them at dinner with this meal-in-one. Everything cooks in the same skillet, so you only dirty one pan.

1 package (8 ounces) brown-and-serve sausage links	1/2 cup chopped sweet red *or* green pepper
2 tbsp. water	1/4 cup chopped onion
2 tbsp. vegetable oil	salt and pepper to taste
3 cups frozen shredded hash brown potatoes	

1) Cut sausage links into bite-size pieces. In a covered skillet, cook sausage in water and oil over medium heat for 5 minutes.

2) Remove sausage with a slotted spoon and keep warm. Carefully add potatoes, red pepper and onion to pan. Cover and cook for 5 minutes. Uncover; cook 5-6 minutes longer or until potatoes are tender. Return sausage to pan; heat through.

nutritional facts: *Per serving: 337 calories • 13g carbohydrates • 9g protein • 29g fat • 549mg sodium • 35mg cholesterol • 1g fiber*

pork medallions with arugula

prep time: 8 minutes • total time: 12 minutes • serves: 4

Pork tenderloin is ideal for on-the-go cooks. Tender, tasty and ready in a flash, the pork pairs well with the arugula, prosciutto and tomatoes.

1 lb. pork tenderloin	1/3 cup balsamic vinaigrette
2 tbsp. olive oil	dressing
1/2 tsp. salt	2 medium tomatoes
1/4 tsp. pepper	4 slices prosciutto
1 medium shallot	4 cups fresh baby arugula
	16 fresh Parmesan shavings

1) Slice pork crosswise into 1/2-inch-thick medallions. Place medallions between 2 sheets of waxed paper; pound lightly with meat mallet to 1/4-inch thickness.

2) In large, nonstick skillet over high, heat oil. Add pork and cook until golden on first side, about 4 min. Turn and cook until golden on second side, about 4 min. Remove from skillet; sprinkle with salt and pepper. Cover and keep warm.

3) Chop shallot to yield 1/3 cup. In same skillet over medium, add shallot and cook, stirring until softened, about 3 min. Stir in balsamic vinaigrette. Remove from heat.

4) Cut tomatoes into 1/4-in. slices. Cut prosciutto slices into quarters. Place 1 cup arugula on each of 4 serving plates. Arrange prosciutto, tomato slices, pork medallions and Parmesan on arugula. Spoon warm vinaigrette over each plate.

nutritional facts: *Per serving: 340 calories • 11g carbohydrates • 35g protein • 17g fat • 1250mg sodium • 95mg cholesterol • 1g fiber • 8g sugar*

cinnamon butter

Combine 1/4 cup softened butter with 4 tsp. brown sugar and 3 tsp. cinnamon. Shape into a log; wrap in waxed paper and freeze 10 minutes. Serve with hot dinner rolls.

boss-worthy roasted pork loin

prep time: 25 minutes • total time: 1-1/2 hours • serves: 10

This tasty pork loin, complete with a side dish of roasted vegetables, will impress guests.

14 sprigs fresh thyme, *divided*	1 (1 lb.) pkg. frozen pearl onions
4 cloves garlic	2 tbsp. olive oil
1 tsp. salt, *divided*	1/4 tsp. pepper
1/4 cup Dijon-style mustard	1 (3 lb.) boneless pork loin roast,
1 large fennel bulb	tied
1 large red onion	3 tbsp. dry plain bread crumbs
1-1/2 lbs. fingerling potatoes	

1) Preheat oven to 425°F. Strip leaves from 10 sprigs thyme to yield 1 tbsp.; place in mini processor. Add garlic and 1/4 tsp. salt; process until finely chopped. Pulse in mustard until combined.

2) Trim fennel. Slice fennel and red onion into 1/2-inch thick wedges, leaving attached at root end. Place in 15- x 11-inch roasting pan. Halve potatoes crosswise if large; add to pan. Add frozen onions, olive oil, pepper, 4 sprigs thyme and remaining salt; toss to combined. Bake 10 min.

3) Meanwhile, trim all visible fat from roast. Brush top and sides of pork with mustard mixture. Sprinkle on bread crumbs to coat. Place pork on vegetables in center of roasting pan. Bake until instant-read thermometer inserted into the center reads 160°F, about 50-60 min., stirring vegetables halfway during cook time.

4) Transfer roast to board; cover with foil and let stand, 15 min. Slice meat and serve with vegetables and pan juices.

nutritional facts: *Per serving: 310 calories • 10g carbohydrates • 34g protein • 14g fat • 480mg sodium • 90mg cholesterol • 2g fiber • 1g sugar*

simple stuffing

A side dish of classic moist stuffing makes a nice addition to this meal. Season your favorite stuffing mix with Italian sausage, mushrooms and celery.

tips for pork, ham & more

cooking time

If the pork chops you're cooking aren't as thick as what was called for in the recipe, go ahead and use them anyway. Just remember to adjust the cooking time. Thinner chops will cook more quickly and thicker chops will take longer.

carving a ham with a bone

1) Place ham fat side up on a carving board. Using a meat form to anchor the ham, make a horizontal cut with a carving knife from the one side of the ham to the bone. Position the cut in about the middle of the ham along  the natural break between the muscles. Make a second cut from the top of the ham to the first cut. Remove the large meaty area of the ham from the bone. Remove the two remaining large meaty sections in the same manner. The meat left on the ham bone may be used for soup or picked off and used in salads or casseroles.

2) Place the meaty piece of ham cut side down on a cutting board. Cut the ham into slices.

about prosciutto

Prosciutto is a thinly sliced Italian-style ham that is salt-cured and air-dried for 10 to 24 months. It is not smoked.

how much to purchase

The cut of pork and ham and the amount of bone in that cut will influence the weight you'll need to buy per serving. Here's a guideline to help you determine the right amount:

- One pound of bone-in roasts, chops or ham yields 2-1/2 to 3 servings.

- One pound of boneless roasts, chops or ham yields 3 to 4 servings.

- One pound of spareribs yields 1-1/4 servings.

super easy italian pork chops

For a fast weeknight dinner, pan-fry some pork chops (boneless or bone-in), then pour a can of Italian diced tomatoes or stewed tomatoes or over them and place slices of provolone cheese on top. You can then either cover the skillet until the cheese melts or, if it's an ovenproof skillet, place it in the oven to melt the cheese. Serve with pasta or noodles and a vegetable of your choice.

cooking pork tenderloins

Many recipes for pork tenderloin say to cook it for a specific length of time per pound. When cooking two 1-pound tenderloins side by side, you would not consider them as one 2-pound roast. Use the roasting time for a 1-pound tenderloin. As long as there is a little space between them in the roasting pan, it doesn't matter if you roast one, two or three tenderloins at the same time.

don't overcook!

Fresh pork cooks quickly and needs only to be cooked to an internal temperature of 160°F. This means a roast should be removed from the oven around 155°F. Tent the roast with foil and let stand for 10 to 15 min. before carving. The temperature should rise to 160°F. during the stand time. If you cook to higher temperatures the pork will be dry and overcooked.

make a fast supper with leftover tenderloin

Leftover cooked pork tenderloin can be turned to a quick and tasty supper. First cut the meat into 1/4-inch-thick slices, then dip them in your favorite barbecue sauce. Coat in a mixture of equal parts flour, bread crumbs and grated Parmesan cheese. Finally fry them in olive oil until they're crispy and heated through. Add a salad and some beans or broccoli and you have a family pleasing dinner.

uses for leftover ham

After serving a large ham, you probably have some leftovers. Cube the meat and toss some into scrambled eggs, bean soup or macaroni and cheese. Ham slices can be heated with barbecue sauce and served on buns for a hearty sandwich.

maple ham slices

A ham slice takes just minutes to heat in a skillet and is perfect for a busy weeknight meal. Add a special touch by pouring a few teaspoons of maple syrup over the ham slices when they're almost done frying. Turn the slices several times so the syrup glazes the meat. The syrup gives the ham a rich flavor. This is great paired with sweet potatoes.

simple ham salad

Another fabulous way to use up little pieces of ham is to make them into ham salad. Finely chop the meat and add mayonnaise, pickle relish, onion if you'd like, and salt and pepper to taste. This ham salad is good in sandwiches or spread on crackers.

give baked ham a flavor boost

A little soda can do wonders for a baked ham. Recommendations are to pour a can of ginger ale, cola or even root beer over the ham before baking. This helps keep the ham moist and adds a touch of flavor to the juices.

making a pocket in a pork chop

Use a sharp knife to cut a pocket in a pork chop. Make a horizontal slit in the middle of the chop by slicing from the edge almost to the bone.

butt or shank

Bone-in half hams are usually labeled butt or shank. The butt half is more rounded and is from the rump area. It is generally more expensive than the shank end since it has more meat and less bone. The shank is lower on the leg and has a narrow end.

meatless & seafood in a snap

pasta puttanesca • p. 136

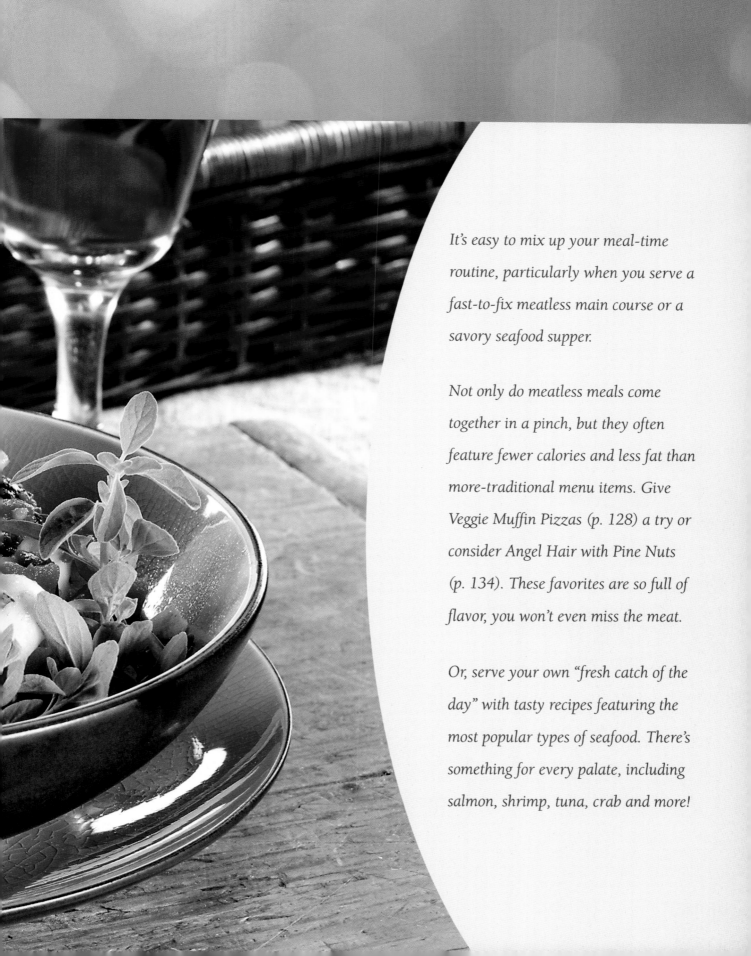

It's easy to mix up your meal-time routine, particularly when you serve a fast-to-fix meatless main course or a savory seafood supper.

Not only do meatless meals come together in a pinch, but they often feature fewer calories and less fat than more-traditional menu items. Give Veggie Muffin Pizzas (p. 128) a try or consider Angel Hair with Pine Nuts (p. 134). These favorites are so full of flavor, you won't even miss the meat.

Or, serve your own "fresh catch of the day" with tasty recipes featuring the most popular types of seafood. There's something for every palate, including salmon, shrimp, tuna, crab and more!

bacon-wrapped maple scallops

prep time: 15 minutes • total time: 27 minutes • serves: 4

Tender, succulent scallops, especially those wrapped in bacon, are a seaside treat. Make them an at-home favorite, too, by preparing them with this simple glaze of maple syrup and honey mustard.

8 pieces thick-sliced bacon (1/2 lb.)	1/3 cup honey mustard
16 sea scallops (about 1-1/4 lbs.)	2 tbsp. maple syrup
	1 lemon

1) Preheat oven to 425°F. Line jelly-roll pan with foil or parchment paper. Place several layers of paper towels on large plate. Place bacon on top and microwave on HIGH until partially cooked, about 3 min. When cool enough to handle, snip slices in half crosswise.

2) In small bowl, combine honey mustard and maple syrup.

3) Rinse scallops and pat dry. Remove small tough muscle on side and discard. Brush each piece of bacon with mustard mixture. Wrap one piece around each scallop and secure with toothpick. Place on prepared baking sheet. Brush top and sides with remaining mustard.

4) Bake until the scallops are opaque, 10-12 min. Cut lemon into 4 wedges. Place 4 scallops on each plate. Garnish with lemon wedge.

nutritional facts: *Per serving: 340 calories • 19g carbohydrates • 16g protein • 22g fat • 640mg sodium • 50mg cholesterol • 1g fiber • 13g sugar*

scallop scam

Some packages of less expensive fish resemble scallops, so be sure to read the label carefully. Or buy your scallops at a reputable fish market.

perfect pasta primavera

prep time: 15 minutes • total time: 25 minutes • serves: 4

Pasta primavera is an Italian specialty which means "spring style." The name is appropriate given to the abundance of vegetables, including asparagus, fresh peas and green onions, found in this garden-fresh dish.

8 oz. shaped pasta, such as penne *or* rotelli	3 tbsp. butter
1/2 cup frozen peas	2/3 cup milk
1 bunch green onions	4 oz. cream cheese, cut into chunks
1/4 lb. asparagus	1/2 cup grated Parmesan cheese
4 cloves garlic, slivered	1/2 cup torn fresh basil leaves, well-packed
1 yellow, red *or* green bell pepper	1/4 tsp. salt
1 cup grape tomatoes (about 20)	1/8 tsp. pepper

1) In large pot over high heat, cook pasta according to package directions. Just before removing pot from heat, stir peas into boiling pasta water. Drain.

2) Meanwhile, cut green onions and asparagus into 2-inch pieces. Thinly slice garlic and bell pepper. Cut tomatoes in half.

3) In large skillet over medium heat, melt butter. Add bell pepper and cook 3 min. Add garlic, green onions and asparagus; cook, stirring frequently, until vegetables are just tender, about 5 min.

4) Add milk and cream cheese; stir over low heat until cream cheese is melted. Stir in grated Parmesan, tomatoes, basil, salt and pepper.

5) Toss pasta with vegetable sauce. Serve immediately.

nutritional facts: *Per serving: 500 calories • 55g carbohydrates • 18g protein • 23g fat • 490mg sodium • 65mg cholesterol • 5g fiber • 9g sugar*

pretty spears

Blanch asparagus to retain its bright, spring-green color. Here's how: simmer for 3 minutes in water. Drain; immediately transfer to a bowl filled with water and ice; soak for 2 minutes. Drain and add to the skillet.

grilled steak and shrimp

prep time: 18 minutes • total time: 2-1/4 hours • serves: 6

This surf-and-turf infuses the beef and shrimp with a wine-based marinade that tastes great hot off the grill. It's perfect for warm-weather entertaining.

3 lbs. beef loin rump steak	1 tsp. Worcestershire sauce
12 jumbo shrimp	2 lemons
1 cup red wine	2 tbsp. dried parsley, *divided*
1 cup olive oil, *divided*	1 cup dry white wine
2 cloves garlic	2 green onions
2 tsp. oregano	

1) Cut beef loin into 6 pieces. Crush 1 garlic clove. Into small bowl, squeeze juice of 1 lemon. Add red wine, 1/2 cup olive oil, crushed garlic, oregano, Worcestershire and 1 tbsp. parsley. Place steaks in large, zippered plastic bag. Pour in marinade; seal and refrigerate 2 hours.

2) Crush remaining garlic. Trim and chop green onions. Squeeze juice of remaining lemon into small bowl. Add garlic, onions, remaining olive oil, parsley and white wine. Place shrimp in large, zippered plastic bag. Pour in marinade; seal and refrigerate for 30 minutes.

3) Preheat grill or grill pan. Remove steaks from plastic bag; discard remaining marinade. Place steaks on grill and cook until browned on first side, about 5 min. Turn and cook until desired doneness, 5-8 min. Remove steaks to platter and keep warm.

4) With tongs holding wadded paper towels, wipe grill grate. Remove shrimp from plastic bag and discard remaining marinade. Place shrimp on grill and cook just until pink, 1 min. Turn and cook until done, 1 min. Add to beef platter; serve immediately.

nutritional facts: *Per serving: 570 calories • 2g carbohydrates • 71g protein • 27g fat • 180mg sodium • 225mg cholesterol • 0g fiber • 0g sugar*

savory skewers

If you can find a piece of sugar cane, slice it into thin spears and use them as skewers for the shrimp. Or try using stalks of fresh rosemary.

halibut provencal

prep time: 6 minutes • total time: 28 minutes • serves: 4

This wonderfully simple dish is a great way to serve seafood—even to those who turn up their noses at fish. Tomatoes and olives form the base for a hearty sauce that complements this meaty fish.

1 (14.5 oz.) can diced tomatoes	2 tsp. herbs de Provence
1/4 cup sliced black olives	1-1/2 tsp. chopped garlic in oil
2 tbsp. olive oil, *divided*	1 lb. halibut
2 tbsp. white wine	1/4 tsp. salt
1 tbsp. capers	1/8 tsp. pepper

1) Preheat oven to 425°F. In glass or other nonreactive 9- x 9-inch pan, combine tomatoes, olives, 1 tbsp. oil, wine, capers, herbs de Provence and garlic.

2) Cut halibut into four equal pieces. Place halibut on top of sauce in pan. Pour remaining oil over halibut, then rub to coat completely. Sprinkle lightly with salt and pepper.

3) Bake until fish flakes when pressed with fork, about 20 min. Remove fish to serving platter, carefully peeling away and discarding any black skin. Spoon sauce over fish and serve.

nutritional facts: *Per serving: 230 calories • 6g carbohydrates • 25g protein • 1.5g fat • 630mg sodium • 35mg cholesterol • 2g fiber • 3g sugar*

keep it cold

Try to buy fish the day you'll be using it. When storing raw fish in the refrigerator, place the fish in a plastic container; set a bag of ice over the fish to keep it very cold.

colorful additions

For even more color, substitute a sweet white Vidalia onion for the red one and add some bright green, fresh basil.

grilled garden sandwiches

prep time: 10 minutes • total time: 29 minutes • serves: 4

This sandwich takes full advantage of late summer's bountiful harvest of fresh zucchini, eggplant and red onions. But it's just as delicious in winter with veggies from the produce section.

1 medium red onion	1/4 tsp. pepper
1 tsp. water	8 thick slices Italian bread, cut from a round loaf (about 1 oz. *each*)
1/3 cup vegetable oil	
2 tsp. garlic salt	
1 lb. eggplant	1/2 cup hummus
2 small zucchini	1 (7 oz.) jar roasted red peppers, drained and patted dry
2 tsp. dried basil	

1) Preheat grill. Meanwhile, cut red onion into 1/2-inch slices. Insert toothpick into one side of each slice to hold. Place on plate; sprinkle with 1 tsp. water. Cover and microwave on HIGH for 1-1/2 min. or until just tender.

2) In small bowl, combine oil and garlic salt. Slice eggplant into 1/2-inch slices. Cut zucchini in half crosswise, then lengthwise into 1/2-inch slices. Lightly brush one side of vegetables with oil mixture. Place on grill, oiled side down. Cook, covered, 3 min. Lightly brush with oil; turn vegetables. Cook, covered, until vegetables are crisp-tender, about 3-4 min. Remove to covered plate. Remove toothpicks from onions and separate slices into rings. Season vegetables with basil and pepper.

3) Lay bread slices on work surface. Spread each slice with 1 tbsp. hummus. On 4 slices, arrange eggplant, red peppers, red onion and zucchini. Top with remaining bread slices. Lightly brush with oil. Place on grill, oiled side down, and cook until browned, about 2 min. Brush bread with remaining oil and turn. Cook until browned, about 2 min. Cut in half and serve.

nutritional facts: *Per serving: 470 calories • 53g carbohydrates • 11g protein • 24g fat • 1430mg sodium • 0mg cholesterol • 7g fiber • 0g sugar*

cheese choices

If you don't have shredded Italian cheese blend, put chunks of whatever hard cheeses you do have in the blender. Options include Gruyere, Jarlsberg, mozzarella, Parmesan, provolone or cheddar.

veggie muffin pizzas

prep time: 8 minutes • total time: 16 minutes • serves: 4

English muffin pizzas are always good, but we've got the secret to making them great: prebake the muffins before topping them with sauce so they stay crispy and stand up to the toppings!

4 English muffins	1/2 cup low-fat jarred tomato sauce
1/2 yellow bell pepper	
1 tsp. olive oil	1/2 cup shredded Italian blend cheese *or* mozzarella
1 cup frozen chopped broccoli	
1/8 tsp. Italian seasoning	4 tsp. grated Parmesan cheese

1) Preheat oven to 425°F. Split muffins and place, cut side down, on baking sheet. Bake until crisp, 6-8 min.

2) Meanwhile, dice yellow pepper. In small nonstick skillet over medium, heat oil. Add pepper, broccoli and Italian seasoning; cook until crisp-tender, stirring occasionally, 5 min.

3) Flip muffins over and spoon 1 tbsp. sauce on each. Top with broccoli mixture. Sprinkle with shredded cheese blend and Parmesan. Bake until heated through and cheese is melted, about 8 min.

nutritional facts: *Per serving: 220 calories • 31g carbohydrates • 11g protein • 6g fat • 540mg sodium • 10mg cholesterol • 4g fiber • 5g sugar*

sassy oven-roasted red snapper

prep time: 10 minutes • total time: 22 minutes • serves: 4

Colorful, flavorful, and a "snap" to prepare, this will become one of your standby recipes. Red snapper fillets are oven-roasted with a delicious crust of sweet, hot and tangy fresh and jarred peppers.

1 lb. skin-on red snapper fillets	1/4 cup jarred sweet pickled pepper strips
1/2 tsp. salt	3/4 cup parsley leaves
1/4 tsp. pepper	3 tbsp. olive oil
3 small red, yellow *or* green peppers	1/3 cup Panko bread crumbs
4 to 8 jarred pepperoncini *or* hot cherry peppers	1 small lemon

1) Preheat oven to 450°F. Line shallow baking sheet with parchment paper. Place snapper, skin side down, on paper; season with salt and pepper.

2) Finely dice enough peppers to equal 2 cups; place in medium bowl. Finely dice pepperoncini and pickled peppers; add to bowl. Finely chop parsley and add to bowl with olive oil. Toss to combine; stir in bread crumbs. Divide mixture evenly among snapper fillets; spread to coat top.

3) Cut lemon into quarters and arrange around the fillets. Bake until the snapper is cooked through and the crust is golden, about 12 min.

nutritional facts: *Per serving: 370 calories • 28g carbohydrates • 33g protein • 13g fat • 620mg sodium • 55mg cholesterol • 4g fiber • 5g sugar*

use foil instead

Don't care for skin on fish? Use aluminum foil rather than parchment paper. The skin will stick to the foil, and you can easily slide a large spatula between the fish and its skin.

whole-wheat herbed spaghetti

prep time: 3 minutes • total time: 18 minutes • serves: 6

Today's whole wheat pasta is a delicious and healthful alternative to typical pasta. When served with a buttery herb sauce, the flavorful spaghetti makes a welcome dinner dish.

1 (1 lb.) pkg. whole wheat spaghetti	1 small bunch fresh dill, thick stems removed
4 tbsp. unsalted butter	1 bunch chives
2 tbsp. olive oil	6 tbsp. grated Asiago cheese, *divided*
2 cloves garlic, peeled	
1 (4 oz.) pkg. prewashed watercress	

1) Bring large pot of water to boil over high heat. Add spaghetti; cook until tender, 10-12 min. Drain, reserving 2 tbsp. cooking liquid and set aside. Return pasta to cooking pot.

2) Meanwhile, in small saucepan over medium-low heat, melt butter with olive oil. Thinly slice garlic cloves. Add to saucepan and cook until softened, 3-4 min. Remove from heat.

3) In food processor, pulse watercress, dill and chives until minced, about 15 seconds.

4) Add reserved cooking liquid, butter mixture and herbs to pasta in pot. Toss to combine. Transfer to 6 serving plates and top each with 1 tbsp. Asiago cheese. Serve immediately.

nutritional facts: *Per serving: 440 calories • 58g carbohydrates • 14g protein • 17g fat • 140mg sodium • 30mg cholesterol • 9g fiber • 2g sugar*

try other herbs

Dill, watercress and chives taste great. So do any fresh herbs from your garden or produce section. Try any combination of basil, parsley, oregano or green onion tops.

traditional stuffed manicotti

prep time: 50 minutes • **total time:** 1-1/2 hours • **serves:** 9

Manicotti is a perfect make-ahead dish for a crowd and for any occasion. The rich, creamy filled pasta and homemade tomato sauce make this a meal to remember.

18	manicotti noodles (two 8 oz. pkgs. with leftovers)	1	(32 oz.) pkg. part-skim ricotta cheese
1	tsp. salt	2	large eggs
3	cloves garlic	2	(8 oz.) pkgs shredded 4-cheese Italian blend, *divided*
1/3	cup olive oil		
2	(28 oz.) cans peeled whole tomatoes, undrained	2	tbsp. packed fresh parsley leaves, finely chopped
1/3	cup packed fresh basil leaves		

1) Bring large pot of water to boil over high heat. Add salt and manicotti; cook until al dente, 7 min. Rinse under cold water; drain and set aside.

2) Meanwhile, peel and thinly slice garlic. In large pot over medium-low, heat oil. Add garlic and cook until fragrant, 1-2 min. Add tomatoes, chopping large pieces into chunks with fork. Roughly chop basil leaves; stir into sauce. Simmer 30 min.

3) In medium bowl, stir together ricotta, eggs, 3 cups shredded cheese and parsley.

4) Preheat oven to 350°F. Spoon 1 cup tomato sauce evenly onto bottom of two 13- x 9-inch baking dishes.

5) Spoon cheese mixture into large zippered bag; close. Snip off small corner with scissors. Insert tip of bag into end of each noodle; press gently to fill. Place 9 noodles in each baking dish.

6) Spoon remaining sauce evenly over top; sprinkle with remaining cheese. Cover tightly with foil. Bake 30 min. Remove foil and bake 10 min.

nutritional facts: *Per serving: 610 calories • 52g carbohydrates • 34g protein • 29g fat • 790mg sodium • 115mg cholesterol • 3g fiber • 7g sugar*

remove seeds

If you don't want the tomato seeds in this dish, just coarsely chop the whole tomatoes and strain with a sieve or a food mill. Discard the seeds.

sportsman's trout fillets

prep time: 8 minutes • **total time:** 15 minutes • **serves:** 4

Tasty trout fillets will broil in only 5 short minutes, so make sure everyone's ready to eat when you begin! A savory lemon-soy butter tops it off beautifully.

4	boneless, brook trout fillets (about 6 oz. *each*)	1	large lemon
4	tbsp. unsalted butter	1/4	tsp. pepper
2	tsp. soy sauce	1/2	tsp. sweet paprika, *divided*

1) Adjust broiler rack to be 4-5 inches below element; preheat broiler. Line large baking pan with aluminum foil, lightly coat with cooking spray.

2) In small saucepan over low heat, melt butter. Stir in soy sauce. Cut lemon in half lengthwise and squeeze juice of 1/2 lemon into pan. Cut remaining half into 4 wedges; set aside.

3) Place fillets on prepared pan in single layer. Brush about 1 tbsp. melted butter sauce over each fillet. Sprinkle each evenly with pepper and paprika.

4) Broil until cooked through, about 4-5 min. Transfer to serving plates, garnish each with lemon wedge and serve.

nutritional facts: *Per serving: 360 calories • 1g carbohydrates • 36g protein • 23g fat • 240mg sodium • 130mg cholesterol • 0g fiber • 0g sugar*

coat with butter

Instead of coating the aluminum foil with cooking spray, brush it with some of the lemon-soy butter to add flavor to the bottom side of the fish.

'bama pan-fried catfish

prep time: 10 minutes • total time: 25 minutes • serves: 4

A favorite throughout Mississippi, Alabama and Louisiana, this sauteed catfish uses a generous measure of lemon, garlic, shallots and plenty of Cajun seasoning to flavor the white-fleshed fish.

1/2 small red bell pepper	2 tbsp. unsalted butter
1/2 small green pepper	4 catfish fillets (4 oz. *each*,
1 large clove garlic	about 1 lb. total)
1 large shallot	2-1/2 tsp. Cajun seasoning
1 lemon	

1) Slice peppers, garlic and shallot. Slice half of lemon into wedges. Juice remaining lemon half to yield 1-1/2 tsp.

2) In small glass bowl, melt butter in microwave on HIGH, 30 seconds. Stir in lemon juice. Place fillets onto baking sheet. Brush both sides of each fillet with butter mixture and sprinkle with Cajun seasoning.

3) Heat large skillet over high. Place fillets in skillet along with any butter and seasonings that may remain on pan. Cook until golden brown on first side, about 5 min. Turn and cook until desired doneness, about 4 min. Remove to platter and keep warm.

4) Add the peppers, shallot and garlic to skillet. Cook and stir until the vegetables are soft, about 5 min. Spoon the vegetables over fillets. Garnish with lemon wedges and serve.

nutritional facts: *Per serving: 170 calories • 4g carbohydrates • 19g protein • 9g fat • 390mg sodium • 80mg cholesterol • 0g fiber • 1g sugar*

use different fish

Any white-fleshed fish can be used in place of the catfish. But because catfish has a distinctive flavor, you may want to increase the amount of seasonings.

veggie ranch wraps

prep time: 15 minutes • total time: 15 minutes • serves: 4

These fun, take-along wraps are a great way to incorporate more vegetables into your diet. Crunchy vegetables are the perfect complement to the soft wrap.

4 spinach wraps	1 small cucumber, peeled and
4 tbsp. reduced-fat mayonnaise	sliced into thin 2-inch long
1 ripe avocado, peeled and	matchsticks
thinly sliced	1 bunch watercress, tough
2 cups shredded carrots	stems removed
1 small green bell pepper,	1/2 cup fat-free ranch dressing
seeded and thinly sliced	
1 small tomato, thinly sliced	
into rounds	

1) Working one at a time, place wrap on top of large piece of plastic wrap.

2) Spread one tbsp. mayonnaise over top. Lay avocado slices horizontally across bottom third of wrap.

3) Top with 1/2 cup shredded carrots and one quarter each of the green pepper slices, tomato slices and cucumber matchsticks. Lay several watercress leaves on top.

4) Drizzle 2 tbsp. ranch dressing over all. Roll wrap tightly from veggie-covered bottom end, pressing firmly. Wrap tightly in plastic wrap to maintain shape until serving time. Repeat with remaining three wraps. Unwrap, cut in half and serve.

nutritional facts: *Per serving: 390 calories • 43g carbohydrates • 7g protein • 23g fat • 640mg sodium • 10mg cholesterol • 5g fiber • 7g sugar*

try other tortillas

If you have fussy eaters at your table, you might prefer to buy plain wraps or tortillas, which have a milder flavor and lighter color than the spinach variety.

fluffy harvest omelet

prep time: 35 min. • total time: 50 min. • serves: 4

With its mushrooms, zucchini and tomato sauce, this hearty omelet isn't just for breakfast. Your family will savor it as a change-of-pace dinner as well.

6 eggs, *separated*	1 (15 oz.) can chunky Italian tomato sauce
1/4 teaspoon salt	
1/4 cup half-and-half cream	1 cup cubed fresh zucchini
1/4 cup grated Parmesan cheese	3/4 cup sliced fresh mushrooms
1/4 teaspoon pepper	1 cup shredded mozzarella cheese
2 tablespoons butter	

1) In a large mixing bowl, beat egg whites until soft peaks form. Add salt; continue beating until stiff peaks form. In a small mixing bowl, beat the egg yolks, cream, Parmesan cheese and pepper until foamy. Gently fold into egg whites.

2) Melt butter in a 10-in. ovenproof skillet; pour egg mixture into skillet; cover and cook over medium-low heat for 8-10 minutes or until eggs are nearly set.

3) Uncover; bake in a 350°F. oven for 5-8 minutes or until top is golden brown and eggs are set. Meanwhile, in a small saucepan, combine the tomato sauce, zucchini and mushrooms. Cook, uncovered, for 10 minutes or until zucchini is tender.

4) Sprinkle mozzarella cheese over omelet; fold in half and top with tomato sauce. Cut into wedges. Serve immediately.

nutritional facts: *Per serving: 311 calories • 11g carbohydrates • 21g protein • 21g fat • 1091 mg sodium • 362mg cholesterol • 2g fiber*

simple swap

If a baked dish calls for half-and-half, you can replace it with 4-1/2 teaspoons melted butter plus enough whole milk to equal 1 cup.

aegean tuna pitas

prep time: 20 minutes • total time: 20 minutes • serves: 8

You won't miss the mayo in these healthy tuna pitas that are inspired by the unforgettable flavors of the Greek Isles. A savory mixture of shallots, capers, celery, parsley and tomatoes adds to the zip.

2 (6 oz.) cans tuna packed in olive oil	2 to 3 sprigs fresh parsley
	2 tbsp. small capers
1 large lemon	1/2 tsp. salt
2 medium tomatoes	1/4 tsp. pepper
1 stalk celery	16 lettuce leaves
1 shallot	8 small (4-inch diameter) pitas

1) Drain and discard oil from 1 can of tuna. Transfer tuna to large bowl. Add second can of tuna, including oil, to bowl.

2) Grate lemon to yield 1 tbsp. zest; set aside. Squeeze lemon to yield 3 tbsp. juice. Sprinkle lemon juice over tuna. With fork, flake tuna into small pieces.

3) Seed and dice tomatoes. Finely chop celery; mince shallot to yield 2 tbsp. Finely chop parsley to yield 3 tbsp. Add tomatoes, celery, shallot, parsley, capers, lemon zest, salt and pepper to tuna mixture. Toss gently with wooden spoon to combine.

4) Cut pita breads crosswise in half. Line each half with lettuce leaf; stuff with heaping spoonful of tuna mixture. Serve immediately.

nutritional facts: *Per serving: 180 calories • 19g carbohydrates • 14g protein • 5g fat • 540mg sodium • 20mg cholesterol • 2g fiber • 2g sugar*

pitas on hand

Fresh, pita breads are a real taste treat. But the packaged ones can be easily frozen and come in handy for toast, pizzas, chips and these sandwiches.

citrus-fennel-topped tilapia

prep time: 15 minutes • total time: 25 minutes • serves: 4

Tilapia is a very mild white fish, and most folks, including kids, love its delicate flavor. When served broiled with a seasoned oil and topped with a citrus salsa, it's truly a special dish.

1 large navel orange	1/2 fennel bulb
1-1/4 tsp. Chesapeake-style seafood seasoning, *divided*	1/2 pink grapefruit
	1 green onion
2 tbsp. olive oil, *divided*	3 tarragon sprigs
4 (6 oz.) tilapia fillets	2 tsp. honey
1/2 red bell pepper	1/4 tsp. salt

1) Line rimmed baking sheet with foil. Adjust broiler rack to 5 inches below element; preheat broiler. Grate 1 tsp. rind from orange; place in small dish. Stir in 1 tsp. seafood seasoning and 1 tbsp. olive oil. Arrange fish on prepared baking sheet. Brush with oil mixture.

2) Core and thinly slice pepper and fennel; cut into 1/2-inch pieces. Place in medium microwave-safe bowl. Microwave, covered, on HIGH until tender-crisp, 2 min. Uncover; set aside to cool.

3) Place fish under broiler and cook until fish is opaque and flakes easily with fork, about 8 min.

4) Meanwhile, trim peel from orange and grapefruit; cut flesh into 1/2-inch pieces. Slice green onion; chop tarragon to yield 1 tbsp. Add honey, salt, orange, grapefruit, green onion, tarragon and remaining oil and seasoning to bowl with red pepper and fennel. Gently toss to combine.

5) Remove fish from broiler and transfer to individual plates. Top with citrus mixture and serve immediately.

nutritional facts: *Per serving: 280 calories • 13g carbohydrates • 35g protein • 10g fat • 440mg sodium • 85mg cholesterol • 2g fiber • 7g sugar*

look at the label

Check the nutrition label on the seafood seasoning. If the sodium count is higher than you prefer, simply omit the salt in the recipe and let each diner season to taste.

well-dressed crispy catfish

prep time: 10 minutes • total time: 22 minutes • serves: 4

An old Southern favorite gets a modern twist when it's oven-baked in a crunchy, spicy pecan crust. The catfish is dressed up even further with a dollop of butter flavored with orange and honey.

1/3 cup Panko bread crumbs	1/2 cup milk
1/2 tsp. paprika	1 tbsp. plus 2 tsp. honey, *divided*
1/2 tsp. salt	
1/4 tsp. cayenne pepper	4 catfish fillets (about 6 oz. *each*)
1/2 cup finely chopped pecans, *divided*	1 small orange
	3 tbsp. softened butter

1) Preheat oven to 425°F. Line large, shallow baking sheet with foil and coat with cooking spray.

2) In shallow bowl, combine Panko, paprika, salt and cayenne; stir in all but 1 tbsp. pecans. In another shallow bowl, whisk together milk and 1 tbsp. honey. Dip catfish in milk mixture; dredge in crumb mixture, patting to help crumbs adhere. Arrange fillets on baking sheet, bake until fish flakes easily, about 12 min.

3) Meanwhile, grate 2 tsp. orange rind into small bowl. Add butter, remaining honey and reserved pecans. Slice orange thinly and arrange on 4 plates. Place catfish on plates; top each with dollop of seasoned butter.

nutritional facts: *Per serving: 480 calories • 18g carbohydrates • 29g protein • 33g fat • 460mg sodium • 105mg cholesterol • 2g fiber • 11g sugar*

stir-in ideas

Does your family like things lively? Add an extra large dash of cayenne to the pecan butter. Or for something really different for adults, stir in a tablespoon of bourbon.

mussels in white wine

prep time: 22 minutes • total time: 29 minutes • serves: 8

These tasty mussels, simmered in fragrant wine and garlic, are a classic dish. It's sure to be a hit with the seafood fans in your family.

5 lbs. fresh mussels	1 tsp. crushed red pepper flakes
1 medium onion	1 tsp. coarse salt
8 cloves garlic	1/2 tsp. dried thyme
1 lemon	1-1/2 cups white wine
1 bunch fresh parsley	2 medium tomatoes
1/2 cup olive oil	

1) Scrub mussels under cold running water. With sharp knife, remove beards. Discard any opened mussels.

2) Thinly slice onion and mince garlic. Slice lemon and set aside. Chop parsley to yield 3/4 cup. In large, heavy stockpot over medium, heat oil. Add onions and garlic; cook, and stir until pale golden, about 3 min. Stir in red pepper flakes, salt, thyme, wine, lemon slices and 1/2 cup of parsley.

3) When wine mixture comes to boil, add mussels and cover pot. Cook, stirring once or twice to evenly distribute mussels, until mussel shells open, about 7 min.

4) Meanwhile, chop tomatoes. With slotted spoon, transfer mussels to large serving bowl, discarding any unopened mussels.

5) Slowly pour remaining broth from pot into small saucepan, leaving any sand or grit behind. Bring broth to boil. Pour broth over mussels. Sprinkle with remaining parsley and chopped tomatoes.

nutritional facts: *Per serving: 430 calories • 16g carbohydrates • 35g protein • 21g fat • 105mg sodium • 80mg cholesterol • 1g fiber • 2g sugar*

crusty bread

You'll want to serve this with lots of crusty bread to sop up all the garlicky goodness of the broth. A loaf of French bread is classic, but try a focaccia or a Portuguese bread, too.

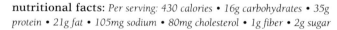

angel hair with pine nuts

prep time: 5 minutes • total time: 15 minutes • serves: 4

This delicious and easy pasta dish is perfect for those really hectic days. Keep a package of pine nuts on the shelf along with some dried herbs, and you'll have dinner on the table at a moment's notice.

1 lb. angel hair pasta	2 tbsp. dried parsley flakes
3 tbsp. butter	1 tbsp. dried basil
1/2 cup pine nuts	1/2 tsp. crushed red pepper flakes
3 tbsp. olive oil	

1) In large pot over high heat, bring 3 qts. water to boil. Add pasta and cook according to package directions.

2) Meanwhile, in small skillet over medium-high heat, melt butter; add pine nuts. Cook, stirring constantly, until golden, 2-3 min. Reduce heat to low. Add oil, parsley, basil and red pepper flakes; heat through.

3) Drain pasta, reserving 1/2 cup cooking liquid. Return pasta to pot; add sauce and reserved cooking liquid. Stir over low heat, tossing gently to coat pasta. Transfer to serving bowl and serve.

nutritional facts: *Per serving: 610 calories • 65g carbohydrates • 15g protein • 34g fat • 290mg sodium • 25mg cholesterol • 5g fiber • 3g sugar*

coarse salt

Add a teaspoon coarse salt— which has larger crystals and no additives—per quart of water after it boils. Adding it earlier makes the water take longer to boil.

red and green gruyere quiche

prep time: 22 minutes • total time: 58 minutes • serves: 6

Loaded with spinach, peppers, onion and garlic, this quiche is particularly tasty and satisfying. The Gruyere cheese adds an elegant touch.

1 (9 inch) refrigerated pie crust	1/4 cup fresh basil leaves
1 (10 oz.) box frozen chopped spinach	1 tbsp. olive oil
1/2 small onion	6 oz. Gruyere cheese
1/2 small red bell pepper	3 large eggs
3 large cloves garlic	1 cup half-and-half
	1/4 tsp. pepper

1) Preheat oven to 400°F. Place pie crust in 9-inch fluted tart pan with removable bottom, pressing it firmly against bottom and sides of pan. Fold down crust to create a 1-1/2-inch-high side. Refrigerate.

2) Place spinach in microwave-safe dish. Microwave on MEDIUM until defrosted, about 2 min. Squeeze dry and set aside.

3) Mince onion, red pepper and garlic. Chop basil. In large skillet over high, heat oil. Add onion; cook and stir until fragrant, 1 min. Add red pepper and garlic. Cook and stir, until softened, 2 min. Add the basil and spinach; stir to the separate spinach.

4) Meanwhile, grate cheese. In small bowl with wire whisk, blend together eggs, half-and-half and black pepper.

5) Sprinkle half of cheese into bottom of pie crust. Top with spinach mixture. Pour on egg mixture. Sprinkle with remaining cheese. Bake until knife inserted in center comes out clean, about 40 min. Let stand before serving, 10 min.

nutritional facts: *Per serving: 410 calories • 23g carbohydrates • 16g protein • 28g fat • 320mg sodium • 160mg cholesterol • 1g fiber • 3g sugar*

fresh side

A side dish of fruit complements this quiche. Use in-season produce or good-quality canned fruit.

passport pepper & shrimp croissants

prep time: 9 minutes • total time: 22 minutes • serves: 4

This sandwich breaks down borders! A French croissant is topped with Thai-inspired warm, sweet shrimp, accented with lime and cilantro. Talk about an international stunner!

1 lb. cleaned and deveined extra-large shrimp	8 sprigs fresh cilantro
1/2 small red bell pepper	1 lime
1 large green onion	2 tbsp. reduced-fat mayonnaise
1 tbsp. canola oil	1/8 tsp. pepper
1/4 cup frozen corn	4 medium-sized croissants

1) Remove tails from shrimp. Cut shrimp in half lengthwise. Slice red pepper into small, thin strips. Thinly slice green onion into diagonal slices.

2) In large skillet over medium, heat oil. Add shrimp, red pepper, green onion and corn. Cook and stir until shrimp is cooked through, 5 min. Meanwhile, chop cilantro. Zest lime to yield 1/2 tsp. zest. Add cilantro, zest, mayonnaise and pepper. Cook and stir until warmed through and combined, 30 seconds. Remove from heat.

3) Cut croissants in half lengthwise. Divide shrimp mixture evenly among bottoms of each croissant. Cover with croissant tops and serve.

nutritional facts: *Per serving: 430 calories • 33g carbohydrates • 28g protein • 1g fat • 650mg sodium • 215mg cholesterol • 3g fiber • 8g sugar*

sandwich filling

The filling for these sandwiches can be made in advance and chilled until serving.

savvy salmon croquettes

prep time: 18 minutes • **total time:** 29 minutes • **serves:** 4

Take this old-fashioned favorite from days gone by and smartly update it for today's tastes by serving the croquettes on a salad with your own flavorful dressing. The zip comes from red pepper flakes and lemon wedges.

1 (14.5 oz.) can salmon	1/2 cup oil
1 small onion	1/2 cup red-wine vinaigrette
1 rib celery	dressing
2 lemons	1 tsp. Dijon-style mustard
1/2 cup dry bread crumbs	1 (10 oz.) bag salad greens
1 egg	1 cup shredded carrots
1/2 tsp. salt	4 sprigs fresh dill
1/4 tsp. crushed red pepper flakes	

1) Drain and flake salmon; discard skin, dark meat and bones. Finely chop onion and celery. Zest and juice one lemon; cut remaining lemon into wedges. In medium bowl, combine salmon, onion, celery, 2 tbsp. lemon juice, bread crumbs, egg, salt and red pepper flakes.

2) In large skillet over medium-high, heat oil. Form salmon mixture into four patties, 3 inches in diameter. Cook salmon patties until first side is golden brown, about 4 min. Turn and cook second side, about 3-4 min.

3) Meanwhile, in large bowl, combine vinaigrette dressing with lemon zest, mustard and remaining lemon juice. Add salad greens and carrots to dressing; snip dill into small pieces and add to bowl. Toss gently; place greens on four plates. Top each with salmon croquette and lemon wedges.

nutritional facts: *Per serving: 520 calories • 23g carbohydrates • 27g protein • 36g fat • 1200mg sodium • 95mg cholesterol • 4g fiber • 7g sugar*

side options

These delicious croquettes can also make a traditional meal when they're served with lemony cream sauce, a side of rice and a fresh vegetable.

pasta puttanesca

prep time: 4 minutes • **total time:** 28 minutes • **serves:** 4

In this traditional dish, long-cut pasta is tossed with a chunky sauce that's so rich and flavorful you'll never even notice it's almost meat-free.

12 oz. fusilli	1/2 cup chopped sun-dried
1 large onion	tomatoes
2 tbsp. olive *or* vegetable oil	1-1/2 tbsp. capers
4 large cloves garlic, minced	2 to 3 tsp. sugar (optional)
1 cup pitted black *or* ripe green	1 tsp. dried oregano
olives, quartered	1 tsp. dried basil
2 anchovy fillets, rinsed and	1/4 tsp. dried red pepper flakes
chopped	1/2 tsp. pepper
1 (28 oz.) can crushed tomatoes	2 tbsp. chopped fresh parsley

1) In large, covered saucepan, bring 1 gallon salted water to boil. Cook fusilli according to package directions. Drain and return to saucepan.

2) Meanwhile, chop onion. In large skillet over medium heat, cook onion with oil until onion is just tender, about 6 min. Add garlic, olives and anchovies; cook until flavors combine, about 2 min. Stir in tomatoes, capers, sugar, oregano, basil, red pepper flakes and pepper. Simmer, partially covered, until sauce is slightly thickened, about 15 min.

3) Add sauce to fusilli; toss to combine. Sprinkle with fresh parsley and serve.

nutritional facts: *Per serving: 600 calories • 94g carbohydrates • 23g protein • 1g fat • 1600mg sodium • 20mg cholesterol • 8g fiber • 20g sugar*

anchovy fillets

Anchovies will "melt" when cooked, adding deep flavor without a fish flavor. So even finicky eaters won't guess they're in this pasta!

peachy french toast

prep time: 15 minutes • total time: 25 minutes • serves: 4

This festive brunch dish is quick enough to serve on a busy morning. Canned peaches are pureed with maple syrup then heated to create a sweet topping for the thick slices of French bread.

3 large eggs	8 (1-in. thick) slices French bread
1 cup milk	1 (15 oz.) can sliced peaches,
2 tsp. vanilla extract	drained
1-3/4 tsp. ground cinnamon	1/3 cup maple syrup
1/8 tsp. nutmeg	1 tbsp. butter
dash salt	confectioners' sugar (optional)

1) Preheat oven to 200°F. In medium bowl, combine eggs, milk, vanilla, cinnamon, nutmeg and salt. Arrange bread in single layer in shallow baking dish. Pour egg mixture over bread. Let stand 5 min. Turn bread over; let stand an additional 5 min.

2) Meanwhile, set wire rack on baking sheet; set aside. In blender, combine peach slices and maple syrup until smooth. Place in small saucepan and heat through.

3) Heat griddle or large skillet over medium heat. Add 1/2 tbsp. butter. Cook half French bread, until golden, about 3 min. per side. Place cooked French toast on wire rack; set in oven to keep warm. Repeat with the remaining butter and bread.

4) Pour the peach puree in a small serving pitcher. Place French toast from rack and skillet on a large platter. Dust toast with confectioners' sugar if desired; serve with the peach puree.

nutritional facts: *Per serving: 800 calories • 142g carbohydrates • 24g protein • 5g fat • 1280mg sodium • 170mg cholesterol • 8g fiber • 38g sugar*

do-ahead delight

Want extra time with your guests in the morning? Prepare the egg mixture and soak the bread; cover and refrigerate overnight. Then cook the bread in the morning.

oven-fried fish

prep time: 15 minutes • total time: 25 minutes • serves: 4

Parmesan cheese and special seasonings add Italian flair to these fillets. Not only is this recipe low in fat, it's delicious as well.

1-1/2 lbs. frozen cod *or* haddock fillets, thawed	2 tbsp. grated Parmesan cheese
2 tbsp. butter	1 tbsp. dried parsley flakes
1/2 cup crushed wheat crackers *or* dry seasoned bread crumbs	1/2 teaspoon Italian seasoning

1) Cut fish into serving-size pieces; place in a greased 13- x 9-in. baking dish. Brush with the butter. In a small bowl, combine the remaining ingredients; sprinkle over the fish.

2) Bake, uncovered, at 425° for 10-15 minutes or until fish flakes easily with a fork.

nutritional facts: *Per serving: 261 calories • 5g carbohydrates • 30g protein • 9g fat • 753mg sodium • 78 mg cholesterol • 0 fiber*

simple substitute

Out of Italian seasoning? For each teaspoon of Italian seasoning, substitute a 1/4 teaspoon each of basil, thyme, rosemary and oregano.

seafood parmesan

prep time: 22 minutes • total time: 29 minutes • serves: 6

When your seafood lovers catch the heavenly aroma of this "Newburg style" classic in the oven, they'll be lined up with their plates. You may even convert all the land-lubbers as well!

1/4 cup butter	1/2 cup, plus 2 tbsp. Parmesan cheese, *divided*
1 tsp. olive oil	4 oz. fresh mushrooms, sliced
1 tsp. minced garlic	1 (4 oz.) jar sliced pimientos, drained
1/4 cup all-purpose flour	1 lb. fresh sea scallops
3/4 tsp. Chesapeake-style seasoning	1/2 lb. medium shrimp, peeled, deveined and tails removed
1 cup seafood stock	2 tbsp. Italian bread crumbs
1 cup light cream	
1 tbsp. cocktail sauce	
1 tbsp. sherry	

1) Preheat broiler to high. In large skillet over medium-high heat, melt butter in olive oil. Add garlic; cook and stir, until fragrant, 1 min. Stir in flour and seasoning; cook and stir for 2 min.

2) Slowly add seafood stock and cream to skillet, whisking vigorously until smooth. Stir in cocktail sauce, sherry and 1/2 cup Parmesan.

3) Add mushrooms and pimientos to skillet. Cook and stir 2 min. Gently stir in scallops and shrimp. Simmer until shrimp turn pink, about 4 min.

4) Transfer mixture to medium casserole. Sprinkle bread crumbs and remaining Parmesan on top. Place under broiler until top begins to brown, about 3 min. Serve immediately.

nutritional facts: *Per serving: 300 calories • 11g carbohydrates • 20g protein • 20g fat • 630mg sodium • 125mg cholesterol • 0g fiber • 1g sugar*

melting butter

If the heat on your stovetop is difficult to regulate, a good trick is to always melt your butter in a bit of olive oil—it will almost always prevent it from scorching.

pasta with crab alfredo sauce

prep time: 15 minutes • total time: 25 minutes • serves: 6

This version of Alfredo is made with milk, butter and cheese, not cream. So you can enjoy the traditional flavor with far less fat. The addition of crabmeat adds a luxurious note to this mouth-watering main course.

1 (1 lb.) pkg. spaghetti	1 tbsp. butter
1 (8 oz.) pkg. cream cheese	1/2 tsp. garlic powder
1-1/2 cups milk	1 (6 oz.) pkg. fresh crabmeat
1-1/4 cups shredded Parmesan cheese	

1) Bring large pot of salted water to boil. Add spaghetti and cook according to package directions. Drain and set aside in large serving bowl.

2) Meanwhile, in medium saucepan over medium-low heat, combine cream cheese, milk, Parmesan, butter and garlic powder. Stir constantly until smooth and creamy but not thick.

3) Add crabmeat and cook until heated through, an additional 2 min. Pour sauce over cooked pasta. Toss gently. Serve immediately.

nutritional facts: *Per serving: 520 calories • 51g carbohydrates • 26g protein • 23g fat • 730mg sodium • 85mg cholesterol • 3g fiber • 4g sugar*

creamy sauce

With a bit of care and a few more minutes, you can make the sauce extra creamy. Allow the cream cheese to reach room temperature; then add the milk a little at a time.

linguine with no-cook sauce

prep time: 17 minutes • **total time:** 29 minutes • **serves:** 4

Of the hundreds of ways to dress pasta, this quick and easy sauce is bound to become one of the most-requested pasta toppers in your house. It's bursting with fresh-from-the-garden flavor.

1 (1 lb.) pkg. linguine	1 orange
1-1/2 tsp. salt, *divided*	2 cloves garlic
3 lbs. plum tomatoes	1/2 tsp. pepper
1 small bunch fresh basil	1/2 cup olive oil
6 to 8 sprigs flat-leaf parsley	1/2 cup grated Parmesan cheese
1 sprig fresh mint	

1) Bring large pot of water to boil over high heat. Add 1 tsp. salt and linguine; cook according to package directions.

2) Meanwhile, halve tomatoes lengthwise. Scrape out seeds with tip of small spoon; discard seeds.

3) Coarsely chop tomatoes and place in large bowl. Chop basil to yield 2/3 cup and parsley to yield 1/4 cup; add to bowl. Finely chop mint to yield 2 tbsp. Grate enough orange rind to yield 2 tsp.; add to bowl. Finely chop garlic, add to bowl with olive oil and pepper. Stir to combine.

4) When pasta is done, drain well and transfer to large serving bowl. Top with tomato mixture and sprinkle with Parmesan.

nutritional facts: *Per serving: 790 calories • 104g carbohydrates • 23g protein • 33g fat • 470mg sodium • 10mg cholesterol • 9g fiber • 17g sugar*

additional ideas

Toss on a few bocconcini (little mozzarella balls) or small cubes of mozzarella for a bit of added protein. For extra flavor and texture, consider adding a tablespoon of pine nuts.

mexican shrimp cakes

prep time: 18 minutes • **total time:** 23 minutes • **serves:** 4

These crisp, savory patties are a fun, south-of-the-border twist on plain crab cakes. Packed with shrimp and spicy jalapenos, they're unusual, delicious and perfect for a quick supper.

1 lime	3 tbsp. canned diced green chiles
8 sprigs cilantro	
2 tbsp. sliced pickled jalapenos	1 egg white
1 green onion	3 tbsp. plus 1/2 cup dry bread crumbs
1/3 cup reduced-fat mayonnaise	
1 lb. peeled and deveined raw shrimp (tails off)	1 tsp. olive oil

1) Grate 1 tsp. rind from lime; cut lime into wedges. Chop cilantro to yield 1/4 cup; chop jalapenos and green onion. In small bowl, stir together mayonnaise, 1 tbsp. cilantro, 2 tsp. jalapeno and 1/2 tsp. lime zest until combined. Set aside.

2) Place shrimp, green chiles, egg white, green onion, remaining jalapeno, cilantro, lime zest and 3 tbsp. of bread crumbs in food processor. Pulse about 10 times just until chopped. Do not overprocess.

3) Place remaining bread crumbs in pie plate. Shape mixture into 8 patties. Coat sides and edges in crumbs.

4) In large, nonstick skillet over medium-low, heat oil. Add patties and cook, covered, until golden on first side, 3 min. Turn and cook until opaque throughout and golden on second side, 2-3 min. Transfer to serving plates. Top with dollop of mayonnaise mixture and serve.

nutritional facts: *Per serving: 280 calories • 19g carbohydrates • 27g protein • 11g fat • 610mg sodium • 180mg cholesterol • 2g fiber • 3g sugar*

pepper pointers

If you think green chiles will give your guests enough heat, you can simply skip the jalapenos. If your crowd really favors the pickle flavor, omit the chiles instead.

asian grilled tuna burger

prep time: 20 minutes • total time: 25 minutes • serves: 4

These are not your mother's fish patties! Seasoned with fresh ginger, cilantro and toasty sesame oil, the grilled patties are served with a refreshing bell pepper and cucumber relish. Serve them on a wedge of focaccia instead of a bun.

1/2 small bunch cilantro	2 tsp. sesame oil
4 green onions	1/4 tsp. salt
2 (6 oz.) cans water-packed albacore tuna, drained	1 small cucumber
	1 red bell pepper
1 tbsp. chopped fresh ginger	1 lime
1 large egg	2 tbsp. low-sodium soy sauce
3 tbsp. dry bread crumbs	2 tsp. sugar
2 tbsp. low-fat mayonnaise	1 large focaccia

1) Adjust broiler rack to 4 inches below element; preheat broiler. Finely chop cilantro to yield 1/2 cup. Thinly slice green onions. In large bowl, combine tuna, cilantro, green onions, egg, bread crumbs, mayonnaise, ginger, sesame oil and salt; stir until blended.

2) With fingers, form mixture into 4 (4-inch) diameter patties, about 1/2-inch thick.

3) Place patties on broiler pan; broil until golden on first side, about 2-3 min. Turn and broil until golden on second side, about 2 min.

4) Meanwhile, peel and seed cucumber. Cut cucumber and red pepper into matchsticks. Squeeze lime to yield 2 tbsp. juice. In medium bowl, toss together cucumber, pepper, lime juice, soy sauce and sugar.

5) Cut focaccia into 4 sections. Place 1 burger on each focaccia and evenly top with pepper-cucumber relish. Serve immediately.

nutritional facts: *Per serving: 350 calories • 42g carbohydrates • 24g protein • 10g fat • 1160mg sodium • 85mg cholesterol • 2g fiber • 7g sugar*

vary the flavor

Canned salmon will be equally delicious and is chock-full of Omega-3 fatty acids. If you'd like, skip the ginger and substitute a few chopped capers or even some olives.

nut-crusted fried fish

prep time: 10 minutes • total time: 20 minutes • serves: 2

It's hard to believe something this tasty comes together in less than half an hour. It's the perfect dish for last-minute company or when you want something special on weeknights.

3 tbsp. dry seasoned bread crumbs	3 tbsp. all-purpose flour
	3 tbsp. milk
3 tbsp. finely chopped pecans *or* pistachios	1/2 lb. fish fillets (about 1/2 inch thick)
1/4 tsp. salt	2 tbsp. vegetable oil
Dash pepper	

1) In a shallow bowl, combine the bread crumbs, pecans or pistachios, salt and pepper. Place the flour in a shallow bowl and the milk in another bowl. Cut fish fillets into serving-size pieces if necessary. Dredge fish in flour, dip in milk, then coat with the crumb mixture.

2) Heat oil in a nonstick skillet over medium heat. Fry the fish for 4-5 minutes on each side or until it flakes easily with a fork.

nutritional facts: *Per serving: 451 calories • 19g carbohydrates • 27g protein • 30g fat • 527mg sodium • 73mg cholesterol • 2g fiber*

the dish on dash

A dash is a very small amount of seasoning added with a quick downward stroke of the hand.

baked salmon with crumb topping

prep time: 10 minutes • total time: 30 minutes • serves: 8

Here's an elegant entree that comes together in no time. A generous topping of bread crumbs, almonds, green onion and seasonings gives moist salmon a tasty treatment.

1 cup soft whole wheat bread crumbs	1-1/2 tsp. minced fresh thyme *or* 1/2 tsp. dried thyme
1/3 cup sliced almonds, coarsely chopped	1/2 tsp. salt
1 tbsp. finely chopped green onion	1/8 tsp. pepper
	2 tbsp. butter, melted
	1 salmon fillet (2 pounds)

1) In a bowl, combine the bread crumbs, almonds, onion, thyme, salt and pepper; mix well. Add butter and toss lightly; set aside.

2) Pat salmon dry. Place skin side down in a 15 x 1-in. baking pan coated with cooking spray. Spritz salmon with cooking spray; cover with crumb mixture. Bake, uncovered, at 350° for 20-25 minutes or until fish flakes easily with a fork.

nutritional facts: *Per serving: 273 calories • 4g carbohydrates • 24g protein • 17g fat • 276mg sodium • 75mg cholesterol • 1g fiber*

on the side

Serve the salmon with a no-fuss side dish of steamed green beans lightly seasoned with rosemary.

chesapeake seafood omelet

prep time: 10 minutes • total time: 15 minutes • serves: 4

If you think omelets are just for breakfast—think again! This elegant, meatless entree can take center stage at a brunch buffet or be a welcome change-of-pace for your supper table.

1 (6 oz.) can canned lump crab meat, drained	1/4 tsp. salt
1 (4 oz.) can baby shrimp, drained	1/4 tsp. dried thyme
8 large eggs	1 tbsp. butter
4 green onions, thinly sliced	1 tbsp. oil
1/2 tsp. Chesapeake-style seafood seasoning	2 slices Swiss cheese

1) Drain crab and shrimp; pat dry with paper towels. Set aside.

2) In large bowl, combine eggs, green onions, Chesapeake-style seasoning, salt and thyme. Heat 12-inch nonstick skillet over medium-high heat. Add butter and oil; tilt pan to coat.

3) Add egg mixture to skillet. Using heat-resistant plastic spatula, push back eggs around rim as they set. Tilt skillet and let uncooked egg mixture run onto empty portion of skillet. Continue until omelet is still moist but evenly cooked, about 3 min.

4) Reduce heat to medium-low. Lay cheese over half of omelet; sprinkle with crab and shrimp. Using two flat spatulas, carefully fold omelet's plain half over filled half. Let stand 2 min. to melt cheese.

5) Slide omelet onto cutting board. Cut into 4 pieces and serve immediately.

nutritional facts: *Per serving: 330 calories • 3g carbohydrates • 31g protein • 21g fat • 660mg sodium •525mg cholesterol • 0g fiber • 1g sugar*

custom omelets

If you feed folks who are fussy about fish, set up the ingredients like a buffet and make each person an individualized omelet, incorporating just their favorites.

shrimp count

Shrimp are classified and sold by size. Shrimp count indicates the number of shrimp of a certain size that are in a pound. The more shrimp it takes to make a pound, the smaller they are. The terms used to describe shrimp are not consistent from store to store. For example, a 16-20 count may be extra jumbo in one market and extra large in another. The count is the best indication of size.

SHRIMP SIZE / NAME	COUNT
COLOSSAL	10 to 15
EXTRA JUMBO	16 to 20
JUMBO	21 to 25
EXTRA LARGE	26 to 30
LARGE	31 to 35
MEDIUM LARGE	36 to 42
MEDIUM	43 to 50
SMALL	51 to 60

peeling and deveining shrimp

1) Start on the underside by the head area to remove the shell from the shrimp. Pull legs and first section of shell to one side. Continue pulling the sup up around the top to the other side. Pull off the shell by tail if desired.

2) To remove the black vein running down the back of the shrimp, make a shallow slit with a paring knife along the back from the head area to tail.

3) Rinse the shrimp under cold water to remove the vein.

cutting cholesterol

Egg substitute is a convenient way to cut back on some of the cholesterol in many types of egg dishes. This product is available in cartons and can be found in the refrigerated and frozen food section of the supermarket. Egg substitute uses egg whites and contains no cholesterol and little or no fat. One-fourth cup of egg substitute is equal to one egg. When experimenting with egg substitute for your breakfast fare, try replacing half of the eggs called for in the recipe with an appropriate amount of egg substitute.

about mussels

Mussels should be tightly closed or, if slightly opened, should close when tapped. Don't purchase mussels that remain open when tapped or have cracked shells. Buy 3/4 to 1 pound of mussels per person. Discard any mussels that do not open after cooking.

dill butter for fish

Dill butter makes a delicious accompaniment to grilled, broiled or sauteed fish. To make, combine minced fresh dill with a half a cup softened butter. Chill for at least 2 hours to blend flavors.

purchasing fish

Buy fresh fish fillets or steaks that have firm, elastic and moist-looking flesh. The skin should be shiny and bright. Fresh fish should have a mild smell. Avoid fish with a strong fish odor, bruised skin and flesh with drying edges.

about brie

Brie is a soft cheese with a rich, creamy texture. Its flavor can range from mild to pungent. Any leftover brie will make a sophisticated snack when served with melon, grapes or berries.

using part of a package of pasta

When a recipe calls for part of a package of long pasta, such as spaghetti or fettuccine, weighting the pasta on a kitchen scale is a great way to get the exact amount. To prevent the pasta from rolling off the scale, place a tall drinking glass on the scale, return the weight to zero and add the pasta to the glass. Keep the pasta in the glass until you are ready to add it to the boiling water.

grading eggs

Eggs sold in the supermarket are graded AA, A or B. The grade is printed on the carton. The higher the grade, the higher and more nicely shaped the yolk will be and the thicker the white will be, which means the white will spread less.

stuffing manicotti shells

Do you get a little frazzled when you try to fill manicotti shells with a cheese mixture? If so, try one of these methods to make quick work of stuffing the shells. If the filling is fairly smooth, place it in a pastry bag or resealable plastic bag with a large round pastry tip. Then squeeze the filling into the shell, filling halfway on one side, then turn the shell around and fill the other half. If the filling is chunky, like a meat and cheese mixture, use a rubber-tipped baby spoon. The spoon fits nicely inside the noodle, and the filling mixture doesn't stick to the spoon's rubber coating.

testing a quiche for doneness

Test quiche or other baked egg dish for doneness by inserting a knife near the center of the dish. If the knife comes out clean, the eggs are cooked.

instant flavor

For a fast and easy seafood marinade, simply set fish fillets in a resealable storage bag. Add lemon juice and salt. Marinate for 15 minutes. Discard the marinade before preparing the fish.

easy side dishes

gingered jicama and pepper stir-fry • p. 148

When it comes to rounding out dinner, nothing fits the bill like a savory side dish. Even the most basic suppertime standby gets a delicious boost when served alongside a bright and colorful accompaniment of vegetables, pasta, beans or rice. (Just take a look at the sensational dish featured at left to see what we mean!)

Your gang won't mind finishing their veggies when Mama's Spaghetti Squash (p. 154) is on the menu. Looking to shake things up a bit? Give Maui Rice (p. 156) a try. And don't forget to fill the bread basket with something unique such as the Sweet & Savory Focaccia found on page 157.

east-side potato latkes

prep time: 26 minutes • total time: 26 minutes • serves: 4

A traditional wintertime dish, these potato pancakes are irresistible. They're simply flavored with green onions quickly fried in hot oil, then served with sour cream.

1 small bunch green onions	2 Idaho baking potatoes
1/2 cup sour cream	(about 14 oz.)
1 egg	1 tbsp. all-purpose flour
1 tsp. salt	6 tbsp. vegetable oil, *divided*
1/4 tsp. pepper	

1) Preheat oven to 250°F. Line baking sheet with paper towels and place in oven.

2) Finely chop green onions. Stir 2 tbsp. of green part into sour cream; set aside. Place remaining green onions in large bowl; stir in egg, salt and pepper.

3) Peel potatoes and shred with box grater or with shredding disk of food processor. Add to bowl with flour; toss well to thoroughly combine.

4) In large nonstick skillet over medium-high, heat 4 tbsp. oil. When very hot, add 1/4 cupfuls of potato mixture, pressing down slightly to form thin cakes. Cook until golden-brown on first side, about 3 min. Turn and cook until brown, about 2 min. Transfer to lined baking sheet and keep warm in oven.

5) Add remaining oil to pan and repeat with remaining potato mixture. Serve immediately with sour cream.

nutritional facts: *Per latke: 360 calories • 22g carbohydrates • 5g protein • 28g fat • 620mg sodium • 65mg cholesterol • 2g fiber • 1g sugar*

other sauces

If you're not a fan of sour cream, you can serve these pancakes with applesauce, apple chutney or for a truly special occasion, a dollop of caviar.

vegetarian delight

prep time: 10 minutes • total time: 29 minutes • serves: 4

Even a meat-loving family will adore this lightly browned tofu side dish. It's seasoned with just a touch of soy sauce. The veggies deliver their fresh flavor with the complement of a tasty sauce and an extra protein punch!

14 oz. extra-firm tofu	1 cup sliced mushrooms
1 large zucchini	2 tbsp. soy sauce
1 medium onion	1/2 tsp. cornstarch
1 small red bell pepper	2 cups fresh bean sprouts
1/4 cup fresh cilantro leaves	1/8 tsp. pepper
2 tbsp. oil, *divided*	

1) Drain tofu, then slice into 3/4-inch squares. Place on double layer of paper towels. Pat and press gently with more paper towels to release liquid. Set aside.

2) Diagonally cut the zucchini into thin slices. Thinly slice the onion and pepper. Chop cilantro.

3) In large skillet or wok over high, heat 1 tbsp oil. Add tofu. Cook until browned on first side, about 3 min. Turn and brown second side, 3 min. Remove to plate. Add remaining oil to skillet. Add onion and mushrooms. Cook and stir 2 min. Add peppers and cook 1 min. Add zucchini; cook and stir, until it starts to soften, 2 min.

4) In small cup, combine soy sauce and cornstarch. To skillet, add bean sprouts, soy sauce mixture, pepper and cilantro. Bring to a boil, stirring to coat with soy sauce. Return tofu to skillet and stir to coat. Transfer to bowl and serve.

nutritional facts: *Per serving: 170 calories • 12g carbohydrates • 12g protein • 9g fat • 540mg sodium • 0mg cholesterol • 3g fiber • 7g sugar*

crisp tofu

For more crisp tofu, dip it in Panko or bread crumbs seasoned with Parmesan cheese before you fry it.

stewed tomatoes

prep time: 7 minutes • total time: 29 minutes • serves: 4

Looking for a great comfort food side dish that is satisfying but not fattening? Then try these sweet, fresh, Italian plum tomatoes that are gently stewed and topped with homemade croutons.

2 lbs. plum tomatoes	1/8 tsp. garlic powder
8 large leaves fresh basil	1 tbsp. sugar
2 slices white bread	1/2 tsp. salt
3 tbsp. unsalted butter, *divided*	1/4 tsp. pepper

1) Fill large pot with hot water. Cover and bring to boil over high heat. Fill large bowl with ice water; set aside. Cut shallow X into bottom of each tomato. Chop basil. Cut bread into 1/2-inch cubes.

2) In small skillet over medium, melt 1 tbsp. butter. Add bread cubes and toss to coat; spread into single layer. Cook until golden on first side, 3 min. Turn; sprinkle with garlic powder. Cook until golden on second side, 4 min. Remove from heat; set aside.

3) Place half of tomatoes in boiling water, about 2 min., Remove to ice water. Repeat with remaining tomatoes. Peel; cut into quarters.

4) Wipe saucepan dry and place over high heat. Add tomatoes, remaining butter, sugar, salt and pepper. Bring to boil. Reduce heat to medium; cook 15 min. Transfer to serving bowl; sprinkle with croutons and serve.

nutritional facts: *Per serving: 160 calories • 19g carbohydrates • 3g protein • 9g fat • 390mg sodium • 25mg cholesterol • 3g fiber • 10g sugar*

prep pointers

When fresh tomatoes aren't in season, canned tomatoes are perfect for this recipe. The croutons are the ideal use for day-old Italian or French bread, too.

thai fried rice

prep time: 23 minutes • total time: 23 minutes • serves: 4

China is not the only country that knows how to create fantastic fried rice. This Thai version is full of fresh flavors and aromatic herbs.

1-1/2 cups quick-cooking rice *or* 3 cups cold, cooked rice	1 bunch green onions
4 cloves garlic	1 cup fresh basil leaves
1 piece fresh gingerroot (1 inch)	1/2 cup cilantro leaves
1/2 small hot pepper	2 tbsp. soy sauce
1 small red bell pepper	1 tbsp. brown sugar
1 cup baby corn	2 tbsp. oil

1) If using quick-cooking rice, prepare according to package directions. Let stand for 5 min. or until water is fully absorbed. Turn out onto shallow baking sheet, place in freezer to chill, 10 min., stirring once halfway through chilling time.

2) Meanwhile, finely chop garlic, ginger, hot pepper and red pepper. Thinly slice corn and green onions; reserve green tops. Chop basil and cilantro.

3) In small bowl, blend soy sauce and brown sugar until dissolved.

4) In large skillet, heat oil; cook garlic, ginger, hot pepper and red pepper until fragrant, 1 min. Add rice, corn and white portion of green onions; cook, and stir, 2 min. Add soy sauce mixture; cook 1 min. Stir in basil, cilantro and green onion tops. Transfer to large bowl and serve immediately.

nutritional facts: *Per serving: 290 calories • 49g carbohydrates • 5g protein • 8g fat • 10mg sodium • 0mg cholesterol • 3g fiber • 5g sugar*

ingredient experiment

Consider mint in place of basil and Jasmine, red or basmati rice for the quick-cooking rice.

indian spiced eggplant

prep time: 8 minutes • total time: 29 minutes • serves: 4

This spicy eggplant dish, inspired by the wonderful and exotic flavors of India, it's fast and easy with the help of a microwave oven. The wonderful aroma in your kitchen will draw everyone to the table in a hurry.

1-1/2 lbs. eggplant (2 small)	1/4 tsp. cloves
2 tsp. coriander	2 tbsp. sugar
1 tsp. cumin	2 tbsp. red wine vinegar
1 tsp. turmeric	4 tbsp. butter
1/2 tsp. ground cinnamon	3/4 tsp. salt
1/2 tsp. cardamom	2 sprigs fresh parsley

1) Cut unpeeled eggplant into 1-inch pieces. Place in large, microwave-safe bowl and sprinkle with 2 tbsp. water. Cover; microwave on HIGH for 3 min. Let stand, covered, 3 min.

2) Meanwhile, in small bowl, combine spices. In another small bowl, combine 1 cup water, sugar and vinegar. Stir until sugar dissolves.

3) In large, heavy nonstick skillet over medium-high heat, melt butter. Add spices; cook and stir, until fragrant, about 1 min. Add eggplant; toss to coat with spice mixture. Sprinkle with salt. Add vinegar mixture; stir to combine. Cover and bring to boil; reduce heat to low. Simmer until eggplant is tender, about 6 min.

4) Uncover; lightly press eggplant down with spatula to cover bottom of pan. Return to boil; cook until liquid is evaporated, about 4 min. Meanwhile, chop parsley. Transfer eggplant to serving dish. Sprinkle with parsley and serve.

nutritional facts: *Per serving: 180 calories • 18g carbohydrates • 2g protein • 12g fat • 520mg sodium • 30mg cholesterol • 7g fiber • 10g sugar*

bread makes it better

Go Indian all the way and serve this dish with a traditional Indian flatbread. If flatbread is not available in your area, substitute a few, warmed pita breads instead.

gingered jicama and pepper stir-fry

prep time: 10 minutes • total time: 22 minutes • serves: 4

Jicama is one of the lesser-known root veggies that you'll absolutely love. Always crisp, jicama in a stir-fry adds crunch unlike anything else! Lightly seasoned with ginger, this side goes well with any main dish.

1 clove garlic	1 tbsp. oil
1 small onion	1 piece piece fresh gingerroot (1 inch)
1 small green pepper	
1 small red bell pepper	2 tbsp. soy sauce
10 oz. jicama (1/2 small)	1 tsp. toasted sesame oil

1) Mince garlic. Thinly slice onion and peppers. Peel, then cut jicama into 2-inch-long x 1/2-inch-wide strips.

2) In large skillet over medium, heat oil. Add onion; cook and stir, 1 min. Add garlic, peppers and jicama. Cook and stir 2 min.

3) Meanwhile, peel and grate ginger. Add to skillet with soy sauce. Cook and stir 2 min., until soy sauce is evaporated. Transfer to serving bowl. Sprinkle with sesame oil; toss to combine and serve.

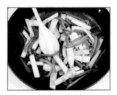

nutritional facts: *Per serving: 90 calories • 10g carbohydrates • 2g protein • 5g fat • 460mg sodium • 0mg cholesterol • 4g fiber • 3g sugar*

other add-ins

If jicama isn't readily available, drained bamboo shoots will also give this dish a good crunch. And a topping of drained, diced black olives will add some zest.

florida green beans

prep time: 12 minutes • total time: 18 minutes • serves: 4

These colorful, orange-infused green beans have a depth of flavor that pairs up very well with beef, pork, seafood or chicken. They cook up quickly and taste so great, you'll want them with almost everything you serve!

1 lb. green beans, trimmed	2 to 3 sprigs parsley
1 orange	2 tbsp. chicken broth
4 tbsp. butter	2 tbsp. orange juice
3 cloves garlic, finely chopped	concentrate, thawed
2 shallots, finely chopped	1/4 tsp. salt
2 to 3 sprigs rosemary	1/8 tsp. pepper

1) Rinse and trim beans. Bring large pot of water to boil over high heat. Add beans; cook until crisp-tender, about 3 min. Drain well.

2) Cut 2 thin slices of orange from center of fruit; set aside. Grate rind of remainder to yield 1 tbsp. zest. In large, nonstick skillet over medium heat, melt butter. Saute garlic and shallots until softened, about 2 min. Mince rosemary and parsley to yield 1 tbsp. each. Add rosemary, parsley, chicken broth and orange juice concentrate. Stir to combine.

3) Add beans to skillet. Cook until beans are heated through and liquid is thickened, about 4 min. Season with salt and pepper.

4) Transfer beans to serving platter. Garnish with orange slices and serve.

nutritional facts: *Per serving: 190 calories • 20g carbohydrates • 3g protein • 12g fat • 260mg sodium • 30mg cholesterol • 5g fiber • 8g sugar*

buy in bulk

Wholesale food markets sell large bags of trimmed, fresh green beans. Use 1 pound for this dish, keep some out for a healthy snack and slice others into salads.

lentils with orange and rosemary

prep time: 8 minutes • total time: 20 minutes • serves: 4

These fresh, creamy lentils make a tasty and healthful side dish for any meal. Fragrant with rosemary and orange, and made slightly sweet with a bit of honey, this dish is destined to become a classic in your home.

1 cup dried lentils	1 navel orange
3 celery stalks	2 tsp. honey
1 red onion	2 tsp. red wine vinegar
1 tbsp. olive oil	1 tsp. salt
1 tsp. chopped dried rosemary	1/4 tsp. pepper

1) In medium saucepan over high heat, bring 6 cups water and lentils to boil. Cook until softened, 18-20 min.

2) Meanwhile, chop celery and red onion. In nonstick skillet over medium, heat oil. Add celery, onion and rosemary. Cook until onion is softened, about 6 min.

3) Meanwhile, grate orange to yield 1 tsp. Trim pith from orange;, cut flesh into 3/4-inch pieces and set aside.

4) Drain lentils and return to pot over medium heat. Stir in orange zest, honey, vinegar, salt, pepper and celery mixture. Cook, stirring occasionally, until heated through, 3 min. Transfer to serving dish. Top with orange pieces and serve.

nutritional facts: *Per serving: 240 calories • 39g carbohydrates • 13g protein • 5g fat • 610mg sodium • 0mg cholesterol • 7g fiber • 7g sugar*

flavor the lentils

You can easily give the lentils a bit of Provencal flavor by adding a piece of celery stalk, a carrot, a thick onion slice and a sprig of fresh rosemary to the cooking water.

fried polenta squares

prep time: 14 minutes • total time: 29 minutes • serves: 4

Break away from the same old side dishes, and serve up this crispy and colorful fried polenta. It's made from cornmeal and cheese and is then topped with a store-bought zesty marinara sauce. You can't ask for an easier accompaniment.

3/4 cup instant polenta	1 tsp. Italian seasoning
1/4 cup plus 2 tbsp. grated Parmesan cheese, *divided*	1 tbsp. olive oil
	1/2 cup prepared marinara sauce

1) Line 9- x 9-inch baking dish with foil, leaving overhang on two sides of pan.

2) In medium saucepan, bring 2 cups water to boil. Add polenta, 1/4 cup Parmesan and Italian seasoning. Cook and stir until thick, about 3 min.

3) Spread mixture in prepared pan. Transfer to refrigerator to cool for 15 min.

4) Lift foil to remove polenta from pan. Cut polenta into 16 squares.

5) In large, nonstick skillet over medium-high, heat oil. Add half of polenta; cook until crispy on first side, 2 min. Turn and cook until crispy on second side, 2 min. Transfer to platter and keep warm. Repeat with remaining polenta squares.

6) Spoon marinara sauce on top and sprinkle with remaining Parmesan. Serve immediately.

nutritional facts: *Per serving: 210 calories • 30g carbohydrates • 6g protein • 7g fat • 260mg sodium • 5mg cholesterol • 4g fiber • 2g sugar*

easy appetizers

Cut the polenta into smaller squares and serve the marinara sauce on the side for an easy snack.

---

rosemary-garlic white beans

prep time: 8 minutes • total time: 25 minutes • serves: 6

Trust the Italians to turn the simple little white bean into something so delicious! With lots of garlic, olive oil, lemon rind, rosemary and hot pepper, this fast-to-fix side pairs well with any meaty entree.

3 cloves garlic	2 tsp. grated lemon zest
2 tbsp. plus 3 tsp. olive oil	1/3 cup dry vermouth *or* water
1 tsp. dried rosemary	6 dry-packed sun-dried tomatoes
1/4 tsp. crushed red pepper flakes	
2 (15 oz.) cans white kidney beans	

1) Peel and finely chop garlic; place in large saucepan with 2 tbsp. oil. Cook over medium-low heat until just beginning to turn golden, 2 min. Add the rosemary and pepper flakes.

2) Drain and rinse beans. Add to pan with lemon zest and vermouth; bring to boil. Reduce heat to simmer; cook, partially covered, 15 min.

3) Meanwhile, cut sun-dried tomatoes into julienne strips. In small, microwave-safe bowl with 1 tbsp. water, place tomatoes and microwave on MEDIUM to soften, 1 min. Let stand.

4) Transfer beans to serving bowl. Drizzle remaining olive oil over beans; garnish with sun-dried tomatoes.

nutritional facts: *Per serving: 280 calories • 39g carbohydrates • 10g protein • 8g fat • 560mg sodium • 0mg cholesterol • 0g fiber • 1g sugar*

garlic oil

Use an entire head of garlic and one cup of olive oil in Step 1. Cool; strain the oil into a jar, leaving 3 tbsp. in the pan for this recipe. Use the garlic oil to add flavor to a vaiety of dishes.

warm cabbage and apple medley

prep time: 5 minutes • total time: 25 minutes • serves: 4

The humble cabbage has never tasted so good. Served warm, the red cabbage's delicate, sweet-and-sour flavor complements any roast or grilled meat.

1/4 cup red wine vinegar	1/2 small head red cabbage
1/4 cup sugar	1 red *or* green apple, cored
2 tbsp. vegetable oil	and diced
1 bay leaf	salt and pepper to taste
1/8 tsp. cloves	

1) In medium saucepan over medium-low heat, stir together vinegar, sugar, oil, 1 tbsp. water, bay leaf and cloves.

2) Core and thinly slice red cabbage. Add to saucepan. Core and dice apple. Add to saucepan.

3) Cover saucepan and cook, stirring occasionally, about 20 min., until cabbage and apple are soft. Season to taste with salt and pepper.

4) Remove bay leaf; transfer to bowl and serve.

nutritional facts: *Per serving: 160 calories • 23g carbohydrates • 2g protein • 7g fat • 40mg sodium • 0mg cholesterol • 3g fiber • 18g sugar*

delicious relish

This crunchy cabbage makes a great topping for sandwiches. Serve any leftovers cold on sliced deli meats such as roast beef or ham on a hearty Kaiser roll.

cheddar-crowned eggplant

prep time: 8 minutes • total time: 29 minutes • serves: 4

Full of flavor from the garlic, tomatoes, onion and basil, this eggplant dish is a keeper, especially when topped with golden cheddar cheese! It all cooks up in one easy-to-clean skillet, so it will be a busy weeknight mainstay.

1-1/2 lbs. eggplant (2 small)	1/2 cup chicken broth
1 medium onion	1/2 tsp. dried basil
2 large cloves garlic	1/4 tsp. salt
1 tbsp. butter	1/4 tsp. pepper
1 tbsp. oil	3 sprigs fresh parsley
1 cup canned petite-cut diced tomatoes	1/2 cup shredded cheddar cheese

1) Trim but do not peel eggplant. Cut eggplant into 1-inch pieces. Place in large, microwave-safe bowl and sprinkle with 2 tbsp. water. Cover and microwave on HIGH, 5 min., stirring after 2-1/2 min. Let stand, covered, 1 min. Meanwhile, slice onion and garlic into thin strips.

2) In large, deep, nonstick skillet over medium heat butter and oil. Add onion and garlic; cook and stir until soft, about 1 min. Add eggplant, tomatoes, chicken broth, basil, salt and pepper. Cover and bring to boil. Reduce heat to medium and cook until flavors are combined, 5 min. Meanwhile, chop parsley; set aside.

3) With slotted spoon, remove eggplant to medium casserole dish and cover to keep warm. Leave all juices in bottom of skillet. Bring to boil over high heat. Cook until reduced by half, about 1 min. Pour juice over top of eggplant. Sprinkle cheddar and then parsley over top. Cover until cheese is slightly melted, 1-2 min. Serve.

nutritional facts: *Per serving: 180 calories • 16g carbohydrates • 6g protein • 11g fat • 410mg sodium • 20mg cholesterol • 7g fiber • 7g sugar*

eggplant tips

Fresh, ripe eggplants have shiny skin and sound hollow when you gently thump them with your fist. Smaller ones tend to be less bitter than the larger varieties.

vegetable-bean medley

prep time: 7 minutes • total time: 22 minutes • serves: 4

An unexpected combination of texture and flavor, this duo of kidney beans and chickpeas features a really fabulous sauce made from spinach and garlic.

8 large mushrooms	1/2 cup vegetable broth
1 small onion	1/4 cup fresh parsley
4 large cloves garlic	4-1/2 cups fresh spinach leaves
1 (15 oz.) can chickpeas	1/4 tsp. salt
1 (15 oz.) can kidney beans	1/8 tsp. pepper
2 tbsp. olive oil	

1) Thinly slice mushrooms, onion and garlic. Rinse and drain beans.

2) In medium saucepan over medium, heat oil. Add onion and garlic; cook and stir until softened, about 2 min. Add mushrooms; cook until they just begin to release liquid, about 2 min. Add beans and broth; bring to boil. Reduce heat; cook, stirring frequently, until the broth is reduced by one-third, about 4 min. Meanwhile, chop the parsley.

3) Add spinach; cover and cook 1 min. Stir in parsley; season with salt and pepper. Transfer to serving dish.

nutritional facts: *Per serving: 410 calories • 60g carbohydrates • 21g protein • 11g fat • 260mg sodium • 0mg cholesterol • 17g fiber • 8g sugar*

fast food processor

With a small food processor, this dish is easy. Pulse the onions and garlic. While they saute, chop the spinach, then the parsley. There's no need to wash the processor in between!

mashed autumn's bounty

prep time: 25 minutes • total time: 29 minutes • serves: 6

Tired of mashed potatoes? Surprise everyone with this rustic combination of fall harvest vegetables. It packs in lots more vitamins than plain potatoes do, too.

1 chicken bouillon cube	4 tbsp. butter
3/4 lb. parsnip	1/4 cup milk
1 lb. carrots	1/4 cup salt
1 lb. Yukon Gold potatoes	1/8 tsp. pepper
1 cup oil	1/8 tsp. nutmeg
1 large shallot	1 to 2 sprigs fresh parsley
1 tbsp. all-purpose flour	

1) Place 2 qts. water in saucepan; add bouillon. Cover and bring to a boil.

2) Peel parsnips and cut into 1/2-inch pieces. Add to saucepan and boil, covered, 5 min. Peel and cut carrots into 1/2-inch slices. Add to pan and boil, covered, 5 min. Peel and cut potatoes into 1-inch pieces. Add to saucepan and boil, covered, 10 min. or until all vegetables are tender.

3) Meanwhile, heat 1/4-inch oil in small skillet. Cut shallot into thin rings. Toss with flour. Add to hot oil and cook, stirring gently with slotted spoon, until golden, about 3-5 min. Remove with slotted spoon to paper towel-lined plate. Set aside.

4) Drain vegetables; return to saucepan. Shake over medium heat to remove moisture, about 30 seconds.

5) Add butter, milk, salt, pepper and nutmeg to saucepan. With hand-mixer, coarsely mash vegetables until combined. Chop parsley. Transfer vegetables to serving bowl; garnish with shallot and parsley.

nutritional facts: *Per serving: 220 calories • 33g carbohydrates • 4g protein • 8g fat • 4960mg sodium • 20mg cholesterol • 6g fiber • 7g sugar*

use other veggies

Cauliflower or turnips can be substituted for the parsnip in this special potato mash.

mushrooms with tricolored peppers

prep time: 8 minutes • total time: 20 minutes • serves: 4

Why serve ordinary sauteed mushrooms when you can make this pretty dish in just minutes? The brightly colored peppers make a wonderful counterpoint to the earthy mushrooms.

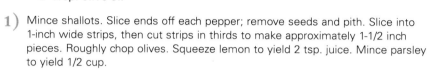

2 medium shallots	10 oz. sliced button mushrooms
3 bell peppers, mixed colors	1/2 tsp. coarse salt
1/2 cup pitted green olives	1/2 tsp. dried oregano
1 lemon	1/4 tsp. red pepper flakes
1 small bunch curly parsley	4 tbsp. goat cheese, crumbled
2 tbsp. olive oil	

1) Mince shallots. Slice ends off each pepper; remove seeds and pith. Slice into 1-inch wide strips, then cut strips in thirds to make approximately 1-1/2 inch pieces. Roughly chop olives. Squeeze lemon to yield 2 tsp. juice. Mince parsley to yield 1/2 cup.

2) In large skillet over medium, heat oil. Add sliced mushrooms; sprinkle with salt, oregano and red pepper flakes. Cook and stir until mushrooms release their liquid, about 5 min.

3) Add peppers to skillet. Cook about 4 min., stirring often. Add 2 tbsp. water and cover pan. Reduce heat to low and cook until tender, 2-3 min.

4) Sprinkle lemon juice over ingredients; turn off heat. Fold in parsley. Remove to serving platter. Sprinkle goat cheese over vegetables. Serve immediately.

nutritional facts: *Per serving: 210 calories • 14g carbohydrates • 8g protein • 16g fat • 720mg sodium • 10mg cholesterol • 4g fiber • 6g sugar*

parsley garnish

Curly parsley makes a beautiful garnish, but so does flat-leaf parsley, which has a little more intense flavor.

lazy potato-egg casserole

prep time: 8 minutes • total time: 28 minutes • serves: 4

This recipe starts with frozen hash browns so you don't waste precious time peeling and dicing potatoes. It's an easy and tasty menu item for a casual supper or a leisurely weekend brunch.

1-1/2 cups frozen hash brown potatoes (diced *or* Southern style)	1 tbsp. cornmeal
	4 green onions
1 tsp. chili powder	1 cup roasted red peppers, *divided*
3 large eggs	3/4 cup shredded reduced-fat cheddar cheese blend
3/4 cup milk	
1/2 cup reduced-fat sour cream	

1) Preheat oven to 425°F. Coat four 1-cup custard cups or individual casseroles with cooking spray. In medium, microwave-safe bowl, microwave hash browns on HIGH for 2 min. Stir in chili powder.

2) Meanwhile, in large bowl, beat eggs, milk, sour cream and cornmeal. Thinly slice green onions and chop 3/4 cup red peppers. Stir into egg mixture along with hash browns and cheese. Ladle into dishes, dividing evenly. Cut remaining red pepper into 8 thin strips and place on top of each casserole.

3) Bake until knife inserted in center comes out clean, 20 min.

nutritional facts: *Per serving: 260 calories • 24g carbohydrates • 16g protein • 11g fat • 260mg sodium • 175mg cholesterol • 3g fiber • 5g sugar*

one-dish wonder

This is a wonderful and unexpected dish for a potluck or buffet. Instead of individual dishes, place the ingredients in a deep-dish pie plate and bake for 30 minutes.

creamy spinach with onions

prep time: 15 minutes • **total time:** 25 minutes • **serves:** 6

This new take on a classic comfort dish incorporates some surprising flavors. Bay leaves, nutmeg, lemon and peppercorns jazz up the creamy spinach and onions for a flavor everyone will love.

1 cup milk	2 tbsp. butter
3 bay leaves	3 tbsp. all-purpose flour
1 tsp. black peppercorns	1 (1 lb.) bag frozen pearl onions
3/4 tsp. salt	1 tsp. lemon zest
1/4 tsp. nutmeg	
1 (10 oz.) pkg. frozen chopped spinach	

1) In small saucepan over medium heat, bring milk, bay leaves, peppercorns, salt and nutmeg just to boil. Remove from heat.

2) Cook spinach according to package directions. Place in strainer; with back of serving spoon, press all excess water from spinach.

3) In medium saucepan, melt butter over medium heat. Stir in flour until smooth. Through sieve or another strainer, gradually add spiced milk, stirring until smooth with wire whisk. Cook until mixture starts to thicken. Add onions, spinach and lemon zest to cream sauce. Cook, stirring frequently, until onions are heated through, about 8 min. Place in serving bowl.

nutritional facts: *Per serving: 100 calories • 17g carbohydrates • 5g protein • 2g fat • 360mg sodium • 5mg cholesterol • 3g fiber • 7g sugar*

mixing in flour

When making a butter and flour roux, cook the flour thoroughly over medium heat. It won't thicken with high heat. This will also prevent lumps and remove the heavy taste of uncooked flour.

mama's spaghetti squash

prep time: 9 minutes • **total time:** 29 minutes • **serves:** 4

Buttery and delicious spaghetti squash goes totally Italian with a garden-fresh topping of fresh zucchini and tomato sauteed with garlic and onion. Your family will delight in this pretty "pasta" change up.

3 lbs. spaghetti squash (1 large)	3/4 cup canned petite-diced tomatoes
1 small red onion	1/8 tsp. salt
1 large garlic clove	1/8 tsp. pepper
1 small zucchini	1 tbsp. butter
2 tbsp. extra-virgin olive oil, *divided*	2 tbsp. shredded Parmesan cheese

1) Cut squash in half lengthwise. With spoon, scrape out and discard seeds. Cut squash into quarters. Place cut side down, in large, microwave-safe dish, overlapping pieces as necessary. Add 2 tbsp. water and cover. Microwave on HIGH until tender when pierced with fork, about 10 min.

2) Meanwhile, thinly slice onion to yield 1 cup. Mince garlic. Thinly slice zucchini.

3) In large skillet over medium, heat 1 tbsp. oil. Add onion and garlic. Cook and stir, until soft, about 3 min. Add zucchini, tomatoes, salt and pepper. Cook and stir, until zucchini is soft, about 4 min.

4) With fork, scrape squash strands from cut side into serving bowl. Add butter and remaining olive oil; toss until butter is melted. Top with zucchini mixture; sprinkle with cheese and serve.

nutritional facts: *Per serving: 190 calories • 20g carbohydrates • 3g protein • 12g fat • 290mg sodium • 10mg cholesterol • 1g fiber • 2g sugar*

make it a meal

For a complete and satisfying vegetarian entree, this delicious dish can be enhanced with fresh parsley or basil and served with crispy cheese toasts.

celery root puree

prep time: 10 minutes • total time: 25 minutes • serves: 4

Celery root puree is a very typical side dish from the French countryside, but not so common in the States. Its smooth, creamy texture and great taste will make it a favorite at your house.

---

  2 medium Yukon Gold potatoes (about 1/2 lb.)

  1 celery root (about 1-1/2 lbs.)

  1/2 lemon

2 to 3 sprigs fresh parsley

  3 tbsp. butter

1/4 cup milk

1/2 tsp. celery salt

1/4 tsp. pepper

1) Peel and dice potatoes into 1/2-inch cubes. Trim and discard tough outer layer from celery root; dice remainder into 1/2-inch pieces.

2) Place potato and celery root in large saucepan. Add enough cold water to just cover. Squeeze lemon to yield 1 tsp. juice; add to water. Cover and bring to boil over high heat.

3) Lower heat to medium and continue cooking, covered, until celery root is tender when pierced with fork, about 15 min. Chop parsley; set aside.

4) In large colander, drain celery root and potato. Place butter and milk in saucepan; cook over medium until butter is melted, 3 min. Remove from heat; stir in celery salt and pepper. Return celery root and potatoes to saucepan. With handheld potato masher, mash until smooth. Transfer to bowl, sprinkle with parsley and serve.

nutritional facts: *Per serving: 180 calories • 21g carbohydrates • 4g protein • 9g fat • 240mg sodium • 25mg cholesterol • 3g fiber • 1g sugar*

have it your way

Make this versatile side any way you want. A dollop of sour cream or heavy cream makes this richer, while a little bit of chicken broth will lighten it up.

curried cauliflower and potatoes

prep time: 12 minutes • total time: 27 minutes • serves: 8

Ginger, onion, curry and garlic add intense flavor to cauliflower florets and red potatoes. Toss in peas and carrots, and this hearty side dish has something to please every taste.

---

 10 tiny red new potatoes

  1 tsp. salt

  1 small onion

  1 piece fresh gingerroot (1 inch)

1-1/2 tbsp. oil

  1 tsp. minced garlic in oil

  1 tbsp. curry powder

  3 cups frozen cauliflower florets

1/2 cup frozen peas

1/2 cup shredded carrots

1) In medium saucepan, place potatoes. Cover with water; add salt. Cover saucepan and bring to boil. Uncover and boil until tender, about 12 min.

2) Meanwhile, chop onion. Peel, then grate ginger.

3) In large skillet over high, heat oil; cook and stir onion until tender. Add ginger, garlic and curry powder. Reduce heat to medium. Cook and stir for 30 seconds. Pour in 1/2 cup water. Stir to release spices from bottom of pan. Add cauliflower and stir to coat. Cover and cook until almost tender, 5 min. Stir in peas and carrots. Cover and cook 3 min.

4) Drain potatoes. Cut in half and add to cauliflower mixture. Stir to coat. Transfer to serving dish.

nutritional facts: *Per serving: 200 calories • 30g carbohydrates • 6g protein • 6g fat • 640mg sodium • 0mg cholesterol • 5g fiber • 3g sugar*

vary the veggies

If cauliflower isn't a family favorite, substitute whatever veggies they'll eat in this dish, such as broccoli florets, button mushrooms or cuts of fresh asparagus.

pretty presentation

For a sunny, sunflower-like presentation, use a large round platter. Place the zucchini boats like petals around a ramekin filled with shredded Parmesan cheese.

sausage stuffed zucchini

prep time: 18 minutes • total time: 28 minutes • serves: 4

Zucchini never tasted so good! Baked with Italian sausage, bread crumbs, pepper and Parmesan, these tender veggie boats take a starring role at any meal.

2 medium zucchini	1/3 cup shredded Parmesan cheese, *divided*
4 oz. (1/2 cup) Italian sausage, removed from casing	1 large egg, slightly beaten
1/4 cup minced red bell pepper	1/4 tsp. salt
1/2 cup dry bread crumbs	1/8 tsp. pepper

1) Preheat oven to 400°F. Place a steam basket in a large pot; fill with 1 inch of water. Bring to a boil. Trim end of zucchini; cut in half lengthwise. Place zucchini in basket and steam until tender, about 4 min. Remove and set aside on baking sheet.

2) Meanwhile, in small skillet, over high heat, cook and stir sausage and peppers, breaking sausage into tiny pieces with a spoon, until sausage is cooked, about 3 min. Remove from heat. Stir in bread crumbs, 1/4 cup Parmesan, egg, salt and pepper.

3) Evenly divide and place sausage mixture onto cut side of each piece of zucchini. Sprinkle with remaining cheese. Bake until heated through and cheese is melted, about 10 min.

nutritional facts: *Per serving: 210 calories • 14g carbohydrates • 10g protein • 12g fat • 440mg sodium • 55mg cholesterol • 2g fiber • 3g sugar*

juicing fruit

Look for the new lemon/lime squeezer tools that are on the market. They squeeze citrus fruits in a flash without getting the juice on your fingers.

maui rice

prep time: 23 minutes • total time: 23 minutes • serves: 6

Try this fresh-tasting side dish with your favorite grilled meats or with a tender roasted chicken. Sweet pineapple, savory ham and tart lime dress up the rice for wonderful island flavor.

1 cup basmati rice	2 green onions
1-1/2 tsp. salt, *divided*	1 small bunch cilantro
1 red bell pepper	1 lime
2 oz. thick-sliced baked ham	1 tbsp. olive oil
1/2 fresh peeled and cored pineapple	1 tsp. honey
	additional cilantro

1) In medium saucepan over high heat, bring 2-1/2 cups water to boil. Stir in rice and 1 tsp. salt. Bring to simmer; cook until almost tender, 10 min. Chop pepper and add to rice. Cook until rice is completely tender, 4 min. Drain excess water and return rice and pepper to pan.

2) Meanwhile, chop ham, pineapple and green onions into 1/2-inch pieces. Chop enough cilantro to yield 1/4 cup. Cut lime in half. Squeeze half of lime to yield 1 tbsp. juice. Cut remaining half into wedges.

3) Add oil, honey, ham, pineapple, green onions, cilantro, lime juice and remaining salt to the rice; toss to combine. Transfer to serving bowl; garnish with additional cilantro and lime wedges and serve.

nutritional facts: *Per serving: 140 calories • 26g carbohydrates • 4g protein • 3g fat • 180mg sodium • 5mg cholesterol • 2g fiber • 10g sugar*

sweet & savory focaccia

prep time: 7 minutes • total time: 25 minutes • serves: 15

This simple bread is a welcome change from more ordinary flatbreads. The difference comes from the special sweetness of raisins and dried apples and apricots. Serve it with roast pork or turkey dinners.

1/3 cup dried apples, *divided*	1/3 cup golden raisins
1/3 cup dried apricots, *divided*	1/2 tsp. course ground pepper, *divided*
2 tsp. butter	
1 (13.8 oz.) pkg. refrigerated pizza dough	1/2 tsp. dried rosemary, *divided*
	1/4 tsp. coarse salt

1) Preheat oven to 400°F. Coat large baking sheet with cooking spray. With kitchen scissors, snip apples and apricots; set aside. Place butter in small, microwave-safe bowl. Microwave on HIGH until melted, 30 seconds.

2) Unroll dough onto pan. Sprinkle with raisins, then half of apples and apricots, and half of pepper and rosemary; press firmly into dough. Fold dough in half lengthwise. Center dough on pan.

3) With fingers, press dough into 8- x 12-inch rectangle. Top with remaining apples, apricots, pepper and rosemary, pressing firmly into dough. Sprinkle with salt; brush with melted butter.

4) Bake until dough is golden, 15-18 min. Remove bread to wire rack to cool slightly; cut into squares and serve warm.

nutritional facts: *Per serving: 120 calories • 23g carbohydrates • 3g protein • 2g fat • 230mg sodium • 0mg cholesterol • 2g fiber • 10g sugar*

season the bread

To please a variety of tastes, divide the focaccia dough in half and top one part with 1/4 cup olive oil seasoned with chopped fresh oregano, rosemary, parsley and basil.

mushroom kasha

prep time: 13 minutes • total time: 25 minutes • serves: 5

A classic Eastern European dish, this combination of buckwheat (also called "kasha"), mushrooms, onions and carrots is hearty and earthy. Serve it instead of brown rice pilaf or potatoes.

2 cups chicken broth	2 tbsp. oil
1 large egg	2 cups sliced mushrooms
1 cup buckwheat	1/2 tsp. pepper
1 medium onion	1/4 tsp. dried thyme
1 carrot	2 to 3 sprigs fresh parsley

1) In small saucepan over high heat, bring broth to boil. Meanwhile, in 2-qt. nonstick pot, lightly beat egg with fork. Add buckwheat and stir to coat completely. Place pot over medium heat. Cook and stir constantly until grains separate, about 4 min.

2) Pour boiling broth over buckwheat, stirring constantly. Reduce heat to low. Cover and cook until buckwheat is tender and liquid is absorbed, about 15 min.

3) Meanwhile, chop onion to yield 1 cup. Chop carrot to yield 1/2 cup.

4) In medium skillet over high, heat oil. Add onions; cook and stir, 2 min. Add carrot, mushrooms, pepper and thyme. Cook until carrot is tender, about 5 min.

5) Meanwhile, chop parsley to yield 1/4 cup. Add buckwheat mixture and parsley to skillet. Stir to combine, then transfer to bowl and serve.

nutritional facts: *Per serving: 220 calories • 30g carbohydrates • 9g protein • 8g fat • 55mg sodium • 40mg cholesterol • 5g fiber • 2g sugar*

add more broth

If the kasha thickens more than you would like while cooking, add boiling water or broth a tablespoon at a time to thin it to your desired consistency.

corn-topped baked potatoes

prep time: 3 minutes • total time: 24 minutes • serves: 4

A buttery blend of corn and green onion, served over piping-hot baked potatoes makes for a two-favorite combo that will win you raves. This simply delicious side pairs well with everyday dinners as well as special-occasion meals.

4 large baking potatoes	1 large green onion, green
1-1/2 cups frozen corn	portion only
8 tbsp. butter	1/4 tsp. pepper

1) Preheat oven to 450°F. Place butter in small oven-proof dish on stovetop to soften. Pierce potatoes several times with fork. Microwave potatoes on HIGH, 5 min. Rotate and microwave on HIGH until softened, 5 min. Transfer to oven and bake until skin is crisp, 10 min.

2) Meanwhile, in medium saucepan with steam basket insert, bring 1/2 inch of water to boil over high heat. Add corn. Cover and steam until heated through, 5 min. Remove steam basket; let cool 1-2 min.

3) Thinly slice green onion. In food processor, pulse 1 cup corn and softened butter. Scrape mixture into small mixing bowl. Add onion, remaining corn and pepper; stir to combine.

4) Remove potatoes from oven. Place each on serving plate. Split to open. Evenly top with corn mixture and serve.

nutritional facts: *Per serving: 530 calories • 76g carbohydrates • 10g protein • 24g fat • 190mg sodium • 60mg cholesterol • 8g fiber • 6g sugar*

spud secrets

For a crispy-skinned baked potato, spray it with olive oil before baking. For a quick side, top it with creamed spinach or leftover garlic-infused broccoli.

tuscan braised cabbage

prep time: 6 minutes • total time: 24 minutes • serves: 6

Italian cuisine treats all vegetables like stars, even the humble cabbage. If you have never had Savoy cabbage, give it a try. With a milder flavor than regular cabbage, it's great with olive oil, pancetta and garlic.

2 oz. pancetta	1/2 tsp. sugar
2 large cloves garlic	1/4 tsp. salt
2 tbsp. olive oil	1/4 tsp. crushed red pepper flakes
1 small head Savoy cabbage (about 1-1/4 lbs.)	2 to 3 sprigs fresh parsley

1) Dice pancetta; cut garlic into slivers. In large, nonstick skillet over medium-high, heat oil. Add pancetta and cook until it begins to brown slightly, 2-3 min. Add garlic, cook just until it begins to turn golden, about 1-2 min.

2) Meanwhile, remove any damaged outer leaves from cabbage and trim core even with base. Cut cabbage through core into 6 wedges. In small bowl, mix together sugar, salt and pepper flakes.

3) Add cabbage to skillet; sprinkle with sugar mixture. Add 1 cup water to bottom of pan. Cover and cook turning once, until tender when pierced with knife, about 15 min. Meanwhile, finely chop parsley. Transfer cabbage to plates; sprinkle with parsley and serve.

nutritional facts: *Per serving: 110 calories • 5g carbohydrates • 3g protein • 9g fat • 200mg sodium • 5mg cholesterol • 2g fiber • 2g sugar*

quick prep

For even faster preparation, shred the cabbage rather than cutting it into wedges; reduce the cooking time to about 10 min.

syrup-sweetened fried corn

prep time: 10 minutes • total time: 26 minutes • serves: 4

This wonderful recipe combines the tastes of the North's maple syrup with the Midwest's staple of corn for a tasty dish that's homey in any region. Try it with your favorite fall suppers.

1 large egg	1 (15.25 oz.) can whole kernel corn, drained
1/4 cup milk	2 tsp. vegetable oil
3/4 cup yellow cornmeal	4 tbsp. maple syrup
1 tsp. baking powder	
1/2 tsp. salt	

1) In medium mixing bowl, beat egg. Stir in milk, cornmeal, baking powder and salt. Add corn and stir to combine thoroughly.

2) In large, nonstick skillet over medium, heat 1 tbsp. oil. Working in batches, drop batter by 1/4 cupfuls into skillet. Cook until firm and lightly browned on first side, about 4 min. Turn and cook until browned on second side, another 4 min.

3) Transfer to plate and keep warm. Repeat with remaining batter, adding more oil, to yield 8 cakes.

4) To serve, place 2 cakes on each individual; top each with 1 tbsp. maple syrup. Serve immediately.

nutritional facts: *Per serving: 290 calories • 57g carbohydrates • 7g protein • 5g fat • 560mg sodium • 55mg cholesterol • 3g fiber • 16g sugar*

kernel of truth

When corn is not in season, try flash-frozen corn, which has almost as much crunch as corn cut right off the cob. Canned corn works, too, but drain it well.

rustic ratatouille

prep time: 10 minutes • total time: 29 minutes • serves: 5

This hearty dish spotlights eggplant, zucchini, tomatoes, onion, bell pepper and fresh herbs. It's a wonderful partner for almost any meat or fish main course.

1 medium eggplant, peeled and chopped	3/4 tsp. dried basil
1 small zucchini, chopped	1/2 tsp. dried oregano
1/4 cup extra-virgin olive oil, *divided*	1 (28 oz.) can petite-diced tomatoes
1 small onion, chopped	2 tbsp. chopped fresh parsley
1 small green pepper, chopped	salt and pepper to taste
2 large cloves garlic, thinly sliced	

1) Preheat oven to 450°F. In large bowl, toss eggplant and zucchini with 2 tbsp. oil. Spread eggplant and zucchini on large baking sheet. Bake until tender, about 20 min.

2) Meanwhile, heat remaining oil in large saucepan. Cook and stir onion until tender, about 1 min. Add pepper, garlic, basil and oregano. Cook 1 min. Add tomatoes. Cover and bring to boil.

3) Stir in eggplant, zucchini and parsley. Return to boil and cook 2 min. to blend flavors. Season with salt and pepper.

nutritional facts: *Per serving: 170 calories • 16g carbohydrates • 3g protein • 11g fat • 210mg sodium • 0mg cholesterol • 7g fiber • 9g sugar*

main or side

Ratatouille is a vegetable stew traditionally served as a side course. But it can be served as a main dish alongside rice or bread.

tasty tabbouleh

prep time: 10 minutes • total time: 29 minutes • serves: 4

This variation of the classic Middle-Eastern side dish replaces the typical parsley with cilantro and mint, fresh lime for vinegar and dried cherries for the tomatoes.

1 cup bulgur	1/4 tsp. allspice
1/3 cup chopped dried cherries	3 to 4 green onions
1 lime	1 cup cilantro leaves
2 tbsp. olive oil	1/3 cup mint leaves
1/2 tsp. sugar	2 tbsp. chopped pistachios
1/2 tsp. salt	

1) In medium, microwave-safe bowl, place bulgur and cherries; add 1-1/4 cups boiling water and stir well. Cover and microwave on HIGH 2 min.; let stand, covered, until bulgur is soft, 25 min.

2) Meanwhile, squeeze lime to yield 1 tbsp. juice; place in small bowl with oil, sugar, salt and allspice. Stir to combine.

3) Finely chop green onions, cilantro and mint; set aside. Fluff bulgur with fork and transfer to serving bowl. Add oil mixture and stir to combine. Stir in green onions, cilantro, mint and nuts. Serve.

nutritional facts: *Per serving: 270 calories • 41g carbohydrates • 6g protein • 10g fat • 310mg sodium • 0mg cholesterol • 9g fiber • 10g sugar*

mid-east mainstay

Tabbouleh is one of those one-dish specialties that gets better as the flavors meld. If you prefer more veggies than grains, add a couple of diced cucumbers.

fresh creamed corn

prep time: 10 minutes • total time: 20 minutes • serves: 4

Celebrate the freshness and sweetness of corn by making this often. Using a can of evaporated milk easily pumps up the creaminess in this dish.

4 large ears fresh corn on the cob	1 tsp. cornstarch
	1/8 tsp. turmeric
1 (12 oz.) can evaporated milk	1/8 tsp. salt
1-1/2 tbsp. fine yellow cornmeal	1/8 tsp. pepper
1 tbsp. sugar	1/4 tsp. paprika

1) Shuck corn. Cut down the length of cob to remove corn kernels from cob. Rotate cob until all kernels are removed. Use dull side of knife to scrape any remaining pulp and milk off cob. Repeat with remaining cobs to yield 3-1/2 cups total corn and pulp.

2) In medium saucepan over high heat, combine corn and pulp, evaporated milk, cornmeal, sugar, cornstarch, turmeric, salt and pepper. Bring to boil, stirring occasionally. Reduce heat to medium-high and cook 5 min., stirring occasionally with rubber spatula to prevent sticking. Transfer to serving bowl. Dust with paprika and serve.

nutritional facts: *Per serving: 220 calories • 44g carbohydrates • 11g protein • 2.5g fat • 250mg sodium • 5mg cholesterol • 4g fiber • 19g sugar*

use extras for soup

If you're a fan of a corn soup, freeze the cobs without kernels from this recipe. Use them along with more fresh corn cobs and chicken stock to create a rich, hearty soup.

sweet 'n' tangy "baby cabbages"

prep time: 9 minutes • **total time:** 20 minutes • **serves:** 4

Get your finicky family's attention by serving brussels sprouts in this sweet and tangy sauce, rich with the flavor of bacon and onions.

1 lb. brussels sprouts	1 tbsp. sugar
1/4 tsp. salt	1 tbsp. vinegar
2 slices thick-cut bacon	1 tsp. prepared mustard
1 small red onion	1/4 tsp. pepper
1 tsp. olive oil	

1) If sprouts are large, cut in half. In large saucepan over high heat, bring 1 qt. hot water to boil. Add salt and sprouts and cook until barely tender, 8-10 min. Drain sprouts; wipe saucepan dry with paper towels.

2) Cut bacon into thin strips; thinly slice onion. In saucepan over medium-high, heat oil. Add bacon and onion and cook, stirring, until bacon is cooked through and onion is tender, about 5 min.

3) Reduce heat to low, then add 2 tbsp. water, sugar, vinegar, mustard and pepper; simmer 1 min. Return sprouts to pan and cook, stirring, until heated through, about 2 min. Transfer to bowl and serve.

nutritional facts: *Per serving: 160 calories • 12g carbohydrates • 6g protein • 10g fat • 360mg sodium • 15mg cholesterol • 5g fiber • 3g sugar*

brussels basics

Don't overcook the sprouts. They should feel barely tender when pierced with the tip of a sharp knife. If they start to take on a cabbage smell, you've cooked them too long.

smoky chipotle 'n' chive potatoes

prep time: 9 minutes • **total time:** 20 minutes • **serves:** 4

These super-creamy sweet potatoes get a flavorful lift from the addition of chive cream cheese, honey and a dash of sweet spices. It's a bold, richly textured side that could become your signature dish!

2 lbs. sweet potatoes	1 tbsp. honey
1 small canned chipotle pepper	1/2 tsp. salt
1/3 cup tub-style cream cheese	1/4 tsp. ground cinnamon
with chives and onions	1/8 tsp. nutmeg

1) Place 1 inch water in medium saucepan. Peel potatoes; cut into 1-inch chunks and place in pan. Cover and bring to boil over high heat. Cook, stirring once halfway through cooking time, until fork-tender, 10 min.

2) Meanwhile, halve chipotle pepper. Scrape out seeds and ribs; discard. Finely chop pepper. Drain potatoes and return to pan.

3) Add cream cheese, honey, salt, cinnamon, nutmeg and chipotle pepper. With potato masher, mash mixture until smooth. Transfer to bowl and serve.

nutritional facts: *Per serving: 290 calories • 53g carbohydrates • 5g protein • 7g fat • 660mg sodium • 20mg cholesterol • 8g fiber • 16g sugar*

honey alternative

For those who find honey a bit too sweet, add another level of flavoring to these potatoes by substituting maple syrup for the honey. Or try brown sugar and raisins.

citrus-glazed baby carrots

prep time: 2 minutes • total time: 18 minutes • serves: 4

Here's the simple secret to pan-steaming carrots: butter and just enough water in a tightly covered skillet means no need for colanders or draining.

2 tbsp. butter, *divided*
1/3 cup water
1/2 tsp. salt
1 lb. baby carrots

3 tbsp. orange juice
2 tbsp. honey *or* brown sugar
1/4 tsp. nutmeg

1) In 10-inch nonstick skillet, bring 1 tbsp. butter, water, salt, carmedium and carrots to a boil. Cover and cook for 10 min., checking after 8 min.; add another 1 to 2 tbsp. water, if necessary.

2) Uncover and raise heat to medium high. Cook, stirring, until water has evaporated and carrots are just tender, 2 min.

3) Stir in orange juice, honey and nutmeg and cook until carrots are completely coated, about 1 min. Add remaining butter and cook, stirring constantly, until glaze thickens slightly, about 2 min.

nutritional facts: *Per serving: 130 calories • 19g carbohydrates • 1g protein • 6g fat • 420mg sodium • 15mg cholesterol • 2g fiber • 15g sugar*

zesty idea

For a "just for the grown-ups" version, substitute bourbon for the orange juice, use brown sugar instead of honey, and replace the nutmeg with the more intense flavor of allspice.

sesame-soy broccoli florets

prep time: 15 minutes • total time: 15 minutes • serves: 2

Here's a side dish with plenty of Asian flair and a touch of sweetness that's sure to satisfy even those who turn up their noses at broccoli. Best of all, it cuts back on fat and cholesterol!

2 cups fresh *or* frozen broccoli florets
1 tbsp. sugar
1 tbsp. olive oil

1 tbsp. soy sauce
2 tsp. rice vinegar
2 tsp. sesame seeds, toasted

1) Place the broccoli in a steamer basket; place in a saucepan over 1 in. of water. Bring to a boil; cover and steam for 5-7 min. or until crisp-tender.

2) Meanwhile, in a small saucepan, combine the sugar, oil, soy sauce and vinegar. Cook and stir over medium heat until sugar is dissolved. Transfer the broccoli to a serving bowl. Drizzle with soy sauce mixture; sprinkle with sesame seeds.

nutritional facts: *Per serving: 156 calories • 16g carbohydrates • 5g protein • 8g fat • 358mg sodium • 0 cholesterol • 4g fiber*

family secret

For an extra flavor punch, sprinkle a dash of Chinese Five-Spice Powder in with the soy sauce and vinegar.

savory potato tortilla

prep time: 5 minutes • total time: 25 minutes • serves: 6

An easy-to-prepare side dish, the potato tortilla is served for breakfast, brunch, as a tapa (little snacks served with cocktails) or for a simple, take-along lunch.

1-1/2 lbs. potatoes	1 tsp. salt
1/4 cup olive oil	1/2 tsp. pepper
4 extra-large eggs	1/4 cup green onions, thinly sliced

1) Peel potatoes and cut into 1/2-inch cubes.

2) In medium nonstick skillet over medium-high, heat oil. Add potatoes and saute, stirring occasionally, until golden, about 15 min.

3) Meanwhile, in medium bowl, beat eggs with salt and pepper until foamy, about 2 min.

4) Stir green onions into skillet; sauté until fragrant, about 1 min. Pour eggs over potatoes, cover and lower heat to medium-low. Cook until egg is almost set on top, about 5 min.

5) Gently slide wooden spoon or rubber spatula around edge of tortilla to loosen. Place large plate over skillet and flip plate and skillet so that tortilla rests on plate Slide tortilla back into skillet, cooked side up.

6) Cook additional 3-4 min. to set completely. Slide onto serving plate, cut in wedges and serve.

nutritional facts: *Per serving: 170 calories • 6g carbohydrates • 7g protein • 13g fat • 440mg sodium • 140mg cholesterol • 3g fiber • 2g sugar*

very versatile

Busy weekend? This dish can be served hot or at room temperature. For a crowd, triple the recipe and add your favorite toppings such as bacon or mushrooms.

buttery peas and carrots

prep time: 20 min. • total time: 20 minutes • serves: 4

This simple side dish is one you'll rely on often to serve with a variety of main courses. The dish offers so much flavor, that you'll find yourself preparing it time and again.

2-1/2 cups baby carrots, halved lengthwise	2 tbsp. water
2 tbsp. butter	1 tsp. sugar
1-1/2 cups frozen peas	salt and pepper to taste

1) In a skillet, saute carrots in butter for 5 minutes. Stir in the remaining ingredients. Cover and simmer for 10-12 minutes or until the vegetables are tender.

nutritional facts: *Per serving: 127 calories • 16g carbohydrates • 3g protein • 6 g fat • 188mg sodium • 15mg cholesterol • 4 g fiber*

sugar busters

Omit the sugar in this dish if you'd like and replace it with garlic salt, onion powder or whatever fresh herb you happen to have on hand. Try it with rosemary or thyme for a delicious change-of-pace.

rosemary-infused potatoes

prep time: 9 minutes • total time: 29 minutes • serves: 4

Adding fresh rosemary to the water for boiling potatoes is a no-muss way to add flavor to red potatoes. Bump up the flavor with a bit of butter, shallots and additional chopped rosemary. Try it tonight!

1-1/2 lbs. petite red potatoes, halved	1/4 cup butter
2 stalks (6 inches *each*) fresh rosemary	3 large shallots, cut into thin strips
	salt and pepper

1) In medium saucepan with enough salted, hot tap water to cover potatoes, place potatoes and one stalk of rosemary. Cover and bring to boil over high heat. Uncover and continue boiling until potatoes are tender, about 12 min.

2) Meanwhile, remove and roughly chop rosemary leaves from second stalk. Set aside.

3) Using tongs, remove and discard rosemary from pot of water. Drain potatoes. Rinse saucepan, wipe dry. Return pot to the stove. Turn on heat to high. Add butter, shallots and chopped rosemary to pan. Stir constantly until butter is melted and shallots are tender, about 3 min. Add potatoes. Stir to coat. Add salt and pepper to taste.

nutritional facts: *Per serving: 270 calories • 36g carbohydrates • 5g protein • 12g fat • 95mg sodium • 30mg cholesterol • 4g fiber • 3g sugar*

green thumb

Rosemary plants are very easy to grow and winter well indoors in cold climates. Even if the plant dies, the dried rosemary leaves and stems are full of flavor.

sun-drenched rice

prep time: 20 minutes • total time: 25 minutes • serves: 6

A robust complement to grilled fish or roast chicken, the rich flavors in this rice are reminiscent of those you might experience while dining in the warm, sunny Italian countryside.

1-3/4 cups chicken broth	1/3 cup pitted green olives
1 cup long-grain white rice	2 tbsp. olive oil
3 tbsp. chopped shallots	3 tbsp. pine nuts
1/4 cup oil-packed sun-dried tomatoes	2 tbsp. white cooking wine

1) In medium saucepan over high heat, bring chicken broth to boil. Stir in rice. Cover, reduce heat to medium-low and simmer until broth is absorbed and rice is tender, 15-20 min.

2) While rice is cooking, finely chop shallots and sun-dried tomatoes. Slice olives crosswise.

3) In medium, nonstick skillet over medium-high, heat olive oil. Add shallots and pine nuts and cook, stirring, until fragrant, about 3 min. Stir in sun-dried tomatoes, olives and wine. Cook, stirring, until tomatoes are softened and heated through, about 2 min. Remove from heat.

4) Fluff rice with fork. Stir olive mixture into rice, tossing well to combine. Transfer to bowl and serve.

nutritional facts: *Per serving: 220 calories • 28g carbohydrates • 4g protein • 10g fat • 460mg sodium • 0mg cholesterol • 1g fiber • 1g sugar*

lively leftovers

Rice is the perfect vehicle for a variety of vegetables: Do you have some leftover mushrooms, peppers or roasted onions in the fridge? Dice them and add them.

crispy couscous cakes

prep time: 26 minutes • total time: 26 minutes • serves: 4

Couscous takes on a whole new personality when it's used to create these crispy, flavorful cakes. Green onions, feta and dill provide light and fresh flavors with a taste of the Mediterranean.

1/2 cup couscous	1/2 tsp. salt
1 bunch green onions	1/4 tsp. pepper
1/4 cup dill	1/4 cup all-purpose flour
1/2 cup crumbled feta cheese	2 tbsp. olive oil, *divided*
2 eggs, lightly beaten	

1) In small saucepan over high heat, bring 1/2 cup water to boil; remove from heat and stir in couscous. Cover and let stand until water is absorbed, 10 min. Fluff with fork.

2) Meanwhile, finely chop green onions and dill. In large bowl, thoroughly blend feta and eggs. Stir in green onions, dill, salt and pepper; blend in flour. Stir couscous into bowl until thoroughly combined. Form mixture into 8 patties.

3) In large, nonstick skillet over medium, heat 1 tbsp. oil. Add 4 patties to oil and cook until light golden on first side, about 3 min. Turn and cook until golden on second side, 3 min. Remove to plate and keep warm. Repeat with remaining oil and patties. Serve immediately.

nutritional facts: *Per serving: 270 calories • 25g carbohydrates • 10g protein • 14g fat • 540mg sodium • 120mg cholesterol • 2g fiber • 2g sugar*

beat the clock

This is a great make-ahead dish, too! Prepare the mixture, then place in a greased baking dish. Bake at 350°F. for 35 minutes before cutting into squares and serving.

lucky sauteed string beans

prep time: 5 minutes • total time: 12 minutes • serves: 4

How fortunate your family will feel when you make these green beans with fresh ginger and garlic— even better than a Chinese restaurant! You'll feel lucky too, because they're so easy to make.

2 square inches fresh ginger	2 tbsp. canola oil
3 large cloves garlic	2 tbsp. reduced-sodium soy sauce
3 large green onions	
1 lb. fresh green beans	1/8 tsp. pepper

1) Peel and grate ginger to yield 1-1/2 tbsp. Mince garlic to yield 1-1/2 tbsp. Thinly slice green onions to yield 1/4 cup. Trim ends of green beans.

2) In large skillet over high, heat oil. Add ginger, garlic and green onions. Cook, stirring, 1 min. Add beans, soy sauce and pepper; stir to coat.

3) Cover and reduce heat to medium-low. Simmer until beans are cooked through, but still slightly crisp, about 5 min. Transfer to bowl and serve.

nutritional facts: *Per serving: 110 calories • 11g carbohydrates • 3g protein • 7g fat • 310mg sodium • 0mg cholesterol • 4g fiber • 2g sugar*

easy idea

Toast slivered almonds in the dry frying pan, first, to top the beans; then, add half canola oil and half butter to the pan to saute the garlic, ginger and green onions.

sauteed potato slices

prep time: 22 minutes • total time: 22 minutes • serves: 4

Using canned potato slices makes this an effortless recipe to prepare. The mixture of fresh thyme, sage, parsley and rosemary goes well with any main dish.

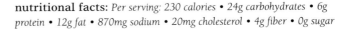

2 (14.5 oz.) cans sliced, new potatoes, drained	1/2 tsp. salt
1 tsp. fresh thyme	2 tbsp. butter, *divided*
1 tsp. fresh parsley	1 tbsp. olive oil, *divided*
1 tsp. fresh rosemary	1/2 cup shredded Parmesan cheese
1 tsp. fresh sage	

1) Lay potato slices in single layer on paper towels. Cover with another layer of paper towel and pat dry.

2) Mince all herbs and place in small bowl. Stir in salt and set aside.

3) In large skillet over medium-high, melt half of butter in half of oil. Working in batches, add enough potato slices to cover bottom of skillet. Cook until browned on first side, 4-5 min. Turn and cook until browned on second side, 4-5 min. Remove to plate and repeat with remaining butter, oil and potato slices.

4) Return all potatoes to pan and sprinkle with herb-salt mixture. Cook, stirring to coat, 1 min. Sprinkle Parmesan over top. Cover and cook until cheese is melted, about 1 min. Carefully transfer to platter and serve.

nutritional facts: *Per serving: 230 calories • 24g carbohydrates • 6g protein • 12g fat • 870mg sodium • 20mg cholesterol • 4g fiber • 0g sugar*

take care

Using a splash guard while browning the potatoes will make cleanup easier. Although the potatoes are dried, they still contain moisture that may make the oil splatter.

austin bbq beans

prep time: 9 minutes • total time: 29 minutes • serves: 6

Beans are the perfect choice for summer, and when combined with chiles, spices, corn and tomatoes, they're almost a meal in themselves. The deep flavor of this version comes from red onions and cilantro.

2 large red onions	2 medium tomatoes
1 tbsp. olive oil	1 small bunch fresh cilantro
2 tsp. chili powder	1/2 tsp. salt
1 (19 oz.) can black beans	1 cup frozen kernel corn

1) Cut each onion in half and thickly slice each half. In medium saucepan over medium, heat oil. Add onions and cook, stirring frequently, until golden brown, about 10 min. Stir in chili powder.

2) Meanwhile, drain and rinse beans. Dice tomatoes; Chop cilantro to yield 1/2 cup. Set aside separately. Add beans, tomatoes and salt to saucepan; bring to boil. Reduce to heat to low and simmer, covered, until flavors have blended, about 5 min.

3) Stir in corn and cook until heated through. Stir in cilantro. Transfer to bowl and serve.

nutritional facts: *Per serving: 200 calories • 34g carbohydrates • 10g protein • 3.5g fat • 210mg sodium • 0mg cholesterol • 10g fiber • 4g sugar*

seeing red

Add even more flavor and texture to this dish. Keep a jar of roasted red peppers packed in oil on hand and slice up a few to add during the last minute or two of cook time.

pesto roasted tomatoes

prep time: 7 minutes • total time: 22 minutes • serves: 4

These delicious roasted tomatoes are as beautiful as they are quick. The bold flavor of the pesto and Parmesan-dressed crumbs will tempt even the pickiest eater who turns away from vegetables.

4 ripe plum tomatoes	2 tbsp. seasoned dry bread
1/8 tsp. pepper	crumbs
3 tbsp. prepared pesto	2 tbsp. grated Parmesan cheese

1) Preheat oven to 450°F. Cut tomatoes in half lengthwise. Gently scrape out seeds with teaspoon and discard. Season tomato shells with pepper; evenly spread in pesto. Arrange on foil-lined baking sheet.

2) In small bowl, combine bread crumbs and Parmesan. Sprinkle over tomatoes. Spray tops of tomatoes with cooking spray.

3) Bake until tomatoes are just tender and topping is golden, about 15 min.

nutritional facts: *Per serving: 90 calories • 0g carbohydrates • 3g protein • 5g fat • 240mg sodium • 5mg cholesterol • 2g fiber • 4g sugar*

instantly homemade

To prepare pesto in a food processor, add a handful of fresh basil, two cloves of garlic, a sprinkle of Parmesan cheese and a splash of olive oil. Puree a bit, and you're done.

toasted walnut noodles

prep time: 5 minutes • total time: 20 minutes • serves: 6

This unique side dish is special enough to take center stage at your next dinner. A simple blend of skillet-toasted nuts, butter, lemon and dill creates a whole new delight that's perfectly delicious!

1 (16 oz.) pkg. wide egg	1/4 cup butter
noodles	1 small bunch dill
1-1/2 tsp. salt, *divided*	1 lemon
1 cup walnuts	1/8 tsp. pepper

1) In large pot over high heat, bring 3 quarts hot water to boil. Add 1 tsp. salt and noodles and cook according to package directions, about 9 min.

2) Meanwhile, coarsely chop walnuts. In large skillet over medium heat, melt butter. Add walnuts and cook, stirring, until lightly toasted, about 3 min. Finely chop dill to yield 1/4 cup; set aside. Grate lemon to yield 1 tbsp. zest. Stir into skillet.

3) Drain noodles; add to skillet and toss well. Add dill, then remaining salt and pepper. Transfer to bowl and serve immediately.

nutritional facts: *Per serving: 410 calories • 41g carbohydrates • 12g protein • 23g fat • 160mg sodium • 65mg cholesterol • 4g fiber • 1g sugar*

wide range

If you're not partial to walnuts, try this easy recipe with pecans, orange rind and parsley for a totally different flavor. Or try it with pine nuts, olive oil and basil.

festive swiss chard

prep time: 15 minutes • **total time:** 15 minutes • **serves:** 6

Eating your way through the rainbow can be fun as well as healthy. Toasted pine nuts, sautéed Swiss chard and dried cranberries are tossed with a splash of balsamic vinegar for an eye-catching dish.

2 oz. pine nuts	1 small onion
1 small bunch *each* red and green Swiss chard, rinsed	1/4 cup dried cranberries
1 tbsp. olive oil	1 tbsp. balsamic vinegar

1) In large skillet over medium-high heat, toast pine nuts until light golden, about 2 min. Remove to plate and set aside.

2) Rinse and thoroughly dry Swiss chard. Thinly slice chard and mince onion.

3) In skillet over medium-high, heat olive oil. Add onion and cook, stirring, until softened, about 2 min. Add Swiss chard and dried cranberries and cook, stirring, until chard is tender and most of liquid has evaporated, about 10 min.

4) Remove from heat and stir in balsamic vinegar before serving. Transfer to serving bowl, sprinkle with pine nuts.

nutritional facts: *Per serving: 130 calories • 12g carbohydrates • 3g protein • 9g fat • 85mg sodium • 0mg cholesterol • 1g fiber • 2g sugar*

switch the swiss

If Swiss chard is too bitter for your taste, check the market for other fresh leafy greens—even large spinach leaves are absolutely delicious when prepared like this.

tangy bacon beans

prep time: 10 minutes • **total time:** 24 minutes • **serves:** 4

Once you try this simple but savory way to cook green beans, you'll want to make them often. Start with a foolproof combination of bacon and onion, and simply saute the green beans.

2 slices bacon	1/2 tsp. salt
1 medium onion	1/2 tsp. pepper
1 lb. green beans	2 tsp. vinegar
1/2 tsp. dried marjoram	1 tsp. sugar

1) Cut bacon into 1/4-inch strips. Thinly slice onion. In large, nonstick skillet over medium-high heat, cook bacon and onions until bacon begins to brown, 5 min.

2) Meanwhile, wash and trim green beans. Add to skillet with any water that clings to green beans. Sprinkle in marjoram, salt and pepper. Cook, covered, until tender, 12-15 min. Add vinegar and sugar and cook 1 min. Transfer to platter and serve.

nutritional facts: *Per serving: 90 calories • 12g carbohydrates • 5g protein • 4g fat • 480mg sodium • 10mg cholesterol • 4g fiber • 4g sugar*

adding herbs

Thyme, dill or parsley would all taste wonderful with these green beans. Or, go a different route with dried herbs de Provence.

cajun country homefries

prep time: 6 minutes • total time: 25 minutes • serves: 4

These oven-roasted homefries are just as crispy and flavorful as traditional fries, but they are much less work—and quite a nice departure from ordinary potatoes.

1 lb. baby red potatoes	1 tsp. dried parsley
2 tbsp. olive oil	1/2 tsp. dried thyme
1 tsp. Cajun spice mix	

1) Preheat oven to 425°F. Rinse potatoes and pat dry with paper towels. Cut potatoes into 1/2-inch chunks.

2) Transfer potatoes to large mixing bowl. Drizzle with olive oil and stir to coat.

3) Sprinkle spice mix, parsley and thyme over potatoes; stir to coat.

4) Coat nonstick baking sheet with cooking spray. Transfer potatoes to baking sheet and spread to single layer.

5) Roast potatoes, stirring every 5 min., until golden and crisp, about 20-22 min.

nutritional facts: *Per serving: 160 calories • 20g carbohydrates • 3g protein • 7g fat • 25mg sodium • 0mg cholesterol • 1g fiber • 0g sugar*

hot, hot, hot

This recipe makes medium-spicy homefries. If your family likes the heat turned up a few notches, increase the Cajun spice mix to 1-1/2 teaspoons or add some hot sauce.

beets in orange sauce

prep time: 15 min. • total time: 50 min. • serves: 8

To ensure your family eats their veggies, we suggest topping beets with this simply irresistible orange glaze. Eating healthy never tasted so good!

8 whole fresh beets	1 cup orange juice
1/4 cup sugar	1 medium navel orange, halved
2 tsp. cornstarch	and sliced, optional
Dash pepper	1/2 tsp. grated orange peel

1) Place beets in a large saucepan; cover with water. Bring to a boil. Reduce heat; cover and cook for 25-30 minutes or until tender. Drain and cool slightly. Peel and slice; place in a serving bowl and keep warm.

2) In a small saucepan, combine the sugar, cornstarch and pepper; stir in orange juice until smooth. Bring to a boil; cook and stir for 2 minutes or until thickened. Remove from the heat; stir in orange slices if desired and peel. Pour over beets.

nutritional facts: *Per serving: 63 calories • 15g carbohydrates • 1g protein • trace fat • 39mg sodium • 0 cholesterol • 1g fiber*

keep it simple

When preparing this colorful side dish, keep in mind that a 15 oz. can of sliced beats can be used in place of the fresh beets. Using canned beats means you can skip right to Step 2.

tips for
easy side dishes

veggie toppers

Steamed, boiled or sauteed vegetables are delicious by themselves but can get a flavor boost or added crunch with these easy toppings:

- Toss with a little butter or spritz with refrigerated butter-flavor spray and sprinkle with bread crumbs.

- Sprinkle with sauteed almonds or pecans, sesame seeds or sunflower kernels.

- Saute some chopped onion, celery or garlic and stir into the cooked vegetables.

- Sprinkle with Parmesan cheese.

- Add a splash of lemon juice or balsamic vinegar.

cilantro or coriander

The fresh green, leafy herb looks similar to flat-leaf parsley, but its flavor is pungent, strong and fresh. When cilantro is dried, it is know as coriander.

super quick pilaf

It's easy to add a bit of interest to plain rice. For each cup of uncooked jasmine, long grain white rice, brown rice or 1-1/2 cups instant rice, saute 1/2 cup each thinly sliced celery and thinly sliced green onions in 1 tbsp. butter. Stir into cooked rice along with 1 to 1-1/2 tsp. grated lemon peel. Season to taste with salt and pepper.

about swiss chard

Swiss Chard has a tangy flavor with a hint of lemon. Its large green leaves are white veined with a white stalk. The red leaf variety has a red stalk. The stalks are usually removed and cooked separately. Swiss chard is good for braising, stir-frying and steaming.

baked potatoes

Russet potatoes are probably the number 1 choice for baked potatoes. Before baking, scrub potatoes with a vegetable brush under cold water. Remove eyes or sprouts. Pierce potatoes with a fork to allow the steam to escape while baking. If you like, you can rub the skin with oil or wrap the potatoes in foil.

buying eggplants

Select a firm, round or pear-shaped eggplant. It should feel heavy for its size. The skin should have a uniform color and be smooth, taut and glossy. The eggplant should be free from blemishes and rust spots with an intact green cap and mold-free stem.

quick side skillet dish

Take leftover cooked rice—white, brown or wild—and leftover veggies to make a super side. Place your leftovers in a skillet with a can of diced tomatoes. Cook over medium heat until heated through. Sprinkle with some grated cheese and serve.

storing bulgur

Once a package of bulgur is opened, store in an airtight container in a cool, dry place for up to 1 month. In warm climates, store in the refrigerator or freezer.

keeping ginger

Peel fresh ginger with a vegetable peeler or small paring knife. To store fresh ginger, place in a small jar that has a tight-fitting lid and cover with dry sherry. Close jar and store in the refrigerator. After you've used the ginger, the ginger-flavored sherry makes a delicious flavor boost to any stir-fry that calls for sherry.

about lentils

 The most commonly available lentil in the supermarket is the brown lentil. Red and yellow lentils may be available in Middle Eastern, Indian or specialty markets. Lentils should be stored in an airtight container at room temperature. They may be stored for up to 1 year.

reviving celery

Give limp celery a second chance to season entrees, soups and stews. Cut the end from each limp stalk. Place in a jar or glass of cold water and refrigerate for several hours or overnight.

make it yellow and green

 Wax beans are yellow string beans and may be used in any recipe that calls for green beans. The next time you have company over, make your green bean recipe, using half green and half wax beans.

caring for vegetables

Handle vegetables gently—they bruise easily. A bruised spot will lead to decay. After purchasing, promptly refrigerate any vegetables that need to be kept cool. Rinse vegetables, including prepackaged vegetables, under cool, running water. Some vegetables, like potatoes or carrots, should be gently scrubbed with a vegetable brush if you are going to eat the peel. Always peel vegetables with a wax coating. Never place raw or cooked vegetables on the same surfaces that came in contact with uncooked meat.

smart shopping for frozen veggies

When buying bags of frozen vegetables, examine the packages for signs that they've been thawed and refrozen. Steer clear of bagged vegetables that are frozen in blocks of large chunks. If the packages are transparent, also check for crystallization. Both indicate thawing and refreezing, which can diminish quality.

favorite cookies

fudge chocolate clusters • p. 180

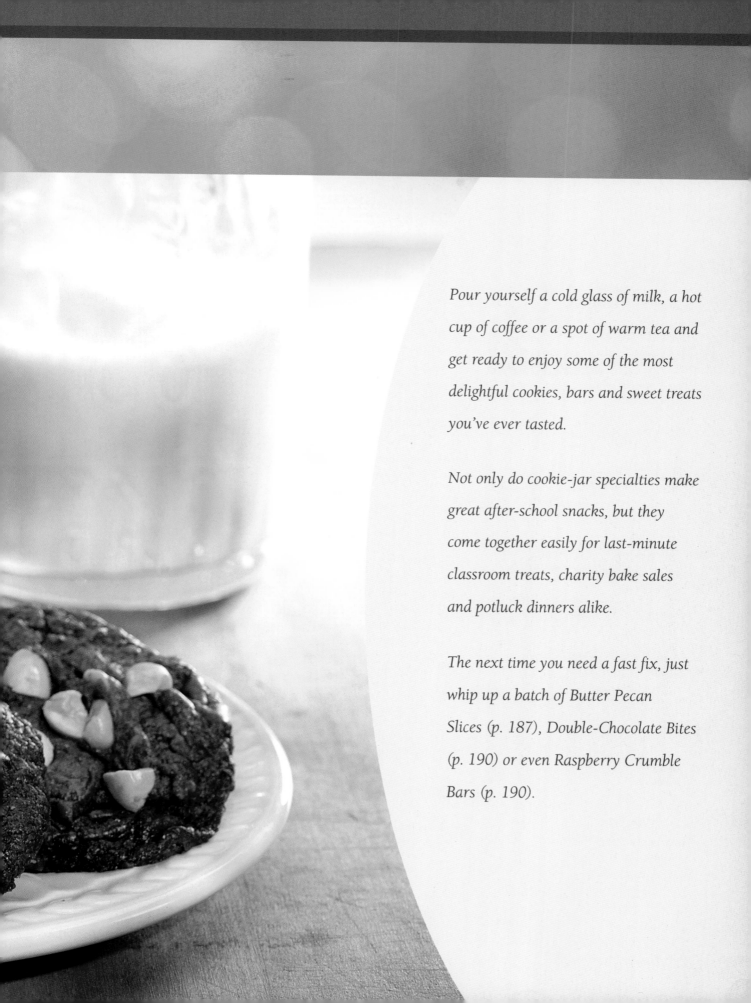

Pour yourself a cold glass of milk, a hot cup of coffee or a spot of warm tea and get ready to enjoy some of the most delightful cookies, bars and sweet treats you've ever tasted.

Not only do cookie-jar specialties make great after-school snacks, but they come together easily for last-minute classroom treats, charity bake sales and potluck dinners alike.

The next time you need a fast fix, just whip up a batch of Butter Pecan Slices (p. 187), Double-Chocolate Bites (p. 190) or even Raspberry Crumble Bars (p. 190).

cinnamon circles

prep time: 29 minutes • total time: 29 minutes • serves: 12

Topped with tiny unpeeled apple wedges and cinnamon-sugar for a truly unique treat, these crispy little morsels are like cookies and pastries all in one. No matter what you call them, they're delicious!

1/2 cup all-purpose flour	4 tbsp. butter
1/2 tsp. plus 1/8 tsp. ground cinnamon, *divided*	1/2 cup old-fashioned oats
1/2 tsp. ginger	1/4 cup plus 2 tsp. sugar, *divided*
1/4 tsp. baking powder	2 tbsp. molasses
	1 small McIntosh apple

1) Preheat oven to 375° F. In food processor, add flour, 1/2 tsp. cinnamon, ginger and baking powder; pulse to blend. Cut butter into pieces and add to bowl; process until blended, about 20 seconds. Add oats and 1/4 cup sugar; pulse to blend. Add molasses; process until well blended and soft dough forms, about 30-45 seconds.

2) On nonstick or lightly greased cookie sheet, divide dough into 12 balls. Flatten with hand into 2-1/2-inch rounds.

3) Core apple but do not peel. Cut horizontally into 1/8-inch slices, then into 1-inch pieces to yield 36 pieces. Arrange three pieces on each cookie.

4) Mix remaining sugar and cinnamon; sprinkle on apples. Bake until edges turn darker brown, 15 min. Let cool on cookie sheet 2 min., then remove to wire rack. Cookies are best when eaten the same day.

nutritional facts: *Per cookie: 100 calories • 15g carbohydrates • 1g protein • 4g fat • 35mg sodium • 10mg cholesterol • 1g fiber • 8g sugar*

cookie pops

Cut six cinnamon sticks in half lengthwise. When you take the cookies out of the oven, immediately poke a cinnamon stick into the bottom of each cookie to make a lollipop.

spiced cookie strips

prep time: 15 minutes • total time: 25 minutes • serves: 12

Convenient refrigerated cookie dough and a few spices from your cupboard are all you need to bake these yummy strips. Your family will want to gobble them up right out of the oven.

1 (18 oz.) tube refrigerated sugar cookie dough	1/2 tsp. nutmeg
2 tbsp. all-purpose flour	1/4 tsp. ground cinnamon
2 tbsp. butter, melted	1/4 tsp. cloves

1) Remove cookie dough from package and coat with flour. Shake excess flour onto work surface. Roll out dough on floured surface into a 12-in. x 8-in. rectangle. Using a pizza cutter or sharp knife, cut rectangle in half lengthwise. Cut widthwise into 1-in. strips. Carefully transfer strips to two ungreased baking sheets.

2) Combine butter and spices; brush over strips. Bake at 425° for 10-12 minutes or until edges are golden brown. Cool for 2 minutes before removing from pans to wire racks.

nutritional facts: *208 calories • 26g carbohydrates • 2g protein • 11g fat • 199mg sodium • 17mg cholesterol • trace fiber*

holiday hostess

These cookie strips make a fun change-of-pace addition to holiday cookie trays and a welcomed present for a hostess.

vanilla puffs

prep time: 10 minutes • total time: 29 minutes • serves: 18

Flecked with bits of vanilla bean, these soft cookies with their creamy glaze are a delight for any occasion. Although the ingredients are simple, they combine for a complex flavor.

1/2 cup butter	2 cups all-purpose flour
2/3 cup sugar	1 tsp. baking soda
2 large eggs	1 tsp. salt
2 tsp. vanilla extract	1 cup confectioners' sugar
1 vanilla bean	1 tbsp. plus 2 tsp. heavy cream

1) Preheat oven to 375°F. Cut butter into chunks and place in large, microwave-safe bowl. Microwave on MEDIUM until softened, 20-30 seconds. Add 2/3 cup sugar, eggs and vanilla extract. Cut vanilla bean in half crosswise; set aside one half. Slice the other half lengthwise. Scrape seeds from each half into bowl with tip of paring knife.

2) With electric mixer on medium, beat until light and fluffy, about 2 min. Add flour, baking soda, and salt to bowl. Beat until ball forms.

3) Roll dough into 1-inch balls. Place 2 inches apart on two ungreased baking sheets. Bake, switching pans halfway through bake time, until lightly golden on bottom, 8 min. Remove from oven and let cool, 1 min.

4) Meanwhile, cut remaining vanilla bean in half lengthwise and scrape remaining vanilla seeds from pod into small bowl. Add confectioners' sugar and cream, stirring until smooth glaze forms. Dip tops of cookies into glaze and place right-side up on rack to cool.

nutritional facts: *Per cookie: 160 calories • 25g carbohydrates • 2g protein • 6g fat • 240mg sodium • 40mg cholesterol • 0g fiber • 14g sugar*

vanilla sugar

Place a leftover vanilla bean pod into a sealed container of sugar. In a few weeks' time, you'll have a wonderful vanilla sugar to flavor baked goods, coffee or tea.

chewy popcorn bars

prep time: 10 minutes • total time: 25 minutes • serves: 16

Crunchy, sweet and slightly salty...these bars are hard to resist. With ready-made popcorn, nuts and a quick homemade buttery caramel, you can quickly create a no-bake cookie that takes just minutes to prepare.

4 cups popped popcorn	1/2 cup packed light brown sugar
1/2 cup salted whole almonds	1/4 cup light corn syrup
1/2 cup salted cashews	1 tbsp. all-purpose flour
4 tbsp. butter	

1) Coat 8-inch square baking pan with cooking spray. Cut and fold 14-inch length of parchment paper to fit bottom of pan, extending up sides to form handles. Place pan in freezer.

2) In large bowl, toss together popcorn, almonds and cashews.

3) In small, nonstick saucepan over medium heat, melt butter. Add brown sugar, corn syrup and flour; bring to boil. Boil 1 min.

4) Gradually pour liquid over popcorn mixture, stirring to coat well. Press into prepared pan and return to freezer to chill, 15 min. Use parchment paper to remove from pan. Cut into 16 bars and serve.

nutritional facts: *Per bar: 130 calories • 15g carbohydrates • 2g protein • 7g fat • 70mg sodium • 10mg cholesterol • 1g fiber • 8g sugar*

stop the stick

To make sure you get the full measure when pouring a sticky liquid, such as corn syrup or honey, into a measuring cup or spoon, spray it first with nonstick cooking spray.

sesame bars

prep time: 3 minutes • total time: 29 minutes • serves: 24

Irresistible and not too sweet, these four-ingredient bars are a delectable cross between a cookie and a candy bar. A unique treat that's rich in both calcium and antioxidants, these are as healthy as they are tasty.

2 cups sesame seeds, untoasted	2 large egg whites
3/4 cup packed light brown sugar	3 tbsp. sesame tahini

1) Preheat oven to 350°F. Lightly coat 9- x 9-inch square pan with cooking spray. Line with baking parchment paper, leaving 1-inch overhang on 2 opposite sides.

2) In medium bowl, mix together sesame seeds, sugar, egg whites and tahini. Stir with rubber spatula until well blended.

3) With small, metal spatula, spread seed mixture evenly into prepared pan. Bake until set, 16 min. Remove from oven. Using overhang, gently lift parchment paper out of pan; place on wire rack. Let stand until cool, about 10 min. Cut into 24 bars. Serve or store in airtight container.

nutritional facts: *Per serving: 110 calories • 10g carbohydrates • 3g protein • 7g fat • 5mg sodium • 0mg cholesterol • 2g fiber • 7g sugar*

save on sugar

Dark brown sugar is only slightly sweeter than light brown sugar. If you have dark brown sugar in your cupboard, use it in this recipe.

dreamy orange cookies

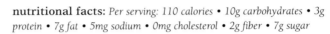

prep time: 15 minutes • total time: 29 minutes • serves: 18

Turn a basic butter cookie into something extra special by flavoring the dough with orange extract and peel, then dipping the cookies in white chocolate. The flavor is reminiscent of the old-fashioned ice cream bar.

6 tbsp. butter, softened	1/8 tsp. salt
1/3 cup confectioners' sugar	3/4 cup all-purpose flour
2 tsp. grated orange peel	1/2 cup white chocolate chips
1 tsp. orange extract	1 tsp. vegetable shortening
1/4 tsp. vanilla extract	

1) Preheat oven to 375°F. Line baking sheet with waxed paper; place in freezer. In food processor, blend butter and sugar until creamy. Add orange peel, extracts and salt; process until blended. Add flour and process until mixture forms ball.

2) Divide dough into 18 portions; roll each into ball. Place on nonstick baking sheet. With bottom of drinking glass, flatten each ball.

3) Bake until lightly browned around edges, 10 min. Remove to cooling rack; place in freezer, 4 min. Meanwhile, place white chocolate and shortening in small, microwave-safe bowl. Microwave on MEDIUM until melted, about 45 seconds.

4) Remove cookies and prepared baking sheet from freezer. Dip cookies in chocolate; place on prepared baking sheet. Return to freezer until chocolate is set, 2 min.

nutritional facts: *Per bar: 100 calories • 10g carbohydrates • 1g protein • 6g fat • 25mg sodium • 10mg cholesterol • 0g fiber • 6g sugar*

go nuts!

Take this up a notch by stirring 1/4 cup chopped almonds or walnuts into the cookie dough. Use an additional 1/4 cup chopped nuts as a crunchy topping for the white chocolate.

whoopie pies

prep time: 14 minutes • total time: 29 minutes • serves: 4

Giant, soft, chocolate cookies are sandwiched with fluffy marshmallow creme to create a truly unforgettable treat. It's part cake, part pie, part cookie...and altogether fabulous!

1 cup all-purpose flour	1/4 cup butter, softened
1/4 cup unsweetened cocoa powder	1/2 cup brown sugar
3/4 tsp. baking soda	1 large egg
1/2 tsp. baking powder	3/4 tsp. vanilla extract
1/4 tsp. salt	1/2 cup milk
	2 cups marshmallow creme

1) Preheat oven to 375°F. In small bowl, combine flour, cocoa, baking soda, baking powder and salt.

2) In medium bowl with electric mixer, beat butter and sugar at high speed until fluffy. Beat in egg and vanilla. At low speed, beat in flour mixture alternately with milk until smooth.

3) Spoon batter into 8 circles onto greased baking sheet. Bake until puffed and set, 10 min. Remove to rack; place in rack in freezer to cool, 5 min.

4) Remove from freezer; place 4 cookies bottom-side up on work surface. Spoon 1/2 cup marshmallow creme onto cookies, then top with remaining cookies, bottom side down. Serve immediately.

nutritional facts: *Per bar: 640 calories • 145g carbohydrates • 8g protein • 3.5g fat • 560mg sodium • 55mg cholesterol • 2g fiber • 81g sugar*

baking cocoa

To assure the finest quality, purchase organic or brand-name cocoa. Look for cocoa that's between 55% and 70% cocoa.

cheery cherry crisps

prep time: 10 minutes • total time: 20 minutes • serves: 12

Crispy, crunchy and very cherry with a double dose of tart and sweet cherries, these pretty little cookies will make the cook cheery, too, since they require no baking.

1 cup crisp rice cereal	1 tbsp. butter
3 maraschino cherries	1/3 cup chopped, dried tart cherries
3 tbsp. light corn syrup	
3 tbsp. light brown sugar	

1) Place nonstick mini-muffin pan in freezer to chill. In medium bowl, place rice cereal. Cut maraschino cherries in quarters; set aside.

2) In small, nonstick saucepan over medium-high heat, combine corn syrup, brown sugar and butter. Cook and stir until sugar and butter are dissolved. Bring to boil; remove from heat. Stir in dried cherries; immediately pour over cereal, stirring thoroughly to combine.

3) Remove muffin pan from freezer. Working quickly, evenly divide cereal mixture among muffin cups. Top each with maraschino cherry quarter. Place in freezer until set, 10 min. Remove crisps to plate and serve.

nutritional facts: *Per serving: 60 calories • 13g carbohydrates • 0g protein • 1g fat • 20mg sodium • 5mg cholesterol • 1g fiber • 7g sugar*

use any fruit

You don't need dried cherries to make this recipe. An equal portion of any chopped dried fruit, such as cranberries or raisins, give texture and sweetness to these treats.

ice cream scoop

An ice cream scoop is an easy way to form uniform balls. But if you don't have one, measure the dough with a heaping tablespoon and form balls with your fingers.

pumpkin balls

prep time: 10 minutes • total time: 25 minutes • serves: 18

Low fat and luscious, these fragrant cookies will fill your home with the wonderful aroma of ginger and pumpkin pie spice. These morsels look great on the dessert table!

12	gingersnap cookies	1/4 cup	finely chopped pecans *or* walnuts
1	cup old-fashioned oats		
3/4	cup all-purpose flour	1	large egg white
1/2	cup packed brown sugar	1/2	cup pumpkin puree
2	tsp. pumpkin pie spice	1	tsp. vanilla extract
1/2	tsp. baking soda	2	tbsp. confectioners' sugar

1) Preheat oven to 350°F. Line a large baking sheet with parchment paper. In a food processor fitted with metal blade, process the gingersnap cookies to fine crumbs.

2) In large bowl, combine crumbs, oats, flour, brown sugar, pumpkin pie spice, baking soda and nuts. Stir until thoroughly blended. Set aside.

3) Using wire whisk, beat egg white in medium bowl until stiff. Add pumpkin puree and vanilla; stir to combine. Add to reserved crumb mixture. Stir well using wooden spoon. (Mixture will be stiff.)

4) With 3/4-oz. ice cream scoop, drop 18 balls onto baking sheet. Bake until just golden at bottom edge, 15 min. Transfer to cooling rack.

5) Place confectioners' sugar in fine sieve. Shaking sieve gently, dust cookies with sugar. Serve warm or cooled.

nutritional facts: Per cookie: 100 calories • 18g carbohydrates • 2g protein • 2g fat • 35mg sodium • 0mg cholesterol • 1g fiber • 9g sugar

effortless dessert

Press refrigerated sugar cookie dough onto a pizza pan. Top with chocolate chips, miniature marshmallows and chopped nuts. Bake at the temperature noted on the dough's package or until the cookie dough is done.

hugs 'n' kisses cookies

prep time: 15 minutes • total time: 25 minutes • serves: 5 dozen

Refrigerated cookie dough takes the work out of these adorable treats that are sure to X-press your O-verwhelming affection for your guests.

1 (18 oz.) package refrigerated sugar cookie dough	Red colored sugar (optional)

1) Cut cookie dough into 1/4-in. slices. On a floured surface, roll each slice into a 6-in. rope. Cut half of the ropes in half widthwise.

2) Form into X's on ungreased baking sheets; seal edges and flatten slightly. Shape remaining ropes into O's on ungreased baking sheets; seal the edges and flatten slightly. Sprinkle with sugar if desired.

3) Bake at 350° for 8-10 minutes or until the edges are lightly browned. Cool for 3 minutes; remove from pans to wire racks to cool completely.

nutritional facts: Per serving: 74 calories • 10 g carbohydrates • 1 g protein • 4 g fat • 72mg sodium • 5mg cholesterol • trace fiber

snowy eggnog cookies

prep time: 10 minutes • total time: 20 minutes • serves: 12

These elegant little cookies feature a rum eggnog filling. By using convenience products, they can be made in moments.

4 tbsp. French vanilla-flavored instant pudding mix (1/2 of 3.4 oz. package)	1 tbsp. rum, bourbon *or* brandy
1 tbsp. milk	1/4 tsp. vanilla extract
1/2 cup sour cream	1/8 tsp. nutmeg
	24 ginger wafer cookies
	1 tbsp. confectioners' sugar

1) In medium bowl with electric mixer, blend pudding mix with milk, sour cream, rum, vanilla and nutmeg at low speed until combined, 1 min. Beat at high speed, about 20 seconds.

2) On baking sheet, arrange half of cookies, bottom side up. Spoon scant tbsp. filling onto center of each; do not spread. Top with remaining cookies, bottom side down. Press gently to spread filling almost to edges.

3) Place in freezer to firm filling, 10 min. Sprinkle with confectioners' sugar; serve immediately.

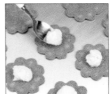

nutritional facts: *Per cookie: 90 calories • 14g carbohydrates • 1g protein • 3.5g fat • 100mg sodium • 10mg cholesterol • 0g fiber • 10g sugar*

rum extract

If you avoid alcohol, purchase the best rum extract available. Use a teaspoon portion of it to flavor vanilla ice cream, fruit, smoothies and these cookies.

nutty graham cracker brownies

prep time: 5 minutes • total time: 27 minutes • serves: 9

Two old favorites...brownies and graham crackers, are combined in a single dessert. With its crunchy crust and sweet, fudgy top, it's sure to be a crowd-pleaser.

9 graham crackers	1 cup sugar
1/2 cup old-fashioned oats	2 large eggs, slightly beaten
3/4 cups butter, *divided*	1 tsp. vanilla extract
2 squares unsweetened baking chocolate	1 cup all-purpose flour
	1/2 cup chopped pecans

1) Preheat oven to 400°F. Line 9- x 9-inch baking pan with foil, leaving overhang on two opposite sides. In food processor fitted with metal blade, process graham crackers and oats until fine crumbs form, about 30 seconds. Transfer crumbs to mixing bowl.

2) Place 6 tbsp. butter in small, microwave-safe bowl; microwave on HIGH until melted, about 45 seconds. Add to crumbs and stir to combine.

3) Spread crumb mixture into bottom of prepared pan, using 1/4-cup measure to flatten. Bake until set, 5 min.

4) Place remaining butter and chocolate in medium, microwave-safe bowl. Microwave on HIGH until melted, 2 min. Add sugar, eggs and vanilla; mix well. Stir in flour. Carefully pour chocolate mixture over graham cracker crust. Sprinkle pecans on top. Bake until set, 15-17 min. Transfer to rack. Lift out with foil and cut into 9 bars.

nutritional facts: *Per brownie: 410 calories • 44g carbohydrates • 6g protein • 25g fat • 170mg sodium • 85mg cholesterol • 3g fiber • 25g sugar*

spread in the pan

Instead of flattening the crumb mixture into the pan with your hand or a spoon, use the bottom of a 1/4-cup measuring cup.

sweet 'n' chewy bars

prep time: 5 minutes • **total time:** 28 minutes • **serves:** 12

These thick bars are chock-full of sweet, chewy dried apricots and crunchy nuts. You'll find they go fast—so make sure to put one aside for yourself!

3/4 cup butter	1/4 cup apricot nectar
3/4 cup sugar	2 cups all-purpose flour
1/4 cup packed light brown sugar	1 tsp. baking soda
2 large eggs	2/3 cup dried apricots
1/2 cup apricot preserves	1/2 cup chopped pecans

1) Preheat oven to 400°F. Grease 13- x 9-inch baking pan. Place butter in small, microwave-safe bowl; microwave on HIGH until softened, about 45 seconds.

2) With electric mixer on medium, cream butter and both sugars until light and fluffy, about 1 min. Add eggs, apricot preserves and apricot nectar. Mix on low speed to combine.

3) Stir in flour and baking soda. Chop dried apricots and add with pecans to dough, stirring to combine. Spread evenly in prepared baking pan.

4) Bake until top is lightly brown and firm, 18-20 min. Cool on rack, about 2 min. Cut into bars and serve warm or cooled.

nutritional facts: *Per serving: 290 calories • 46g carbohydrates • 4g protein • 10g fat • 130mg sodium • 55mg cholesterol • 1g fiber • 25g sugar*

great glaze

If time allows, make a glaze using 1 cup confectioners' sugar and 4 teaspoons apricot nectar. Drizzle over warm individual servings or entire bar cookie when cooled.

fudgy chocolate clusters

prep time: 15 minutes • **total time:** 22 minutes • **serves:** 8

The perfect mix of salty and sweet, this can't-miss combination of chocolate, peanut butter and peanuts will have everyone reaching for "just one more."

1/3 cup plus 1 tbsp. salted peanuts	1/2 cup sweetened condensed milk
1/2 cup semisweet chocolate chips	1/2 cup creamy peanut butter

1) Preheat oven to 350°F. Coarsely chop 1 tbsp. peanuts. Set aside in small bowl.

2) Place chocolate chips in medium, microwave-safe bowl. Microwave on HIGH until halfway melted, about 90 seconds. Stir until chips are completely melted.

3) Stir in sweetened condensed milk and peanut butter until well blended. Stir in remaining whole peanuts.

4) Line baking sheet with parchment paper. Drop batter by tablespoonfuls onto baking sheet. Sprinkle reserved chopped peanut pieces on top of cookies; with fingers, press nuts lightly to adhere.

5) Bake until just beginning to set, about 6 min. With thin metal spatula, carefully transfer cookies to cooling rack to cool completely.

nutritional facts: *Per serving: 270 calories • 22g carbohydrates • 8g protein • 18g fat • 190mg sodium • 5mg cholesterol • 2g fiber • 18g sugar*

melting chocolate

To prevent scorching, check the microwaved chocolate every 30 seconds. Or, melt the chocolate in a small, heavy pot atop another pot with boiling water (or in the top of a double boiler).

coconut marmalade bars

prep time: 5 minutes • total time: 29 minutes • serves: 20

This recipe is so simple to prepare, you'll have time to make fresh cookies any time you want. And since you just use the food processor and one pan, there's little mess.

1/2 cup butter, softened	1/2 tsp. baking powder
1/2 cup sugar	2/3 cup quick-cooking oats
1/3 cup marmalade	1/2 cup chopped pecans *or*
1 large egg	walnuts
1 tsp. vanilla extract	1-1/4 cups shredded coconut,
1/2 tsp. salt	*divided*
2/3 cup all-purpose flour	

1) Preheat oven to 375°F. Coat 9-inch square pan with cooking spray. In a food processor, combine butter, sugar, marmalade, egg, vanilla and salt until blended, 30 seconds. Add flour, baking powder, oats, pecans and 1 cup of coconut. Pulse together just until combined.

2) Scrape into prepared pan and spread to make level. Top with remaining coconut. Bake until toothpick inserted in center comes out clean, about 24 min. Cut into 20 bars and serve warm or cooled.

nutritional facts: *Per serving: 750 calories • 83g carbohydrates • 8g protein • 46g fat • 610mg sodium • 115mg cholesterol • 5g fiber • 48g sugar*

baking mat

A silicone baking mat will prevent the bars from sticking to the pan and will make cleanup easy...just rinse the mat and dry.

pizza pan cookie pie

prep time: 5 minutes • total time: 25 minutes • serves: 12

Pick a night when pizza's on the menu, and then give your family a pleasant surprise for dessert by serving this clever cookie. It's fun, tasty and super easy. It's great for kids' parties, too!

1 (18 oz.) pkg. refrigerated sugar cookie dough	1 extra-large egg
1 cup seedless raspberry jam	1 tsp. vanilla extract
1-1/2 cups shredded coconut	1/4 cup green sprinkles
1 tbsp. butter, melted	1/2 cup chocolate brownie flavor glazed walnuts
1/3 cup sugar	1/4 cup dried cherries
1/4 cup all-purpose flour	

1) Preheat oven to 350°F. Grease 12-inch round pizza pan. Press cookie dough evenly into pan.

2) Spread jam over cookie dough leaving 1/2-inch border all around.

3) In medium bowl, stir together coconut, butter, sugar, flour, egg and vanilla. Sprinkle mixture over top of pizza to resemble cheese.

4) Bake until topping mixture just starts to brown, about 15 min. Remove from oven and cool 10 min. Scatter walnuts and cherries over top. Drop sprinkles in small clusters over cookie's surface. Cut into 12 wedges and serve.

nutritional facts: *Per serving: 390 calories • 61g carbohydrates • 4g protein • 16g fat • 220mg sodium • 35mg cholesterol • 1g fiber • 37g sugar*

switch the "sauce"

For a tomato-red variation on this pizza cookie, use either strawberry jam or cherry preserves. Both are chunkier than raspberry jam, so you may need to break up any lumps.

chocolate-layered mint bars

prep time: 15 minutes • total time: 24 minutes • serves: 18

Always a tasty and winning combo, chocolate and mint make a truly pretty pair in this delicious, layered bar. Serve a batch at your next lunch buffet or picnic, and just wait for the oohs and ahhs.

1 (9 oz.) pkg. chocolate wafer cookies	4 oz. cream cheese
6 tbsp. butter	1/2 cup marshmallow creme
1-1/4 cups semisweet chocolate chips, *divided*	1/4 cup heavy cream
	1 tsp. peppermint extract
	6 to 8 drops green food coloring

1) Line 9- x 9-inch baking dish with foil, leaving overhang on 2 opposite sides. In a food processor, pulse cookies to fine crumbs.

2) Place butter and 1 cup chocolate chips in microwave-safe bowl. Microwave on HIGH until partially melted, 1 min. Remove; stir until melted. Pour over crumbs; stir to combine. Transfer crumb mixture to prepared pan; press to form even layer. Place pan in freezer.

3) With electric mixer on medium-high, beat cream cheese, marshmallow creme, heavy cream, peppermint extract and food coloring until thick and smooth. Remove crust from freezer. Spoon mixture over crust. Return to freezer; chill 10 min.

4) Place remaining chocolate chips in small, microwave-safe bowl. Microwave on HIGH until partially melted, 30 seconds. Remove and stir until chips are melted. Transfer to small, zippered plastic bag. Remove pan from freezer. With foil ends, gently remove cookie from pan. Snip off corner of plastic bag. Squeezing bag gently, drizzle chocolate over mint layer. Cut into 18 bars.

nutritional facts: *Per bar: 200 calories • 23g carbohydrates • 2g protein • 13g fat • 135mg sodium • 20mg cholesterol • 1g fiber • 14g sugar*

vary the flavor

Substitute raspberry extract and red food coloring to make an unforgettable chocolate-raspberry bar. Or try it with orange extract and orange food coloring for a different flavor.

salted peanut clusters

prep time: 13 minutes • total time: 23 minutes • serves: 18

These quick-to-fix treats combine a buttery caramel flavor with crunchy, salty peanuts. Simple to make and hard to resist, they're just perfect for warm weather because there's no baking!

2 tbsp. butter	1/2 cup semisweet *or* white chocolate chips
1/4 cup packed light brown sugar	
2 tbsp. corn syrup	1 cup salted peanuts
2 tsp. all-purpose flour	

1) Line baking sheet with waxed paper or parchment paper; place in freezer.

2) In medium, nonstick saucepan over medium heat, bring butter, sugar, corn syrup and flour to boil; cook, stirring constantly, 1 min.

3) Remove from heat and stir in chocolate chips until melted. Stir in peanuts.

4) Using 2 spoons, drop 18 clusters onto cookie sheet. Place in freezer until firm, 10 min. Transfer to plate and serve.

nutritional facts: *Per cluster: 70 calories • 9g carbohydrates • 1g protein • 3.5g fat • 25mg sodium • 5mg cholesterol • 1g fiber • 7g sugar*

even easier

For two-ingredient clusters, melt the chocolate chips over hot water. Stir in the peanuts and drop onto the baking sheet. Refrigerate or freeze.

nutty flax morsels

prep time: 7 minutes • total time: 29 minutes • serves: 36

Flaxseeds have a mild, nutty flavor. They add crunch as well as valuable Omega-3 nutrients to these whole-grain cookies. No one will suspect that something so tasty is good for you, too!

1/2 cup unsalted butter, softened	1 tsp. ground cinnamon
1 cup packed light brown sugar	1 tsp. baking powder
2 large eggs	1/8 tsp. salt
2 tsp. vanilla extract	1/2 cup chopped walnuts
1 cup whole wheat flour	1/4 cup flaxseeds
1/2 cup all-purpose flour	

1) Preheat oven to 375°F. Line 2 baking sheets with parchment paper. In large mixing bowl with electric mixer on medium, cream together the butter and sugar until light and fluffy, about 2-3 min. Add the eggs and vanilla; beat until combined, about 1 min.

2) Sift together flours, cinnamon, baking powder and salt. Gradually stir into butter mixture.

3) Fold in all but 2 tbsp. nuts and all of flaxseeds. Drop by rounded tablespoons onto prepared sheets, about 2 inches apart. Sprinkle tops with remaining walnuts. Bake until beginning to brown around edges, 9-11 min. Remove to rack. Serve warm or cooled.

nutritional facts: *Per cookie: 90 calories • 11g carbohydrates • 2g protein • 4.5g fat •25mg sodium • 20mg cholesterol • 1 fiber • 6g sugar*

fruity flavor

Customize your recipe with a half cup of raisins or cranberries or chopped dried apricots or cherries. Folks will love the flavorful, healthy treats.

california spice cookies

prep time: 10 minutes • total time: 28 minutes • serves: 36

Want a different cookie? Try these deliciously spicy morsels. They use a cake mix as the base, so you can whip up a batch in no time. You add the special touches, so they're filled with goodness from your kitchen.

1 (18.25 oz.) pkg. spice cake mix	3/4 cup sunflower seeds
1/2 cup butter, melted	3/4 cup raisins
2 large eggs	3/4 cup shredded coconut, *divided*
1/4 cup maple syrup	
1 carrot	

1) Preheat oven to 375°F. Coat 2 large baking sheets with cooking spray. In large bowl with electric mixer, beat together cake mix, butter, eggs and maple syrup until well blended, about 1 min.

2) Shred carrot to equal 1 cup. Add to bowl with sunflower seeds, raisins and 1/2 cup of coconut. Stir until combined. Drop by rounded tablespoonfuls onto prepared baking sheets, spacing 1-1/2 inches apart. Flatten slightly with back of spoon or moistened fingers. Sprinkle with remaining coconut.

3) Bake until cookies spring back when lightly touched in center and are golden brown on bottom, 8-10 min. Transfer cookies to rack to cool.

nutritional facts: *Per cookie: 130 calories • 17g carbohydrates • 2g protein • 6g fat • 125mg sodium • 20mg cholesterol • 1g fiber • 11g sugar*

try other ideas

You can substitute golden raisins, chopped dates, dried apricots, blueberries, cranberries or even chopped dried mango bits for the raisins.

chocolate option

If your family prefers chocolate, omit the nuts from the recipe. Roll these goodies in sugar, then in chocolate sprinkles.

sugared nut balls

prep time: 9 minutes • total time: 27 minutes • serves: 7

Also called Mexican Wedding Cakes, these tender little cookie balls are flaky and not overly sweet. They're just perfect for an afternoon snack or a tasty ending to the evening meal.

5 tbsp. unsalted butter, softened	1/4 tsp. vanilla extract
3/4 cup all-purpose flour	pinch salt
1/2 cup confectioners' sugar, *divided*	1/3 cup chopped walnuts

1) Preheat oven to 350°F. In medium bowl, combine butter, flour, 3 tbsp. confectioners' sugar, vanilla and salt. Knead with your hands until thoroughly combined. Add the nuts.

2) Using 1/2 oz. ice cream scoop, shape into 14 balls. Place onto ungreased baking sheet. Bake until very lightly browned on bottom, about 12-15 min.

3) Roll warm cookie in remaining confectioners' sugar. Cool on wire rack, then roll again in confectioners' sugar.

nutritional facts: *Per serving: 190 calories • 19g carbohydrates • 3g protein • 12g fat • 0mg sodium • 20mg cholesterol • 1g fiber • 9g sugar*

tasty topping

For added flair, top these bars with a tasty, decorative drizzle of melted white chocolate. Sprinkle with chopped macadamia or pistachio nuts.

pina colada bars

prep time: 8 minutes • total time: 25 minutes • serves: 16

All you'll need are a pair of sunglasses to feel like you're in the tropics when you bite into one of these pretty and exotic bars. Chock-full of sweet pineapple and coconut, they're all at once light and flavorful.

1-1/4 cup all-purpose flour, *divided*	1/2 cup pina colada mixer frozen concentrate
3 tbsp. confectioners' sugar	1/2 tsp. rum extract
3/4 cup flaked coconut, *divided*	1/2 tsp. baking powder
6 tbsp. butter, softened	1/4 tsp. salt
3 large eggs	
1 (8 oz.) can crushed pineapple	

1) Preheat oven to 400°F. Grease an 8- x 8-inch baking dish.

2) In small bowl, mix 1 cup flour and confectioners' sugar. Add 1/4 cup coconut and butter; mix with pastry blender or two knifes until mixture resembles coarse crumbs. Press into bottom of prepared baking dish. Bake until edges just start to brown, about 8 min.

3) Meanwhile, drain pineapple and set aside. Thaw pina colada concentrate by placing in zippered plastic storage bag and running under warm running water for 1 min. In medium mixing bowl, whisk together eggs and pina colada concentrate. Stir in drained pineapple, rum extract, baking powder, salt and remaining flour and coconut. Spoon filling over crust.

4) Bake until filling is set, 15-18 min. Transfer to rack to cool and cut into 16 squares.

nutritional facts: *Per square: 120 calories • 14g carbohydrates • 2g protein • 6g fat • 55mg sodium • 50mg cholesterol • 1g fiber • 7g sugar*

buttery orange rounds

prep time: 6 minutes • total time: 29 minutes • serves: 30

These delicate little circles have all the wonderful texture of a butter cookie with the added kiss of orange. The creamy citrus frosting adds a luscious richness.

1 large orange	1 tsp. vanilla extract, *divided*
1/2 cup plus 4 tbsp. unsalted butter, softened	1-1/4 cups all-purpose flour
2/3 cup sugar	1/2 tsp. baking soda
2 large egg yolks	1/4 tsp. cream of tartar
	1 cup confectioners' sugar

1) Preheat oven to 350°F. Line 2 baking sheets with parchment paper. Grate orange to yield 1 tsp. zest. Squeeze orange to yield 1 tbsp. plus 2 tsp. juice.

2) Place 1/2 cup butter and granulated sugar in medium bowl. Beat with an electric mixer on medium until fluffy. Stir in egg yolks, 2 tsp. orange juice and 1/2 tsp. vanilla.

3) Sift flour, baking soda and cream of tartar. Add dry ingredients to butter mixture one-third at a time, mixing well after each addition.

4) With fingers, evenly divide batter into 30 balls; place 3 inches apart on baking sheets. Bake until lightly golden on edges, 10-12 min.

5) Meanwhile, in clean mixing bowl, cream remaining butter. Add confectioners' sugar and remaining orange juice and vanilla. Mix on medium until smooth. Fold zest into icing. Remove cookies from oven. With small spatula, spread icing onto warm cookies. Serve warm or cooled.

nutritional facts: *Per cookie: 110 calories • 13g carbohydrates • 1g protein • 6g fat • 20mg sodium • 30mg cholesterol • 0g fiber • 9g sugar*

prep pointers

These cookies will spread as they bake so don't flatten them before putting them in the oven or they will be too thin. Leave a full 3 inches of space between each ball.

mallow ball munchies

prep time: 15 minutes • total time: 15 minutes • serves: 30

This no-bake recipe is easy to assemble, even for little hands. The combination of sweet and salty is sure to please grown-up tastes, too.

1 cup creamy peanut butter	1 cup swirled peanut butter and milk chocolate chips
1 (7.5 oz.) jar marshmallow creme	1/4 cup chopped dry roasted salted peanuts

1) In large mixing bowl, stir together peanut butter and marshmallow creme until combined.

2) Stir in chips until combined, then peanuts.

3) With fingertips, squeeze dough into 1-inch clusters. Serve immediately or store in airtight container.

nutritional facts: *Per cookie: 230 calories • 22g carbohydrates • 6g protein • 14g fat • 130mg sodium • 5mg cholesterol • 2g fiber • 14g sugar*

go nuts!

If you like chunky peanut butter, you can use it in this recipe instead of adding additional peanuts. You'll still get the crunch with the smoothness of peanut butter.

no-guilt gourmet cookies

prep time: 15 minutes • total time: 27 minutes • serves: 24

These quick-to-make and truly tasty cookies actually have real nutritional merit, courtesy of a hearty helping of oatmeal and zucchini! So feel free to dig right in to a warm, soft, home-baked treat.

1 cup all-purpose flour	1 medium zucchini
1 cup old-fashioned oats	1/2 cup oil
3/4 tsp. ground cinnamon	1 large egg
1/2 tsp. baking soda	3/4 cup packed brown sugar
1/4 tsp. nutmeg	1/2 cup flaked coconut (optional)
1/4 tsp. salt	

1) Preheat oven to 375°F. In medium bowl, mix flour, oats, cinnamon, baking soda, nutmeg and salt.

2) Shred enough zucchini to equal 1 cup. In large bowl, mix oil, egg and brown sugar until well blended. Stir in zucchini and coconut until blended. Stir in flour mixture until thoroughly combined.

3) Drop dough by tablespoonfuls onto two nonstick cookie sheets to form 24 cookies. Bake until lightly browned, 10-12 min. Remove to cooling rack. Serve warm or cooled.

nutritional facts: *Per cookie: 110 calories • 14g carbohydrates • 1g protein • 6g fat • 60mg sodium • 10mg cholesterol • 1g fiber • 7g sugar*

switch out zucchini

Some folks have an aversion to zucchini. If your family doesn't like zucchini or if it's out of season, simply substitute a large banana instead.

spiked walnut brownies

prep time: 11 minutes • total time: 29 minutes • serves: 12

Chocolaty-rich and crunchy with nuts, these brownies feature two kinds of chocolate, chopped walnuts and almond-flavored liqueur. A bit more of liqueur is brushed on top after baking for even more flavor.

8 tbsp. butter, cut into pieces	3 tbsp. almond-flavored liqueur, *divided*
2 oz. unsweetened chocolate, chopped	2 large eggs
2 oz. semisweet chocolate, chopped	1-1/4 cups all-purpose flour
1-1/4 cups sugar	1 cup coarsely chopped walnuts
	12 walnut halves (optional)

1) Preheat oven to 400°F. Coat 8- x 8-inch baking pan with cooking spray.

2) In large saucepan over low heat, melt butter and chocolate, stirring constantly. Remove from heat; stir in sugar and 2 tbsp. liqueur. Beat in eggs, one at a time. Blend in flour, then stir in walnuts.

3) Spread in pan and top, with walnut halves. Bake until brownies just start to pull away from sides of pan, 18-20 min. Remove from oven and place on racks to cool. Immediately brush with remaining liqueur. Cut into 12 squares when cooled.

nutritional facts: *Per serving: 290 calories • 28g carbohydrates • 5g protein • 20g fat • 65mg sodium • 55mg cholesterol • 2g fiber • 25g sugar*

taste twists

You can substitute 1 cup semisweet or white chocolate chips for the chopped walnuts and add rum instead of the liqueur for a totally different taste treat.

spicy applesauce oaties

prep time: 11 minutes • total time: 25 minutes • serves: 18

Applesauce keeps these oat cookies extra moist, while pie spice, raisins and walnuts bump up the taste for a chewy treat your kids will love as a lunchtime or snacktime treat. Try a batch today.

1/4 cup butter	1/2 tsp. baking soda
1/2 cup packed light brown sugar	1/4 tsp. salt
1 large egg	3/4 cup all-purpose flour
1/2 cup applesauce	1-1/2 cups old-fashioned oats
1 tsp. vanilla extract	1/2 cup chopped walnuts
1 tsp. apple pie spice	1/4 cup raisins

1) Preheat oven to 350°F. Place butter in medium, microwave-safe bowl. Microwave on MEDIUM until softened, but not melted, about 15 seconds.

2) Add brown sugar to bowl. Using electric mixer, blend until smooth and creamy. Beat in egg, applesauce and vanilla. On low speed, add pie spice, baking soda and salt.

3) Stir in flour, oats, walnuts and raisins. Drop dough by tablespoons onto ungreased baking sheets. Bake until golden, 12-14 min. Remove to wire racks to cool.

nutritional facts: *Per cookie: 130 calories • 19g carbohydrates • 3g protein • 5g fat • 80mg sodium • 20mg cholesterol • 1g fiber • 8g sugar*

sweet 'n' savory
Add 1/3 cup shredded cheddar cheese to the batter of these applesauce cookies.

butter pecan slices

prep time: 5 minutes • total time: 25 minutes • serves: 24

Crunchy and loaded with nuts, these cookies—reminiscent of bakery-made cinnamon rolls—are truly elegant but so easy to prepare when you use the secret ingredient: refrigerated pie crust!

1 tbsp. butter	1/2 tsp. ground cinnamon
1 ready-roll pie crust (1/2 pkg.)	2/3 cup chopped pecans
1/3 cup packed light brown sugar	

1) Preheat oven to 425°F. Place butter in small, microwave-safe dish and microwave on HIGH until softened, 5-10 seconds. Unroll pie crust onto large cutting board. Spread butter in thin layer over crust.

2) In small bowl, combine the brown sugar and cinnamon. Sprinkle evenly over the dough. Spread the nuts over sugar mixture; roll lightly with rolling pin to press nuts into the dough.

3) Roll dough tightly from one end into log. With sharp knife, slice dough into 1/2-inch rounds. Place rounds 2 inches apart on ungreased baking sheets.

4) Bake until cookies just start to brown lightly, 8-10 min. Remove to rack to cool.

nutritional facts: *Per serving: 160 calories • 16g carbohydrates • 1g protein • 10g fat • 110mg sodium • 5mg cholesterol • 1g fiber • 7g sugar*

change the shape
Instead of spirals, cut the dough circle into wedges. Roll from the wide edge into a crescent shape before baking.

favorite sandwich cookies

prep time: 15 minutes • total time: 15 minutes • serves: 9

So simple to make, these creamy on-the-outside and crispy on-the-inside cookies will be the hit of any after-school gathering. And don't forget to enlist the help of those after-school snackers in the making!

1/2 cup roasted peanuts	2 tbsp. butter, softened
1/2 cup peanut butter	32 chocolate wafer cookies,
1/2 cup confectioners' sugar	about 2-inch diameter

1) Finely chop peanuts in mini processor. Remove 1/4 cup; place on small plate and reserve for coating edges.

2) Add peanut butter, sugar, and butter to processor; process until blended. Drop 1 level measuring tbsp. of mixture on flat side of 18 cookies. Top with remaining cookies, rounded side up. Press cookies together so that filling just comes to edges.

3) Roll edge of each cookie in chopped peanuts to coat. Serve immediately or store in airtight container.

nutritional facts: *Per serving: 310 calories • 27g carbohydrates • 9g protein • 21g fat • 200mg sodium • 10mg cholesterol • 3g fiber • 15g sugar*

mix it up

This filling can be used with any store-bought cookies, including sugar, vanilla wafers and chocolate chip.

chocolate chip cookie squares

prep time: 8 minutes • total time: 26 minutes • serves: 16

Once you've made this speedy cookie bar recipe, you'll make it again and again. It has all the great flavors of fresh-baked chocolate chip cookies without the fuss of making multiple batches, every time!

1/2 cup butter, cut into small chunks	1 cup all-purpose flour
	1/4 tsp. baking powder
3/4 cup packed light brown sugar	1/4 tsp. salt
1 large egg	1 cup chocolate chips
1/4 tsp. vanilla extract	3/4 cup chopped walnuts

1) Preheat oven to 375°F. Line a 9- x 9-inch baking pan with aluminum foil and coating with cooking spray.

2) In food processor, blend together butter, sugar, egg and vanilla until combined, about 1 min. Add flour, baking powder, salt, chocolate chips and walnuts. Process using pulses, just until combined.

3) Drop dough into mounds in prepared pan. Place sheet of waxed paper on top and pat dough into even layer with fingers. Discard paper.

4) Bake until toothpick or cake tester inserted in center comes out clean, about 18-20 min. Set on rack to cool; cut into 16 squares.

nutritional facts: *Per square: 210 calories • 23g carbohydrates • 3g protein • 13g fat • 95mg sodium • 30mg cholesterol • 1g fiber • 16g sugar*

at the ready

This is such a popular recipe, you may want to double or triple all the dry ingredients and keep them sealed in a glass container until the next time you want to bake.

butterscotch oatmeal bites

prep time: 10 minutes • total time: 20 minutes • serves: 14

You can make these no-bake cookies at a moment's notice for a quick snack or dessert. Plus, they travel well, so you can tuck them into brown-bag lunches for a midday surprise.

2-1/2 cups miniature marshmallows	3 cups Cheerios
1 cup butterscotch chips	1/2 cup raisins
1/4 cup peanut butter	1/2 cup flaked coconut
2 tbsp. butter	

1) In a heavy large saucepan, combine the marshmallows, chips, peanut butter and butter. Cook and stir over medium-low heat until chips and marshmallows are melted. Remove from the heat; stir in Cheerios, raisins and coconut.

2) Drop by 1/4 cupfuls onto waxed paper. Let stand for 10 minutes.

nutritional facts: *Per serving: 191 calories • 26g carbohydrates • 3g protein • 9g fat • 108mg sodium • 5mg cholesterol • 1g fiber*

chips mix

For an easy change of pace, replace the butterscotch chips in this recipe with semisweet chocolate chips.

cocoa-almond meringue cookies

prep time: 20 minutes • total time: 1 hour 40 minutes • serves: 24

These yummy chocolate, almond and coconut treats taste just like a popular candy bar.

4 large egg whites	1/8 tsp. salt
1/4 tsp. cream of tartar	1 cup sugar
1/2 tsp. coconut extract	1/4 cup plus 1 tablespoon
1/4 tsp. almond extract	unsweetened cocoa powder,
1/4 tsp. vanilla extract	*divided*

1) In a mixing bowl, beat egg whites, cream of tartar, extracts and salt on medium speed until soft peaks form. Beat in sugar, 1 tbsp. at a time, on high until stiff peaks form. Sift 1/4 cup cocoa over egg whites; fold in. Place mixture in a pastry or heavy-duty resealable plastic bag; cut a small hole in a corner of bag.

2) Pipe meringue in 2-in. circles onto parchment paper-lined baking sheets. Bake at 250° for 50-60 minutes or until set and dry. Turn off oven; leave cookies in oven for 1-1/2 hours. Dust with remaining cocoa. Store in an airtight container.

nutritional facts: *Per serving: 26 calories • 6g carbohydrates • 1g protein • trace fat • 14mg sodium • 0 cholesterol • trace fiber*

parchment pointer

There is no right or wrong side to parchment paper, so either side can be used. For the best baking results, use a fresh sheet of paper for each pan of cookies.

raspberry crumble bars

prep time: 7 minutes • total time: 29 minutes • serves: 20

These irresistible bar cookies are incredibly easy to make, but are chock-full of flavors. A sweet, crumbly layer of oats serves as the base for stripes of raspberry jam, chocolate and almonds.

1-1/2 cups old-fashioned oats	1/4 tsp. almond extract
1 cup all-purpose flour	2/3 cup seedless raspberry jam
3/4 cup butter, softened	1/4 cup mini chocolate chips
2/3 cup packed brown sugar	1/4 cup sliced almonds

1) Preheat oven to 400°F. Line 9- x 9-inch baking pan with foil.

2) In medium bowl, using an electric mixer, combine oats, flour, butter, sugar and almond extract until mixture is crumbly. Remove and reserve 1 cup mixture. Press remaining mixture into prepared pan.

3) Spread on jam and crumble on reserved oat mixture. Top with chocolate chips and almonds.

4) Bake until golden, about 20 min. Remove pan to wire rack to cool completely. Remove cookies from pan and peel off foil. Cut into bars.

nutritional facts: *Per bar: 180 calories • 24g carbohydrates • 2g protein • 5g fat • 50mg sodium • 20mg cholesterol • less than 1g fiber • 15g sugar*

potluck favorite

Need a dessert for an informal party? Cut these bars in half and you'll have several dozen, bite-size treats. Chilling the pan makes cutting the cookies easy.

double-chocolate bites

prep time: 8 minutes • total time: 29 minutes • serves: 24

Surprise your family with the wonderful aroma of freshly baked chocolate cookies. Cocoa powder and chocolate chips provide a double dose of flavor to delight the taste buds, too.

4 tbsp. butter, softened	1/2 cup unsweetened cocoa powder
1/2 cup sugar	1 cup all-purpose flour
1/2 cup packed light brown sugar	1/2 tsp. salt
1 extra-large egg	1/2 tsp. baking soda
1-1/4 tsp. vanilla extract	1/2 cup mini chocolate chips

1) Preheat oven to 350°F. Adjust rack to center of oven. Cover two baking sheets with parchment paper; set aside. In large bowl, beat butter with electric mixer until creamy, 2 min. Add sugars and beat until fluffy, 2-3 min., scraping down sides as needed. Mix in egg, then vanilla. Add cocoa and mix until well blended.

2) Sift together flour, salt and baking soda. With mixer on low speed, add flour to chocolate mixture and beat until just combined. Fold in chocolate chips.

3) Drop batter by tablespoonfuls onto baking sheets. Bake until edges just start to brown, 10-12 min. Let cool slightly on pan, then remove cookies to rack.

nutritional facts: *Per cookie: 100 calories • 16g carbohydrates • 1g protein • 3.5g fat • 80mg sodium • 15mg cholesterol • 1g fiber • 11g sugar*

kids in the kitchen

Get the kids involved in the kitchen. Little helping hands can measure the dry ingredients, divide the stick of butter and add the egg and chips to the batter.

fruity oatmeal nut bars

prep time: 9 minutes • total time: 29 minutes • serves: 8

It doesn't get much easier than this. Start with a mix, add a layer of delectable, spreadable fruit and crown it with a topping of walnuts and oats for a soft, chewy bar.

1/2 cup unsalted butter, softened	1/3 cup blueberry spreadable fruit
1 large egg	1/3 cup finely diced walnuts
1 (17.5 oz.) pkg. oatmeal chocolate chip cookie mix	2 tbsp. quick-cooking oats

1) Preheat oven to 375° F. Line 13- x 9-inch pan with foil. In large bowl using hand mixer, combine butter and egg. Add cookie mix. Blend until thoroughly combined.

2) Place large spoonfuls into prepared pan. Place sheet of waxed paper over top. Pat dough into even layer with fingers. Discard paper.

3) Spread blueberry fruit over dough. Sprinkle walnuts and oats on top. Bake until lightly browned, about 18 min. Cut into 8 bars.

nutritional facts: *Per bar: 470 calories • 51g carbohydrates • 6g protein • 28g fat • 250mg sodium • 60mg cholesterol • 2g fiber • 14g sugar*

kid appeal

Have kids pat the dough in the pan, flatten the mixture with wax paper, smear on their favorite spreadable fruit and sprinkle with the topping.

luscious seven-layer bars

prep time: 5 minutes • total time: 25 minutes • serves: 36

These simple-to-prepare bars don't even require a bowl. Layers of buttery graham cracker crumbs, nuts, chocolate chips, oats and coconut bake together in just 20 minutes.

1/2 cup butter	1-1/2 cups old-fashioned oats
1-1/2 cups graham cracker crumbs	1 (14 oz.) can sweetened condensed milk
1 (12 oz.) pkg. semisweet chocolate chips	1-1/3 cups coconut
1 cup chopped pecans *or* walnuts	

1) Preheat oven to 375°F. Line 13- x 9-inch baking pan with foil, leaving 1-inch overhang on 2 short sides. Cut butter into 8 to 12 pieces and place in pan; place pan in oven until butter is melted, about 1 min.

2) As soon as butter melts, remove pan from oven; tilt pan to evenly distribute butter. Cover with even layer of graham cracker crumbs, then chocolate chips, pecans and oats. Drizzle condensed milk evenly over all, then top with coconut.

3) Bake until golden, about 20 min. Cool on wire rack, then lift out with foil and cut into 36 bars.

nutritional facts: *Per serving: 160 calories • 19g carbohydrates • 3g protein • 10g fat • 60mg sodium • 10mg cholesterol • 1g fiber • 14g sugar*

lunch-time treat

This recipe makes more than enough for several snack times. Pack the extras individually in plastic wrap. Freeze so they'll be handy for popping in lunch boxes.

parchment paper

If you have parchment paper on hand, you can line the baking pan with that instead of foil. You'll probably need to lay two sheets across each other.

candy bar blondies

prep time: 5 minutes • **total time:** 29 minutes • **serves:** 6

What do you get when you cross a butterscotch brownie with caramel-chocolate candy bars? A dessert that's chewy with just a bit of toffee crunch and a guarantee you'll keep coming back for more.

1/4 cup unsalted butter	1 tsp. baking powder
1 cup packed light brown sugar	1/2 tsp. salt
1 large egg, beaten	2 (2.07 oz.) peanut and caramel
1 tsp. vanilla extract	chocolate-covered candy bars
1 cup all-purpose flour	1 cup milk chocolate toffee bits

1) Preheat oven to 375°F. Line 8- x 8-inch baking dish with aluminum foil, allowing overhang on two sides. Lightly coat with cooking spray. Set aside.

2) In medium saucepan over low heat, melt butter. Remove from heat. Add brown sugar, stirring well. Stir in egg and vanilla extract.

3) Add flour, baking powder and salt, stirring just until combined. Chop candy bars into 1/2-inch pieces; stir into brownie batter.

4) Pour into prepared baking dish, spreading evenly. Bake until top is just firm to touch, about 22 min. Remove brownies from oven.

5) Sprinkle toffee bits over top, pressing gently onto brownie. Allow bits to melt slightly, about 1 min. Gently lift brownie from pan using foil overhang. Cut into squares; serve warm or cooled.

nutritional facts: *Per serving: 570 calories • 87g carbohydrates • 7g protein • 24g fat • 160mg sodium • 70mg cholesterol • 1g fiber • 65g sugar*

more chocolate

For added chocolate flavor, stir in 1/2 cup mini chocolate morsels. If you can find white mini morsels, use them: They'll look wonderful with the green decorating sugar.

mint crinkles

prep time: 10 minutes • **total time:** 27 minutes • **serves:** 1-1/2 dozen

Why save the cookie baking for the holidays? Mix, roll and bake these chocolate-minty treats in a jiffy. They're so easy, you'll be able to have cookies, warm from the oven, any time you want.

1/3 cup butter	1-1/4 cups all-purpose flour
1/4 cup unsweetened cocoa powder	1/2 tsp. baking soda
1/2 cup sugar	1/2 tsp. baking powder
2 large eggs	1/2 tsp. salt
1-1/2 tsp. mint extract	1/4 cup green decorating sugar

1) Preheat oven to 375°F. Place butter in large, microwave-safe mixing bowl. Microwave on MEDIUM until softened, about 20 seconds.

2) With electric mixer, cream together butter, cocoa, sugar, eggs and mint extract until light and fluffy, about 1-2 min. Add flour, baking soda, baking powder and salt to mixing bowl. Stir just until combined.

3) Place decorating sugar in shallow bowl. With fingers, roll dough into 1-inch round balls. Roll dough balls in sugar to cover completely. Place 2 inches apart on ungreased baking sheet.

4) Bake until tops are cracked and cookies are firm, 10-12 min. Transfer to rack to cool or serve warm.

nutritional facts: *Per serving: 110 calories • 16g carbohydrates • 2g protein • 4g fat • 140mg sodium • 30mg cholesterol • 0g fiber • 8g sugar*

moonbeam munchies

prep time: 15 minutes • total time: 25 minutes • serves: 36

This simple from-scratch sugar cookie dough can be mixed in a flash and is easy to roll and cut. Need to move at "light speed?" Use purchased refrigerator cookie dough instead.

2 cups sugar	1 tsp. baking soda
1 cup shortening	1/2 tsp. salt
1 large egg	1 cup sour milk
2 tsp. lemon extract	1/2 cup water
5-1/4 cups all-purpose flour	5 drops yellow food coloring

1) In a mixing bowl, cream sugar and shortening. Add egg and extract. Combine flour, baking soda and salt; add to the creamed mixture alternately with sour milk. Mix well. Refrigerate for 2 hours or overnight.

2) On a lightly floured surface, roll dough to 1/4-in. thickness. Cut with a round cookie cutter. If desired, cut some circles in half and form into half moon shapes. Place on greased baking sheets.

3) Bake at 350° for 8-10 minutes or until the edges begin to brown. Remove to wire racks to cool. Combine water and food coloring; brush over cooled cookies. Allow to dry completely. Store in airtight containers.

nutritional facts: *Per serving: 66 calories • 25g carbohydrates • 2g protein • 6g fat • 73mg sodium • 7mg cholesterol • trace fiber*

swift solution

To sour milk, place 1 tablespoon white vinegar in a measuring cup. Add milk to equal 1 cup.

lavender shortbread

prep time: 45 minutes • total time: 1 hour 15 minutes • serves: 24

Lavender flowers can be used fresh or dried in cooking. The flowers have an intense flavor, so they are best used sparingly.

2 cups confectioners' sugar	2/3 cup sugar
2 tbsp. plus 2 tsp. finely snipped dried lavender flowers, *divided*	2 cups all-purpose flour
	1/2 cup cornstarch
	1/8 tsp. salt
1 cup butter, softened	

1) In a bowl, combine confectioners' sugar and 2 tsp. lavender; cover and set aside at room temperature for 24 hours. In a mixing bowl, cream butter, sugar and remaining lavender. Combine flour, cornstarch and salt; add to the creamed mixture. Divide dough in half. Cover and refrigerate for 2 hours or until easy to handle.

2) On a lightly floured surface, roll out one portion of dough to 1/4-in. thickness. Cut into 1-1/2-in. squares. Repeat with remaining dough.

3) Place 1 in. apart on ungreased baking sheets. Prick with a fork several times. Bake at 325° for 18-22 minutes or until edges are lightly browned. Cool for 1 minute before removing to wire racks to cool completely. Sift reserved lavender sugar; discard lavender. Dust cookies with the sugar. Store in airtight containers.

nutritional facts: *Per serving: 175 calories • 26g carbohydrates • 1g protein • 8g fat • 90mg sodium • 20mg cholesterol • trace fiber*

flower power

Dried lavender flowers are available from Penzeys Spices at www.penzeys.com.

tips for
favorite cookies

pretty crisscross pattern

A fork is used to make the crisscross pattern on peanut butter and other types of cookies. If the fork is sticking to the cookie dough, try spraying the fork with cooking spray.

mixing it up

Drop cookie dough is usually so thick that it can be dropped from a spoon and requires no shaping. If while you're mixing the dough the mixer begins to strain, use a wooden spoon to stir in the last of the flour or all of the nuts, chips and dried fruit.

spread too thin

If cookie dough spreads too thin when it's baked, make sure the baking sheet is completely cooled before placing the next batch of dough on it. Also, try chilling the dough before baking it.

about biscotti

Biscotti (bee-skawt-tee) is an Italian cookie that is baked twice. First it's baked as a loaf and cut into individual cookies. Then the cookies are baked again, which produces dry, crunchy cookies that go great with coffee.

make quick work of cutting brownies or bars

A large pizza cutter will quickly and cleanly cut a pan of brownies into bars.

crumbling cookies

If cookies crumble when you remove them from the baking sheet, let them cool for 1 to 2 min. first. But if cookies cool too long, they become hard and can break when removed. If this happens, return the baking sheet to the oven to warm the cookies slightly so they'll release more easily.

don't forget to floss

To easily slice refrigerated cookie dough, slide a 1-inch piece of dental floss under the chilled roll. Crisscross the ends above the roll and pull until you've cut a perfectly round slice.

storing cookies

Cookies should always be completely cooled and icings should be completely dry before storing. Store crisp cookies separately from soft cookies and strong-flavored cookies separately from delicate-flavored cookies.

uniform drop cookies

To ensure drop cookies bake up to a uniform size, use an ice cream scoop with a spring release. A 1-tbsp.-size scoop will give you a 2-inch cookie. Just scoop the dough, and then even off the top with a flat-edge metal spatula and release onto a baking sheet.

coating the edges

To give a little twist to refrigerated cookies, coat the edge in nuts, colored sugar or jimmies. Spread the coating lengthwise down a piece of waxed paper. Place the roll of dough on top of the coating and roll gently, pressing coating onto dough with your hands.

making layered bars

When the bottom layer of a bar cookie needs to be pressed into a pan, try this trick. Place the mixture into the pan then cover with waxed paper. Press dough evenly into pan. Discard the waxed paper. This way your hands and fingernails stay clean.

remove bars easily from pan

To pop bars out of the pan without any fuss, line the pan with foil. First cut a piece of foil that is larger than the pan. Turn the pan upside down and mold the foil around the bottom and sides of the pan. Turn the pan right side up and insert the foil, allowing the edges to overhang the pan. Grease foil if recipe directs to grease the pan. Bake and cool as directed. After the bars are completely cooled, lift out of the pan using the foil.

keeping brownies

Store most brownies in an airtight container at room temperature. Brownies with a pudding layer, cream cheese or other perishable ingredients should be stored in the refrigerator.

storing bars

Most bars can be stored directly in the pan. Just cover the pan with foil or slip into a large plastic food storage bag. Close the bag and store at room temperature. If the bars were made with perishable ingredients, such as cream cheese, they should be stored in the refrigerator.

dusting with confectioners' sugar

To achieve a light coating of confectioners' sugar over the top of bars, brownies, cakes or other desserts, place some confectioners' sugar in a small fine mesh strainer. Tap the rim of the strainer gently as you move it over the top of the dessert.

evenly baked bars

When pouring batter into the pan or pressing the crust into the pan, make sure the corners are evenly filled. If one corner is thinner than the others, it will be overbaked.

shaping cookies

Cookies bake more evenly if all the cookies on the baking sheet are the same size. A 1-1/2-inch ball of dough will require about 1 tbsp. of dough per cookie. Fill a teaspoon or tablespoon with dough. Use another spoon or small rubber spatula to push the mound of dough off the spoon onto a cool baking sheet. Place dough 2 to 3 in. apart or as recipe directs.

delicious desserts

coconut joy pie • p. 205

Dig in! It's no wonder dessert is everyone's favorite course. After all, sweet sensations tempt taste buds by putting the spotlight on chocolate and caramel…getting mouths watering with the promise of sweet fruits and buttery crusts…or turning heads by delivering creamy puddings or crunchy nuts. What's not to like?

Turn the page, and you're sure to find sweet sensations that come together with ease as well as impressive edibles that are perfect for weekend dinner parties. You'll even find a few treats to top off Sunday brunches or to serve as surprise after-school snacks.

freezer pleaser

When peaches are in season, buy extra. Cut them in half, pit or core them and freeze. Use them in this recipe for a winter treat that recalls summer.

shortbread-stuffed peaches

prep time: 18 minutes • total time: 18 minutes • serves: 4

A great dessert any time of year, it's especially welcome in the dog days of summer. Even though the peaches are prepared in the microwave, the topping has that crispy, oven-baked taste everyone loves.

2 tbsp. butter	1 tbsp. brown sugar
2 peaches, halved and pitted (1 lb.)	3 tbsp. pecans, coarsely chopped
1/4 cup butterscotch sauce	
6 pecan shortbread cookies, crushed	

1) In small microwave-safe bowl, heat butter on HIGH to melt, 1-2 min. Set aside.

2) With a teaspoon, increase hollows in peach halves, making them about 1 inch in diameter. With sharp paring knife, trim rounded side of peaches so they sit level, cut side up. Place in 9-inch, microwave-proof baking dish.

3) Spoon 2 tbsp. butterscotch sauce into the hollows; cover with plastic and cut 2 slits for venting. Microwave on HIGH for 5 to 6 min. or until fork tender.

4) Meanwhile, in medium bowl, combine cookie crumbs, butter, brown sugar and pecans. Place peaches on serving plate, leaving juices in dish. Evenly divide crumb mixture and mound on peaches. Stir remaining butterscotch sauce into fruit juices in dish. Spoon over peaches.

nutritional facts: *Per serving: 280 calories • 35g carbohydrates • 3g protein • 15g fat • 170mg sodium • 10mg cholesterol • 2g fiber • 12g sugar*

all about orange

This cake can be made with orange juice, zest and extract instead of the lemon counterparts.

lemon pound cake

prep time: 20 minutes • total time: 2 hours • serves: 16

Like most pound cakes, this delicious dessert ideally is made a day in advance to allow the flavors to develop. It can be stored for a week in an airtight container or frozen for up to two months.

1 large lemon	2-1/2 cups sugar
2-3/4 cups all-purpose flour	6 large eggs
1-1/2 tsp. baking powder	2 tsp. lemon extract
1/2 tsp. salt	1-1/2 cups confectioners' sugar
1 cup unsalted butter, softened	
1 (8-oz.) pkg. cream cheese, softened	

1) Preheat oven to 325°F. Grease and flour 10-inch tube pan. Zest, then juice lemon; set aside. In medium bowl, combine flour, baking powder and salt.

2) With electric mixer, cream butter and cream cheese until smooth. Gradually add 2-1/2 cups sugar; beat on high speed until creamy, about 3 min. Add eggs, one at a time; beat 1 min., scraping sides of bowl.

3) Reduce to lowest speed; beat in extract. Gradually add flour mixture, beating until just combined. Stir in zest by hand and scrape into prepared pan; spread level. Bake until toothpick inserted near center comes out clean, about 1 hour, 15 min. Cool on rack 15 min.; remove from pan and set on rack (right-side up) to cool completely.

4) In medium bowl, whisk confectioners' sugar and 4-5 tsp. lemon juice to glaze consistency. Place in small zippered bag. Snip off one corner. Drizzle glaze over cake.

nutritional facts: *Per serving: 420 calories • 60g carbohydrates • 6g protein • 18g fat • 180mg sodium • 125mg cholesterol • 1g fiber • 43g sugar*

quickie coconut cake

prep time: 9 minutes • total time: 29 minutes • serves: 8

This classic cake makes a great dessert for any and all occasions. Not only does it taste so good, it's also pretty and quick and simple to make.

2/3 cup low-fat milk	1/2 cup jarred lemon curd
1 tsp. vanilla extract	1-1/2 cups marshmallow creme, *divided*
1/4 tsp. coconut extract	
1/3 cup sugar	3/4 cup shredded coconut, *divided*
2 cups reduced-fat instant baking mix	

1) Preheat oven to 425°F. Coat 8-inch round cake pan with cooking spray. In large bowl, stir together milk, extracts and sugar. Stir in baking mix just until combined. Scrape into cake pan and spread level.

2) Bake until top is golden brown and toothpick inserted in center comes out clean, 14-16 min. Invert onto rack and place in freezer to quickly cool, 8 min.

3) Meanwhile, in medium bowl, stir together lemon curd and 1/2 cup marshmallow creme. Slice cake in half and spread curd mixture on bottom half of cake. Sprinkle with 1/4 cup coconut. Top with cake layer. Spread with remaining marshmallow creme; sprinkle with remaining coconut.

nutritional facts: *Per serving: 280 calories • 55g carbohydrates • 3g protein • 5g fat • 410mg sodium • 0mg cholesterol • 1g fiber • 32g sugar*

beat the clock

Make this cake even more quickly by using a lemon-flavored or vanilla cake mix, then make the filling and topping as directed.

creme de menthe parfaits

prep time: 10 minutes • total time: 10 minutes • serves: 4

This green-and-white delight looks so elegant and fresh, no one will guess how easy it is. Just a few minutes in the kitchen produces a dessert that dazzles the eye and the taste buds.

1/4 cup plus 4 tsp. green creme de menthe liqueur	2 cups chocolate-chip mint ice cream, slightly softened
3/4 cup heavy cream	4 chocolate mint candies
1 tbsp. confectioners' sugar	4 sprigs fresh mint

1) In medium bowl, combine 1/4 cup liqueur, cream and sugar. Beat at high speed with electric mixer until cream is stiff.

2) In each of 4 parfait, dessert or wine glasses, place 1 tsp. remaining liqueur.

3) Layer 3 tbsp. cream mixture, 1/2 cup ice cream, and another 3 tbsp. cream mixture. Cut mint candies in half diagonally. Garnish parfaits with candies and sprig of mint. Serve immediately.

nutritional facts: *Per serving: 380 calories • 37g carbohydrates • 4g protein • 19g fat • 80mg sodium • 70mg cholesterol • 1g fiber • 31g sugar*

kid-friendly version

This one isn't for the kids, but you can make them their own version. Layer chocolate-chip mint ice cream with chocolate sauce and crumbled chocolate cookies.

chocolate raspberry roll

prep time: 25 minutes • total time: 70 minutes • serves: 10

This charming dessert is both old-fashioned and sophisticated. A light chocolate sponge cake is rolled with a blend of raspberries and whipped cream and flavored with raspberry liqueur for luxury in every bite.

1/4 cup unsweetened cocoa powder plus 4 tbsp., *divided*	1 cup sugar
3/4 cup all-purpose flour	1 tsp. vanilla extract
1 tsp. baking powder	1 pint fresh raspberries
1/4 tsp. salt	4 tbsp. confectioners' sugar
4 large eggs	4 tbsp. raspberry liqueur
	1 cup heavy cream

1) Preheat oven to 375°F. Line 15-1/2 x 10-1/2 jelly-roll pan with foil; spray with cooking spray. Lay clean towel on work surface; dust with 2 tbsp. cocoa. In small bowl, blend flour, 1/4 cup cocoa, baking powder and salt.

2) In large bowl, beat eggs at high speed with electric mixer, 3 min. Beat in 1 cup sugar, 1/4 cup water and vanilla. At low speed, beat in flour mixture. Spread batter evenly in pan. Bake until cake springs back when touched in center, 12-15 min. Invert cake onto towel. Remove foil and roll cake up in towel from 1 short end. Place seam-side down on rack until cool, 30 min.

3) Reserve 1/2 cup berries. In small bowl with spoon, crush 3/4 cup berries with 1 tbsp. confectioners' sugar and 1 tbsp. liqueur; stir in whole berries. In medium bowl, whip cream with remaining sugar and 1 tbsp. liqueur. Fold in berry mixture.

4) Unroll cake and remove towel. Sprinkle cake with remaining liqueur, then spread cream to within 1 inch of edges. Re-roll cake; dust with remaining cocoa. Place on tray; garnish with reserved berries. Chill 20 min.; serve.

nutritional facts: *Per serving: 280 calories • 37g carbohydrates • 6g protein • 14g fat • 140mg sodium • 115mg cholesterol • 4g fiber • 24g sugar*

make it mocha

If your family likes a deep chocolate flavor, try adding a tablespoon of instant coffee or espresso powder to the cake batter with the other dry ingredients.

exotic fruity sherbet

prep time: 10 minutes • total time: 16 minutes • serves: 4

This gorgeous dish is a delicious and healthy alternative to a traditional cake or pie. A great light dessert, it's especially welcome when served as the crowning touch to a festive brunch or luncheon.

3 tbsp. sugar	2 kiwifruit
2 tbsp. fresh mint leaves	1/2 pint fresh raspberries
1 ripe mango	1 quart orange sherbet

1) In microwave-safe measuring cup, combine sugar and 1/4 cup water. Microwave on HIGH until slightly thickened, 5-6 min.

2) Meanwhile, mince mint leaves. Stir mint into syrup and set aside.

3) Peel and slice kiwi into 1-inch chunks; place in medium mixing bowl. Slice mango from pit; remove skin and cut into 1-inch chunks. Add to kiwi. Add raspberries to bowl; toss gently to combine.

4) To serve, evenly divide fruit among 4 serving dishes. Place 1 large scoop sherbet on top of fruit. Spoon mint syrup over sherbet and fruit; serve immediately.

nutritional facts: *Per serving: 260 calories • 59g carbohydrates • 1g protein • 0.5g fat • 860mg sodium • 0mg cholesterol • 4g fiber • 51g sugar*

serving suggestions

Freeze this into molds, putting whole mint leaves in each. Then use it as a centerpiece for a party punch with mango juice, seltzer and orange juice.

coffee-crunch ice cream cake

prep time: 12 minutes • total time: 29 minutes • serves: 10 to 12

Now you can make one of those ice cream shop cakes at home with this clever layering of chopped cookies, ice cream, fudge sauce and espresso beans. Have the fun of making it and eating it!

11 chocolate sandwich cookies	1 (1/2 gallon) box coffee
1/2 cup chocolate-covered	ice cream
espresso beans	1 (8 oz.) container frozen
1-1/4 cups hot fudge sauce	whipped topping, thawed

1) Set serving platter near work space. Reserve 6 cookies and 6 espresso beans for garnish. On cutting board, chop remaining cookies and espresso beans together. Microwave 1/2-cup fudge sauce just until softened, but not hot, about 30 seconds.

2) Unwrap ice cream and cut horizontally into 3 slabs. Place one slab on serving dish. Sprinkle on half of chopped cookies and espresso beans. Drizzle 1/4-cup fudge sauce evenly on top. Cover with second ice-cream slab. Repeat layers. Place in freezer to firm, about 10 min.

3) Meanwhile, with serrated knife, slice remaining cookies in half. Spoon whipped topping into disposable pastry bag with star tip or food storage bag with corner snipped off. Remove cake from freezer. Pipe topping on long sides of cake and in 3 rows on top.

4) Garnish with cookie halves on two outer rows on top and espresso beans down center row. Serve with remaining hot fudge sauce.

nutritional facts: *Per serving: 620 calories • 60g carbohydrates • 10g protein • 37g fat • 290mg sodium • 170mg cholesterol • 1g fiber • 38g sugar*

it's in the bag

No pastry bag? Is the plastic storage bag just too flimsy for a firm filling? Make a sturdy and disposable funnel with four sheets of clean, letter-size, white printer paper.

rocky road pizza

prep time: 5 minutes • total time: 20 minutes • serves: 6 to 8

Looking for an interesting dessert to offer your hungry clan? Chocolate lovers will relish this palate-pleasing pizza that cleverly captures the flavor of rocky road ice cream.

Pastry for single-crust pie (9 inches)	1/2 cup mini marshmallows
3/4 cup semisweet chocolate	1/4 cup salted peanuts
chips	

1) On a lightly floured surface, roll pastry into a 9-in. circle; place on a lightly greased baking sheet. Prick with a fork. Bake at 450°F. for 8-10 minutes or until lightly browned. Sprinkle with chocolate chips. Bake 1-2 minutes longer or until chocolate is softened.

2) Spread chocolate over crust to within 1/2 in. of edges. Sprinkle with marshmallows. Bake for 1-2 minutes or until marshmallows puff slightly and are lightly browned. Sprinkle with peanuts. Remove to a wire rack to cool.

nutritional facts: *Per serving: 232 calories • 26g carbohydrates • 3g protein • 14g fat • 123mg sodium • 5mg cholesterol • 1g fiber*

tiny helpers

Let your little chef into the kitchen to help prepare this treat. Tots can sprinkle on the chips, marshmallows and peanuts. Older kids can spread the chocolate over the crust.

fruit-filled cupcakes

prep time: 15 minutes • **total time:** 26 minutes • **serves:** 12

The texture of these cupcakes is light and airy. And they've got a wonderful surprise—a sweet, fruity center. If you need a cupcake for a special occasion, this one will surely do the trick!

1-1/4 cups all-purpose flour	1-1/2 tsp. almond extract, *divided*
3/4 cup sugar, *divided*	1 large egg, *separated*
1-1/2 tsp. baking powder	1 cup confectioners' sugar
1/2 tsp. salt	1/4 cup raspberry preserves
2 tbsp. vegetable oil	1/2 pint fresh raspberries
1/2 cup, plus 2 tsp. milk	1/4 cup sliced almonds

1) Preheat oven to 400°F. Line 12-cup muffin tin with paper liners. In medium bowl, stir together flour, 1/2 cup sugar, baking powder and salt.

2) Add oil, 1/4 cup milk and 1 tsp. almond extract. With electric mixer, beat until smooth. Separate egg; place white in small bowl. Add yolk to batter with 1/4 cup milk. Beat 1 min. With clean beaters, beat egg white until soft peaks form. Gradually beat in remaining sugar to whites until stiff peaks form. Fold in egg white.

3) Spoon 1 tbsp. batter into prepared cups. Top each with rounded 1/2 tsp. raspberry preserves, then additional tbsp. batter, covering jam completely. Bake until cakes are firm to touch, 8-10 min. Place on rack.

4) Meanwhile, combine confectioners' sugar and remaining milk and almond extract to form glaze. Dip cupcakes into glaze. Press 3-4 raspberries on top of glaze and sprinkle with almond slices.

nutritional facts: *Per serving: 230 calories • 45g carbohydrates • 3g protein • 4.5g fat • 160mg sodium • 20mg cholesterol • 1g fiber • 33g sugar*

less trans fat

For health benefits, do more homemade baking with light, healthy vegetable or canola oil whenever possible.

chocolate pots de creme

prep time: 6 minutes • **total time:** 27 minutes • **serves:** 5

No one will ever believe this elegant, chocolate-and-cream dessert uses just five ingredients and takes mere minutes to prepare.

1 cup semisweet mini chocolate chips, *divided*	2/3 cup half-and-half
1 tbsp. sugar	5 tbsp. refrigerated ready-to-use whipped cream
1/2 tsp. vanilla extract	

1) In small dish, set aside 1 tsp. mini chips. Place remaining chips, sugar and vanilla in food processor; pulse several times to combine.

2) Pour half-and-half into microwave-safe bowl. Microwave, uncovered, on HIGH just until it begins to boil, about 1 min. Stir. Microwave 15 more seconds or until boiling but not boiling over.

3) Into food processor, slowly add half-and-half; process until mixture is smooth and creamy, about 30 seconds. Pour into 1/4 cup demitasse cups or dessert dishes. Freeze for 20 min. Remove from freezer. Garnish each with 1 tbsp. whipped cream, sprinkle with remaining chocolate chips. Serve immediately.

nutritional facts: *Per serving: 230 calories • 26g carbohydrates • 2g protein • 14g fat • 15mg sodium • 10mg cholesterol • 2g fiber • 21g sugar*

yuletide treat

For the winter holidays, make a festive and memorable dessert by replacing the vanilla extract with mint extract and sprinkling the top with a crushed candy cane.

coconut pecan tartlets

prep time: 4 minutes • total time: 28 minutes • serves: 4

Once you've made these fabulous tartlets, your family will be requesting them again and again. And you'll be happy to oblige because pre-rolled pastry and a one-bowl filling make them a snap!

1 refrigerated ready-made pie crust (1/2 of 15-oz. pkg.)	1 tbsp. lemon juice
4 tbsp. butter	1 tsp. vanilla extract
1 large egg	1/4 tsp. coconut extract
1/2 cup sugar	3/4 cup shredded coconut
1/4 cup all-purpose flour	1/3 cup chopped pecans plus 4 whole pecans

1) Preheat oven to 425°F. Cut pie crust in fourths and fit into 4 (4- x 3/4-inch) tartlet pans. Trim off excess dough by pressing with thumb against edge of pan. Place tartlet pans on baking sheet; bake until crust is firm, about 8 min. Reduce oven temperature to 375°F.

2) Meanwhile, place butter in medium, microwave-safe bowl. Microwave on HIGH until melted, about 45 seconds. Into bowl add egg, sugar, flour, lemon extract, whisk to combine. Stir in coconut and chopped pecans.

3) Spoon mixture into hot tart shells and spread level. Place 1 pecan in center of each tart. Bake tartlets until puffed slightly and set in center, 12 min. Serve warm or at room temperature.

nutritional facts: *Per serving: 560 calories • 59g carbohydrates • 6g protein • 35g fat • 220mg sodium • 95mg cholesterol • 1g fiber • 28g sugar*

toasted coconut

For even more texture and flavor, first toast the coconut in butter before using it in this recipe.

orange-raspberry fool

prep time: 10 minutes • total time: 25 minutes • serves: 4

Often served in an elegant parfait dish, this very English dessert looks quite fancy. The best-kept secret is that it's actually a cinch to prepare, and will "fool" your guests into thinking it's difficult to make.

1 large navel orange	1 (12 oz.) container frozen whipped topping, thawed
1/3 cup sugar	1 (7 oz.) container plain nonfat Greek-style yogurt
1 (12 oz.) pkg. frozen raspberries	

1) Grate orange to yield 1 tsp. zest. Squeeze juice from orange into medium saucepan. Add zest and sugar; bring to boil. Boil 1 min.; stir in frozen raspberries and return to boil, 2 min.

2) Remove half of raspberry mixture to medium bowl and half to blender. Puree in blender for 15 seconds. Stir puree into fruit bowl. Place bowl in freezer to cool, 15 min.

3) Meanwhile, in large mixing bowl, place whipped topping and fold in yogurt.

4) Remove fruit sauce from freezer; reserve 1/2 cup sauce. Fold remaining sauce into whipped topping mixture, leaving some streaks of sauce.

5) Spoon into 4 parfait dishes. Serve topped with drizzle of reserved fruit sauce.

nutritional facts: *Per serving: 430 calories • 66g carbohydrates • 3g protein • 14g fat • 30mg sodium • 0mg cholesterol • 5g fiber • 50g sugar*

it's all greek

Drain your favorite plain or vanilla nonfat yogurt to give it the texture of Greek yogurt. Then sprinkle some cinnamon, coconut flakes or slivered almonds on top.

festival funnel cakes

prep time: 5 minutes • total time: 25 minutes • serves: 4

When you can't get to a country fair, you can have one at home! Use a glass measuring cup to pour the batter for these classic funnel cakes and taste a summer treat any time of the year.

3 cups vegetable oil	2 tsp. vanilla extract
3/4 tsp. baking powder	1 large egg
1/4 tsp. salt	1-1/4 cups all-purpose flour
1 cup milk	2 tbsp. confectioners' sugar
1/4 cup sugar	

1) In deep, large skillet, heat 1/2-inch oil to 375°F over medium heat. Place paper towels on 4 plates; set aside.

2) In medium bowl, stir together baking powder and salt. Add milk, sugar, vanilla and egg; stir thoroughly to combine. Stir in flour to create thin batter. If necessary, add additional 1 tbsp. of flour or milk to achieve consistency of thin pancake batter.

3) For each cake, fill glass measuring cup with scant 1/2 cup batter. Pour batter into hot oil in continuous circular motion, crossing over batter occasionally to connect rings. Fry until golden color reaches from bottom partly up sides, about 2-3 min. Carefully turn with two long metal spatulas. Fry until second side is golden, about 1 min. Remove from oil and place on prepared plate.

4) Return oil temperature to 375°F and repeat with remaining batter. Sprinkle cakes with confectioners' sugar. Serve immediately.

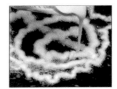

nutritional facts: *Per serving: 340 calories • 37g carbohydrates • 8g protein • 18g fat • 260mg sodium • 60mg cholesterol • 1g fiber • 7g sugar*

a bit of cocoa

Instead of sprinkling funnel cakes with confectioners' sugar, dust with some unsweetened cocoa powder.

petite mississippi mud pies

prep time: 15 minutes • total time: 25 minutes • serves: 4

This version of the deliciously rich mud pie has a chocolate cookie crust, dressed-up hot fudge sauce and just a hint of coffee flavoring. The result is a speedy, special dessert.

16 chocolate sandwich cookies	1/2 cup hot fudge sauce
1/4 cup butter, melted	4 cups coffee ice cream
1 tbsp. brewed coffee *or* water	3/4 cup whipped topping
1 to 2 tsp. instant espresso *or* coffee powder	

1) Place cookies in zippered plastic bag; crush with rolling pin. Add melted butter and combine well. Press crumb mixture into 4 (4- x 1-inch) tartlet pans with removable bottoms. Place in freezer for 10 min.

2) Meanwhile, in small microwave-safe bowl, combine coffee and espresso powder, stirring to dissolve powder. Add hot fudge sauce. Microwave until mixture can be stirred smooth, about 15 seconds.

3) Remove each tart shell from pan and place on individual serving plate. Spoon 1 tbsp. espresso sauce in bottom of tart. Top with one large scoop ice cream. Drizzle with additional sauce. Spoon whipped topping on side.

nutritional facts: *Per serving: 960 calories • 100g carbohydrates • 11g protein • 56g fat • 570mg sodium • 180mg cholesterol • 2g fiber • 70g sugar*

easy garnish

In addition to drizzling the tops with hot fudge sauce, top with a few chocolate-covered coffee beans.

blueberry yogurt delight

prep time: 5 minutes • total time: 22 minutes • serves: 4

These parfaits have the decadence of the richest cheesecake with the health benefits of yogurt and fresh blueberries. They're a not-too-sweet treat.

- 1 cup frozen blueberries
- 1/4 cup grape juice
- 4 rectangular pure-butter shortbread cookies
- 3 (6 oz.) containers vanilla custard-style yogurt
- 3 (6 oz.) containers blueberry custard-style yogurt
- 1/4 cup frozen whipped topping, thawed

1) In blender, puree blueberries and grape juice until smooth. Place cookies into zippered plastic storage bag. With rolling pin, crush into crumbs.

2) Into each of 4 parfait glasses, spoon 1/4 cup vanilla yogurt, 1 tbsp. blueberry puree and 1/4 cup blueberry yogurt. Evenly divide and spoon the cookie crumbs into each glass.

3) Spoon 1/4 cup blueberry yogurt, 1 tbsp. blueberry puree and 1/4 cup vanilla yogurt into each. Top each with 1/2 tbsp. blueberry puree and 1 tbsp. whipped topping. Serve immediately.

nutritional facts: *Per serving: 350 calories • 59g carbohydrates • 13g protein • 7g fat • 280mg sodium • 15mg cholesterol • 2g fiber • 44g sugar*

sweet topping

A fresh, homemade whipped topping is great when you have the time. Whip a cup of heavy cream with a tablespoon of sugar and a teaspoon of vanilla.

coconut joy pie

prep time: 14 minutes • total time: 29 minutes • serves: 8

All the flavors of a classic candy bar are combined in this light and creamy pie. It all starts with a simple chocolate crumb crust and ends with a coconut and almond topping.

- 2/3 cup flaked coconut, *divided*
- 1-1/2 cups cold milk
- 1 (3.4 oz.) pkg. instant vanilla pudding mix
- 2 cups low-fat whipped topping
- 2 cups mini marshmallows
- 1/4 tsp. coconut extract
- 1 (6 oz.) prepared chocolate crumb crust
- 1/3 cup hot fudge sauce
- 1/4 cup sliced almonds, *divided*

1) Spread coconut on microwave-safe plate. Microwave on HIGH for 1 min., stirring halfway through. Set aside 2 tbsp. of coconut for garnish.

2) Meanwhile, fill large bowl one-fourth full of ice and water. Set medium bowl over ice water. Add milk and pudding mix; whisk for 2 min. or until thickened. Fold in whipped topping, marshmallows, coconut extract and remaining coconut.

3) Spoon half of pudding mixture into crust. Drizzle on about 3 tbsp. of fudge sauce; sprinkle on 2 tbsp. of almonds. Top with remaining pudding mixture. Drizzle with fudge; scatter remaining almonds and reserved coconut on top. Freeze for at least 15 min. or until set.

nutritional facts: *Per serving: 330 calories • 46g carbohydrates • 5g protein • 15g fat • 220mg sodium • 5mg cholesterol • 2g fiber • 24g sugar*

slim substitutes

You can cut some of the calories without reducing the flavor by substituting skim or 2% milk for whole milk and incorporating sugar-free vanilla pudding into the mixture.

tasty topping

If your family likes an extra-sweet topping, add 1/4 cup dark or golden raisins or even dried cherries to the topping. You could also make a confectioners' sugar glaze.

cinnamon cake

prep time: 5 minutes • total time: 29 minutes • serves: 9

The fragrant aroma of this simple cinnamon cake will awaken even the soundest sleeper in the morning or bring the kids running in after school. The delicate cake and crumbly topping are just perfect!

2-1/2 cups buttermilk baking mix, *divided*	1 tsp. ground cinnamon, *divided*
1/4 cup sugar	1/2 cup packed brown sugar
1/2 cup sour cream	3 tbsp. butter
1/4 cup milk	1/4 cup chopped walnuts
1 large egg	1/4 cup semisweet chocolate chips
1 tsp. vanilla extract	

1) Preheat oven to 400°F. Grease 9- x 9-inch baking pan. In medium bowl, combine 2 cups buttermilk baking mix, 1/4 cup sugar, sour cream, milk, egg, vanilla and 1/2 tsp. cinnamon. Pour batter into prepared pan.

2) In small bowl, combine remaining buttermilk baking mix, brown sugar, butter and remaining cinnamon. Cut mixture with pastry blender (or 2 knives) until mixture resembles coarse crumbs. Stir in walnuts.

3) Sprinkle crumb mixture over batter. Bake until golden and set, about 22 min.

4) Meanwhile, place chocolate chips in small, microwave-safe bowl. Microwave on HIGH until very soft, 30 seconds. Stir until completely melted. Transfer chocolate to small, zippered plastic bag; seal bag. Squeeze chocolate into corner and snip off tip of bag.

5) Remove cake from oven and transfer to rack. Squeeze chocolate onto cake in crisscross pattern. Serve warm or cooled.

nutritional facts: *Per serving: 400 calories • 54g carbohydrates • 7g protein • 18g fat • 590mg sodium • 45mg cholesterol • 2g fiber • 24g sugar*

frosty sensation

For a cooler dessert without any more effort, replace the yogurt with the sorbet of your choice.

summer melon parfaits

prep time: 15 minutes • total time: 15 minutes • serves: 4

Even kids who don't care for fruit will gobble up this treat that features yogurt and frozen whipped topping. It will refresh you and your family in the heat of summer, no matter what time of day.

1/4 cup lemonade concentrate	1 cup diced honeydew
1/4 cup lemon, orange *or* raspberry yogurt	1 cup diced cantaloupe
8 oz. frozen whipped topping, thawed	

1) In a large bowl, combine the lemonade concentrate and yogurt; fold in the whipped topping.

2) In each of four dessert glasses, layer with 1/4 cup honeydew, 1/4 cup lemon mixture, 1/4 cup cantaloupe and remaining lemon mixture.

nutritional facts: *Per serving: 234 calories • 31g carbohydrates • 1g protein • 10g fat • 17mg sodium • 1mg cholesterol • 1g fiber*

red, white & blue trifle

prep time: 15 minutes • total time: 29 minutes • serves: 10 to 12

Need a last-minute dessert that's perfect for a block party or potluck dinner? This cake, jam and fruit confection serves a crowd, tastes like a dream and is gorgeous to behold.

1/4 cup lemon juice	1/4 cup seedless raspberry jam
1/4 cup sugar	2 (6 oz.) containers raspberries
1 cup white chocolate chips, *divided*	1 pint blueberries
	1/2 tsp. lemon extract
1/4 cup milk	1 (8 oz.) container frozen
1 (1 lb.) angel food cake	whipped topping, thawed

1) In small saucepan over high heat, bring lemon juice, sugar and 1/4 cup water to boil, stirring occasionally to dissolve sugar. Boil until mixture is syrupy, about 3 min.

2) In small, glass bowl, combine 3/4 cup white chips and milk. Microwave on medium until chips are melted and smooth when stirred, about 1 min. Set aside.

3) Remove crust from cake, if desired. Cut cake into 1-inch slices. Brush both sides of cake with sugar syrup. Spread one side of half the cake slices with jam; "sandwich" with other half of cake slices. Cut each sandwich into 1-inch cubes. In medium bowl, gently combine raspberries and blueberries.

4) Fold melted chocolate and lemon extract into whipped topping. In 2-1/2-qt. serving bowl or trifle dish, place half of cake sandwiches; top with half of whipped-topping mixture. Spoon in half of mixed berries. Repeat layers; sprinkle remaining chips over top. Serve immediately or chill, covered, until ready to serve.

nutritional facts: *Per serving: 300 calories • 57g carbohydrates • 5g protein • 8g fat • 170mg sodium • 0mg cholesterol • 1g fiber • 28g sugar*

for adults only

This family-friendly version is alcohol free, but traditional trifles can feature a variety of berries plus a sugar syrup laced with Scotch, bourbon, brandy or sherry.

---

blueberry extravaganza

prep time: 15 minutes • total time: 15 minutes • serves: 4

Ready-made crepes enclose a blueberry filling sparked with the tang of fresh lemon. A warm fruity sauce is the crowning glory to this simple, yet elegant dessert.

1 lemon	4 (8-inch) ready-made crepes
1/4 cup sugar	1/2 cup blueberry preserves
1-1/2 tsp. cornstarch	
2 cups fresh blueberries, *divided*	

1) Grate lemon to yield 2 tsp. zest; squeeze lemon to yield 4 tsp. juice; set aside. In medium saucepan, blend sugar with cornstarch; stir in 3/4 cup cold water until smooth. Add 1-1/4 cups blueberries. Cook over medium heat, stirring constantly, until mixture comes to boil and thickens, about 5 min. Remove from heat; stir in half of lemon juice and half of zest.

2) Chop remaining 3/4 cup blueberries. In small bowl, combine preserves and remaining lemon juice and lemon rind; stir in blueberries. Spread onto crepes. Serve immediately.

nutritional facts: *Per serving: 230 calories • 56g carbohydrates • 2g protein • .5g fat • 50mg sodium • 5mg cholesterol • 2g fiber • 46g sugar*

crepe capers

Crepes, which are nothing more than a pancake batter thinned with milk, melted butter and a teaspoon of vanilla, are easy and fun to make yourself.

easy apricot-cherry crisp

prep time: 12 minutes • total time: 28 minutes • serves: 6

An unusual twist on a typical crisp, this great-tasting apricot and cherry version will win you over. It's easily made at any time of year with canned apricots, dried cherries and instant oatmeal.

5 tbsp. butter	1/2 cup plus 1 tbsp. all-purpose flour, *divided*
1 tsp. chopped fresh gingerroot	1 (1-1/4 oz.) package instant oatmeal mix
3 (16 oz.) cans apricot halves in juice	
1/2 cup dried cherries	
1/2 cup packed brown sugar, *divided*	

1) Preheat oven to 425°F. Place butter in medium, microwave-safe bowl. Microwave on HIGH just until melted, 35-45 seconds; set aside. Sprinkle ginger in 8-inch square microwave-safe baking dish.

2) Drain apricots; reserve 1/4 cup liquid. Place apricots, reserved liquid, cherries, 1/4 cup brown sugar and 1 tbsp. flour in baking dish with ginger. Stir to combine; cover with vented plastic. Microwave on HIGH until beginning to bubble, 5-6 min., stirring once about halfway during cooking.

3) Meanwhile, add oatmeal mix and remaining brown sugar and flour to butter. Stir until crumbly. Sprinkle evenly over fruit. Bake until topping is golden, 15 min. Serve hot, or slightly warm.

nutritional facts: *Per serving: 340 calories • 58g carbohydrates • 5g protein • 10g fat • 10mg sodium • 25mg cholesterol • 5g fiber • 39g sugar*

other oats

Vary the flavor by using different kinds of instant oatmeal, such as maple and brown sugar or peaches and cream.

---

mexican ice cream

prep time: 7 minutes • total time: 13 minutes • serves: 6

A cinnamon-chocolate-orange sauce takes ordinary ice cream to a whole new level. Top it off with a couple of crisp, cinnamon tortilla chips for a dramatic look.

2 (8 inch) honey wheat flour tortillas	1/2 tsp. cornstarch
3 tsp. sugar	1/2 cup chocolate-flavored syrup
1 tsp. ground cinnamon	1/8 tsp. orange extract
1/2 cup orange juice	1 pint chocolate ice cream
1/4 cup unsweetened cocoa powder	1 pint coffee ice cream

1) Preheat oven to 375°F. Stack tortillas and cut through both at once to form 12 wedges. Place in single layer on baking sheet. Lightly coat tortillas with cooking spray. In small bowl, combine sugar and cinnamon. Reserve 2 tsp. and set aside. Sprinkle remainder over tortillas. Bake tortillas until lightly browned, 7 min.

2) Meanwhile, in small saucepan over medium heat, combine the orange juice, cocoa, cornstarch and reserved cinnamon mixture. Bring to boil; cook and stir, until thickened, about 5 min. Remove from heat; stir in the chocolate syrup and orange extract.

3) Spoon 2 tbsp. sauce into bottom of 6 bowls. Spoon 1 scoop of chocolate and 1 scoop of coffee ice cream into each bowl. Drizzle remaining sauce over top. Garnish each with 2 tortilla chips and serve.

nutritional facts: *Per serving: 510 calories • 59g carbohydrates • 9g protein • 25g fat • 160mg sodium • 155mg cholesterol • 2g fiber • 45g sugar*

authentic taste

For some south-of-the-border-style heat, add a couple of red pepper flakes to the chocolate sauce. Or stir in 1/8 tsp. espresso powder for a rich, mocha sauce.

fresh plum tartlets

prep time: 7 minutes • total time: 28 minutes • serves: 4

These scrumptious tartlets, with a crisp, cookie-like crust, are topped with both prune butter and sliced fresh plums for a deliciously sweet dessert. It's packed with a heart-healthy dose of fiber.

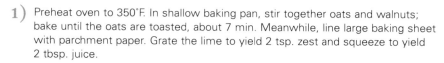

1 cup old-fashioned oats	2 large egg whites
1/2 cup walnuts	1 lb. fresh plums
1 lime	1/4 cup prune butter
1 cup corn flakes cereal	
1/2 cup sugar	

1) Preheat oven to 350°F. In shallow baking pan, stir together oats and walnuts; bake until the oats are toasted, about 7 min. Meanwhile, line large baking sheet with parchment paper. Grate the lime to yield 2 tsp. zest and squeeze to yield 2 tbsp. juice.

2) Transfer oats and walnuts to food processor with corn flakes and sugar; process to fine crumbs, about 1 min. Add egg whites and 1 tbsp. lime juice; pulse until evenly moistened, 30 seconds.

3) Divide dough into sixths and place on prepared baking sheet. With moist hands, pat each portion into 4-inch round. With tips of fingers, raise edge of dough all around, about 1/4 inch. Bake until crisp, 10 min. Cool on baking sheet, 2 min.; transfer to rack.

4) Meanwhile, halve and pit plums. Slice into thin wedges and set aside. In small bowl, combine remaining lime juice, half of zest and prune butter. Spread mixture over bottom of each round. Arrange sliced plums over prune butter. Garnish with remaining lime zest and serve.

nutritional facts: *Per serving: 400 calories • 71g carbohydrates • 10g protein • 11g fat • 100mg sodium • 0mg cholesterol • 6g fiber • 43g sugar*

crisp or soft?

These crisp tarts are meant to be picked up and eaten like a big cookie. But if you let them sit overnight, they soften enough to be eaten from a plate with a knife and fork.

citrus mousse

prep time: 12 minutes • total time: 12 minutes • serves: 4

Here's a luscious mousse mixture that's quick to make and very versatile. With just five ingredients plus your choice of fresh fruit, it's a delicious ending to a special lunch.

1 lime	1/2 cup prepared lemon curd
1 (3 oz.) pkg. Neufchatel cream cheese (1/3 cup)	2 cups reduced-fat whipped topping
1 tbsp. orange juice concentrate, undiluted	1/2 pint fresh raspberries

1) Over medium mixing bowl, grate 1 tsp. rind from lime. Add cream cheese and orange juice concentrate. Beat with electric mixer on high until smooth, 30 seconds. Add lemon curd and beat together just until blended, 30 seconds. With rubber spatula, fold in whipped topping until combined.

2) Set aside 12 raspberries for topping. Evenly divide remaining raspberries among bottoms of 4 dessert dishes. Spoon or pipe mousse into dishes. Garnish each with 3 raspberries. Serve immediately or refrigerate, covered, until serving.

nutritional facts: *Per serving: 210 calories • 27g carbohydrates • 3g protein • 10g fat •85mg sodium • 10mg cholesterol • 0g fiber • 16g sugar*

berry basics

Raspberries are very perishable. If the fresh ones you find aren't perfect, use individual, flash-frozen berries in their place. Or, try this recipe with fresh or frozen blueberries instead.

it takes the cake

If you have slices of pound or sponge cake or some lady fingers in the house, use them as a base for the bananas. For a trifle-like dessert, soak the cake in a bit of rum.

chocolate banana pudding

prep time: 15 minutes • **total time:** 1-1/4 hours • **serves:** 6

Perfect for a potluck or make-ahead supper, this dessert will wow your guests. Or make just the rich pudding as the ending to a weeknight dinner.

2 oz. dark chocolate	2-3/4 cups milk
1/3 cup unsweetened cocoa powder	2 large egg yolks
1/2 cup sugar	14 thin chocolate wafer cookies, *divided*
3 tbsp. cornstarch	3 bananas, *divided*
1/2 tsp. instant coffee granules	1/2 cup whipped cream

1) Roughly chop chocolate; set aside. In medium saucepan, whisk together cocoa, sugar, cornstarch and instant coffee. Whisk in milk. Set pan over medium heat, cook, stirring frequently, until mixture comes to boil, 5 min.

2) Meanwhile, beat egg yolks in small bowl. Remove pudding from heat; gradually stir 1/2 cup of pudding into yolks until blended. Slowly stir yolk mixture into pan. Return to stove; bring to simmer over low heat, stirring constantly. Remove from heat; stir in chocolate until melted.

3) Scrape into bowl; cover with plastic touching surface. Set aside to cool to room temperature, about 1 hour. (Can be made 1 day in advance; store refrigerated.)

4) Set aside 2 cookies and one-half banana. Peel and slice remaining bananas; halve cookies. In 8-cup glass serving bowl, layer one-third bananas, one-third pudding and half of cookies. Repeat layers, ending with pudding. Cover and refrigerate for 4 hours or overnight. To serve, slice remaining banana. Top pudding with whipped cream; garnish with reserved cookies and sliced banana.

nutritional facts: *Per serving: 380 calories • 59g carbohydrates • 8g protein • 14g fat • 135mg sodium • 95mg cholesterol • 4g fiber • 41g sugar*

serving suggestion

Flan makes the perfect finale for spicy meals. Serve it after a dinner of Southwestern or Cuban foods.

quicker caramel flan

prep time: 15 minutes • **total time:** 3 hours 45 minutes • **serves:** 6

Enjoy ordering flan at your favorite restaurant? Now you can savor the flavor of this popular dessert in your own home. The fantastic treat is much easier than you think.

5 large eggs	2-1/2 cups milk
1/2 cup sugar	2 tbsp. caramel ice cream topping
1 tsp. vanilla extract	
1/8 tsp. salt	

1) In a bowl, whisk eggs, sugar, vanilla and salt. Gradually stir in milk. Spoon 1 tsp. caramel topping into each of 6 ungreased 6-oz. custard cups. Place cups in a 13- x 9-in. baking dish. Pour egg mixture into each cup. Fill baking dish with 1 in. of hot water.

2) Bake, uncovered, at 350°F. for 30-35 minutes or until centers are almost set. Remove cups from water to a wire rack; cool for 30 minutes. Refrigerate for 3 hours or until thoroughly chilled. Invert onto dessert dishes.

nutritional facts: *Per serving: 208 calories • 26g carbohydrates • 9g protein • 8g fat • 176mg sodium • 191mg cholesterol • trace fiber*

taste-of-the-tropics fruit soup

prep time: 15 minutes • total time: 15 minutes • serves: 4

Soup for dessert? You bet! On a hot summer's evening, nothing tops off dinner like this pretty, cool and refreshing fruit soup. It's easy to make and so beautiful that you'll be serving it at every barbecue.

2 kiwifruit	6 ice cubes
3 cups seedless, cubed watermelon	2 tbsp. coconut *or* regular rum (optional)
2 mangos	8 mint sprigs, *divided*
2 cups guava-passion fruit drink	1 cup coconut sorbet
5 tbsp. frozen limeade concentrate	

1) Peel kiwi and slice into 1/4-inch rounds. Cut watermelon into 3/8-inch pieces. Peel and pit mangos; cut one mango into 3/8-inch pieces; set aside.

2) Quarter remaining mango and place in blender. Add fruit drink, limeade concentrate, ice cubes, rum if desired and 12 mint leaves. Blend until smooth, about 1 min.

3) Pour into 4 shallow bowls. Scatter on kiwi, watermelon and mango. Place 1/4-cup scoop of sorbet into each bowl. Garnish with mint sprigs and serve.

nutritional facts: *Per serving: 340 calories • 77g carbohydrates • 2g protein • 2g fat • 30mg sodium • 5mg cholesterol • 4g fiber • 63g sugar*

money saver
Cut your grocery bill by omitting the kiwifruit and replacing it with more watermelon.

peanut passion pie

prep time: 5 minutes • total time: 27 minutes • serves: 8

This crunchy, sweet and unforgettably delicious pie has it all—peanuts, chocolate and butterscotch—in one wonderfully rich serving.

1/4 cup butter	1/4 cup semisweet chocolate chips
1/4 cup packed brown sugar	1/4 cup butterscotch chips
1/4 cup sugar	1 (6 oz.) prepared chocolate crumb crust
1 large egg	
1/2 tsp. vanilla extract	
1/2 cup roasted and salted peanuts	

1) Preheat oven to 350°F. Place butter in small, microwave-safe dish and microwave on HIGH until melted, 30 seconds.

2) In medium bowl, use wooden spoon to stir together melted butter and sugars. In small bowl, beat egg. Add to medium bowl with vanilla; stir vigorously to combine.

3) Stir in peanuts, chocolate chips and butterscotch chips.

4) Pour the mixture into crust. Bake until golden and set, 22 min. Place on rack to cool. Serve completely cooled or slightly warm.

nutritional facts: *Per serving: 250 calories • 33g carbohydrates • 3g protein • 12g fat • 190mg sodium • 40mg cholesterol • 1g fiber • 23g sugar*

perfect pair
A scoop of creamy vanilla ice cream turns each slice into a special dessert.

rise and fall

Remember that souffles begin to fall the moment they come out of the oven…that's part of their charm! Always plan to serve souffles the moment they're done baking.

super chocolate souffle

prep time: 20 minutes • total time: 40 minutes • serves: 8

Here's a richly intense (but not too sweet) souffle that's not tricky to make. This recipe makes eight individual servings but can easily be adapted for a single souffle in a 2-quart dish by baking for 25 minutes.

3 tbsp. butter, *divided*	5 oz. dark *or* bittersweet
1/4 cup plus 2 tbsp. sugar, *divided*	chocolate
3/4 cup milk	5 large eggs, at room
2 tbsp. all-purpose flour	temperature
1 tbsp. unsweetened cocoa powder	2 tsp. vanilla extract
1 tsp. instant espresso *or* coffee powder	

1) Preheat oven to 350°F. Place 1 tbsp. butter in small, microwave-safe dish. Microwave on HIGH until softened, 30 seconds. Brush 8 (6-oz.) custard cups with butter. Sprinkle bottom and sides with 2 tbsp. sugar; set on jelly-roll pan. In saucepan over medium heat, whisk together milk, flour, cocoa, coffee powder and 2 tbsp. sugar; bring to simmer, stirring constantly. Simmer until thickened, 1 min.

2) Meanwhile, chop chocolate. Add chocolate and remaining butter to pan. Remove from heat; let stand until chocolate is melted, 2 min. Separate eggs, placing whites in medium bowl and 4 yolks in saucepan. Add vanilla; stir chocolate mixture until blended.

3) With an electric mixer on high, beat the egg whites until frothy, 1 min. Add the remaining sugar and beat until stiff peaks form, 2 min. Add about one-fourth whites to chocolate mixture, stirring until blended. With spatula, fold in remaining whites by hand, half at a time, just until combined. Spoon into prepared dishes.

4) Bake until puffed and moist in center, 20 min. Serve.

nutritional facts: *Per serving: 220 calories • 18g carbohydrates • 6g protein • 16g fat • 290mg sodium • 145mg cholesterol • 2g fiber • 14g sugar*

fruity finale

Use up any over-ripe fresh bananas, peaches, pears, mangoes or pineapples in this recipe. Just slice and saute them with butter, brown sugar, cinnamon and the rum.

rum-glazed fruit

prep time: 10 minutes • total time: 10 minutes • serves: 6

Peaches, pears and banana are simmered in a quick-to-make creamy rum sauce for a decadent dessert that's practically ready before you can even clear the dinner dishes!

1 (15 oz.) can peach halves	3 tbsp. brown sugar
1 (15 oz.) can pear halves	1/4 tsp. ground cinnamon
1/2 cup heavy cream	1 firm, ripe banana
1/4 cup rum	

1) Drain peaches and pears. Pat dry thoroughly with paper towels.

2) In medium, nonstick skillet over medium heat, combine cream, rum, brown sugar and cinnamon. Bring to boil for 1 min.

3) Add peaches and pears. Reduce heat to simmer. Cook 2 min., turning once. Slice banana into 1/2-inch slices and add to skillet. Simmer 30 seconds. Evenly divide fruit among 6 dessert dishes. Spoon sauce over and serve.

nutritional facts: *Per serving: 230 calories • 35g carbohydrates • 1g protein • 8g fat • 15mg sodium • 25mg cholesterol • 3g fiber • 29g sugar*

chocolate lemon cakes

prep time: 13 minutes • total time: 29 minutes • serves: 9

These pretty little lemon cakes are moist, tender and bursting with flavor from lemon zest, juice and extract. Topped with a drizzle of chocolate, they're surefire winners!

1 lemon	1 cup sugar
1 cup all-purpose flour	2 large eggs
1/2 tsp. baking powder	1/2 tsp. lemon extract
1/8 tsp. salt	1/4 cup heavy cream
3 tbsp. unsalted butter, softened	1/3 cup semisweet chocolate chips
1-1/2 oz. cream cheese, softened	

1) Preheat oven to 425°F. Coat 9 muffin cups with cooking spray. Grate lemon to yield 1-1/2 tsp. zest; squeeze lemon to yield 1 tbsp. juice. In medium bowl, combine flour, baking powder and salt.

2) In another medium bowl, cream butter and cream cheese with electric mixer until smooth. Add sugar and beat on high until creamy, about 1 min. Add eggs; beat on high, 2 min. Add lemon juice and extract.

3) Add flour mixture and 1 tsp. zest. With rubber spatula, stir just until combined. Divide batter among muffin tins, carefully filling any empty spaces with 1/8-inch water. Bake until toothpick comes out clean when inserted in center, 15 min.

4) In small saucepan over high, heat cream to boiling point. Remove from heat and, with rubber spatula, stir in chocolate until melted. Let cool to frosting consistency.

5) Place cakes on wire rack set over waxed paper. With spoon, drizzle on chocolate. Sprinkle with remaining lemon zest and serve.

nutritional facts: *Per cake: 270 calories • 39g carbohydrates • 4g protein • 11g fat • 90mg sodium • 70mg cholesterol • 1g fiber • 27g sugar*

change of pace

Instead of adding the chocolate topping, poke holes in the cakes and drizzle with a slurry— a tbsp. each of lemon juice and confectioners' sugar.

jewel-topped sherbet

prep time: 8 minutes • total time: 22 minutes • serves: 4

These citrus "jewels" are so easy to make and can be stored in airtight containers for months. They're a surprising treat on their own but are even better atop smooth, sweet sherbet.

3/4 cup plus 1 tbsp. sugar	1/4 cup turbinado sugar
1/2 cup water, *divided*	1 pint orange sherbet
1 orange	

1) In small saucepan, bring 3/4 cup sugar and 3/4 cup water to boil. Meanwhile, with vegetable peeler, remove orange peel in long strips. Slice lengthwise into 1/8-inch-wide strips. Place in glass measure and add 3/4 cup water. Microwave on HIGH 1 min.

2) Drain peel in sieve and add to saucepan; reduce heat to low and simmer 12 min. Sprinkle turbinado sugar and remaining 1 tbsp. sugar in small, shallow bowl. Drain rind, add to bowl and toss until coated with sugar.

3) Place sherbet in each of 4 dessert dishes. Top with sugared peel and serve.

nutritional facts: *Per serving: 320 calories • 79g carbohydrates • 1g protein • 1.5g fat • 35mg sodium • 0mg cholesterol • 3g fiber • 74g sugar*

citrus zest

Use sugared peels to top other desserts such as cheesecakes, ice creams and parfaits. Or add them chopped to cakes, cookies and quick breads for a burst of citrus flavor.

freezer pleaser

Don't let any leftover coconut go to waste. Set the remaining coconut in a freezer-proof storage bag. To reuse, simply thaw in the refrigerator.

tropical banana compote

prep time: 10 minutes • **total time:** 20 minutes • **serves:** 5

Don't limit your use of bananas to the cereal bowl. Instead, send your taste buds on a "trip" to the tropics with this special, speedy dessert. Bananas are available in every season so this is bound to become a favorite all year-round.

3 medium firm bananas	2 tbsp. flaked coconut, toasted
1/4 cup orange juice	maraschino cherries *or* strawberries
2 tbsp. butter	(optional)
3 tbsp. brown sugar	

1) Cut bananas in half lengthwise, then cut widthwise into quarters. Arrange in a greased 11- x 7-in. baking dish.

2) In a saucepan, combine orange juice, butter and brown sugar; cook and stir until sugar is dissolved and butter is melted. Pour over the bananas.

3) Bake, uncovered, at 350°F. for 10-12 minutes. Spoon into individual serving dishes; sprinkle with coconut. Garnish with cherries or strawberries if desired.

nutritional facts: *Per serving: 192 calories • 34g carbohydrates • 1g protein • 7g fat • 70mg sodium • 15mg cholesterol • 2g fiber*

tiny taste

If your family is counting calories, serve this oh-so-creamy dessert in demitasse cups or shot glasses. It's so rich that even a small portion will satisfy.

heavenly berries and chocolate cream

prep time: 12 minutes • **total time:** 27 minutes • **serves:** 4

Berries and chocolate are a match made in heaven. Your family will think you are an angel for creating this luxurious dessert that layers delectable chocolate cream and fresh berries.

1 cup heavy cream, *divided*	1/2 cup mascarpone
6 oz. semisweet chocolatechips	2 cups raspberries, blackberries,
2 tbsp. raspberry jam	strawberries *or* a combination
1 tsp. vanilla extract	mint leaves (optional)

1) In microwave-safe bowl, combine 1/4 cup heavy cream and chocolate. Microwave on HIGH, stirring frequently, just until chocolate is melted and smooth, about 1-2 min. Add jam and vanilla; microwave in 20-second intervals, stirring until smooth and combined.

2) In medium bowl with electric mixer, blend mascarpone with 2 tbsp. heavy cream.

3) Stir in chocolate mixture and beat until smooth.

4) Add remaining heavy cream and beat at high speed until fluffy and peaks form.

5) In 4 parfait, dessert or wine glasses, layer chocolate mixture with berries, beginning with chocolate. Chill at least 15 min. Garnish with mint leaves if desired.

nutritional facts: *Per serving: 590 calories • 38g carbohydrates • 7g protein • 52g fat • 40mg sodium • 120mg cholesterol • 1g fiber • 7g sugar*

chocolate-cherry sponge cakes

prep time: 20 minutes • total time: 20 minutes • serves: 6

This event-worthy dessert is rich in flavor from the chocolate, ricotta cheese, cherries and chocolate sauce, while the sponge cake gives it great texture. It's truly impressive.

24 frozen dry-pack sweet cherries, *divided*	2 tbsp. corn syrup
2/3 cup part-skim ricotta cheese	2 tbsp. confectioners' sugar
2-1/2 oz. dark chocolate, *divided*	1 pkg. (6 pieces) individual sponge cakes
1/4 cup fat-free half-and-half *or* whole milk	

1) Rinse cherries in sieve under running water to thaw; place on several layers of paper towels to drain. Lay double layer of paper towels on plate; spread ricotta on towels. Top with 2 more layers of paper towels; press down lightly to absorb excess moisture. Chop chocolate and reserve 3 tbsp.; set aside.

2) In small saucepan over medium-low, heat half-and-half until just beginning to simmer. Add remaining chocolate, stirring just until melted. Remove from heat. Stir in corn syrup; set aside to cool slightly. Scrape ricotta into small bowl. Stir in confectioners' sugar and reserved chopped chocolate.

3) Spoon 1 tbsp. chocolate sauce into indentation on sponge cakes. Set aside 6 whole cherries. Halve remaining cherries and divide among sponge cakes. Top with ricotta mixture, mounding in center. Top each with 1 cherry and drizzle with remaining chocolate; serve immediately.

nutritional facts: *Per serving: 250 calories • 42g carbohydrates • 7g protein • 7g fat • 140mg sodium • 50mg cholesterol • 1g fiber • 27g sugar*

here's the scoop
To make perfect ricotta mounds atop the cakes, use a two-ounce ice cream scoop.

tempting tortoni parfait

prep time: 10 minutes • total time: 29 minutes • serves: 4

A popular Italian dessert, this rich treat relies on ice cream flavored with Marsala wine. The ice cream is combined with chopped almonds, cookie crumbs and fudge sauce.

1/2 cup sliced almonds	1 quart vanilla ice cream
16 small crisp almond-flavored cookies	1/2 cup hot fudge sauce, warmed
1/4 cup Marsala wine	4 maraschino cherries

1) In medium skillet over medium heat, cook almonds, stirring occasionally, until toasted; remove from heat.

2) In food processor, combine almonds and cookies. Process until crumbs form. Remove to medium bowl; toss in Marsala wine. Place half of mixture in small bowl and half in medium bowl.

3) Spoon ice cream in food processor and pulse until barely smooth. Add to medium bowl with cookie crumb mixture and stir until just combined.

4) Working quickly, alternately layer 1 tbsp. reserved crumb mixture, 1 scoop ice cream and 1 tbsp. fudge sauce in each of 4 parfait glasses. Repeat layers of crumb mixture, ice cream and fudge sauce. Top each with 1 maraschino cherry. Place each parfait in freezer when finished. Freeze up to 10 min.

nutritional facts: *Per serving: 740 calories • 75g carbohydrates • 13g protein • 44g fat • 170mg sodium • 60mg cholesterol • 5g fiber • 58g sugar*

fruit fact
Fresh or frozen strawberries can be used in place of the maraschino cherries in this recipe.

natural sweetner

Consider using a spoonful of honey as a nice alternative to confectioners' sugar. It adds healthy sweetness to this dish.

mango-melon split

prep time: 20 minutes • **total time:** 20 minutes • **serves:** 4

Fresh fruit and cottage cheese are a healthy variation on a banana split. A tasty sauce of preserves and pomegranate is the finishing touch.

1 (16 oz.) container low-fat cottage cheese	1/4 cup pomegranate juice
2 tbsp. confectioners' sugar	1 mango
1/4 tsp. ginger	1/2 small cantaloupe *or* honeydew melon
1/2 cup apricot, peach *or* raspberry preserves	1 kiwifruit
	4 strawberries

1) In medium bowl, combine cottage cheese, sugar and ginger; whip with fork until fluffy.

2) In small bowl, blend preserves and pomegranate juice for topping.

3) Peel mango with vegetable peeler. Cut into thin slices parallel to pit, then cut into 16 long strips. Finely dice any remaining fruit adhering to the pit, add to the cheese.

4) Cut melon into very thin wedges and lay flat to remove peel. Reserve 16 wedges, trimming as needed to match length of mango. Finely dice remaining strips or trimmed pieces; add to the cottage cheese mixture.

5) Peel kiwi with vegetable peeler. Dice finely and add to cheese. Stir to combine well. Cut strawberries in half.

6) In each of 4 banana-split bowls or dessert plates, arrange 4 strips of mango and 4 strips of melon. Top with scoop of cottage cheese mixture. Garnish with 2 strawberry halves; spoon topping over. Serve.

nutritional facts: *Per serving: 270 calories • 57g carbohydrates • 12g protein • 2g fat • 410mg sodium • 10mg cholesterol • 3g fiber • 41g sugar*

ideal dessert

No matter what the occasion, these truffles fit the bill. They're perfect to serve for everyday treats as well as special occasions. Take them to a potluck or plate them for a bake sale contribution.

mint truffles

prep time: 20 minutes • **total time:** 30 minutes • **serves:** 12

These chocolaty candies have such an appealing look and sweet flavor, it's hard to believe they take only minutes to prepare.

1 (6 oz.) cup milk chocolate chips	1/4 tsp. peppermint extract
3/4 cup whipped topping	2 tbsp. baking cocoa

1) In a small microwave-safe mixing bowl, melt chocolate chips; let cool to lukewarm, about 7 minutes. Beat in whipped topping and extract.

2) Place in the freezer for 15 minutes or until firm enough to form into balls.

3) Shape into 1-in. balls. Roll in cocoa. Store in a covered container in the refrigerator.

nutritional facts: *Per serving: 91 calories • 10g carbohydrates • 1g protein • 5g fat • 11mg sodium • 3mg cholesterol • 1g fiber*

mini apricot turnovers

prep time: 10 minutes • total time: 30 minutes • serves: 8

Turnovers don't have to be time-consuming when you use prepared pie pastry and fruit preserves. These oven-fresh goodies are just right for breakfast, lunch and dinner as well as late-night snacks.

1 (15 oz.) pkg. refrigerated pie pastry	2 tbsp. milk
1 (12 oz.) jar apricot *or* peach preserves	1 tbsp. sugar
	1/4 tsp. ground cinnamon

1) Cut each pastry into four wedges. Place a rounded tbsp. full of preserves in the center of each. Moisten edges with water. Fold pastry over filling; press edges with fork to seal.

2) Place turnovers on an ungreased baking sheet. Cut a small slit in the top of each. Brush with milk. Combine sugar and cinnamon; sprinkle over turnovers. Bake at 425°F. for 16-18 minutes or until golden brown. Serve warm.

nutritional facts: *Per serving: 348 calories • 55g carbohydrates • 2g protein • 14g fat • 216mg sodium • 10mg cholesterol • 1g fiber*

sweet substitution

Feel free to experiment with other fruit preserve flavors. Try strawberry or raspberry for a change of pace.

strawberry-pineapple sundaes

prep time: 15 minutes • total time: 22 minutes • serves: 6

Your family will love this oh-so-yummy sundae that's just bursting with fruit. The homemade sauces are better than any store-bought varieties.

pineapple sauce:	2 tbsp. sugar
1 cup crushed pineapple with juice	2 tsp. cornstarch
2 tbsp. orange marmalade	**sundae:**
1 tbsp. sugar	3 bananas
1 tbsp. cornstarch	1 quart vanilla ice cream
strawberry sauce:	1/2 cup prepared whipped topping
1 pint strawberries	6 maraschino cherries

1) Drain pineapple and reserve juice. In small saucepan over medium heat, whisk together pineapple, 2 tbsp. reserved juice, marmalade sugar and cornstarch. Cook, stirring until thickened, about 2 min. Thin with additional pineapple juice if needed. Set aside.

2) For strawberry sauce, hull and slice berries. Reserve 1/2 cup. Place remaining berries, 2 tbsp. water and sugar in blender. Puree. Transfer to small saucepan. In small bowl, stir together cornstarch and 2 tbsp. water. Stir into strawberry mixture in saucepan. Cook and stir over medium heat until thickened, about 2 min. Add reserved berries; cook and stir 1 min. Set aside.

3) For sundaes, peel bananas; cut lengthwise and crosswise into 2 pieces. Place 2 scoops ice cream in each of 6 serving dishes. Place 2 banana pieces in each dish. Drizzle 1 scoop of ice cream with strawberry sauce and the other with pineapple sauce. Top with spoonful of whipped topping and a cherry; serve immediately.

nutritional facts: *Per serving: 350 calories • 61g carbohydrates • 4g protein • 11g fat • 80mg sodium • 40mg cholesterol • 4g fiber • 49g sugar*

sundae bar

Fill dishes with the sauces, fruit and whipped topping so that friends and family can make their own sundaes.

combining hot and cold

When adding egg yolks to hot liquid, be very careful because the liquid could cook the eggs. Let the chocolate-cream mixture stand a bit before adding the sugar and yolks.

warm chocolate creme brulee

prep time: 24 minutes • total time: 29 minutes • serves: 4

The classic creme brulee recipe requires long, slow baking in a water bath and melting sugar with a torch. This version is made in the microwave and is served warm with a crust that's crispy from the broiler.

1 cup heavy cream	3 large egg yolks
1/2 cup whole milk	1 tbsp. orange flavored liqueur (optional)
2 oz. high-quality bittersweet chocolate, very finely chopped	
1/4 cup sugar	4 tbsp. light brown sugar

1) In 4-cup glass measuring cup, microwave cream and milk on HIGH until very hot but not boiling, about 3-4 min. Remove and add chocolate, but do not stir. Let stand 2 min., then stir with whisk until smooth. Add sugar and egg yolks, one at a time, and whisk until blended. Whisk in orange liqueur.

2) Pour into 4 shallow creme brulee dishes. Microwave on LOW for 8-12 min., rotating dishes a quarter turn every 2 min. Mixture should be just barely set in center. Do not overcook. Remove and place onto shallow baking pan. Let stand 3 min.

3) Meanwhile, preheat broiler to high. Adjust oven rack to highest position. If needed, place an inverted shallow baking pan onto rack, so that creme brulee dishes will be less than 2 inches from broiler element.

4) Sprinkle each creme brulee evenly with 1 tbsp. brown sugar. Place pan under broiler until sugar is melted and bubbling, about 45 seconds. Let stand 2-3 min. Place in freezer for 5 min. before serving. (Can also be placed in refrigerator for up to 3 hours.)

nutritional facts: *Per serving: 460 calories • 40g carbohydrates • 5g protein • 31g fat • 60mg sodium • 240mg cholesterol • 1g fiber • 36g sugar*

seasonal substitution

When the holidays roll in, replace the almond extract with peppermint for a little more seasonal flair.

quick chocolate cream

prep time: 10 minutes • total time: 10 minutes • serves: 4

Sometimes a creamy chocolate dessert is all you need to end a satisfying meal. This fantastic finale will surely disappear before your eyes, so you may want to double the recipe!

2/3 cup hot fudge sauce	1 cup heavy cream, whipped
1/2 cup sour cream	additional hot fudge sauce and sliced almonds (optional)
1/4 tsp. almond extract (optional)	

1) In a bowl, combine fudge sauce, sour cream and extract if desired. Fold in the whipped cream. Spoon into dessert dishes.

2) Drizzle with additional fudge sauce and sprinkle with almonds if desired.

nutritional facts: *Per serving 439 calories • 35g carbohydrates • 5g protein • 30g fat • 104mg sodium • 102mg cholesterol • 1g fiber*

no-bake chocolate torte

prep time: 20 minutes • total time: 30 minutes • serves: 4 to 6

Here's a delightful dessert that only looks like you fussed all day. With its attractive appearance and wonderful taste, no one will know that you saved time by spreading an easy-to-prepare frosting on a store-bought pound cake.

1 frozen pound cake (10-3/4 ounces), thawed	6 tbsp. baking cocoa
2 cups heavy tsp. cream	1/2 tsp. almond extract
6 tbsp. confectioners' sugar	1/2 cup sliced almonds, toasted (optional)

1) Slice pound cake lengthwise into three layers and set aside. In a large mixing bowl, beat cream until soft peaks form. Gradually add sugar and cocoa; beat until stiff peaks form. Stir in extract.

2) Place one layer of cake on a serving platter; top with 1 cup of the frosting. Repeat layers. Frost top and sides with remaining frosting. Garnish with almonds if desired. Chill at least 15 minutes. Refrigerate any leftovers.

nutritional facts: *Per serving: 511 calories • 38g carbohydrates • 6g protein • 38g fat • 215mg sodium • 181mg cholesterol • 2 g fiber*

slimming down?
Consider trying the layered torte with prepared angel food cake instead of buttery pound cake. It's still a no-bake delight.

tapioca cherry-berry parfaits

prep time: 22 minutes • total time: 22 minutes • serves: 4

The satisfying taste of tapioca gets the star treatment when it's served in alternating layers with a supporting cast of a tasty fruit mixture and a dollop of flavored whipped cream.

1 (10 oz.) pkg. frozen dry-pack cherries	1 cup heavy cream
2 cups strawberries	2 cups prepared tapioca pudding
2 tsp. lemon juice	
1/3 cup plus 3 tbsp. seedless raspberry jam, *divided*	

1) Place frozen cherries in a sieve under cold running water until partially thawed, 1 min. Cut cherries in half and return to sieve to drain.

2) Hull strawberries and cut into 3/4-inch chunks; place in medium bowl. Add lemon juice, 1/3 cup jam and drained cherries; stir to combine.

3) With electric mixer on high, whip cream and remaining jam in medium bowl until stiff peaks form.

4) In each of 4 wine glasses or parfait dishes, alternately layer 1/4 cup each tapioca, cherry mixture and whipped cream, ending with dollop of cream. Serve immediately.

nutritional facts: *Per serving: 500 calories • 66g carbohydrates • 6g protein • 26g fat • 125mg sodium • 120mg cholesterol • 2g fiber • 46g sugar*

types of tapioca
Some prepared tapioca pudding brands are more natural than others. Some even offer a creamy "no sugar added" product that works very well in this recipe.

black forest brownie trifle

prep time: 15 minutes • total time: 25 minutes • serves: 6

If you like cherries and chocolate, you'll definitely want to try this tempting, no-bake treat that makes use of ready-made ingredients for a quick remake of the classic, black forest cake.

1 pint vanilla ice cream	1 (15 oz.) can pitted dark, sweet
1/4 cup sugar	Bing cherries
1/8 tsp. salt	3 tbsp. grenadine
1/3 cup sliced almonds	1/2 tsp. almond extract
15 bite-size brownies	

1) Remove ice cream from freezer; allow to soften slightly. Line baking sheet with parchment or waxed paper; set aside.

2) In small cast-iron pan over medium-low heat, melt sugar and salt, stirring until liquid and golden in color, about 7 min. Remove pan from heat; mix in almonds. Pour mixture onto prepared pan to cool.

3) Empty cherries into small bowl. Stir in grenadine and almond extract. Slice brownie bites in half horizontally.

4) In individual dessert dishes, layer 5 brownie slices, 1/2 cup scoop of ice cream and 1/3 cup cherries. With fingers, break sugared almonds into bite-size pieces. Sprinkle evenly over cherries and serve immediately.

nutritional facts: *Per serving: 320 calories • 48g carbohydrates • 4g protein • 13g fat • 105mg sodium • 35mg cholesterol • 2g fiber • 34g sugar*

sweet substitute

Can't find bite-size brownies? Buy a frozen dark chocolate layer cake and divide it into bite size portions. Layer the slices in individual dishes and enjoy.

chai-strawberry smoothie

prep time: 5 minutes • total time: 18 minutes • serves: 2 (10-oz.) servings

The spicy flavors of Chai tea pair beautifully with luscious, sweet strawberry and banana in this refreshing smoothie. You may just need to make a double batch, since everyone will want seconds!

1 Chai tea bag	1 cup frozen strawberries
1 (6 oz.) container strawberry-banana yogurt	1/2 cup frozen vanilla yogurt
	1 tsp. vanilla extract
1 banana	2 fresh strawberries (optional)

1) Place partially filled kettle on to boil over high heat. Place tea bag in glass measure; add 1 cup boiling water. Steep 3-5 min. Remove tea bag and allow tea to cool, about 10 min.

2) Meanwhile, peel and slice banana. Place yogurt, banana slices, frozen strawberries, frozen yogurt and vanilla extract in blender with cooled tea. Puree on high speed until mixture is smooth, about 45 seconds.

3) Evenly pour into 2 tall glasses. Garnish each with fresh strawberry if desired and serve.

nutritional facts: *Per serving: 270 calories • 52g carbohydrates • 6g protein • 3.5g fat • 75mg sodium • 10mg cholesterol • 3g fiber • 31g sugar*

smoothie secret

Vary the flavor of this smoothie with different fruits, teas or juices. Even skim milk plus ice cubes can be delicious.

very cherry turnovers

prep time: 15 minutes • total time: 29 minutes • serves: 9

A quick and easy alternative to pie, turnovers are wonderfully versatile. They can serve as an on-the-go breakfast or can be packed for lunches. Of course, they're great after dinner, too.

3/4 cup dried cherries	3 oz. farmer's cheese *or* cream cheese, softened
1/4 cup cherry *or* raspberry jam	1 large egg
1 tbsp. all-purpose flour	1 tbsp. confectioners' sugar
1 puff pastry sheet (from 17.25 oz. pkg.), thawed	

1) Heat oven to 400°F. In medium, microwave-safe bowl, combine cherries and jam. Microwave on HIGH until warmed through and softened, about 1 min.

2) Dust work surface with flour. Unfold pastry and roll out to 12-inch square. With sharp knife, cut into nine 4-inch squares. Spoon 1 rounded tsp. cheese onto center of each square. Top with 1 tbsp. cherry mixture, leaving 1/2-inch border of pastry all around.

3) Beat egg in small bowl. With pastry brush, brush egg on edges of pastry. Fold one corner of pastry diagonally to opposite corner to form triangle. Press edges together to seal. Repeat with remaining pastry squares. Place on baking sheet. Bake in lower third of oven until puffed and golden brown, about 12 min. Transfer to rack and dust with confectioners' sugar. Serve warm or cooled.

nutritional facts: *Per serving: 220 calories • 26g carbohydrates • 4g protein • 11g fat • 170mg sodium • 35mg cholesterol • 2g fiber • 13g sugar*

use any fruit

You don't need dried cherries to make this recipe. An equal portion of any chopped dried fruit, such as cranberries or raisins, give texture and sweetness to these treats.

refreshing lemon cream

prep time: 10 minutes • total time: 4 hours 15 minutes • serves: 6

Fresh lemon juice provides the tangy flavor in this smooth, rich ice cream recipe from Sunkist. The refreshing, make-ahead treat can be prepared without an ice cream maker and looks splendid and summery when served in individual cups made from lemon halves.

2 cups heavy cream	lemon boats (optional)
1 cup sugar	fresh mint and shredded lemon peel (optional)
1/3 cup lemon juice	
1 tbsp. grated lemon peel	

1) In a bowl, stir cream and sugar until sugar is dissolved. Stir in lemon juice and peel (mixture will thicken slightly).

2) Cover and freeze until firm, about 4 hours. Remove from the freezer 15 minutes before serving.

3) Serve in the lemon boats or individual dishes. Garnish with the mint and lemon peel if desired.

nutritional facts: *Per serving 407 calories • 37g carbohydrates • 2g protein • 29g fat • 31mg sodium • 109mg cholesterol • trace fiber*

berry delightful

You can add 1/2 cup mashed strawberries to the lemon mixture before freezing if you'd like.

tips for
delicious desserts

water bath for custards

Place baking dish in a larger baking pan, then place on a rack in the oven. Use a kettle to pour hot water into the larger pan, according to the recipe's directions.

easy peel cupcake liners

Spray cupcake liners with cooking spray before you fill them with batter. Then when the liners are peeled off, the cupcakes will be less likely to tear or crumble.

pouring cupcake batter without a mess

Place the cupcake batter into a large resealable plastic bag. Press out air and seal the bag. Snip off one bottom corner with scissors, then squeeze out the batter into muffin cups.

what's in a name?

Cobbler, crisp or fool...what do they mean? A cobbler has a biscuit-like topping over a fruit base. The topping can be either a single layer or dropped over the fruit to give it a cobblestone effect. Crisps have a crumb topping of flour, sugar and butter that is sprinkled over the fruit base. A crisp topping may also include oats, nut and spices. A fool is a traditional British dessert made by folding whipped cream into pureed fruit.

beating egg whites

To achieve the highest volume when beating egg whites, follow these tips. Allow whites to warm up by standing at room temperature for 30 minutes. Make sure there are no flecks of egg yolks in the whites. Beat the whites in a clean, dry metal or glass bowl with clean, dry beaters.

frosting too thick or thin?

If your frosting is not the right consistency for spreading, it's easily fixed. If it is too thick, add milk a teaspoon at a time until it's the right consistency. If it's too thin, let it stand for 10 to 20 min.; it may thicken up by itself. If it's still too thin, beat in some sifted confectioners' sugar until it is spreadable.

in a pinch cake tester

If you don't have a long wooden spick or metal cake tester to check for doneness for a cake baked in a tube or fluted tube pan, use a strand of uncooked, dry spaghetti. Insert it as you would a toothpick. Discard spaghetti after use.

creaming butter

To get the best volume in your cakes, butter should be soft before creaming. If a table knife glides through the butter, it is perfect for creaming. If you softened it in the microwave and butter is partially melted, it will not cream properly and the cake will not rise as high as it should.

making a rope edge

To make a rope edge, line the pie plate with the pastry and trim 1/2 inch beyond the edge of the pie plate. Turn the overhanging pastry under to form a rolled edge. Then make a fist with one hand and press you thumb at an angel in the pastry. Pinch some of the pastry between your thumb and index finger. Repeat at about ½-inch intervals around the crust. For a looser-looking rope, position your thumb at a wider angel and repeat at 1-inch intervals.

timing is everything

A souffle will begin to fall shortly after it is removed from the oven. Plan the serving time well and have the guests waiting for the souffle.

preventing soggy tart crusts

Brush tart crusts with melted jelly before layering with fruit. That will help seal the crust and keep the fruit juices from absorbing into the crust.

checking doneness

Check for doneness at the shortest time given in the recipe using the stated doneness test. If the baked good does not test done, continue baking and check again.

making crumbs for crusts

Graham crackers, chocolate or vanilla wafers, gingersnaps and even macaroons can be crushed to use in a crumb crust. The two easiest ways to crush the cookies is to break them up and place in a food processor until they are finely crushed. The other way is to place the broken cookies in a resealable plastic bag (with the air removed) and crush with a rolling pin.

take time to cool off

A wire rack is used for cooling baked goods because it allows air to circulate around the food, which prevents moist, soggy spots. In general, cakes need to rest for 10 minutes in their pans. The resting time helps prevent these items from crumbling when they are removed. Still other cakes—angel food and chiffon—that are baked in tube pan are cooled completely in their pan.

separating eggs

It's easiest to separate eggs when they are cold. Use an egg separator, which is available in the housewares section of stores. Place the separator over a custard cup. The yolk stays in the separator while the white drips into the custard cup.

12 weeknight menus

menu 1

Korean Steak, p. 63

Oriental Salad, p. 28

Exotic Fruity Sherbet, p. 200

menu 2

Mexican Cheese Steaks, p. 72

Rosemary-Infused Potatoes, p. 164

Citrus Mousse, p. 209

menu 3

Spicy Meatball Sandwich, p. 54

Vegetable Chowder, p. 28

Nutty Graham Cracker Brownies, p. 179

menu 4

Saucy Beef in Bread Baskets, p. 70

Tangy Bacon Beans, p. 168

Coconut Joy Pie, p. 205

menu 5

Blackened Chicken, p. 84

Cajun Country
Homefries, p. 169

No-Bake Chocolate Torte, p. 219

menu 6

Basil Balsamic
Chicken, p. 86

Pesto Roasted
Tomatoes, p. 167

Heavenly Berries and
Chocolate Cream, p. 214

menu 7

Chicken Enchiladas
Picante, p. 103

Roasted Corn and
Bean Salad, p. 33

Cinnamon Cake, p. 206

menu 8

Buffalo Chicken
Burgers, p. 88

Austin BBQ Beans, p. 166

Peanut Passion Pie, p. 211

change-of-pace pork

menu 9

Balsamic Maple-Glazed Pork, p. 110

Warm Cabbage and Apple Medley, p. 151

Easy Apricot-Cherry Crisp, p. 208

menu 10

Three-Bacon Pizza, p. 53

Field Greens with Basil Vinaigrette, p. 37

Black Forest Brownie Trifle, p. 220

seafood suppers & meatless menus

menu 11

Well-Dressed Crispy Catfish, p. 133

Summer Harvest Chopped Salad, p. 39

Petite Mississippi Mud Pies, p. 204

menu 12

Veggie Ranch Wraps, p. 131

Poppy Seed Citrus Salad, p. 24

Fudgy Chocolate Clusters, p. 180

general recipe index

This handy index lists every recipe by food category, major ingredient and/or cooking method, so you can easily locate recipes to suit your needs.

alphabetical index

substitutions & equivalents

equivalent measures

3 teaspoons	=	1 tablespoon		16 tablespoons	=	1 cup
4 tablespoons	=	1/4 cup		2 cups	=	1 pint
5-1/3 tablespoons	=	1/3 cup		4 cups	=	1 quart
8 tablespoons	=	1/2 cup		4 quarts	=	1 gallon

food equivalents

grains

Macaroni	1 cup (3-1/2 ounces) uncooked	= 2-1/2 cups cooked
Noodles, Medium	3 cups (4 ounces) uncooked	= 4 cups cooked
Popcorn	1/3 to 1/2 cup unpopped	= 8 cups popped
Rice, Long Grain	1 cup uncooked	= 3 cups cooked
Rice, Quick-Cooking	1 cup uncooked	= 2 cups cooked
Spaghetti	8 ounces uncooked	= 4 cups cooked

crumbs

Bread	1 slice	= 3/4 cup soft crumbs, 1/4 cup fine dry crumbs
Graham Crackers	7 squares	= 1/2 cup finely crushed
Buttery Round Crackers	12 crackers	= 1/2 cup finely crushed
Saltine Crackers	14 crackers	= 1/2 cup finely crushed

fruits

Bananas	1 medium	= 1/3 cup mashed
Lemons	1 medium	= 3 tablespoons juice, 2 teaspoons grated peel
Limes	1 medium	= 2 tablespoons juice, 1-1/2 teaspoons grated peel
Oranges	1 medium	= 1/4 to 1/3 cup juice, 4 teaspoons grated peel

vegetables

Cabbage	1 head	=	5 cups shredded	Green Pepper	1 large	=	1 cup chopped
Carrots	1 pound	=	3 cups shredded	Mushrooms	1/2 pound	=	3 cups sliced
Celery	1 rib	=	1/2 cup chopped	Onions	1 medium	=	1/2 cup chopped
Corn	1 ear fresh	=	2/3 cup kernels	Potatoes	3 medium	=	2 cups cubed

nuts

Almonds	1 pound	=	3 cups chopped	Pecan Halves	1 pound	=	4-1/2 cups chopped
Ground Nuts	3-3/4 ounces	=	1 cup	Walnuts	1 pound	=	3-3/4 cups chopped

easy substitutions

when you need...		use...
Baking Powder	1 teaspoon	1/2 teaspoon cream of tartar + 1/4 teaspoon baking soda
Buttermilk	1 cup	1 tablespoon lemon juice *or* vinegar + enough milk to measure 1 cup (let stand 5 minutes before using)
Cornstarch	1 tablespoon	2 tablespoons all-purpose flour
Honey	1 cup	1-1/4 cups sugar + 1/4 cup water
Half-and-Half Cream	1 cup	1 tablespoon melted butter + enough whole milk to measure 1 cup
Onion	1 small, chopped (1/3 cup)	1 teaspoon onion powder *or* 1 tablespoon dried minced onion
Tomato Juice	1 cup	1/2 cup tomato sauce + 1/2 cup water
Tomato Sauce	2 cups	3/4 cup tomato paste + 1 cup water
Unsweetened Chocolate	1 square (1 ounce)	3 tablespoons baking cocoa + 1 tablespoon shortening *or* oil
Whole Milk	1 cup	1/2 cup evaporated milk + 1/2 cup water

cooking terms

Here's a quick reference for some of the cooking terms used in Taste of Home recipes:

Baste—To moisten food with melted butter, pan drippings, marinades or other liquid to add more flavor and juiciness.

Beat—A rapid movement to combine ingredients using a fork, spoon, wire whisk or electric mixer.

Blend—To combine ingredients until just mixed.

Boil—To heat liquids until bubbles form that cannot be "stirred down." In the case of water, the temperature will reach 212°.

Bone—To remove all meat from the bone before cooking.

Cream—To beat ingredients together to a smooth consistency, usually in the case of butter and sugar for baking.

Dash—A small amount of seasoning, less than 1/8 teaspoon. If using a shaker, a dash would comprise a quick flip of the container.

Dredge—To coat foods with flour or other dry ingredients. Most often done with pot roasts and stew meat before browning.

Fold—To incorporate several ingredients by careful and gentle turning with a spatula. Used generally with beaten egg whites or whipped cream when mixing into the rest of the ingredients to keep the batter light.

Julienne—To cut foods into long thin strips much like matchsticks. Used most often for salads and stir-fry dishes.

Mince—To cut into very fine pieces. Used often for garlic or fresh herbs.

Parboil—To cook partially, usually used in the case of chicken, sausages and vegetables.

Partially Set—Describes the consistency of gelatin after it has been chilled for a small amount of time. Mixture should resemble the consistency of egg whites.

Puree—To process foods to a smooth mixture. Can be prepared in an electric blender, food processor, food mill or sieve.

Saute—To fry quickly in a small amount of fat, stirring almost constantly. Most often done with onions, mushrooms and other chopped vegetables.

Score—To cut slits partway through the outer surface of foods. Often used with ham or flank steak.

Stir-Fry—To cook meats and/or vegetables with a constant stirring motion in a small amount of oil in a wok or skillet over high heat.

additional photo credits

Stack of Dishes Photo
Page 20
Luxe/Shutterstock.com

Fondue Pot Photo
Page 21
Paul Maguire/Shutterstock.com

Beets Photo
Page 43
matka_Wariatka/Shutterstock.com

Crockpot Photo
Page 43
trailexplorers/Shutterstock.com

Star Cookie Cutters Photo
Page 56
Jasna/Shutterstock.com

Spaghetti Photo
Page 57
Elke Dennis/Shutterstock.com

Pita Bread Photo
Page 57
Olga Lyubkina/Shutterstock.com

Chicken Skewer Photo
Page 105
Olga Lyubkina/Shutterstock.com

Meat Thermometer Photo
Page 105
Scott Rothstein/Shutterstock.com

Eggs Photo
Page 143
Monkey Business Images/Shutterstock.com

Lentils Photo
Page 163
PixAchi/Shutterstock.com

String Beans Photo
Page 163
Harris Shiffman/Shutterstock.com

Frosted Cupcakes Photo
Page 222
Igor Kisselev/Shutterstock.com